Russian Exploration,
from Siberia to Space

Russian Exploration, from Siberia to Space
A History

BRIAN BONHOMME

McFarland & Company, Inc., Publishers
Jefferson, North Carolina, and London

Maps not otherwise credited are by the author.

LIBRARY OF CONGRESS ONLINE CATALOGUING DATA

Bonhomme, Brian, 1962–
Russian exploration, from Siberia to space : a history /
Brian Bonhomme.
p.   cm.
Includes bibliographical references and index.

ISBN 978-0-7864-6687-0
softcover : acid free paper ∞

1. Discoveries in geography — Russian — History.
2. Russia, Northern — Discovery and exploration — Russian.
3. Eurasia — Discovery and exploration — Russian.
4. Outer space — Exploration — Soviet Union.
I. Title.
G292.B66 2012   910.947 — dc23   2012001224

BRITISH LIBRARY CATALOGUING DATA ARE AVAILABLE

Front cover design by David K. Landis (Shake It Loose Graphics)

Manufactured in the United States of America

*McFarland & Company, Inc., Publishers
Box 611, Jefferson, North Carolina 28640
www.mcfarlandpub.com*

#757461962

For Lena and Isabel — the two lights of my life

Table of Contents

Introduction

This book is about Russian explorers and expeditions from the late sixteenth century to recent times. It has three main aims: first, to introduce to a broad, nonspecialist audience a relatively under-studied area of both Russian history and the history of exploration; second, to bring together a series of Russian narratives and developments usually treated separately but which can more usefully be viewed as related parts of a coherent larger Russian story; and third, to offer an outline of recent and current scholarly research — in both English and Russian — of the major matters treated here, and thus to serve as a basis for further study. It will be useful at the outset to examine each of these objectives a little further.

1. Russia, Russians, and the History of European Exploration

In the Western, and especially the English-speaking, world the history of geographical discovery and exploration offers a well-known European cast of characters and events: Columbus, the Italian in Spanish pay, and his fateful discovery of the Americas; Cortés's and Pizarro's conquests of the Aztec and Incan Empires for Spain; the Portuguese global circumnavigation under Magellan that finally proved the spherical shape of the world; the eighteenth-century Pacific voyages of the remarkable English sailor James Cook; Lewis and Clark's great American expedition into the Louisiana Purchase at the start of the nineteenth century; and Neil Armstrong's "one giant leap for mankind" onto the moon, for example. Recent scholarship has brought to greater public attention a handful of important adventurers from other parts of the world — most famously, perhaps, the Chinese-Muslim admiral Zheng-He, and his seven early-fifteenth-century voyages from China, across the Indian Ocean, to East Africa (and perhaps still further). While the importance of the canonical Western explorations and conquests — measured in terms of their overall impact on the shaping of the modern world — is unassailable, it is equally true that *Russia* participated fully in the European era of exploration, conquest, expansion, and colonization and has continued a rich tradition of exploration up to the present — facts that still seem not to have been incorporated all that well in the English-speaking countries into either the World History curriculum or popular knowledge. Partial exceptions may perhaps be made for Ermak, the Russian Cossack conqueror of Siberia whose increasingly well-known exploits delivered for Russia, in the long term, an empire as great and rich as that yielded to Spain by Cortés and Pizarro — but one that has proved much more enduring; and for Vitus Bering, usually credited as discoverer of the Bering Straits and Alaska. Beyond Ermak and Bering, however, lie many other Russian contributions — mostly unknown outside of narrow academic circles.

An extreme case, highlighted in the prodigious labors of the Canadian historian Glynn Bar-ratt, concerns the exploration and study of Polynesia in the nineteenth-century — to which enterprise, says Barratt, "Russians ... contributed at least as much as Frenchmen, Americans, or Spaniards, though not as much as British subjects.... We in the West almost always over-look this."[1] We overlook, or underappreciate, much else as well, including pioneering Russian explorations and studies in Australia, Brazil, Tibet, western China, Papua New Guinea, the discovery of Antarctica, and more.

Why do we overlook these things? Perhaps it is partly the relative secrecy under which many Russian and Soviet explorations were carried out, or the lack of publicity many of them originally received in the West (the Space Race clearly excepted). In other words, maybe it is because the Russians themselves, at least prior to the twentieth century, kept many of their achievements quiet. More likely, perhaps we in the West feel less directly impacted by Russian and Soviet discoveries than by those of Columbus, Louis and Clark, and the rest. Although this sentiment is easy to sympathize with, it is far from bulletproof — especially nowadays, as the world rapidly shrinks and the histories, achievements, and des-tinies of all nations become increasingly intertwined. Western ignorance of Russian explorations, incidentally, is not mirrored by Russian ignorance of Western ones. Whether this is proof of the greater importance of Columbus, Magellan, and the rest over Russian counterparts; of greater interest by Russians in foreign histories; or something else entirely, cannot be resolved here.

There are a few other possible reasons for the obscurity of Russian explorers. I will put off their discussion until the concluding section, however, since they will make more sense following, rather than preceding, the accounts and circumstances of the explorers them-selves.

2. Separate Narratives or a Coherent History?

In researching and writing this book I have come to suspect that the history of Russian exploration, rather than being simply a concatenation of discrete (if compelling) narratives, displays certain generalizable traits. Russian exploration is, of course, tied closely to imperial expansion, and this, in turn, has been much more geographically contiguous than that of the other major Western empires. Basic geography has largely determined this distinction, but noticeable cultural patterns have followed in its wake. For Iberians and northern Euro-peans, exploration almost inevitably involved travel by sea to distant lands. Thus, the Western explorer inhabited, in turn, three separate spaces: home, a featureless oceanic middle space, then the destination. Put more abstractly, the traveler moved among three fairly clearly delineated cultural circumstances: familiar, empty, and "other." This is, of course, over-simplified, but the contrast with the Russian experience is notable. Russians expanded and explored, for the most part, simply by traveling step-by-step farther and farther from their homeland or other point of departure. Rarely was there any middle stage comparable to the Western European's experience of the ocean. Only once most of contiguous Eurasia had been reached and at least provisionally explored was their any real necessity for sea travel comparable to that undertaken by the Westerners. But by this time — the start of the nine-teenth century — the mentality of contiguity, if you will, had already become firmly entrenched. Thus, although Russians pressed on — across the North Pacific then around the world — they were never quite such comfortable and instinctive global explorer-imperialists as, say, the British or French. Annexation of distant, utterly non-contiguous, far-flung lands — such as Hawaii, the Tuamotus, or New Guinea — while of passing interest, could never be reconciled with the vision of a contiguous nation-empire. Consequently, such places were visited, charted, and sometimes fairly well explored; but all were ultimately left more or less alone, at least by the Russians.

With a little imagination one might even continue this line of analysis — emphasizing the importance of contiguity — through the Space Race and to the present day. In the 1950s and 1960s, the Russians' focus — and their greatest successes — involved near-earth space (satellites and cosmonauts in orbit). When the Americans explicitly shifted the target to landing a man on the moon — a far greater distance — the Russians quickly fell behind. This was, perhaps, more a matter of available technology and financial resources than a specific Russian fixation with relatively contiguous low-orbit spaces. But nonetheless, from 1969 forward, after the race to the moon had been won by the Americans, Russians continued to develop their near-earth capabilities, quickly becoming — and still somewhat remaining — dominant in the development of orbiting space stations and human space endurance, while the Americans increasingly floundered in search of a clear focus for their space program. More recently still, in 2007, the Russians planted their flag on the sea floor under the North Pole. Although the event was written off by many in the West as a meaningless publicity stunt, the Russians appear to have done it in some seriousness — simultaneously asserting their resurgent national and economic vigor and laying claim to potential oil and gas riches under the North Polar sea floor. The latter consideration was facilitated by provisions of the 1994 United Nations Convention on the Law of the Sea, which recognizes states' legitimate claims over territory extending from their coastline to the edge of their undersea continental shelf. Although this affects the Northern Polar rights of several nations (including the United States and Canada), so far the Russians, true to their exploring and expansion traditions, have been particularly assertive about the supposed physical-geological contiguity of the Russian landmass and the sections of sub–Arctic sea floor in question.

Returning to terrestrial Russian exploration, the question arises: was there a point at which Russians tended to "draw the line" — so to speak — between contiguous (and thus annexable) and noncontiguous (unannexable) territory? If there was, then Alaska (and the period 1741–1867) is probably the best fit. Here, distances from the consolidated frontier across the Bering Sea were relatively small, and shrank still further as navigation improved. This encouraged a little more than a century of Russian efforts to explore, claim, and develop their new American frontier. But ultimately the distance proved too great. Official Russian commitment to Alaska grew weak, resulting in its sale to the USA in 1867.

The points raised here intersect strongly with assertions made by other scholars working from somewhat different angles. The blurring, in Russia, of lines usually drawn more clearly by other imperial peoples between their "nation" and their "empire" has been noted and treated by several people, including Geoffrey Hosking, for example.[2] Richard Pipes has offered a possible explanation by noting that unlike some of its Western neighbors Russia became an empire first and a nation only thereafter.[3] (Perhaps it is worth pointing out too that — for the most part unlike the Russians — the Iberians and northern Europeans also had those broad, empty oceans to help them conceive the boundaries between nation and empire far more clearly.)

Particularly relevant to the book at hand, the geographer-historian Valerie Kivelson has recently and persuasively assessed Russian expansion, at least into Siberia, as a kind of building project, with each newly incorporated area or people conceived by the Russian state as contiguous "building blocks" in a growing imperial edifice (one might interpret Kivelson's notion as a projection — into the non–Russian world of Siberia — of the venerable metaphor that casts early modern Muscovite unification as a "gathering" of the Russian lands). But rather than seek simply or quickly to assimilate the various peoples they encountered (though they did indeed do this to some degree), the Russians, Kivelson argues, built from these "blocks" a "taxonomy of nations" ruled over by tsars whose primary goals were not just to "tax [and] protect" but also to "count like gold and treasure" the various peoples and lands thus acquired.[4] Kivelson only treats Russian expansion into Siberia, but I suspect that a comparable framework — focused on the question of contiguity or its absence — could accommodate a much larger spread of Russian expansion and exploration. Perhaps New Guinea, the Polynesian islands, and even Alaska, lacking contiguity with the mother country, were inassimilable into Kivelson's notional "taxonomy" — were, in other words, too distant to "tax," "protect," or "count like gold and treasure."

Perhaps herein lies another reason why Russian explorers are not well-known in the West: much of what they explored was subsequently locked up like treasure within the Russian empire and has become — or seemed — inaccessible and distant to us. Conversely, those places the Russians did not lock up — especially, those remote, un-contiguous islands and shores — consequently lost their Russian connections. So we associate them with other explorers and traditions.

Russia's path toward the front rank of exploring began slowly, and from relatively far behind. During the fifteenth and sixteenth centuries, when first the Iberians, then increasingly the Dutch, French, and British, seemed insatiably fascinated with the wider world — and as they endlessly traveled and plundered their way through it — Muscovite Russians, in contrast, evinced a marked "lack of curiosity about their environment" and about what lay beyond it.[5] As Kivelson has also noted, when they did raise their gaze, at least until around 1700, Russians tended to focus less on the natural environment than on supernatural ones, preferring either Orthodox theology and devotion or folk superstition to natural history and practical geography. Western visitors of the time, such as the Dutchman Isaac Massa (1586–1643), noticed and frequently remarked upon such things. At least two separate events, separated by more than a century, jolted the Russians out of this complacency, however, and mark important watersheds in the story told here. The first, the subject of chapter 1, was Ermak's conquest of the Khanate of Sibir'. The second, background to matters treated in chapters 3 and 4, was Russian Emperor Peter the Great's famous wrenching of his medieval domains into the modern and Western worlds during the first quarter of the eighteenth century. If the exploring tradition developed slowly, however, it has nonetheless become a defining characteristic of Russian culture and history and a unique contribution to the history of European exploration more generally.

3. Historiography: The Writing of Russian Exploration in History

Throughout the book I have attempted to give the reader a sense of the historiographical terrain — that is, of the changing ways in which historians and others have thought and written about Russian exploration history. Some of the periods, episodes, or individuals surveyed here have attracted much scholarly attention and continue to provoke lively debate or disagreement. This is the case with the Russian presence in far eastern Eurasia, the northern Pacific, and Alaska. Here, unresolved questions range from the factual (how many of Semen Dezhnev's boats made it through the Bering Straits in 1648?) to the interpretive (who best deserves to be remembered as the discoverer of Alaska?). These and other uncertainties derive from various conditions: the paucity of original source materials, errors and ambiguities in those that *do* exist (including missing or inaccurate navigational data, unattributable place names, or unidentifiable natural features), and much else. Sometimes, they are driven also by the biases of Western, Soviet, and Russian historians and biographers eager to promote a particular hero or view. The fact that the pantheon of Russian explorers features a lively mix of native sons and foreign recruits only adds to the dynamic, with historians and biographers occasionally seeming to take sides in defense of "their own." The Space Race, too, continues to attract great attention. Here, the events are far more recent. The source material, though much richer, has only recently become accessible; so historians have just begun to pierce the veils of secrecy, hagiography, and outright misinformation with which the Soviets shrouded their endeavors. These and other debates are treated throughout the book, as appropriate.

Other episodes of Russian exploration, by contrast, have begun gathering dust — most of the major studies and biographies now being of some vintage. Examples might include the Central Asian travels of N. M. Przheval'skii or G. N. Potanin, and even Ermak's initial conquest of Siberia. Many questions remain regarding these and other expeditions, and it is to be hoped that this book may provoke a little renewed interest in some of them.

There have been encouraging recent trends in the scholarship of Russian explorers and expeditions. Women have begun receiving more attention. For example, the travels and observations of Baroness Elizabeth von Wrangell (or Wrangel), who accompanied her husband Ferdinand across Siberia and remained with him in Alaska during his tenure as governor of the Russian-American Company, have recently been published.[6] Other important and fascinating women remain obscure however, including Mariia Pronchishcheva (sometimes considered the world's first female Arctic explorer; see chapter 3) and A. V. Potanina, wife and travel companion of the explorer Grigorii Nikolaevich Potanin (see chapter 6). Overall, women's contributions and experiences remain a lacuna. A dearth of sources underlies this unfortunate scholarly silence, however, and puts a great obstacle in the way of easy remedy.

Rather more energy has been given recently to filling another gap in our knowledge — the experiences of the many indigenous peoples whom the Russians encountered and conquered. Traditionally relegated to passive victims or contextual factors in stories of Russian exploration, the original or earlier inhabitants of Siberia and many other areas are now finding increasing voice in studies by James Forsyth, Yuri Slezkine, Michael Khodarkovsky, and others.[7]

Comparing Russian- and English-language accounts of Russian exploration one quickly finds that while the two traditions bear much in common, there are also some tensions. Russian (and especially Soviet-era) writers have been highly (and understandably) vocal about their compatriots' achievements and have sometimes reacted testily to Western ignorance or skepticism. Equally importantly, they have also argued against (and continue in some cases to counter) certain interpretations of Western scholarship, so that occasionally the appearance arises of "Western" versus "Russian" positions. The ongoing minor battle over whom to credit for the discovery of Alaska — the Dane Vitus Bering or the Russian Aleksei Chirikov — is only the most famous of several examples. In other instances, however, English- and Russian-language scholarship has come together in recent years, with the Russians now distancing themselves from some of the propositions and articles of faith that characterized Soviet scholarship. One hears less and less, for example, of how "comradely" the interactions were of Russian colonists and conquered Siberian, Alaskan, or other native peoples.[8]

Organization

Some readers may wonder about the order in which events are treated here, especially the division of Siberian exploration into "terrestrial" (chapter 2) and "coastal" stages (chapter 3) in spite of the fact that the two are largely inseparable parts of a single process. Part of my answer would be that although for the most part the book is arranged chronologically, where this presents problems I have tried to impose a workable order on a bewilderingly complex set of movements by operating geographically. Beyond mere convenience, however, I have also sought to reinforce the notion of "geographical contiguity" by presenting Russian expansion as a series of moving concentric circles or ripples radiating out—if very unevenly—from the historical Muscovite core. Thus, progressing rather than leapfrogging, we move from Eastern Europe eastward into Siberia (chapters 1–2), outward to the coasts of Eurasia (chapter 3), then across to Alaska (chapter 4). Thereafter we follow Russians by sea across the Pacific (chapter 5), by land into Central Asia (chapter 6), and to both Poles (chapter 7), noting as we go the far greater Russian interest in the Arctic than Antarctic, based in part on facts of contiguity. Finally we move beyond the earth during the era of the Space Race (chapter 8).

Not all of the explorers discussed here are unambiguously Russian. Many, though born and raised within the confines of the Russian Empire, are of German or other extraction. Others still are "Russian" only by employment or association. All, however, operated under Russian auspices and properly belong within the narrative of Russian history. One might add, of course, that similar caveats obtain regarding the explorers and expeditions of other countries, too: John Cabot, who claimed Newfoundland for England in 1497, was born Giovanni Caboto in Italy, just to name one of many examples.

In researching this book I have grown somewhat fond, and certainly respectful, of many of the historical personalities I encountered. No less than their better-known and more celebrated Western counterparts, Russians and their agents faced and overcame stupendous hardships, showed unfathomable fortitude and courage in the face of great deprivation and discomfort, and discovered, charted, and documented innumerable new wonders—places, peoples, flora, fauna, and natural phenomena. On the other hand, I am also struck—at times repelled—by the harsh cruelty of at least some of the same men; at the execrable treatment sometimes meted out to native peoples; at the rape, kidnapping, and slaughter of innocents; at the wanton destruction of populations of animals for their fur—and all for mere profit. But here too my sense is that the Russians were more like than unlike their Western counterparts. Both, in turn, seem neither better nor worse than the average of humanity globally. In other words, although the details may be unique, the story of Russian exploration is very much a common human story, part of our shared, global history.

***

Geographical coordinates given throughout are generally those supplied in the accounts of the explorers themselves and are thus subject to inaccuracy, typically the more so the further back in time one goes. Where appropriate, such errors are noted. Similarly, dates are given according to the Julian calendar in use in Russia at the time (with exceptions noted). This means that during the eighteenth century dates are eleven days behind those in the West. In the nineteenth century the difference is twelve days, and thirteen in the early twentieth. Russia adopted the Gregorian (Western) calendar in February 1918. I have used the standard simplified (no diacritical marks) Library of Congress spelling throughout for Russian personal and place names, though with exceptions for words commonly used in English (thus, "Tsar Nicholas I," not "Tsar Nikolai I"). This system, like all others, is not perfect and on occasion generates its own peculiarities, such as the attribution of the discovery of the Pribilof Islands to a man named Pribylov, or of the naming of Zavadovski Island after a man named Zavadovskii.

The research and writing of this book was supported in part by release time granted by the School of Graduate Studies at Youngstown State University, and by funds from the same institution's School of Technology. I am most grateful for this support. For assistance with bibliographical work and images, I also wish to thank Jennifer Hanuschak, Nathan Pavalko, and Clayton Ruminski. Special thanks to my brother Paul for help with some of the maps.

Chapter 1

The "Conquest of Siberia": Ermak's Expedition of 1581–1585[1] and Its Aftermath

As late as the 1530s, and speaking geographically, Russia (or "Muscovy" as it was then properly known) remained a European, rather than a Eurasian, state. Its easternmost boundaries fell short of the Ural Mountains and far shy of the lower Volga River.[2] In reality, Russian political control ran thin and increasingly nominal even *before* these distant borders, especially toward the Urals. The land beyond was largely *terra incognito*.[3] But a mere century later, Russians would stand nearly 3,000 miles to the east on the Pacific coast at the Sea of Okhotsk, having also reconnoitered by then the major river basins and some sections of the Arctic coastline in-between. (Exploration and assimilation of the remoter *land* areas between and beyond the rivers would continue well into the twentieth century, however.) A network of strategic forts, churches, and other buildings was one sign of Russia's growing political and economic domination of Siberia and the northern Far East. Others included growing disruption of ancient patterns of life among this huge area's various native peoples and the wholesale destruction of sea otter, mink, and other fur-bearing animal populations. During the eighteenth and nineteenth centuries, the Russians' eastward momentum would carry them further still: to Kamchatka, the Chukchi Peninsula, and then across the Bering Straits to Alaska (including its islands, coasts, and a little of the interior), and then south to California and other Pacific points. The American thrust was not to last, however. The sale of Alaska to the United States in 1867 marked its end. Much of this story is told in later chapters of this book.

Ermak Timofeev

The credit for launching Muscovite Russia on its incredible drive to the east is given to a rough and somewhat mysterious Russian Cossack adventurer and riverboat pirate named Ermak Timofeev. In terms of his historical importance, Ermak stands with Cortés and Pizarro, a Russian *conquistador* who opened for his country and monarch the gates of a grand and (Alaska excepted) enduring empire — for such was the ultimate effect of the defeat he and his several hundred followers inflicted in the early 1580s on Muscovy's eastern neighbor, the Khanate of Sibir', and on its Muslim Turkic ruler, the Khan Kuchum. Maddeningly little is known of Ermak, and much mythology clings to him. Although a few reliable primary sources exist — mainly letters and orders from the 1580s mentioning Ermak and written by the tsar — they illuminate only small parts of his life. Other, more expansive narratives exist also — various chronicles, epic folk-tales (*byliny*), songs, and legends. But these were composed decades after the fact and on hearsay by parties who have embellished his legend for their own purposes.[4] Unfortunately, these sources differ greatly on important details: time, place, and order of events — even the manner of Ermak's death.[5] Modern scholarship has only partially sorted out this confusion. Most likely, a completely accurate and definitive reconstruction of Ermak's movements and achievements will never be achieved.[6] On the other hand, the main contours of the narrative — and its ultimate significance — are both clear and compelling.

Prelude to the Conquest: Russia and the Mongols

Ermak's eastward conquest contains an element of historical irony in that it came at the expense of the Khanate of Sibir', a successor state to the Mongol hordes who had themselves invaded Russia from the east 300 years earlier, in the mid-thirteenth century. The Mongols, in turn, were only the latest in a long series of eastern invaders stretching back two millennia to the ancient Cimmerians and Scythians. Thus, Ermak's contribution was not just the conquest of Siberia — a historical watershed in its own right — but the reversal of an ancient pattern of migration and invasion. Never again would eastern nomads — Sarmartians, Huns, Mongols, and the rest — find significant opportunity to move west. Instead, the Russians were coming east to stay.

It is worth noting additionally that before and while sweeping Russia, the Mongol hordes also conquered much of Siberia itself, with further important consequences. It was from the Mongols, for example, that Russians learned something of the extent of Siberia's potential fur wealth — raising the likelihood of eventual Russian expansion into the area. The Mongols even helped — inadvertently — to lay the ground for the eventual Russian conquest and absorption of Siberia, as their own campaigns there — through to the sixteenth and early seventeenth centuries — undermined native peoples' social cohesion, agricultural activity, long-distance trade, and important crafts, such as metalworking. This significantly weakened Siberian societies, leaving them more vulnerable to Russian encroachment.[7]

Any irony present in these various circumstances must have been (and no doubt remains) lost on the region's wide- but thinly spread native Siberians. Few of them participated in either the Mongol or the Russian tide, but all were washed by both. The latter one changed them forever.

The Mongols and Sibir'

Originating in the steppe lands north of the Gobi Desert, the Mongols were a nomadic horse-riding people fragmented into numerous tribes headed by chiefs known as khans. Though illiterate, shamanic by religion, and numbering only about three-quarters of a million as of 1200, they would leave an indelible mark on history, building and maintaining the single largest contiguous empire the world has known, stretching at its height, around 1279, from Eastern Europe, through the Middle East, and to the Pacific coast of China. The foundations for this remarkable achievement were laid in the early thirteenth century by the legendary Mongol leader Chingiss (or Genghis) Khan, who welded a disparate array of nomadic peoples into a single nation-army. To this day the Mongols' reputation endures, especially in the field of combat, where they constituted one of the fiercest, most merciless, and successful war machines in history. In their day and since, Mongol armies enjoyed a reputation of near invincibility. Dedicated almost entirely from birth to warfare, they trained for every conceivable battlefield scenario and perfected structures and practices of military organization that time and again set them apart from their many and varied adversaries. They were master military strategists, skilled in the use of siege weaponry, but even more effective in motion. Consummate horseback archers, they wielded a compound bow more powerful than any other hand-held weapon of the day and for centuries thereafter. They sported effective light armor that provided maximum protection without compromising movement. And when they attacked, they did so with blinding speed, in huge formations, and with legendary brutality. Those who resisted, and especially their leaders, were regularly flayed alive, pulled apart, or otherwise made into horrific examples. Entire towns were razed completely. The effect of such savagery was to terrorize the next target into immediate submission, since the Mongols usually offered each settlement or town this choice. Surrender usually meant incorporation into the Mongols' massive forces, creating a cascading steamroller of various peoples, under Mongol rule, hurtling ever further west, through Russia and beyond to Poland and Hungary. The tide stopped abruptly in early 1242 after — and because of — the death of Chingiss's successor, the fearsome Ugedei Khan. Europe was thus saved. For Russia, however, the reprieve came too late. The Muscovite state would spend the next two-and-a-half centuries under the so-called Mongol Yoke.

Mongol achievements and abilities went far beyond the battlefield, however, as does their historical significance overall. To facilitate intertribal cooperation and keep the Mongol confederation from degenerating into factionalism, Chingiss outlawed many of the practices over which component tribes had earlier fought, including the kidnapping and sale of women and the theft of animals. To promote trade and prosperity, record-keeping was introduced, efforts were undertaken to have the Mongol dialect made into a written language, and property and hunting rights were established and codified. An efficient pony-express postal system functioned. Order and stability were prized and rigorously enforced. Harsh punishments, often death, were meted out to offenders. The famed silk-road — then the primary artery of global trade — was effectively policed and protected so that merchants and merchandise could pass along it largely unmolested. Under the khans, it was said that a girl, carrying valuables, could travel alone and unmolested the entire distance of the empire. Whether or not one did, history does not record, though the famed Italian traveler Marco Polo, at least, did safely undertake a similar journey in the late thirteenth century.

The historical importance of these and other Mongol achievements is unlikely to have been either apparent or interesting to the Russian and other Slavic peoples who found themselves on the receiving end of a series of massive onslaughts that commenced in earnest in 1237. For the most part, Russia was attacked by Tatars — nomadic Turkic-speaking peoples earlier hostile to the Mongols but now part of their irresistible military confederation. The Tatars overran most of the Russian lands, though the heavily forested areas of the north were less affected. Rather than occupy the territory they conquered, the Tatars mostly settled along a wide crescent south and east of Russia, with a capital established at Sarai on the Volga River. From here they collected taxes. When these were delivered Russians were left largely to manage their own affairs. When they stopped or were inadequate, violent punitive raids soon got them coming again. Over time, this Tatar khanate came to be known as the Golden Horde.

A Shift in the Balance of Power

At their most deadly and efficient in the thirteenth century, the Mongols overall — and the Golden Horde in particular — were by the mid-fourteenth century still formidable, but clearly a waning and increasingly fragmented force. In 1368 Mongol domination came to an end in China — a major loss. Further west, a Russian force under the celebrated Prince Dmitri Donskoi won the first ever Russian victory over the Tatars in 1380 at the Battle of Kulikovo by the Don River. Though the Tatars returned in force shortly thereafter, their aura of invincibility was shattered irreparably. Slowly, momentum began to shift to the Russian side.

But still great challenges remained. The slowly "vanishing Siberian tide," as one writer has called it,[8] threatened to create a power vacuum in its wake, leaving Russia dangerously exposed and vulnerable. Lithuania, an ambitious and rapidly growing western neighbor, inflicted defeats upon the Russians in battles during 1368 and 1371. By the late fourteenth century it "had grown into an empire of 350,000 square miles, extending from the Baltic to the Black Sea. Lithuania had defeated the Teutons in 1410 [at the momentous Battle of Grunwald]; it was closely associated with Poland.... One bold bid by the rulers of Lithuania could have incorporated the Russian heart lands into the new empire."[9] Yet it never happened. "Interruptions in the Baltic trade and political disarray" following the death in 1430 of the great Lithuanian monarch, Vytautus (r. 1401–1430), reduced the Lithuanians' potency.[10] Instead, the Muscovite princes were able eventually to turn the Mongol-Tatar disaster to their advantage, forging in their opposition to a common enemy, an unbeatable unity and strength.

From the early days of their submission to the Golden Horde, Russia's many princes had struggled against one another in a desperate competition to give to the invaders the only things they really wanted — taxes and tribute. If at first thought this competition seems obsequious or even treasonous, it was in fact purely self-serving, since a significant portion of what was collected could be skimmed off and pocketed. The khans of the Golden Horde were also the chief powerbrokers across most of the Russian lands. Their favor was a formidable political tool and Russian princes courted it aggressively. It was his connections with Khan Uzbek, for example, that enabled Michael of Tver to become prince of the politically critical city of Vladimir in 1308. Not to be outdone, a rival prince, Iurii, from Moscow (not yet the powerful principality it would soon become), courted and bribed the same khan, and then married into his family. His efforts were rewarded when the khan transferred Michael's throne to Iurii. So pleased was the khan with his new protégé's efficiency in collecting taxes from other princes that Uzbek himself ended Michael's counterclaims by having him murdered. In subsequent decades the princes of one city in particular — Moscow — would spin this sort of diplomacy into the basis for rule over all the Russian lands, leading to the rise of a new incarnation of Russia named *Muscovy*.[11] Eventually, Muscovite-Russian princes would outgrow their Tatar patrons altogether and push them aside.

The Expansion of Muscovy prior to Ermak[12]

By around 1400 Moscow and the independent north–Russian city-state of Novgorod were the chief rivals for access to Siberia and its wealth. A treaty of 1456 resolved in Moscow's favor the competition over lands "between the Northern Dvina and the Urals, with their population of Komi-Zyrians and Samoyeds."[13] Occasional Muscovite raids over the following years pushed the Russian presence slowly but inexorably further east still, beyond the Pechora region — whose native Komi tribes were recruited for campaigns against their eastern neighbors across the Urals, the Mansi and Khanty peoples — during the 1460s. Furs flowed west. In 1478 Moscow annexed Novgorod. Increasingly, Russia was becoming one state — Muscovy — rather than many. Subsequent military expeditions beyond the Urals during 1483 and 1499 yielded fur-tribute from the peoples along the Pelym, Northern Sosva, Ob', and Irtysh Rivers and helped solidify Muscovite influence in the area. At the same time, glimmerings of knowledge emerged about Siberia's potential mineral wealth — further raising Muscovite interest in the region. An Arctic sea route, linking the White Sea with the mouth of the Ob', was added in the early 1600s.[14]

The consolidation of Russian lands under Muscovite domination, which continued apace during the fifteenth and sixteenth centuries, contrasts markedly with the fragmentation and decay of the Golden Horde into seven separate khanates.[15] In 1480, Muscovite prince Ivan III or "the Great" (1462–1505; and the first Russian ruler to claim the title of "tsar") successfully repelled a half-hearted Tatar raid, thereby marking the effective end of Tatar domination of Russia. As the tide turned, Muscovite expansion brought the Russian presence and influence washing back up against Tatar domains. The founding of Solikamsk in 1430, the conquest of the Perm/Komi lands in 1472, and in 1489 the capture of a Novgorod settlement along the Viatka River, all combined, left Russians pressed against the northern flank of the Khanate of Kazan and the western flank of the Khanate of Sibir'.[16] Through the mid–1500s, Muscovite energies remained focused primarily on consolidation of the Slavic Russian lands, not on further eastward expansion. This would change, however, shortly after the accession of Ivan IV or "the Terrible," who ruled Muscovy from 1533 to 1584.

Early Muscovite Expansion against the Tatars

In the early 1550s, hunger for territorial expansion and concern about the resurgent power of the Khanate of Kazan inspired Ivan to attack both it and its southern neighbor and potential ally, the Khanate of Astrakhan. In one of the earliest Russian campaigns to make decisive use of gunpowder, Kazan was defeated and annexed in 1552. Astrakhan fell in 1556. Thereafter, the eastward flow of Russian colonists and settlers increased steadily. Most went into the Perm lands north of Kazan, others closer toward the ill-defined domains of the Khanate of Sibir', beyond the Urals.

Though described in one seventeenth-century account of Ermak's exploits as "of exceeding height, so as to reach with some of its peaks up to the clouds of heaven,"[17] the Ural Mountains are in fact a less-than-formidable natural barrier. Across them, on the Irtysh River near where Tobol'sk now stands, lay the citadel of Isker[18] — the center and heart of the entire Khanate of Sibir' — whose influence extended along the Irtysh and the larger Ob', to which it soon joins, then down to the lower reaches of the Ob' and south and west to the Volga-Kama region. The population of the whole Khanate of Sibir' has been variously estimated but was certainly no more than 30,000 by Ermak's time (the population of whole the of geographical Siberia out to the Pacific was perhaps only 200,000[19]). This number included an assortment of peoples. The Tatars ruled the area and counted among their subject or tributary peoples various, mostly Finnic-speaking, natives whose shifting territories overlapped each other and that of Sibir' — Khants and Mansis, and further north, the Nenets being the main groups.[20]

The inevitable conflict with Sibir' was delayed, however. Russia's efforts in the disastrous Livonian War (a futile and decades-long effort to expand in the Baltic at the expense of Sweden, Poland, and Lithuania) and years of political and social chaos — both the result of Ivan's personal mania for power — took up Russian energies for the next two decades. At the same time, the rulers of Sibir', hoping to avoid the fate of their neighbors in Kazan and Astrakhan, pursued friendly relations with Ivan after 1555, and paid him tribute. This last circumstance changed, however, when in 1563 Sibir's rulers — the brothers Yediger and Bekbulat — were murdered and replaced by the more belligerent and anti–Russian Khan Kuchum (r. 1563–1598).[21] Within a decade Kuchum had had Ivan's tribute-collector murdered, reneged on tribute payments, and apparently given his blessing to raids against Russian territories west of the Urals. The stage was now set for confrontation.

Ermak before the Conquest

Of Ermak's background, birth, and childhood, little is known. One tradition holds that his proper name was Vasilii Timofeevich Alenin; that he worked on a "river fleet on the Kama and Volga," much as his father and uncle had; and that he was the grandson of a poor man originally from Suzdal (northeast of Moscow).[22] Only one brief description exists: "flat-faced, black of beard and with curly hair, of medium stature and thickset and broadshouldered."[23] Although at least one specialist believes Ermak to have been a veteran of Ivan IV's wars who had subsequently headed east,[24] most accounts describe him as a free-booting Cossack river-boat pirate who had by the end of the 1570s already spent many years preying on Russian and non–Russian victims alike on the Volga or Don Rivers. He appears to have been a man without a plan, who lived day-to-day, and who fell into greatness by accident.

The forces that were to thrust him into history were already well in train when, around 1580, Ermak and a loyal detachment headed north into the Kama River, a Volga tributary originating in the Perm lands west of the Urals. They were in search of refuge — the tsar was cracking down on piracy, and floating gallows designed especially for outlaws of Ermak's sort were already plying the Volga waters. The lands to which they fled were only nominally under the tsar's control. The more immediate authority was a single family — albeit one of Russia's most significant ever and at the height of its powers: the Stroganovs.[25] An old, apparently discredited, story has it that the Stroganovs were descendants of a Mongol who had been "chopped into small pieces for having engaged in treacherous dealings with an early grand duke of Vladimir."[26] In fact, the family hailed from the White Sea coast of Novgorod, later settling along the Dvina River where they laid the foundations of a trading and financial empire centered on Sol'vychegodsk on the Vychegda River, not far from modern-day Kotlas, and running from Vologda and Ustiug in the north to Riazan and Kaluga in the south. Expansion of trade east into nearer Siberia was a primary Stroganov ambition, already under way well before Ermak's time.

The Stroganovs' wealth lay mainly in salt production, and then in grain, minerals, and furs. They did brisk business both domestically and abroad, primarily with the English and Dutch, but also, via intermediaries, with merchants as far apart as Paris, Central Asia, and perhaps even China. Fleets of Stroganov vessels plied the rivers and seas connecting these places.[27] Their landholdings were immense — perhaps 600,000 square miles by the early 1500s and destined to grow far beyond this over the coming decades.[28] Their wealth was unparalleled. These assets purchased great political influence. The ambitions and successes of a string of rising Muscovite princes had been sewn together with free Stroganov loans.

The Stroganovs also maintained a private militia, which Ivan IV had relied upon to defend his eastern frontier since the 1550s while most of his regular forces were tied up in the Livonian War. Partly in return for this service; partly to pay off the debt of generations of his princely forebears; and partly because the Stroganovs were talented salesmen who laid before Ivan the promise of control of a fantastically rich (but essentially imagined) "kingdom" far beyond the Urals — his for the taking if only the Stroganovs might be allowed certain privileges and controls over lands in-between this distant vapor and the tsar's own lands — Ivan granted the Stroganovs large swaths of land in the Russian northeast, thereby further cementing their dominion in this region. Of particular importance was a charter of 1558 granting to Grigorii Stroganov, paterfamilias at the time, "the uninhabited lands, black

Portrait of the Cossack Ataman Yermak, by Alexei Gavrilovich Venetsianov, 1818. Lithograph (The State Hermitage Museum, St. Petersburg. Photograph © The State Hermitage Museum. Photo by Sergey Pokrovsky).

[coniferous] forests, wild rivers and lakes and uninhabited islands and marshlands ... which extend for some 88 versts [about 58 miles] along the [west] bank of the Kama from the mouth of the Lysvaia, and along the [east] bank of the Kama opposite Pyznovskaia backwaters, and along both banks of the Kama [along which Ermak would later flee] to the Chussovaia River." The charter also allowed Grigorii to "build a small town," "place cannon and defense guns," establish agriculture, bring in settlers (so long as they were not already registered taxpayers elsewhere in the tsar's domains), and prospect for salt. He was also given "complete judicial authority over his settlers." The arrangement was to last twenty years, after which time the Stroganovs would be required to "bring to [the tsar's] Treasury in Moscow ... whatever settlement our officials call for." The area was, of course, far from "uninhabited"—despite repeated use of the word in Ivan's letter. And Ivan himself admitted as much, noting that the "Perm people [local populations] may keep their established enterprises which they have held from ancient times."[29]

Over the following years, Ivan added more privileges and territories to the Stroganovs' original grant. In 1572 he authorized them to make war on a Siberian people called the Cheremis, whom he blamed for recent attacks on Russian settlements. A "letter patent" of 1574 allowed construction of forts "in Takhcheia" and along the Tobol' River and its tributaries. Ivan offered protection for any Siberian natives who would pay him tribute, and to any who would ally with him and the Stroganovs against Khan Kuchum of Sibir'. Significantly, near the end of the letter — almost as an afterthought — the tsar authorized the Stroganovs to build and garrison forts "on the Irtysh and Ob' and other rivers."[30] This was a virtual *carte blanche* for further expansion.

In return, the Stroganovs agreed to develop mining, industry, and agriculture in the area. As their interests in the region grew, so did the tools of their colonization, so that a "lengthening chain of military outposts and watchtowers soon dotted the river route to the east"—especially along the Chosva and Sylva Rivers.[31] This caused growing resentment among the Mansi and other affected Siberian peoples. Inevitably, and with a ferocity that sometimes took the Russians by surprise, these peoples fought back, taxing the Stroganovs' forces heavily. With the tsar reluctant to spare men from the Livonian War and the Stroganovs determined to pacify the area, it became vital to find new recruits. These were the circumstances into which Ermak and his men arrived in or around 1580.

A condition of Ivan's charters with the Stroganovs was that the latter should under no circumstances accommodate "brigands, outlaws or any persons who have run off from [nobles] with their possessions."[32] This should have excluded Ermak and his men. But of more immediate concern to both Ivan and the Stroganovs was the threat posed by Kuchum and his efforts to drive Russian settlers and Muscovite ambitions out of his domains. Kuchum used for these attacks his army of Mansi, Khanty, Bashkir, and Mari vassals.[33] These raids continued through 1581. The necessity of finding men to fight against Kuchum ran contrary to considerations about whom to accept for the job, especially as Ivan continued to extend the Stroganovs' charter to include lands further and further east, across the Urals and towards the river Ob'. On this basis alone, Ermak and his followers may well have been acceptable. Conversely, some recent historical accounts have emphasized the possibility that Ermak may have deliberately volunteered as a way to receive forgiveness and an official pardon for his earlier crimes. In this version of affairs, Ermak may simply have been availing himself of an existing and well-known willingness on the part of the tsar to swap an official pardon for useful state service.[34] In any case, it seems Ivan himself did not officially endorse Ermak's mission nor even knew of it at first, thus setting the scene for tensions down the road.

Ermak's Campaign

Ermak would not be the first Russian to lead an attack across the Urals and into Siberia, but he would be the first to make a real mark. Detachments from Novgorod had raided into the so-called Iugra land all the way back in 1187 and 1193, and much more recently, Ivan III (1462–1505) had sent two separate forces, led by members of the noble Kurbskii family, all the way to the Ob' River in 1483 and 1499. The best any of these had achieved was a one-time tribute payment.

Arriving in Stroganov territory, Ermak probably headed a group of about 540 Cossacks and others, though the number is variously assessed. According to one account, they had recently departed from the camp of one Ivan Kol'zo — a notorious *hetman* and pirate whose 7,000-strong force had recently been neutralized by a Russian formation of about 10,000.[35] At least according to some of the traditional sources, Ermak may not at first have brought great joy to the Stroganovs. Suggestions exist that he and his men raided and looted in the Stroganovs' territories before coming to terms and, even, that the Stroganovs sent him to Siberia in part just to get rid of him.

Whatever Ermak's relations with the Stroganovs, the campaign began, most likely, on 1 September 1581 (the conquest itself came in 1582).[36] Debate continues as to who formally initiated it, the Stroganovs or Ermak himself.[37] If the chronicles are to be believed, the affair was marked throughout by profound religious fervor. Prayers were offered "to the all merciful God of the Holy Trinity and to the Virgin Mother and all the heavenly powers and saints." The stated goal was to "drive out the godless barbarian"[38] and to "destroy the abominable gods" of the "infidel" (meaning the Muslim Tatar rulers rather than their subject pagan Siberians).[39] Ermak's army — probably swelled by now to about 840, including men given by the Stroganovs[40] — was well supplied. "[F]ine clothing and cannon, volley guns, seven-barreled muskets, and provisions [were] in abundance."[41] In fact, the supplies were so copious that, according to tradition, Ermak's boats began to sink, requiring some items be left behind.

Matters quickly deteriorated, however. Intending to cross the Urals before winter cold and snow presented impassable barriers, Ermak and his party apparently got lost along the Chussovaia River.[42] The wasted time forced a postponement. Ermak eventually set up camp among the mountains, built a small wooden church, and waited for the spring thaw. (Some folk legends also have him hiding treasure in caves in the area.) Not until May or June 1582 did the Russians finally find themselves on the far side of the Urals, sailing into the khan's domains.[43]

Ermak progressed almost entirely by river — sometimes following the current, at other times progressing under sail — in flat-bottomed boats, probably of the type known later as *doshchanki*. He did not pioneer a new route to the east but followed a series of rivers and portages already known to fur traders and others, including the above-noted Muscovite ambassador earlier killed on Kuchum's orders. The route (map 1) followed the Kama River into the Chussovaia, then into the smaller Serebrianka. A portage — estimated by a seventeenth-century chronicler at about 300 miles[44] but more likely only about eighteen — brought Ermak to a series of other rivers: the Zhuravlia, the Tagil, the Tura, the Tobol' (where much of the fighting was to take place), and finally along the Irtysh to Sibir' itself.[45] By late spring, Ermak was well inside Kuchum's realm and meeting increasing resistance. A captured Tatar reportedly provided useful information about the ruler, his forces, and about Isker — the primary settlement and capital of Sibir'. At about the same time, Kuchum learned of the approaching Russians.

Though native resistance was often fierce, Ermak and his men always had the huge advantage of firearms: "muskets, small volley guns, fowling pieces, small caliber fortress cannon, Spanish guns and harquebuses."[46] Neither Siberians nor Tatars had any such weapons (nor, it seems, had they ever seen such things before). They relied instead on arrows, horses, and other more traditional methods. Nonetheless, the defending Siberians showed great resourcefulness. At one point (probably in late June), they managed to stop Ermak's boats by stringing iron chains across the River Tobol'. It was a short-lived victory, however. The Russians simply disembarked and — with their vastly superior firepower — inflicted heavy casualties, broke the chains, and continued along the river.

As Ermak approached the confluence of the Tobol' and Irtysh Rivers, Kuchum prepared to make a stand. Sending his heir, Mametkul (described in several sources as his son, but usually regarded now as his nephew) to a hill called Chuvashevo, beside the Irtysh River, he ordered the construction of an abatis — a defensive structure made of felled trees — and earthworks. This done, Mametkul and his forces — perhaps ten thousand strong — then retired to a nearby location on the Tobol' River, called Babasan. Here they erected more fortifications and awaited their enemies and a fateful battle.

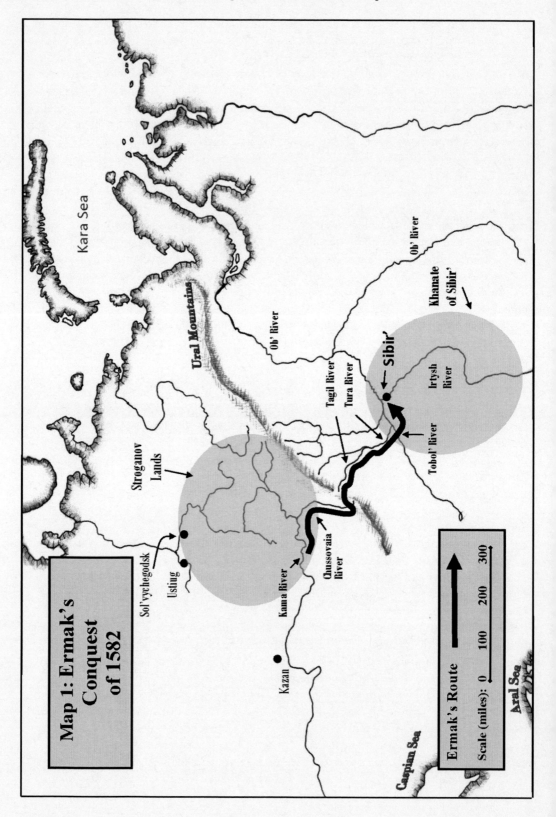

It is not known for certain when the Battle of Babasan occurred — 21 July 1582 is favored by some scholars. As the Siberians poured out of their defenses and gathered for attack, many on horseback, it became clear that Ermak's men were vastly outnumbered by a motley assortment of native Siberians and Tatars. The seventeenth-century Remezov Chronicle puts the Russians' disadvantage at thirty-to-one, though this is probably exaggerated. Then the battle was on, the Siberians attacking "the invading forces mercilessly ... and wound[ing] the Cossacks with their lances and sharp arrows."[47] The two sides fought "hand to hand, slashing one another" so that — in the colorful language of one of the chronicles — "the horses were up to their bellies in ... blood and corpses."[48] Predictably, however, modern firearms turned the tide in Ermak's direction. A large number of the native contingent of Kuchum's forces fled, and the rest soon withdrew.[49] The Cossacks then continued along the Tobol', suffering renewed arrow attacks but few if any casualties.

Eleven days later, on August 1, Ermak found himself again in the thick of battle, this time for control of an important encampment belonging to Karacha, one of Kuchum's chief advisors. The encounter in large part replayed its predecessor, with firearms proving decisive and the enemy sustaining heavy losses before fleeing. With the Tatar and native forces quickly resorting to guerrilla tactics, the summer growing old, and the real prize still ahead, Ermak opted to remain only two weeks, long enough to loot Karacha's compound of its food and valuables — "gold and silver, and precious stones and pearls, and money in quantity." Cattle were taken, too. Despite this temptation, the Remezov Chronicle has Ermak and his men "fervently praying and fasting" at this time, in honor of the Assumption.[50] Few modern writers take this seriously, presenting Ermak's army instead gorging itself to the point of sickness whenever opportunity allowed. Probably in the middle of August the company left the compound and pressed along the Irtysh under periodic harassment from Siberians hidden in the woods alongside. Further confrontations ensued over the coming weeks — none, as yet, decisive.

October was to be the most important month of the expedition. According to one account, things began auspiciously for the Cossacks on the 4th, when, having temporarily backtracked along the Tavda River, perhaps in search of supplies, they forced a grain tribute on the surrounding people — thereby beginning a tradition of tribute and tax collection among the Siberians that would continue in varied forms to the present. Then, around the third week of the month, Ermak came upon a settlement close to Kuchum's fort at Chuvashevo, belonging to a Tatar prince (or *murza*) named Atik. The Russians occupied it without great difficulty then contemplated their next move. Quickly, however, the situation became precarious. With Ermak now camped, and the rivers freezing over, Mametkul and Kuchum's forces began to gather in large numbers, preparing for the crucial showdown.

The chronicles place great emphasis on preparations for this battle, noting how greatly Ermak's forces were outnumbered (ten or twenty to one), how hopeless the odds seemed, and the impossibility of flight now that the weather was turning. Fervent prayers were offered for divine intervention, and rousing speeches were made to raise sinking morale. The following extract is from the Stroganov Chronicle and is, presumably, in Ermak's voice:

> Oh, brother comrades in arms, how can we retreat? Autumn has already set in. Ice is freezing in the rivers. We cannot take to flight and bring reproach and disgrace upon ourselves. Rather let us place our trust in God, for victory does not come from having a great mass of warriors, but from the help of God on high. It is possible that God will help even the helpless. Brothers, have we ourselves not heard what evil this godless and cursed heathen of the Siberian land, Sultan Kuchum, has brought on our Russian land of Perm, how he

has laid waste the towns of our Sovereign, and murdered and enslaved Orthodox Christians? Do we not know of the number of the Stroganovs' *ostrozheks* [small forts] he has destroyed? Almighty God will punish the cursed one for shedding Christian blood. Brothers, let us recall our oath, which we swore before God in the presence of honest men. We gave our word and promised, kissing the cross, that if Almighty God helped us, we would not retreat, even though we might die to the last man. We cannot turn back. We cannot dishonor ourselves and break the oath we have sworn. If the Almighty Glorious God of the Trinity will help us, then even if we fall, our memory will not die in these lands, and our glory will be eternal![51]

Apparently, this did the trick, for the men "all shouted an oath in one voice," that they were "ready to die for the holy church of God," to "suffer for the Orthodox faith," to "serve the devout Sovereign Tsar and Grand Prince" Ivan. As morning broke, good omens were seen: the sun "shone forth and pierced the clouds with radiant light."[52] It was the feast of St. James, October 23. Led by Ermak, more prayers were offered — to God, the Virgin, and the Saints. Then, as dawn appeared, the Cossacks headed toward the enemy fort, intending a reconnaissance but soon finding themselves in pitched battle as the defenders poured out of the abatis.

It must have been a terrifying event. Ermak's forces, though heavily outnumbered, "were all breathing with rage and fury, clad in iron, holding copper shields, bearing spears and firing iron shot." "The pagans shot innumerable arrows, and against them the Cossacks fired from fire-breathing harquebuses, and there was dire slaughter; in hand to hand fighting they cut each other down."[53] Though the Siberians had managed somehow to lay their hands on two cannons, these helped them little, if at all. Inexperienced in their use, they crowded too closely around the barrels, endangering themselves as much as the attackers, while also reducing their own freedom of movement and offering the Russians an easier target.

The battle raged on and off over four days. Slowly, the invaders began to gain the upper hand, driving their enemy back. By the 25th, victory was within sight — large numbers of Siberians began to desert. And in a dramatic turn of events that day, Mametkul himself sustained a serious wound and was evacuated along the Irtysh. Kuchum — watching from the relative safety of a neighboring hill — was now supposedly overcome with a bout of self-recrimination and repentance. He cried out: "My evil has fallen back upon my own head, and my own injustice has overtaken me. I was joyous when I attacked the Russian lands, Great Perm and the Stroganov *ostrozheks*, but now I have lost all that was mine, and I have been conquered."[54] Whatever his actual thoughts at the time, Kuchum hastily retired to Isker, gathered some possessions, and fled.

The next day, October 26 — diminished in number by more than a hundred — Ermak's forces arrived to claim their prize: Isker. The main stronghold, measuring about 300 feet in diameter, was ringed with palisades and other obstacles, and perched at the top of a steep-sided hill. The main gates, however, were wide open and Ermak and his men moved in without resistance. Looting ensued, with the Cossacks acquiring "a great amount of gold and silver, cloth of gold, precious stones, sables, martens and valuable foxes."[55] More prizes were on their way. Four days later a party of native Siberians arrived, this time not to fight but to deliver tribute — an acknowledgement that Ermak, not Kuchum, was now the accepted power. Furs, women, trinkets, and food poured in.

While the conquerors enjoyed their spoils, Ermak set about the urgent business of consolidating his gains. A messenger was sent to inform the almost-forgotten Stroganovs of the glorious results of the expedition they had funded. The messenger later returned, though with depressing news. Bearing on his back a swath of welts — results of a beating administered on behalf of the Stroganovs — he presented a letter from the same. Addressed to Ermak, it demanded repayment of 30,000 rubles earlier advanced — with interest. Ermak himself was ordered to return immediately to face trial for his "misdeeds." It must have seemed a strange reward for victory.

The Stroganovs' apparent ingratitude had good reason, however. They had recently received an angry missive from Ivan himself accusing *them* of "disobedience amounting to treason"[56] for sending Ermak to Sibir' without proper authorization. Ivan's anger stemmed from a recent surge of attacks against Russian villages and outposts in the Upper Kama Valley carried out by native Mansis in retaliation for some of Ermak's early raids. Ivan, of course, had no way of knowing at that point that the troublesome Cossack had gone on to conquer Sibir' itself.

Ermak pondered his choices. One of his company suggested bypassing the Stroganovs altogether and trying instead to curry favor directly with the tsar. Surely he would come round once he knew of the great prize that had been won. To this end a sizeable shipment of furs or other tribute should be sent. With the tsar on his side, what need would Ermak and his band have of the Stroganovs?

As these plans were hatching, further numbers of natives, Tatars, and their women returned to the area around Ermak's stronghold. Hopes of an easy rest for the Cossacks were soon dispelled, however. On December 5,[57] Mametkul reappeared. His men ambushed a party of twenty Russians fishing at "a place called Iabolak,"[58] killing them all. Ermak mounted a quick counterattack that cost numerous lives on both sides, then returned to the fort at Isker while his enemies vanished into the forest. There were no other major confrontations over the winter.

The need to make direct contact with Ivan was made all the more urgent by the difficulty Ermak and his men faced holding, with only a few hundred men, a fort in the middle of what was still essentially hostile territory. Consequently, despite the winter having set in hard, an embassy was sent to Moscow during December in search of recognition and forgiveness, supplies and reinforcements. There is at least one contemporary report that Ermak himself went to Moscow at this time, but that is almost certainly untrue.[59] One "Kol'zo" (the same name, but not the same man mentioned earlier), an *ataman* from Ermak's company, went instead.

Kol'zo's embassy, laden with furs, reached Moscow in February 1583. Initially mistaken for the notorious riverboat pirate of the same name, Kol'zo was brought in bonds before his tsar, who immediately fell to salivating over "2,400 dark sables, 2,000 beavers, and 800 big black foxes."[60] This was much more than the value of the annual tribute Kuchum had earlier broken off. No doubt it soothed Ivan, who quickly accepted all that was explicitly offered and, it seems, much that was not: complete personal dominion over Ermak's conquest (apparently without reference even to the Stroganovs) and all the potential riches it offered. In exchange, Ermak and his men were granted royal pardons, clothing, and cash — the latter likely of modest value. Ivan also sent Ermak two suits of chain mail bearing the royal insignia. Received in Isker in March, the armor would soon acquire great significance.

Back in Isker, Ermak and his men continued to enjoy the influx of tribute, including Siberian women, and to bully and terrorize the local population. The Native Siberian men, increasingly outraged at the Cossacks' behavior, attacked and harassed them at every opportunity. Efforts by Ermak's men to spread Christianity — especially the burning of local totems — outraged more than it converted. Around this time also, Ermak sent a detachment of his men northward down the Irtysh in order to also bring under control Siberian settlements at Nazym.

Mametkul, injured but still in action, also organized raids. During the late winter of 1583, news came to Ermak that his nemesis was encamped on the nearby Vagai River. The Cossack sent sixty men to intercept him and, during a nighttime raid, inflicted significant casualties. Mametkul himself was taken prisoner. This latter piece of news, which soon reached Kuchum himself at his camp on the Ishim River, only added to the probability that another major offensive would soon be launched against Ermak's diminishing forces. Mametkul was apparently treated well by Ermak, held for quite some time, and then sent to Moscow, probably in 1584.

Before this, on 10 May 1583, Tsar Ivan finally authorized the dispatch of a force of several hundred men to Isker. They were not quite the reinforcements Ermak had hoped for. In command were Prince Semen Bolkhovskii and Ivan Glukhov. Ivan intended to make Bolkhovskii governor of the region, effectively pushing Ermak aside. But fortune had not yet deserted the Cossack adventurer. The tsar's men, unused to the rigors of western Siberia, made slow progress, and were forced to winter over in Perm. Ermak and company were left to their own devices for the time being.

They were hardly having an easy time of it, however. Meager food supplies and illness made life inside the compound difficult while constant native harassment made forays beyond it highly risky. At some point in 1584, Ermak suffered a blow at the hands of his earlier victim Karacha, who arranged to have envoys sent to Ermak posing as men loyal to the tsar. They asked for help against the Nogais — another declining but still formidable remnant of the Golden Horde. Ermak apparently took the request at face value and, perhaps seeing an opportunity to ingratiate himself with his sovereign, sent a trusted lieutenant — the same Ivan Kol'zo who had earlier visited the tsar in Moscow — and forty men. Arriving in Karacha's camp, all were killed. Emboldened by this victory, Karacha advanced on Isker and then blockaded it, hoping to starve out Ermak. After some weeks, however, Ermak and some of his men counterattacked under cover of darkness. Karacha's forces suffered heavy losses and the remainder fled. The siege was ended. But with his retinue further reduced, Ermak's circumstances remained precarious.

Sometime after the end of summer 1584, the "reinforcements" Ivan had sent under the command of Bolkhovskii and Glukhov finally arrived. The journey had not been kind to them. All of the horses had been lost, along with most of the weapons and food supplies they had set out with. Too weakened and wretched to constitute a threat to Ermak, the new arrivals brought disaster nonetheless by further draining the Cossacks' already precarious food reserves. The Russians spent the winter of 1584-1585 in a severe famine. Bolkhovskii did not survive.

Matters improved the following spring with the melting of the snows. Various Tatars, Khants, and Mansis delivered game, livestock, furs, and other valuable items. But for Ermak and most of his men these were to be the last of the good times.

The Strange Death of Ermak Timofeev

The circumstances of Ermak's death, like much in his life, remain unclear. Different chronicles, folk songs, and legends have him expiring in various ways, and it is virtually certain the matter will never be resolved. All accounts agree, however, that a trap was laid near the start of August. In one version, representatives of Bukhara merchants contact Ermak to report that Kuchum was preventing them from passing. Others have Ermak simply resolving to rob a food-laden caravan he had been told was moving along the Irtysh River. Whatever the truth, Ermak and about a hundred of his men headed along the river to meet the travelers. Finding nothing, and with darkness gathering, they headed their boats back toward Isker. It already being late, they camped for the night, probably on a small island. Then the trap was sprung. In heavy rain, while Ermak and his men slept, Kuchum's forces silently attacked, slitting throats.

Was Ermak this easily and ignominiously dispatched? Perhaps. But other, more romantic endings to his story are also told, any of which could be true. Some have Ermak waking during the slaughter and attempting an escape. In one version, he lurches for his boat, slips, badly hits his head, and is then finished off. But the most appealing and dramatic ending of all — rich with symbolic import — is outlined in the Remezov Chronicle, and embellished in other legends. As his men are slaughtered, Ermak, wakened by the mayhem, desperately throws on his chain-mail armor — the very suit given to the Conqueror of Siberia by Tsar Ivan himself. Thus protected, Ermak makes a desperate leap from a high embankment into his boat. But the vessel has drifted a little way out from the bank. He falls short — or perhaps hits the boat at its edge, causing it to capsize — and is dragged down by the weight of his armor to a watery grave, watched by Kuchum. It was, perhaps, the night of August 5–6, 1585.

However it happened, Ermak's death came too late to change the fate of Sibir'. Though the few Cossacks still in the fortress quickly fled after hearing of their leader's fate, other Russians, sent directly from Moscow, soon arrived to chase the returned Tatars and Siberians back out for good. The end of the Livonian War in 1583 generally facilitated the dispatch of troops east, while the death of Ivan the Terrible the following year did nothing to diminish Russian commitment to full annexation and further eastward expansion. Western Siberia had fallen.

* * *

In the wake of Ermak's demise, Tsar Ivan made it a priority to secure access to the Tura River, and so to consolidate the victory. Running east from the foothills of the Urals into the Tobol', the Tura constituted the primary entryway into Sibir' from the west at this time and had been Ermak's way in. Along its banks Russia consequently founded the town of Tiumen' in 1586. The following year, a little further east, Tobol'sk was established near the confluence of the Tobol' and Irtysh Rivers, close to the important sites of Babasan and Isker itself. Less than two decades later, the two main arteries of western Siberia, the Irtysh and Ob' Rivers, had been effectively secured with a string of forts and settlements running from Tara and Tomsk in the south (1594 and 1604) to Obdorsk on the Arctic coast (1595). Decades of uprisings and pacifications lay ahead, however.

The Stroganovs benefited less from these developments than they had perhaps hoped. They never got to possess or control the new lands or settlements east of the Urals, though they did manage to win numerous trade concessions. The family, in any case, was to remain wealthy and influential for many more generations.

But what of Kuchum? He too has been written off in various ways. For sure, he remained at large — and a thorn in the Russians' side — for well over another decade. Efforts to catch and kill him were undertaken by the Muscovite government throughout the 1590s, but succeeded only in 1598 when, by now an old man, he appears to have been dispatched by Nogai agents of the tsar. Alternative versions have him drowning in the Ob' River or killed by Bukharans.[61]

His nephew and thwarted heir, Mametkul (who had earlier been captured and sent to Moscow), enjoyed a kinder fate. Along with other members of Kuchum's immediate family, he had his loyalty to the Russian state purchased with noble titles, marriage, and high offices.

Ermak's "Afterlife"

Posthumously, Ermak became a hero of mythical proportions in Russian, Christian, and even Tatar memory. Old legends have it that his corpse was eventually recovered by a fisherman, who recognized it by the royal suit of armor. The body, though dead, continued for a long time to bleed whenever pierced. And it did not decompose. Miraculous healings were reported. And when the corpse was finally buried beside a pine tree, flames leapt from the grave for many years.

Notions such as these have kept Ermak an enduring icon of Russian history and imagination to the present day — and have granted him a long and interesting historiography.[62] He looms large in folk traditions — his life and death being celebrated in songs and tales. Even now he is among the pantheon of heroes both of Russian nationalists (who revere him for enlarging the Russian state) and within the Orthodox Church (to whose faith and influence he opened the whole of Siberia). The historical anthropologist James Forsyth has noted the following symbols of Ermak's legend in more recent times: "An Orthodox banner depicting St. Dmitri, which ostensibly belonged to [Ermak], is preserved in the cathedral in Omsk; a monument to him was erected in Tobol'sk in 1839; he was made the subject of a famous ballad by the Romantic poet Ryleev (also Ryleyev); and his (Christian) victory over the 'pagans' is celebrated in a vast painting made by V. I. Surikov in 1895 which hangs in the Russian Museum in Leningrad."[63]

Ermak is also an adaptable hero. The Soviets — foes (theoretically) of Russian nationalism and of the Orthodox Church alike — admired him no less. For them, the rough-and-ready river-boat pirate and his companions exemplified the tradition of history being made by common, "proletarian" folk, and also the forward march of (Russian) modernity in the face of (Siberian) "backwardness." This latter point is reflected in the wider tendency of Soviet-era historiography to emphasize — often to the point of sheer distortion — the supposedly "comradely" and mutually beneficial relations between Russians and Native Siberians, not just in the time of Ermak, but over centuries of Russian expansion. Post-Soviet Russian scholars, by contrast, are increasingly rejecting this interpretation and instead accepting that Russian expansion and colonialism were no less brutal and exploitative than their Western European counterparts.[64]

It is possible that excessive emphasis has been placed on Ermak and his one expedition as the moment when Russia assimilated nearer Siberia. The Russian historian S. V. Bakhrushin has argued as much, noting that the way had been paved earlier, not only by Novgorodians or by the forces of Ivan III noted above, but by Russian hunters and merchants — mostly nameless individuals and small groups who had presumably begun making their way beyond the Urals decades before Ermak and who continued to do so afterwards.[65] Other Soviet-era Russians, perhaps in keeping with their Marxist framework, have also emphasized the more important but less visible role played (before and after the 1580s) by ordinary Russian migrants — peasants especially. These, it is claimed, were the real "conquerors" of Siberia.[66] Finally, the existence of other "unknown" Russian expeditions into

Siberia, dating to the late fourteenth century, has also been argued, though with little success.[67]

The Conquest of Middle and Further Siberia

Scarcely was Russian domination of western Siberia even nominally achieved when the seeds of further expansion were already germinating. Five years after the founding of Obdorsk in 1595, an intrepid group of about one hundred Cossacks in four small vessels used it as the setting-off point for the main stage of a journey east along the Arctic coast. They landed at Taz Bay, whence they accessed the Taz River, sailing south. Here they built the fort of Mangazeia. Though they did not know it at the time, they were less than 150 miles from Siberia's next great river system to the east—and from the next major phase of Russian expansion—onto the Enisei.

Suggestions for Further Reading in English and Russian

Almazov, Boris. *Ataman Yermak so tovarishchami* [Ataman Yermak with his Comrades]. St. Petersburg: Terra, 1997.

Andreev, A. I., *Ocherki po istochnikovedeniiu Sibiri*. Vol. 1, *XVII vek*. Outline of Source Studies of Siberia. 2nd ed. Moscow-Leningrad: Akademiia Nauk SSSR, 1960.

Armstrong, Terence, ed. *Yermak's Campaign in Siberia: A Selection of Documents*. Translated by Tatiana Minorsky and David Wileman. London: Hakluyt Society, 1975.

Bobrick, Benson. *East of the Sun: The Epic Conquest and Tragic History of Siberia*. New York: Poseidon Press, 1992.

Buzukashvili, M. I. *Ermak: Geroicheskoe proshloe nashei rodiny*. Moscow: Voennoe izdatel'stvo, 1989.

Collins, D. N. "Russia's Conquest of Siberia: Evolving Russian and Soviet Historical Interpretations." *European Studies Review* 12, no. 1 (1982): 17–43.

De Hartog, L. *Russia Under the Mongol Yoke: The History of the Russian Principalities and the Golden Horde, 1221–1502*. London: British Academic Press, 1996.

Dmytryshyn, Basil. "Russian Expansion to the Pacific, 1580–1700: A Historiographic Review." *Slavic Studies* 25 (1980): 1–26.

Dmytryshyn, Basil, E. A. P. Crownhart-Vaughan, and Thomas Vaughan, eds. *Russia's Conquest of Siberia: A Documentary Record, 1558–1700*. Vol. 1. Portland: Western Imprints, Press of the Oregon Historical Society, 1985.

Dvoretskaia, N. A. "Ofitsial'naia i fol'klornaia otsenka pokhoda Yermaka v XVII v." [Official and Folklore Evaluations of Yermak's Campaign in the 17th Century]. *Trudy Otdela drevnerusskoi literatury* 14 (1958): 330–34.

Fedorov, E. A. *Yermak*. Moscow: Novaia, 1995.

Forsyth, James. *A History of the Peoples of Siberia: Russia's North Asian Colony, 1581–1990*. Cambridge: Cambridge University Press, 1992.

Funk, Dmitry, and Lennard Sillanpää, eds. *The Small Indigenous Nations of Northern Russia*. Vaasa, Finland: Åbo Akademi University, Social Science Unit, 1999.

Gorelov, A. A. "Trilogiia o Ermake iz sbornika Kirshi Danilova." In *Russkii fol'klor: materialy i Issledovaniia*. Moscow-Leningrad: Akademiia nauk, 1961, 345–76.

Hellie, Richard. "Migration in Early Modern Russia, 1480s–1780s." In *Coerced and Free Migration: Global Perspectives*. Edited by David Eltis. Stanford, CA: Stanford University Press, 2002.

Istoriia Sibiri: s drevneishykh vremen do nashykh dnei. 5 vols. Leningrad: "Nauka," 1968–69.

Khodarkovsky, Michael. *Russia's Steppe Frontier: The Making of a Colonial Empire, 1550–1800*. Bloomington: Indiana University Press, 2002.

Lantzeff, G. V., and R. A. Pierce. *Eastward to Empire: Exploration and Conquest on the Russian Open Frontier to 1750*. Montreal: McGill-Queen's University Press, 1973.

Lessner, Erwin. *Cradle of Conquerors: Siberia*. Garden City, NY: Doubleday, 1955.

Mueller, G. F. *Istoriia Sibiri*. 2 vols. Moscow, 1937–41.

Naumov, Igor V., and David N. Collins. *The History of Siberia*. Routledge Studies in the History of Russia and Eastern Europe, vol. 6. New York: Routledge, 2006.

Ogorodnikov, V. I. *Ocherk istorii Sibiri do nachala XIX stoletiia*. Irkutsk, 1920.

Ostrowski, D. *Muscovy and the Mongols: Cross-Cultural Influences on the Steppe Frontier, 1304–1589*. Cambridge: Cambridge University Press, 1998.

Pierre, Maureen. "Outlawry (*vorovstva*) and Redemption through Service: Ermak and the Volga Cossacks." In *Culture and Identity in Muscovy, 1359–1584*. Edited by A. M. Kleimola and G. D. Lenhoff. Moscow: ITZ-Garant, 1997.

Sergeev, V. I. "K voprosu o pokhode v Sibir' druzhiny Yermaka" [On the Siberian Campaign of Yermak's Band]. *Voprosy istorii* 1 (1959): 117–29.

Severin. T. "Conquistadors of Siberia." In *The Oriental Adventure: Explorers of the East*. Boston, 1976, 40–60.

Skrynnikov, R. G. "Ermak's Siberian Expedition." *Russian History/Histoire Russe* 13 (1986): 1–39.

_____. *Sibirskaia ekspeditsiia Ermaka*. 2nd ed., Novosibirsk: "Nauka," 1986.

Slovtsov, P. A. *Pis'ma o Sibiri* [Letters about Siberia]. St. Petersburg, 1826; Tiumen: Mandriki, 1999.

Svin'in, P. P. *Shemiakin Sud; Yermak, ili Pokorenie Sibiri* [Shemiaka's Tribunal. Yermak, or Siberia's subjugation], Moscow: Kronos, 1994.

Wieczynski, Joseph L. "Toward a Frontier Theory of Early Russian History." *The Russian Review*. 33, no. 3 (1974):284–95.

Williams, Robert C. *Ruling Russian Eurasia: Khans, Clans, and Tsars*. Malabar, FL: Krieger, 2000.

Chapter 2

Into the Siberian Interior: The Crossing and Early Investigation of Terrestrial North Eurasia

The Khanate of Sibir' turned out to be the last significant barrier to Russian eastward expansion short of the distant Pacific coast (reached in 1639, see chapter 3) and north of the mighty Chinese Empire. With some exceptions (mainly the Kirghiz, Buriats, and Chuckhi), Siberia's numerous native peoples — the inhabitants of all these spaces — were, to their great misfortune, relatively easy to defeat and dominate. And Russians found compelling reasons to do so, for their lands, forests, and rivers teemed with priceless furs: mink, sable, ermine, otter, and others. There were also valuable minerals, particularly iron and copper. Tribute and plunder, and secondarily the propagation of Orthodox Christianity, became the engines of a contiguous expansion that quickly and permanently turned Russia into the world's largest state.

Although many different kinds of Russians poured into Siberia in the decades following Ermak's death — including state peasants, runaways, and clerics — the advance guard of exploration comprised two main groups: state soldiers (often Cossacks) and *promyshlenniki*. The former were official men, dispatched by the Muscovite government on its behalf and for its benefit. Their names are often well known. Ermak himself was, arguably, of this type[1]; certainly those who were sent to consolidate his conquest were.

The other type was the *promyshlennik*. The word connotes a person engaged in commerce and is translated variously as *hunter-entrepreneur*, *trader*, or *prospector*. *Promyshlenniki* were essentially self-directed opportunists. Though some were able to turn their skills into official commissions, the greater part lived, worked, and sometimes died on the fringes of society as fur-trappers, traders, and looters — often all three at once. One apt recent description has them as persons determined to make something of themselves either "by feat or by crime."[2] They came from all over Russia, but especially from what, prior to the penetration of Siberia, had been the northeast, on the European side of the Ural Mountains. These were towns such as "Great Ustiug, Sol'vychegodsk, Solikamsk, Kargopol', Kholmogor, Vologda, and so on."[3] They typically lacked most of the qualifications one might expect of great explorers — geographical and navigational training, proper equipment, and state backing. The first of these things they generally learned on the job (or perished from the lack thereof); the second they often made do without, negotiating some of the world's most hostile and forbidding terrains and climates in incredibly basic fashion; and the third, if it came at all, tended to be granted after the fact, by a state anxious to reap the benefits of their prodigious labors.

What the *promyshlenniki* possessed in abundance was courage. Here were men — and probably some women[4] — who sailed uncharted and wild Arctic coasts, sometimes in tiny boats barely fit for river duty; who followed unknown frozen rivers or treacherous rapids through hostile lands with minimal equipment and strategy; who trudged by foot across some of the most desolate territory anywhere on earth, in bitter cold and stifling heat, amid clouds of biting insects, and through periods of hunger and starvation. They improvised virtually every aspect of their lives day-to-day — all in search of the wealth that could be attained by bringing home a cargo of furs (or less frequently, walrus ivory or other commodities). In the seventeenth century in particular, some of the best furs were literally worth more than their weight in gold, especially on Chinese markets. (Fur values declined in the eighteenth century in the face of new supplies from North America.) A person could physically carry sufficient pelts to make himself rich. Some of the *promyshlenniki* triumphed and became wealthy. Others died, poor and unknown. The ratio can only be guessed at. The Soviet explorer G. A. Ushakov offers the following poignant example: "In 1940 a group of Soviet sailors carrying out hydrological work disembarked on the small, empty island of Faddei, lying close to the eastern coast of the Taimyr Peninsula [the northernmost extension of Eurasia]. On the shore the sailors suddenly came upon some copper cauldrons sticking out of the ground." Upon further inspection they found also "frying pans, scissors, a copper bell, tin plates, and some blue glass beads."[5] The following year similar finds, including datable coins, were made on the mainland of the Taimyr Peninsula. By 1945 a picture had emerged telling of an ill-fated expedition — made by entirely unknown Russians in 1617 or earlier — that had rounded the Taimyr Peninsular from west to east before losing their fight against the harsh elements.

Though they often worked separately, official men and *promyshlenniki* ultimately complemented one another, each providing a vital part to the overall process of Russian exploration and expansion. Typically, the *promyshlenniki* were first into any given area, often serving as vital sources of information for the state and even as a link between the state and Siberian natives, whose culture and languages some assimilated.

From Ermak's Sibir' to the Enisei Valley

Eurasia's main riparian arteries — the Ob', Enisei, Lena, Iana, Indigirka, and Kolyma — all run south to north and are very roughly parallel to each other. They thus serve as consecutive, incremental frontiers, and in the decades following Ermak's adventures, Russia's eastward expansion may usefully be reckoned in terms of progress from one to the next (map 2). Though these river valleys are separated by many hundreds of miles — or by more than a thousand in the case of the Enisei and Lena — they are all nearly joined in many places by a network of tributaries running east and west. With some (or much) effort these gaps could often be bridged by portage. It was along these routes that the Russians focused almost all their efforts during the seventeenth century — so much so that the first Russian empire in Eurasia, so to speak, was almost entirely river based.

Ermak's contribution had been to bring Russians to the Irtysh River, and more generally onto the larger Ob' basin of which it is part. Almost immediately thereafter, other Russians, unknown *promyshlenniki* for the most part, pushed on towards the next major river, the Enisei, approaching it first from downstream at high northern latitudes, later pushing south. They traveled both by sea, hugging the Arctic coast, and by land, crossing passes in the

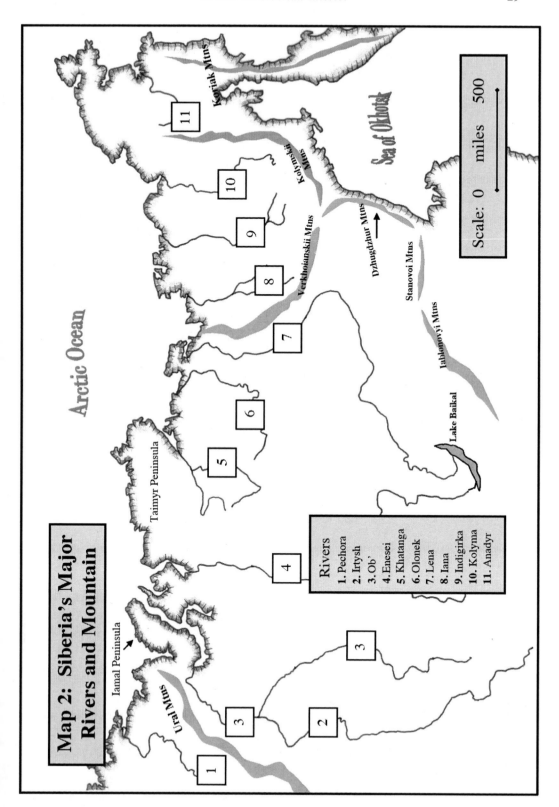

Map 2: Siberia's Major Rivers and Mountain

Arctic Ocean

Iamal Peninsula

Ural Mtns

Taimyr Peninsula

Koriak Mtns

Kolymskii Mtns

Verkhoianskii Mtns

Dzhugdzhur Mtns

Stanovoi Mtns

Iablonovyi Mtns

Lake Baikal

Sea of Okhotsk

Scale: 0   miles   500

Rivers
1. Pechora
2. Irtysh
3. Ob'
4. Enesei
5. Khatanga
6. Olonek
7. Lena
8. Iana
9. Indigirka
10. Kolyma
11. Anadyr

Ural Mountains. The first of them were on the river well before 1600.[6] The first settlement — a small winter camp at Turukhansk — was founded in 1607 near the confluence of the Lower Tunguska. Eniseisk, a larger fort-settlement farther south, near the influx of the Angara, followed in 1619. These forts, and the official Russians who came to build them, were in some cases opposed not only by local native peoples, but also by the *promyshlenniki* who had preceded them — the latter fearing the loss of their own profitable positions as fur-trade pioneers. During 1600, for example, Russian military personnel came into conflict with both groups on the Taz, directly west of the Enisei itself.[7] By the 1620s the trickle of Russians was becoming a flood. By now, too, the more southerly upwaters of the Enisei were being explored and settled, leading to the establishment of Krasnoiarsk in 1628 and Bratsk in 1630 (map 3).

From the Enisei to the Lena

Once on the Enisei, Russians quickly and frequently clashed with the native Evenk (or Tungus) and Buriat peoples whose territory spread far to the east and south. From their first encounters with the Evenks, Russians learned of the existence of the next great river to the east, the Lena; of the Iakuts ("horsepeople") who lived along its banks; and of the reputed great fur wealth of the region. Predictably, by the early 1620s the first *promyshlenniki* had already found their way there, setting off from Tobol'sk and Tomsk. They found, and quickly decimated, an especially abundant population of sable, along with other furs.

The first official men were not far behind. Perhaps first was the military captain, V. Bugor, who may have reached the Lena itself as early as 1628 via portages from the Angara. Two years later another military captain, I. Galkin, not only reached the great river, but went beyond, venturing during the spring of 1631 into entirely unknown Iakut lands to the east.[8] More speculatively, a little earlier, at the end of the 1620s, state servitors A. Dobrynskii and M. Vasil'ev — accompanied by a *promyshlennik* named A. T. Lupachko — may have pushed as far as the Aldan, a major tributary east of the upper reaches of the Lena.[9]

A more well-known Russian pioneer on the Lena is the Cossack military captain Petr Beketov. During 1628, Beketov had made a name for himself extracting tribute from the Buriats and Evenks of the Angara River, west of the upper Lena. Under Beketov's boot the native peoples quickly acceded to Muscovite control, allowing the Russian to return a hero to his base in Eniseisk. Three years later he left on another state-sponsored mission, this time to the Lena. Setting out in May 1631 he "portaged from Ilimsk[10] (founded the previous year) to the Lena with about thirty men, proceeded [down] the river, built a fortified camp of fallen trees, and imposed tribute" on the local population.[11] The following year he founded the settlement of Iakutsk. It quickly became the capital of eastern Siberia, eventually growing into a great city. In 1635, Beketov founded Olekminsk, located higher up the Lena, at a point he had previously passed en route to Iakutsk.

Of course, these things are easier said than they were done. In 1633, Beketov himself filed an official report, now often quoted. Besides noting the great quantities of furs he had so far procured for his tsar, he described how over the course of two-and-a-half years he and his men had "shed our blood, suffered every privation, starved, eaten every unclean thing [he specifically mentioned grass and fir bark], and defiled our souls."[12] Like most Cossack explorers of the time he shed plenty of other people's blood too. During 1631, dissatisfied with the amount of "tsar's tribute" he had been able to get from a group of sixty Buriats of

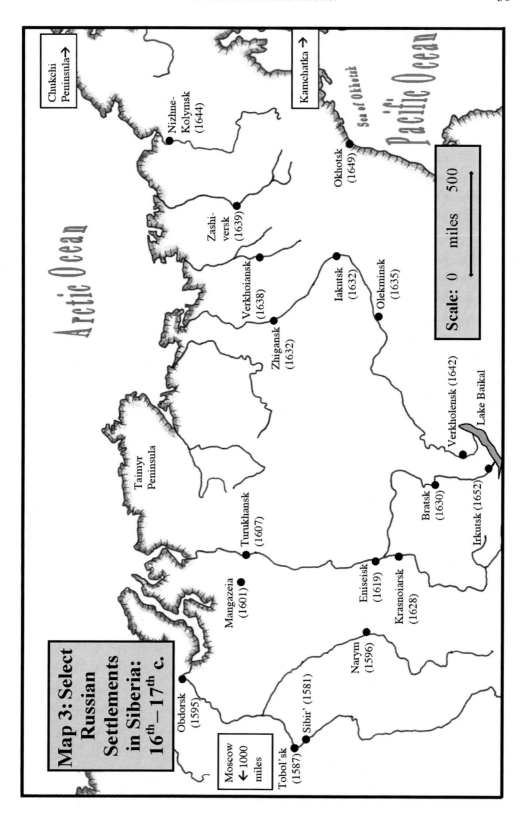

Map 3: Select Russian Settlements in Siberia: 16th – 17th c.

Arctic Ocean

Pacific Ocean

Chukchi Peninsula →

Kamchatka →

Sea of Okhotsk

Nizhne-Kolymsk (1644)

Okhotsk (1649)

Zashi-versk (1639)

Verkhoiansk (1638)

Iakutsk (1632)

Olekminsk (1635)

Zhigansk (1632)

Verkholensk (1642)

Lake Baikal

Taimyr Peninsula

Turukhansk (1607)

Bratsk (1630)

Irkutsk (1652)

Mangazeia (1601)

Eniseisk (1619)

Krasnoiarsk (1628)

Obdorsk (1595)

Narym (1596)

Sibir' (1581)

Moscow ← 1000 miles

Tobol'sk (1587)

Scale: 0 miles 500

the upper Lena, he "upbraided and threatened them," eventually provoking a confrontation in which "forty of the Buriats were ... massacred on the spot and the rest left wounded."[13] Other common Russian tactics of the time, designed to win tribute from Siberian natives, included the kidnapping of wives and children. Rape was utterly commonplace. Siberian native communities could be equally barbaric, of course, although they at least could fairly claim to be acting against unprovoked attack in defense of their lands and ways.

The further east Russians penetrated into Siberia the further away Moscow lay. Once the Lena had been reached the capital was almost impossibly distant. Travel to and from it typically took a year or more, and the tsar's authority in these remote Siberian lands, consequently, was at first more nominal than real, making mayhem and disorder almost inevitable. Though the government did occasionally reprimand military captains and others for excessive use of force (beginning with Ermak himself) and for acting more in their own interests than those of the state, often even the most gross violations of conduct were overlooked if the end result was useful to the state.

In the meantime, Russians — both the independent *promyshlenniki* and those sent by the government — continued to push through Siberia, now using Iakutsk as a base, and heading northeast, east, and south. The conquest of these growing expanses took another important turn when, in 1637, the Russian government established the Bureau of Siberian Affairs (*Sibirskii prikaz*). With jurisdiction over all Siberia, including lands not yet even glimpsed, its purview was comprehensive: administration, military affairs, justice, transportation, finance and trade, and natural resources. Its functions were transferred by Tsar Peter the Great in 1710 to a provincial chancery at Tobol'sk.[14]

From the Lena to the Iana and Indigirka

With almost dizzying speed, the Lena passed from frontier to stepping stone, as the Russians leapfrogged farther and farther east, river by river by river. Beyond the Lena, spaced at almost even intervals of several hundred miles, lie three nearly parallel waterways: the Iana, Indigirka, and Kolyma. In 1633 S. Kharitonov and Posnik Ivanov crossed the imposing Verkhoianskii mountain range and stumbled upon a dry-land route that led them during 1636–1637 onto the upper reaches of the Iana and on to the Indigirka.[15] During the same years — 1633–1638 — working from Arctic coastal waters, their compatriots, I. Rebrov and M. Perfil'ev, found the mouths of the same two rivers.

Another early pioneer beyond the Lena was the Cossack Elisei Buza. Setting out in 1637 from Iakutsk, Buza followed the Lena downstream (north), passing through the forest zone, then tundra and mountains, then the river delta, before finally entering the frigid Arctic Ocean. Here, he and his party headed a little way back west to a winter camp near the mouth of the Olonek River. The following season Buza turned east, this time traveling, largely overland, as far as the Iana River then, like Kharitonov and Ivanov before him, through the Verkhoianskii Mountains and on to the Indigirka. Here he may have become the first Russian to meet the native Iukaghir people who lived "wedged between the Iakuts [Sakha] in the interior and the Tungus [Evenks] on the coast."[16] Buza discovered three or possibly four new tributary rivers in the region. Tales of rich hunting grounds and possible silver deposits ensured others would soon follow in his wake.

One who quickly did so was Dmitri Zyrian, another Cossack, who in 1640 took fifteen men north down the Indigirka River. After collecting tribute from the local Iukaghirs he too entered the Arctic Ocean. Turning east into uncharted waters he sailed along the coast, further than any Russian previously, to the Alazeia River. Here he learned of still another major river further east.

This was the Kolyma, fated three hundred years later to host many of Stalinist Russia's notorious labor camps. The river enters the Arctic Ocean near 160° east longitude. Declining to travel further himself, Zyrian left the way open for his compatriot Mikhail Stadukhin, who reached the river in 1644, became the first European to encounter the native Chukchi, and the same year founded Srednekolymsk. In this case, a state servitor (Stadukhin) preceded the *promyshlenniki*, who came to the Kolyma in search of furs in 1646. Both the *promyshlenniki* and official state servitors soon went beyond, however, trading with the local Chukchis (often exchanging iron and other metal products for furs) and from them learning of destinations yet further to the east. It must have seemed to the Russians that the land — and the opportunities — went east forever. In fact, the Pacific Ocean and the end of Eurasia were now only a few hundred miles away.

Relations with the Chukchi, and with the neighboring Iukaghirs, both of whom were fiercely independent, deteriorated quickly and steadily, however, in the face of brutal treatment meted out by the advancing Russians — who, as well as forcing the native people to deliver ever larger quantities of fur tribute or compelling them to purchase metalwares at extortionate rates, frequently resorted to kidnapping, murder, rape, enslavement, the destruction of winter clothing and fishing equipment, the humiliation of shamans, and spoliation of religious items.[17] Though lacking all modern weapons and tactics, the Chukchis, especially, nonetheless put up such a fight that it would take the Russians well over a century after first contact to bring them more-or-less under control.

The terrain and climate in these most northeasterly areas of Siberia also presented the Russians some of their greatest challenges. Verkhoiansk, for example, founded in 1638 is one of the coldest spots in the Northern Hemisphere, with winter temperatures recorded in recent times as low as -90° F. The summer, though sometimes hot (above 90°), is short and plagued with horrific clouds of biting insects. The region is a patchwork of high mountains and endless lakes. This made the going both longer and more difficult. Nonetheless, small groups of *promyshlenniki* continued to move east in search of richer pickings. In 1649 some found a route up the Aniui River and into the Anadyr via a portage. Some 350 miles down the latter river they founded Anadyrsk[18] from which would be conducted much of the exploration and conquest of the northeasternmost extremity of Siberia.

Southward from Siberia: The Collision with China

While the northern and central Lena routes brought furs and tribute, the southern reaches of the river promised not only more of the same, but enticing extras. Rumors abounded of rich deposits of silver, lead, and copper. And most attractive of all — after decades of exploration in some of the world's most hostile climates — relatively mild, fertile lands fit for settlement and agriculture. Consequently, once begun, exploration and domination in this direction progressed quickly. Parties moving upstream founded numerous settlements during the 1640s: Verkholensk (1642), Verkheangarsk (1646), Verkhneudinsk and Barguzin (both 1648). Also in 1648, the Lena route to Lake Baikal was found by Kurbat Ivanov, opening up to Russians the largest and still today one of the purest bodies of freshwater in the world.[19] Irkutsk, on the Angara River west of the lake itself, was established in

1652 and quickly became a major regional center. Pressing still further south, in 1652 the aforementioned Petr Beketov was sent by Tsar Alexis to explore the Selenga, Ingoda, and Shilka rivers, the last of which is tributary to the mighty Amur. He founded a fort at Irgensk (near the confluence of the Shilka and Ingoda rivers) the same year, and the fort of Nerchinsk in 1653–1654. These developments brought the line of Russian settlement and exploration perilously close to China, raising the likelihood of conflict.

In fact, during the mid and late 1640s two particularly aggressive Russian explorers had already been pushing matters in this direction: Vasilii Danilovich Poiarkov and Erofei Pavlovich Khabarov.

Vasilii Danilovich Poiarkov

Poiarkov is celebrated as the first European to reach the Amur River, now the frontier between the Russian Far East and China. Like Ermak before him, he was of humble stock, the son of state serfs born in Kashin, to the north of Moscow. Sometime during the 1630s he entered the employ of the governor of Siberia. By 1638 he was working on construction of a fort at Iakutsk, subsequently the Russian capital of eastern Siberia, on the Lena River. Here, Poiarkov became intrigued by rumors circulating of another great river — this one far to the south — whose adjacent lands were fertile and rich in mineral deposits. The following summer he was sent by Petr Golovin, military commander of Iakutsk, to investigate these claims. His brief was to "collect the Sovereign's iasak [tribute]," to "search for new non-iasak-paying people," and to seek out "silver, copper, and lead ores" and grain.[20]

Setting off in June 1643, Poiarkov took about 130 men upstream for about a month along the Aldan, a tributary of the Lena descending from the Stanovoi Mountains. Anticipating violence, the group was well-armed with powder and shot. For good measure, and "in order to strike fear into the people of the hostile lands" they also took "a cast iron cannon of ½ pound caliber and 100 cannon balls."[21] Their route would prove difficult —filled with cataracts — and highly circuitous. From the Aldan it led into the Uchur River and then, ten days later, into the Gonam. A five-week struggle against this river's many rapids, involving numerous portages, brought Poiarkov close to the top of the mountains, though with the loss of some supplies.

At this point, with winter setting in, the party camped for a fortnight then divided into two. Forty-nine men[22] remained at altitude while the rest, including Poiarkov, traveled on up the Niukzha for six days. A grueling two-week portage brought them to the Brianda, along which they traveled for two-and-a-half more weeks upstream. Then they came over the top of the Stanovoi Range and down the far side using the Zeia River, one of the Amur's main feeders.

Along the river a detachment of Poiarkov's men encountered a group of Daurs (a local people of Mongolic background). They proved friendly, providing food and furs. Poiarkov, on the other hand, was ungracious and imperious. Noticing that the Daurs had objects made of copper, lead, and silver, and assuming this indicated the presence of these ores somewhere nearby, he demanded to be shown their sources. The Daur prince, whom Poiarkov took hostage, tried to make clear that all such items had been purchased from a Mongol khan named Borboi, to whom they paid tribute in sables. The khan in turn traded the sables to the Chinese in exchange for silver, copper, and lead. In other words, there were no mines, except those far away in China. A similar story explained the origins of the Daurs' silk and cotton possessions, in which Poiarkov also took great interest.

It is unclear whether Poiarkov did not believe what he was told or was merely frustrated by it. Either way, his response was both reprehensible and counterproductive. Rather than pursue relations with the Daurs or simply leave them and head further south, he and his men apparently harassed and punished them mercilessly, quickly provoking a fight in which both sides suffered casualties. The Daurs quickly stopped all cooperation, causing a famine among the Russians over the winter of 1643-44. To alleviate the situation, Poiarkov sent a force of about seventy men under the command of one of his deputies, Iurii Petrov, to a nearby Daurian fort—either to force tribute or just steal some food. The effort resulted in another battle and several wounded but few supplies. Over the course of the winter, forty of Poiarkov's men died of hunger and were, apparently, eaten by their desperate compatriots.

Although the spring thaw brought some relief in the form of new supplies from the splinter group earlier left behind, Poiarkov's self-inflicted misfortune soon continued. Setting off again downstream along the Zeia, the Russians noted several settled areas and a wide variety of agricultural crops, including "barley, oats, millet, buckwheat, pease, and flax ... cucumbers, poppyseed, beans, garlic, apples, pears, walnuts, and Russian nuts."[23] Poiarkov dispatched a contingent of twenty-six men to scout the route ahead, which led quickly into the Amur itself. The advance group themselves were attacked further along the Amur, near the mouth of the river Sungari, by locals who had, no doubt, been warned of Poiarkov's brand of international relations. Only two survived.

Poiarkov continued along the Amur all the way to its confluence with the Ussuri River then followed the Amur as it turned north. Throughout the long journey the group faced periodic harassment from various local peoples—including Diuchers, Evenks (Tungus), Nanai (Goldi) and then Nivkh. In late fall the Russians finally arrived at the river's mouth by the Sea of Okhotsk.

With winter setting in, the Russians, friendless in a harsh wilderness, camped for another miserable season. They were, however, able to take three Nivkh hostages, and in this manner collect a valuable fur tribute. Only sixty men made it through to the following spring (1645), at which time, his main objective already achieved, Poiarkov resolved to return home, taking the furs and hostages with him. Not liking his chances traveling with a weak and reduced force back over the route by which he had arrived, he made the decision to circle back via the Sea of Okhotsk—recently discovered by his compatriot I. I. Moskvitin (see chapter 3). After three arduous months, a north tack along the coast brought him to the mouth the Ulia River where the party again rested, this time in an abandoned blockhouse constructed six years previously by Moskvitin. Here they spent the winter of 1645-1646 without quite the level of hardship of previous winters. Tribute exacted from the local Even (Lamut) people swelled the party's holdings of sable and provided one more hostage. (Hostages were always useful in helping discourage their kinsmen from attacking; could provide further information on local resources, routes, and conditions; and provided potential interpreters for the future.)

The next spring, after ordering twenty of his men and the one Even hostage to remain behind and collect further tribute, Poiarkov set off for Iakutsk. Traveling much of the way on sleds and skis, he and his remaining party of about forty followed the river into the mountains, crossed successfully, then followed the Maia River to the Aldan, whence they accessed the Lena and sailed home, arriving 12 June 1646.

Despite having established sour relations between Russians and a variety of Siberian peoples, Poiarkov's voyage was still a significant piece of exploration that resulted in the first mapping of many of the major features along the riparian route and part of the coast of the Sea of Okhotsk. Poiarkov also glimpsed the coast of the island of Sakhalin — the first European to do so. Unfortunately for the Daurs and other local peoples, Poiarkov's expedition also confirmed that from the Russian point of view the Amur region was well worth colonizing, being of moderate climate, rich in forests and furs, and full of agricultural possibilities.

Erofei Pavlovich Khabarov

Erofei Pavlovich Khabarov (c. 1610–1671) was born in Velikii Ustiug. He would eventually achieve fame in Poiarkov's footsteps for discovering a much more viable Russian route to the Amur, following the Olekma River. His introduction to Siberian life and exploration seems to have come through the Stroganovs, whose saltworks he managed at Sol'vychegodsk, probably in the early 1630s. Thereafter, he moved further east — to the Enisei basin around 1636 and then — via a stint hunting furs in the forbidding Taimyr Peninsula — on to the richer lands along the Lena, including a spell at Iakutsk. In these areas he invested in various colonization and development schemes and quickly built up interests in farming, saltworks, furs, and the transport trade. Despite having his Iakutsk saltworks seized by the government, Khabarov grew wealthy. His ambitions, however, were not sated.

Sometime in the late 1640s he heard of Poiarkov's discovery of the Amur and of the potential riches to be had there. Determined to cash in, he set off in March 1649 on a self-financed expedition with government approval. Leaving from Iakutsk he took a party (variously estimated between seventy and 150 men) and proceeded up the Lena (west). This brought him to the Olekma River and then to the Tungir River, which he followed south past the Stanovoi Range and close to its source high in the Iablonovyi Mountains. Crossing the peaks on foot, the party then descended the southern slopes of the mountains by river, sailing into the Amur itself sometime early in 1650 in winter. His approach had been spotted, however, by Russian *promyshlenniki* already in the area and perhaps also by some of the Daurs. As word spread, the native people, remembering Poiarkov's cruelty, quickly disappeared. Khabarov consequently encountered several empty villages.

The Daurs and other local peoples had not fled in vain. Khabarov proved just as unpleasant as his compatriot. One of the few left behind was an old woman. Khabarov — who, like Poiarkov, wanted to know the sources of Daur copper, lead, and silver — tortured her for information. He learned only what he had already heard: that all such objects had come in trade from the Manchu Chinese to whom the Daurs paid tribute.

Leaving a detachment to defend a newly constructed fortification, Khabarov quickly returned to Iakutsk, arriving on 26 May 1650. His official report echoed Poiarkov's in its estimation of the region's potential for profit. The Daurs' tributary status vis-à-vis China was troubling, however. China would likely intervene to protect its interests in the region, meaning a hugely larger Russian force — thousands, not tens, of men — would be needed than those used so far elsewhere in Siberia.

While the report wound its way to Moscow, Khabarov immediately set off again for the Amur, departing in autumn 1650 with 138 men, soon swollen by reinforcements to more than 200. This time the native peoples stood and fought bravely, but to no avail. Khabarov and his men established a fort at Achansk (near what is now Komsomol'sk-na-Amur). They then hacked, blasted, and ravaged their way downstream to the confluence of the Amur and the Sungari before turning south into Nanai territory. By now Khabarov and his party had their blood up. They appear to have behaved hideously at every contact with locals. Sparing neither women nor children, they reputedly massacred hundreds and damaged productive agricultural areas. These depredations finally brought Manchu China into the fray, setting in motion a series of battles and negotiations that would end decades later, in 1689, with the establishment of an official Russian-Chinese border along a line primarily favorable to the Chinese.

Khabarov's ham-fisted jaunt through the Amur is not the only example of Russian incompetence in dealings with China at the time. Ivan Petlin, Russia's first ambassador to China — and an important explorer of the route to Pekin — had visited back in 1618–1619. He seemed to make a promising start — obtaining in particular a letter from the Chinese emperor authorizing limited Russian trade. But it was to no avail. The Russians remained uncertain of the letter's meaning (and of the emperor's original intent) all the way up to 1675, when it was properly translated. In a sense, then, during the 1650s and thereafter, Russian depredations against native peoples, along with subsequent fights with the Chinese, took place in order for the Russians to obtain privileges in the Amur region that they had already been at least partially granted, but which — thanks to the current conflicts — they were now losing. On the other hand, both Poiarkov and Khabarov had not come only to trade but also to colonize — to add at least the north flank of the Amur to the growing Muscovite Empire. This, of course, the Chinese could never have tolerated. The result was a major Manchu-Chinese attack on the Russian fort at Achansk in March 1652 and a subsequent Russian withdrawal.

At around the same time, worse developments — for the Daurs — were afoot in Moscow, where Khabarov's report had been eagerly read. Deeming the prize worth the investment, the government agreed to organize a force 3,000 strong — by far the largest yet to be deployed by Russia in Siberia. It was put under the command of Prince Lobanov-Rostovskii, however, not Khabarov. Preparations for deployment commenced. Moscow's pleasure at this point, however, was far more with Khabarov's discoveries than with the man himself, whose brutality was complicating Russian prospects in the region. An arriving Russian military commander, Dmitrii Zinov'ev, had him arrested in late 1653. Brought to Moscow and tried, Khabarov ultimately was treated lightly: he was told off and mothballed for a short time. Later, he was forgiven, promoted, and sent back to Siberian service. His contributions were too great for any other result. His heavy-handedness may even have ultimately saved lives as well as taken some, since it encouraged Moscow to recall Lobanov-Rostovskii's forces en route and try instead to reestablish diplomatic relations with China. With an eye especially to commencing fur-trading relations, an embassy was readied for dispatch during 1654, to be headed by Fedor Isakovich Baikov (c. 1612–c. 1664).

To smooth the embassy's way (the Russians were becoming aware by now of the importance the Chinese attached to proper protocol), an emissary was sent ahead — a man named Setkul Ablin. Unfortunately, Ablin was competent neither in the Chinese language nor Chinese court formalities. His Manchu hosts were unsure who he was or what he wanted. On the other hand, they were quite convinced the Russian had brought with him neither the obligatory tribute nor appropriate official letters. His efforts to explain that his master, Baikov, was bringing exactly such things failed. When Baikov eventually did turn up, nearly two years later, matters went poorly again. Other Russian ambassadors dispatched in his wake over the following couple of decades were no more successful in establishing working relations with the Chinese. Each did, however, contribute more usefully to Russian knowledge of the routes, landscapes, peoples, and resources encountered on their long journeys east.

Interestingly, ambassadors from other European nations to China frequently encountered almost the same circumstances as the Russians, so that when reading the history of such embassies, all the way through to British efforts in the late eighteenth and early nineteenth century, one gets the impression that the Chinese must have been very tired indeed of the unending influx of "barbarian" ambassadors who simply could not — or would not — figure out and play the niceties of Oriental diplomacy.

Russia and China Establish a Border

With diplomacy on the rocks once again, Russia resumed building up its forces north of the Amur. Many of the men sent, however, found the combination of local riches and the great distance from Moscow an irresistible temptation. Desertion and lawlessness became common, and many Russians plundered the locals for their own benefit across the Amur region. A series of Russian military captains sent on Moscow's orders were unable to restore order adequately. The inevitable conflicts with the Chinese began in 1652 (as Khabarov moved toward the Amur) and continued through the decade and long thereafter. Generally, the Chinese had the upper hand. The Russians fell back further and further north of the Amur.

In 1665 a raiding party of outlaw Cossacks and *promyshlenniki* established a fort and settlement at Albazin, right on the north bank of the Amur itself. This unauthorized *fait accompli* was legalized after the fact and integrated into the Russian state under the aegis of the governor of Nerchinsk. The fort soon began serving as a base for Russian forays into and across the Amur. Unregulated expansion of the Russian presence south of the Amur continued through the 1660s, aided in at least one case by the defection from Chinese to Russian protection of a Tungus chieftain, who brought with him nearly 350 others. Surprisingly, the Chinese — who by now had been dealing for millennia with unwelcome invaders from the north — at first made only minor and sporadic efforts to stem Russian encroachments. This changed during 1680–1681, however, as the Emperor K'ang Hsi began a major buildup of Chinese forces, garrisons, and supply lines behind and along the southern bank of the Amur and along many of its southern tributaries. The emperor sent the Russians offers of prisoner exchanges and trade in return for a Russian withdrawal toward Iakutsk. The Russians turned him down, thus provoking a Chinese attack during 1682–1683 that successfully pushed the invaders back to the Amur and then across it to the fort at Albazin. From here the Russians, well-armed and fortified, could not so easily be dislodged.

The Chinese opted for a slow, methodical approach, spending two years constructing earthworks, bringing in cannons, gunboats, and other weapons and supplies. In May 1685 the Chinese, numbering about 6,000, suddenly attacked. The Russians suffered heavy casualties. When the Chinese began to burn the fort itself, its Russian commander, Aleksei Tolbuzin, surrendered. The Chinese let him and all survivors leave. Tolbuzin, declining to take the hint, quickly returned with reinforcements of men, weapons, and powder, along with a Germany military engineer named Afanasii Beiton. The fort was soon rebuilt, resulting in a decisive Chinese counterattack, employing 11,000 men, the following summer.[24]

With its efforts simply to grab the Amur by force having obviously failed, the Russian government abruptly changed tack once again. The last sixty or so Russians in the Albazin garrison were saved from starvation when the Chinese agreed to end hostilities in return for peace talks at Selenginsk, south of Lake Baikal. Though the process was somewhat extended and tortuous, these talks eventuated in a durable treaty signed at Nerchinsk on 27 August 1689 that set the Chinese-Russian border for the next century and a half. The line ran along the Argun River to its meeting with the Shilka (the beginning of the Amur), then swept 200 miles north of the Amur and east along the crest of the Stanovoi Range to the Okhotsk coast. Albazin was lost. The treaty, though useful in formalizing Russo-Chinese commercial relations, thus kept Russia away from the entire Amur. This latter condition would change, however, when, many decades later, the Russians were able to exploit developing Chinese weaknesses to force the Treaty of Aigun. Signed in 1858, this established the current Russian-Chinese border along the long-coveted Amur.

Viewed from a Western perspective — with Russian expansion into Siberia constituting an extension of imperial control into what were at that time clearly non–Russian areas — the encounter with China seems unambiguously a case of Russian expansion checked and Chinese defense secured (at least for the time being). Russian writers, perhaps operating from a sense of Russia's Manifest Destiny in Siberia, do not always agree. A scholarly Russian account published as recently as 2006 relates Sino-Russian encounters of the 1680s in terms of "China's active northward expansionist drive" and designates territories on the north bank of the Amur as "Russian territory."[25]

Early Scientific and Inventorying Expeditions in Siberia

The Treaty of Nerchinsk, along with Moskvitin's attainment a half-century earlier of the Pacific coast (see chapter 3), represent a clear milestone in the history of Russian exploration and expansion. Geographical Siberia was now effectively incorporated and the borders of a greatly swollen Russian empire-state more or less established. Accordingly, efforts were increasingly directed towards scientific explorations geared less to conquest and tribute than to inventorying this massive new territory, along with its still largely unknown native peoples, and its potential riches of minerals and metals, flora, fauna, and soils.

Anecdotal impressions of the land and its resources had filtered back to Moscow throughout the seventeenth century. The explorer-conqueror of Kamchatka, Vladimir Atlasov (see chapter 3), for example, reported on the region in 1700: "In the Kurile lands [southern Kamchatka] there are lots of birds — ducks and gulls — on the ocean in the winter, and lots of swamp swans [geese? wading birds?], too, because the swamps don't freeze in the winter. And in the summer the birds fly in, but few of them remain, because in summer the sun is terribly hot, and there are huge rains and thunder and lighting often. And they say that the land caves in or collapses at midday."[26] And many, many other such reports exist, noting all manner of impressions.

Somewhat more methodical expeditions and reports began to appear around the same time. Most were inspired, directly or indirectly, from the top down, by the accelerating Westernization campaigns launched around the turn of the century by Tsar Peter the Great. A few, however, were self-motivated. One such involves the cartographic contributions of Semen Ul'ianovich Remezov (1642–c. 1720).[27] Remezov was born into a minor gentry family and raised in the Siberian city of Tobol'sk, not far from the scene of Ermak's earlier victories. Inspired by the epic pedigree of his hometown, Remezov would later author his eponymous chronicle, one of the three main Siberian chronicles from which Ermak's story is primarily known to this day and a source dripping with Orthodox Christian teleology. Remezov is also renowned, however, as one of Siberia's first accomplished map makers. At first independently of any guidance from his reforming tsar, Remezov sought out western scientific and technological knowledge of his subject on his own initiative. Though based always in his beloved Tobol'sk, he visited at least neighboring parts of Western Siberia, collecting cartographic, natural historical, ethnographical, and historical information as he went. His lasting contribution — based on a synthesis of firsthand experience and collected materials — is a series of three important Siberian atlases.[28]

Also during the first quarter of the eighteenth century, the father and son industrialists-metallurgists Nikita (1656–1725) and Akinfii Demidov (1678–1745) organized searches for iron and copper across several areas of Siberia, with major finds of the former in the far north and of the latter in the Altai region. Akinfii also found silver in the Altai.

More comprehensive and academically oriented surveys followed, and expanded dramatically as the eighteenth century progressed. An important and relatively comprehensive early survey of Siberian nature was carried out by Daniel Gottlieb Messerschmidt (1685–1735), a German-born naturalist and ethnographer invited to Russia by Peter the Great. During 1720–1727 Messerschmidt traveled widely in western and central Siberia, turning his eye to nearly everything — including flora, fauna, minerals, ethnology, and history. Of most interest at the time, he "confirmed major deposits of copper in the Urals, iron around Tobol'sk, and silver at Nerchinsk."[29] The work of Messerschmidt and the Demidovs ensured that henceforth metals and minerals would attract Russians into Siberia as much as furs — ultimately much more so. During 1721–1722, Messerschmidt traveled with the Swede P. J. T. Strahlenberg (along with Remezov, an early student of the resources of the Tobol'sk region).[30] An accounting of the then-current state of knowledge about Siberian geography and history, along with basic statistical information, was published in 1727 by Ivan Kirilovich Kirilov (1696–1737).[31]

Particularly important surveying and inventorying work was carried out in connection with Russia's overall greatest eighteenth-century exploration — the Kamchatka Expeditions of 1725–1728 and 1733–1743. Although focused especially on the coastal geography of north Eurasia and the discovery of Alaska (treated in chapters 3–4), these expeditions — which constitute a major watershed in the history of Russian exploration generally — were also a major contribution to the study of inland and riverine Siberia and so warrant mention here as well. The relevant work was carried out by the transplanted Germans G. F. Müller (1705–1783) and J. G. Gmelin (1709–1755),[32] the Frenchman Louis Delisle de la Croyère (1690–1741), and the Russian S. P. Krasheninnikov (1711–1755). Muller focused on historical and ethnographical work. His efforts in various local archives yielded the first primary sources on Ermak and other early Siberian explorers, including Semen Dezhnev, whose maritime exploits are detailed in chapter 3 of this book. Gmelin, trained in medicine, studied and collected specimens of flora and fauna. De la Croyère, an astronomer usually described as incompetent, undertook mapping and charting duties.

The only one of the four to travel all the way to the Kamchatka peninsula — at that time the most remote and difficult part of the journey — was the Russian Krasheninnikov. Only twenty years old at the expedition's start, inferior to the other three in wealth and status but certainly not in courage and fortitude, he eventually clocked eight years valuable service, traveling in relatively spartan style with a small entourage. Arriving on Kamchatka in October 1737 in a decrepit ship that wrecked and literally fell to pieces upon arrival, Krasheninnikov spent four years and pursued with great energy and dedication in often terrible conditions one of the great expeditions of Russian history. In W. Bruce Lincoln's eloquent summary, the young Russian "collected the specimens needed to piece together a full-scale portrait of the primeval land of earthquakes, volcanoes, geysers, quaking bogs, tidal waves, and avalanches into which his passion for science had brought him. He charted Kamchatka's rivers, mapped its trails and passes, crisscrossed its many mountains, discovered its hot springs, and struggled to understand the materials he had gathered and the things he had seen."[33] The results were published in 1745 as the *History of Kamchatka and the Kurile Islands with Countries Adjacent*,[34] even today a classic and vital source. Krasheninnikov was still on Kamchatka when in the autumn of 1740 a young German naturalist and physician named Georg Wilhelm Steller arrived. Steller and Krasheninnikov collaborated for several months before the German headed onward to Okhotsk where he would begin his role in the great events of the Second Kamchatka Expedition and the Russian discovery of Alaska (see chapter 4).

Finally, even the quickest overview of eighteenth century Siberian exploration would be woefully incomplete without mention also of Peter Simon Pallas (1741–1811). Like many of his peers, Pallas was a foreigner whose service to Russia flowed from Peter the Great's Westernization projects. Educated in the natural sciences in Germany, the Netherlands, and Britain, Pallas was invited to Russia, and to membership of the prestigious Academy of Sciences, in 1767. He originally planned to spend a few years at most, but ended up giving Russia four decades of his life. He is best known for the Academy Expedition of 1768–1774, which he primarily organized and led. Focused broadly on the scientific study of natural resources, flora, and fauna, the expedition traveled widely — visiting central Russia and the lower Volga region, the Caspian Sea, the Urals, southern Siberia and the Altai, Lake Baikal, and beyond. Pallas is credited with the discovery of numerous species, including mammals, birds, fish, insects, and plants. He also made contributions in paleontology, ethnology, metallurgy, and many other fields. His major publications — including guides to plants and animals across much of the empire — remained authoritative for many years and are still highly regarded works.[35]

By the mid-eighteenth century, then, the exploration and inventorying of natural resources within Siberia was well under way. At the same time, however, the enormous size of the region — along with the challenges of terrain and climate — ensured that important work — even basic geographical discoveries — would continue through the nineteenth and into the twentieth century. An entire separate book would be needed to do any justice at all to the many, many persons and expeditions who picked up where Pallas and others left off.

Interpreting the Russian Conquest of Central and Eastern Siberia

Russian expeditions and conquests in Siberia are frequently described with the words *epic, heroic,* or are reckoned a "saga." There can be no doubt that these words are merited. The hostility of terrain and climate, the "tyranny of distance" separating the Russian pioneers from familiar places, the enormity of the landscapes — in short, the difficulty of the task and the scale of the victory — all make this so. This is history viewed, of course, from the point of view of the Russians. In recent times, by contrast, writers have begun to assume different perspectives: those of the native Siberians, of Siberian wildlife, even of the land itself. Here, more suitable terms include tragedy, collapse, and despoliation. Western authors, free of the political restraints of their Soviet counterparts, were first to make this shift of viewpoint. Soviet-era writers often took pains to emphasize cooperative aspects and examples of interaction among Russians and Native Siberians — which no doubt did also occur — while glossing over the rest. From such points of departure it has not been hard to construct almost hagiographic accounts — and stirring novels — of some of the main personalities.[36] Native Siberian perspectives were treated first in anthropological writings and only more recently in works by historians. The two fields now often intermix productively, however, as in the recent work of James Forsyth, Yuri Slezkine, and others.[37]

The importance to Russia of Siberia — primarily of its natural resources — has grown exponentially in recent times. Siberia is now fundamental to any definition of modern Russia's place in the world. The region's oil and gas reserves rival, or perhaps exceed, those of the Middle East. Huge quantities of many metals and minerals are mined, smelted, and used domestically and around the world. In post–Soviet times major forest-law reforms have been carried out, aimed primarily at massively increasing the profitability of Siberia's huge forest reserves.[38] This has all come at significant costs, however, both to Siberia's natural environment and to its many native peoples, all of whose destinies were forever altered by the train of events set in motion by Ermak, Beketov, Poiarkov, Khabarov, and their ilk some four centuries ago.

Suggested Readings in English and Russian

Website

Meeting of Frontiers. http://frontiers.loc.gov/intldl/mtfhtml/mfhome.html. This is a vast and highly useful collection of primary and secondary sources, bibliographies, and other matter organized by the Library of Congress.

Books and Articles

Andreev, A.I. *Ocherki po istochnikovedeniiu Sibiri.* Vol. 1, *XVII vek.* Outline of Source Studies of Siberia. 2nd ed. Moscow-Leningrad: Akademiia Nauk SSSR, 1960.

Bassin, Mark. "Expansion and Colonialism on the Eastern Frontier: Views of Siberia and the Far East in Pre-Petrine Russia." *Journal of Historical Geography* 14 (1988): 3–21.

_____. *Imperial Visions: Nationalist Imagination and Geographical Expansion in the Russian Far East, 1840– 1865.* New York: Cambridge University Press, 1999.

Black. J. L., "J.-G. Gmelin and G.-F. Müller in Siberia, 1733–43: A Comparison of their Reports." In *The Development of Siberia: People and Resources.* Edited by Alan Wood and R. A. French. Basingstoke, UK: Macmillan Press, Ltd., 1989.

Bobrick, Benson. *East of the Sun: The Epic Conquest and Tragic History of Siberia.* New York: Poseidon Press, 1992.

Breyfogle, Nicholas B., Abby Schrader, and Willard Sunderland, eds. *Peopling the Russian Periphery: Borderland Colonization in Eurasian History.* London: Routledge Publishers, 2007.

Cheng, Tien-fong. *A History of Sino-Russian Relations.* 2nd ed. Westport, CT: Greenwood Press, 1975.

Collins, David N., "Bibliography [of] English Language Publications Related to Siberia and the Russian Far East, 1991–1993. *Sibirica: Journal of Siberian Studies* 2, no. 1 (2002): 120–24.

_____. "Bibliography [of] English Language Publications Related to Siberia and the Russian Far East, 1996–1999." *Sibirica: Journal of Siberian Studies* 3, no. 1 (2003): 117–128.

_____. *Siberia and the Soviet Far East.* Oxford, UK: Clio Press, 1991.

Fischer, J. E., *Sibirskaia istoriia s samogo otkrytiia Sibiri do Zavoevaniia sei zemli rossiiskim oruzhiem...* [Siberian History from the Discovery of Siberia to Its Conquest by Russian Arms...], St Petersburg: Akademiia, 1774.

Forsyth, James. *A History of the Peoples of Siberia*. Cambridge: Cambridge University Press, 1992.

Funk, Dmitry, and Lennard Sillanpää, eds. *The Small Indigenous Nations of Northern Russia*. Vaasa, Finland: Åbo Akademi University, Social Science Unit, 1999.

Gol'denberg, Leonid A. *Semen Il'inovich Remezov, sibirskii kartograf i geograf, 1642–posle 1720*. Moscow: "Nauka," 1965.

Istoriia Sibiri. Vol. 2., *Sibir' v sostave feodal'noi Rossii*. Leningrad: Izd-vo nauka, 1968.

Khodarkovsky, Michael. *Russia's Steppe Frontier: The Making of a Colonial Empire, 1550–1800*. Bloomington: Indiana University Press, 2002.

Kivelson, Valerie. *Cartographies of Tsardom: The Land and Its Meanings in Seventeenth-Century Russia*. Ithaca: Cornell University Press, 2006.

Lanzeff, C. V., and Richard A. Pierce. *Eastward to Empire: Exploration and Conquest on the Russian Open Frontier to 1750*. Montreal: McGill-Queen's University Press, 1973.

Lincoln, W. Bruce. *The Conquest of a Continent: Siberia and the Russians*. New York: Random House, 1994.

Mancall, Mark. *Russia and China: Their Diplomatic Relations to 1728*. Cambridge, MA: Harvard University Press, 1971.

Naumov, Igor V. *The History of Siberia*. Edited and translated by David N. Collins. Routledge Studies in the History of Russia and Eastern Europe 6. London: Routledge, 2006.

Nikitin, N. I. *Zemleprokhodets Semen Dezhnev*. Moscow: Rosspen, 1999.

Paine, P. C. M. *Imperial Rivals: Russia, China, and Their Disputed Frontier*. Armonk, NY: M. E. Sharpe, 1997.

Preobrazhenskii, A. A. *Ural i Zapadnaia Sibir' v kontse XVI[-]nachale XVIII veka* [*The Urals and Western Siberia in the Late Sixteenth to Early Eighteenth Century*]. Moscow: Nauka, 1972.

Slezkine, Yuri. *Arctic Mirrors: Russia and the Small Peoples of the North*. Ithaca: Cornell University Press, 1994.

Stolberg, Eva-Marie, ed. *The Siberian Saga: A History of Russia's Wild East*. Frankfurt: Peter Lang, 2005.

Wood, Alan, ed. *The History of Siberia: From Russian Conquest to Revolution*. London: Routledge, 1991.

Chapter 3

The Edges of Empire: Russian Explorations along Coastal North Eurasia from the Earliest Times to the Final Conquest of the Northeast Passage

Though presented here in a separate chapter, the Russian exploration and charting of coastal north Eurasia — from the White Sea region in the west, east across the immense Arctic littoral, to the Bering Straits, then south around the coasts of Kamchatka and the shores of the Sea of Okhotsk — was not carried out as a discrete set of voyages. Rather, as should be clear from the preceding chapter, coastal explorations freely overlapped and intersected with the more river-based eastward movement of the Russian frontier. As with the final exploration and assimilation of interior Siberia, mapping and possessing Russia's new coasts proved a long-term undertaking. Turning the hypothetical (and more romantic-sounding) Northeast Passage into a practical Northern Sea Route took until the mid-twentieth century, for example.

As with the early conquest of terrestrial Siberia, economic and political goals remained the primary motivations: exacting tribute from native peoples, extending Russia's frontiers, finding and exploiting mineral wealth, and — the eternal theme — procuring furs. There were new developments also. From the time of Peter the Great (r. 1682–1725), Russian exploration became increasingly scientific, both in its planning and goals, and it became better funded and more ambitious, with the state playing an ever-greater role. New organizations contributed to these developments, especially the Russian Academy of Sciences (founded in 1724) and — much later — the Russian Geographical Society (1845). Though heroic individuals long continued to occupy center stage, after about 1700 they increasingly functioned within organized frameworks under state supervision. Consequently, the venerable independent *promyshlenniki*, critical up to about 1700, became more peripheral.

Increasing amounts of time, energy, and money were given to inventorying, collecting, and studying all manner of flora, fauna, and mineral resources; to ethnological study, astronomical observations; and so on. These were hardly matters with which Ermak or his near contemporaries had concerned themselves. These trends are in evidence especially in the two great Kamchatka Expeditions (1724/1725–1730 and 1732–1743[1]) led by Vitus Bering. The second one, known also — and more evocatively — as the Great Northern Expedition, was the single largest and most ambitious expedition of the eighteenth century, in Russia or anywhere.

Compared to the conquest of Siberia, coastal exploration also presented certain distinct challenges and circumstances, primarily associated with the shift from rivers to seas and oceans: deeper and more unpredictable waters, and new and more treacherous ice conditions, for example. It also brought Russians into competition with other maritime powers: the British, Dutch, French, Spanish and eventually the United States, all of which had their own ambitions and interests in play.

Early Interest in the Northeast Passage

Arguably Russia's most important coastal questions — indeed, the preponderance of its actual (or potential) coast — stretched along the Arctic. Though this was obviously not the place to seek out the warm-water ports that would prove so important in the modern period, the area was critical because of the tantalizing possibilities it held out of a maritime route from Europe to the Far East — from the Atlantic to the Pacific. Interest in this question far predates the earliest efforts to answer it. In 1246, for example, the Minorite friar Johannes de Plano Carpini "traveled with three companions to Tartary [an old name for Siberia] at the behest of the Pope." Carpini later opined in an account of his travels that both north and east Siberia were "invironed with the Ocean Sea." In other words, Siberia was bordered, at least on these two sides, by water, making the ocean trip from west to east possible in theory.[2] Marco Polo's travels in the thirteenth century inspired a similar idea, as did contemporary tips from Siberian fishermen and a report in the late fifteenth century by Baron Sigismund von Herberstein, ambassador to Moscow for Holy Roman Emperor Maximilian I.[3]

Though hearsay and speculation dominated thinking about the Siberian coasts much beyond the Ob' River, more westerly points were better understood. A Novgorodian Russian named Uleb is reported to have entered the Kara Sea through the Iugorskii Strait in 1032.[4] By the early twelfth century, Russians had ventured — fleetingly — east as far as the Ob' itself. Further north, as early as 1136 a Russian monastery was established at the Arctic mouth of the Dvina River, at the place that would later become Arkhangel'sk.

Most of the early pioneers in these regions came from mixed Russian-Nordic stock and are known to us as the *Pomory* (literally "those by the sea"). Settling and expanding along the White Sea coast, the *Pomory* developed a maritime culture based on fishing and hunting the frigid Arctic waters. They discovered the Arctic islands of Kolguev and Vaigach. And by the mid-sixteenth century they were familiar with the conditions and approximate geography of what we may now conceive of as the western end of the Northern Sea Route: as far north as Spitsbergen and east past Novaia Zemlia to the mouth of the Enisei River.[5] Much of this skill and knowledge remained in local hands and minds, however.

Maps produced during the European Age of Expansion also promoted the idea of a viable northern passage to China. The anonymously produced "King-Hamy" map of 1502 or later, shows the east of Eurasia completely washed by water.[6] Martin Waldseemuller published in 1507 the first world map to show America and Asia "unambiguously" as separate continents.[7] This fashion became increasingly common after mid century, as can be seen on maps by, for example, Zaltieri (1566), Mercator (1569), and others.[8] From about these times, the waters linking the Arctic and Pacific Oceans (the future Bering Strait) came to be known

by the name "Anian." A particularly accurate rendition of the disposition of the area (remarkable, given that it would not be properly encountered and charted until the eighteenth century), was given in the Barents Map, published in 1611 by Pontanus.[9]

Not all mapmakers of the time bought into the idea of Anian, however. *De Orbe Novo*,
a world map published in Paris in 1587 by Petrus Martyr, showed America and Russia
joined across the Pole by a great icy continental bridge. Another, published only shortly
before Bering's first voyage by Guillaume Delisle, the French geographer royal, was both
provocative and refreshingly honest, stating of eastern Siberia's mountains: "It is not known
whether the range ends here or continues into another continent."[10]

Early Searches for the Northeast Passage

Among the first advocates for finding the Northeast Passage were Dmitri Gerasimov,
a Russian diplomat who spoke on the subject in 1525, and the English merchant Robert
Thorne (d. 1527) who in 1527 proposed to King Henry VIII the possibility and benefits to
English trade of such a route.[11] Richard Hakluyt the lawyer (d. 1587) and John Dee (1527–
1608) seconded this opinion a half-century later, basing their arguments on the writings of
ancient authors, including Pliny and Ishmael Abulfeda.[12]

Whatever the provenance of the idea of finding the Northeast Passage, priority in actually undertaking to navigate it is given to the English, whose motivations, we have seen,
were commercial and imperial. The age of global trade was opening. Opportunities
abounded for Europeans who could trade or colonize in the Americas and the Far East; yet
Spanish and Portuguese shipping dominated the early, critical routes in the Atlantic and
Indian Oceans. The Northeast Passage offered a potential shortcut between east and west:
a backdoor route into the European-Asian-American trading triangle. With this in mind,
in May 1553 the Englishmen Hugh Willoughby and Richard Chancellor led an expedition
into the White Sea, departing from London. The ships crossed the North Sea but were
tossed and separated in a storm while rounding the top of Norway. Willoughby made it to
Novaia Zemlia, but then was forced by ice conditions to land on the Kola Peninsula. Here,
he and his entire crew died. Their frozen corpses were discovered the next year by Russian
fur-trappers. Chancellor was more fortunate. He washed up near the mouth of the Northern
Dvina, whence he and his men were brought to Moscow. A meeting with Tsar Ivan IV and
lucrative Anglo-Russian trade followed.

Efforts to navigate the north Eurasian coast continued apace thereafter. Stephen Burrough (1525–1584),[13] who had sailed with Chancellor, made two further attempts in 1556
and 1557, reaching Vaigach Island (between Novaia Zemlia and the Russian mainland) on
the first trip and falling short of the Ob' Estuary on the second. Dithmar Blefken led a
Danish expedition in 1564 that reached Novaia Zemlia but was unable to proceed beyond
it. A Russian report from 1616 claims Dutch sailors made it by sea as far as the Enisei in
1603 (causing Tsar Michael to issue a new ban on foreigners in the area).[14] But this was the
limit. The celebrated Dutch sailor Willem Barents lost his life testing the higher Arctic latitudes around Spitsbergen and northern Novaia Zemlia in the 1590s. In 1608, after two
failed attempts by the Englishman Henry Hudson, the London-based Muscovy Company
(set up to manage the trade Chancellor and Ivan had initiated) "concluded that no usable
North-east passage existed."[15]

West European attempts at the passage were viewed somewhat schizophrenically by the Russian state. On the one hand, commercial intercourse with the English, especially the sale of Russian furs, brought profit and held out also the possibility (not to be realized) of an important military alliance. On the other hand, from the Russian viewpoint, these were *Russian* coasts — not international waters (a concept that did not then exist, anyway). One could not simply allow foreigners to sail and exploit them at will. Yet, lacking a proper navy (until around 1700), Russian options were limited.

Tsar Ivan IV's approach was to ban foreign ships from the emerging eastern routes in the White, Baltic, and Kara Seas (to the Ob' Estuary), while simultaneously making exceptions for ships of England's Muscovy Company.[16] An expedition of 1580, carried out by the company in cooperation with Ivan and headed by Arthur Pett and C. Jackman left England at the end of May, headed for Novaia Zemlia, the Ob' Estuary, and points further east. The ultimate goal was China. Early progress was excellent. By late August they had passed Vaigach and entered the Kara Sea, but here they encountered heavy ice and turned back.[17]

English fortunes in the region subsequently declined. Two years later, Ermak and his entourage set out to conquer Sibir' (see chapter 1). Their successes, and in particular the arrival in Moscow in 1583 of Ermak's fur-laden mission, convinced Ivan and his advisors of the immense fur-wealth of Siberia and of the ability of Russians to access it themselves. Foreign presence in the region suddenly seemed unnecessary — even unwise. The English found themselves increasingly unwelcome; then they too were banned.[18] Russians, at the same time, began to press harder than ever to master their own coasts.[19]

Russian Efforts Toward the Northeast Passage

In 1696 Tsar Peter the Great founded the Imperial Russian Navy. The previous lack, however, was not the critical obstacle to Russia's maritime success one might imagine. This is largely thanks to the well-developed shipbuilding and sailing culture long ago developed by the aforementioned *Pomory*. Especially during the seventeenth century, both service persons and *promyshlenniki* came disproportionately from this region (known as *Pomor'e*). On the other hand, the absence of a state navy partly explains the relative obscurity of Russian maritime achievements before Peter. Official expeditions undertaken by national navies (such as the English Royal Navy) are generally well recorded in history. The more haphazard and unorganized efforts of various Russians were not always so. A sense of the problem, and of the possibilities, is indicated by the fact that the Englishman Burrough, previously noted, was able to make it as far as he did in the 1560s due in large part to assistance from *Pomor* sailors he met en route. These, it seems, already knew quite well the eastward route at least to the Ob' Estuary and were willing to show it to him. He did not acknowledge their assistance, however. Burrough, apparently, was only able to follow part of the way, eventually falling behind the Russians and turning back.[20]

Russians of the late sixteenth and early seventeenth centuries sailed in a great variety of vessels. Many, especially those of the *promyshlenniki*, were often minimally seaworthy — improvised with whatever materials and expertise were available at the site of construction, usually "entirely without iron ... and held together by wooden nails and leather thongs. As often as not, they had only a single mast with a deerhide sail."[21] Larger and better quality boats were also common, though. The *koch*, in particular, was specially designed for Arctic waters. Typically about seventy feet in length and twin masted, the *koch* had a shallow keel and was covered with an extra layer of "skin" planking, usually of oak or larch, which gave it superior protection from ice damage. Among several other adaptations, the bottom of the *koch* was very flat, so that ice tended simply to lift it up rather than crush it, as was the case with more conventional hull designs.

When it came to navigating the treacherous waters of the Arctic coast, Russians enjoyed one particularly crucial advantage over foreigners. Rather than having to approach from the Norwegian and Barents Seas and then sail as far east as possible, Russians could access the Arctic coast at many points from rivers and land bases spread across their own rapidly expanding country. In such ways the Stroganovs had developed their own trade routes along stretches of the White Sea coast before 1600. The founding of Mangazeia in 1601, noted in chapter 1, is a further case in point, since it involved a trip down the Ob', then partway along the Ob' Estuary (which Russian sailors had first accessed in the 1570s[22]), and finally back south into the Taz Estuary and River (map 4). At no point on this significant eastward trip was it necessary to sail away from the comparative shelter of inland and coastal waterways.

Thus, the Russians were able to approach the overall passage puzzle piece by piece. Beginning in 1633, for example, traveling sometimes together and sometimes separately, I. I. Rebrov (d. 1666) and M. Perfil'ev (dates unknown), led a mixed group of service people and *promyshlenniki* down the Lena, into the Arctic, and then east along the coast, progressing or resting with the seasons. By 1636 they had made it all the way to the Indigirka, having earlier stopped also at the mouths of the Olonek and Iana. They traveled more than 700 miles on the open sea, point to point, and greatly further in fact. Rebrov and Perfil'ev also navigated several hundred miles up the Indigirka and were perhaps the first Russians, at least officially, to reach the lands of the Iukaghirs.[23]

Following close behind, but sticking closer to shore, in 1637 the Cossack Elisei Buza obtained further information along the same stretch as he sailed from the Lena Delta east to the mouth of the Omolon River (after which he proceeded further by land). During 1641–1644, traveling by river and land, Dmitri Zyrian reached the next major river, the Alazeia.[24] His expedition was complemented by that of Mikhail Stadukhin, who at about the same time, but working instead by sea, also reached the mouth of the Alazeia River. Stadukhin — a Iakut Cossack and merchant born sometime after 1610 — did not stop there, but carried on to the Indigirka River and — a new discovery — the Kolyma River in July 1643. (His further travels even beyond this point are treated below.) In 1646 Isai Ignatii Mezenets made the "first documented attempt to round the Chukchi Peninsula." He reached, however, only to about 170° east, near Chaun Bay.[25] Thus, in the space of only a decade, Russians had pioneered well over 1,000 miles of Arctic coast east of the Lena delta.

Semen Ivanovich Dezhnev

Perhaps the most critically important part of the overall Passage was first navigated by the Russian Siberian Cossack, Semen Ivanovich Dezhnev (c. 1605–c. 1673) who, beginning from the Kolyma River in eastern Siberia, sailed east along the Arctic coast in 1648–1649, all the way to the end of the continent, then south around the Chukchi Peninsula until re-entering the Siberian mainland, possibly at the Anadyr Estuary, but more likely farther south, at the Oliutorskii Peninsula (map 5). Dezhnev, in other words, sailed right through the straits that Vitus Bering was to discover officially nearly a century later. Disagreement persists — especially along national lines — about whether the Russian or the Dane deserves

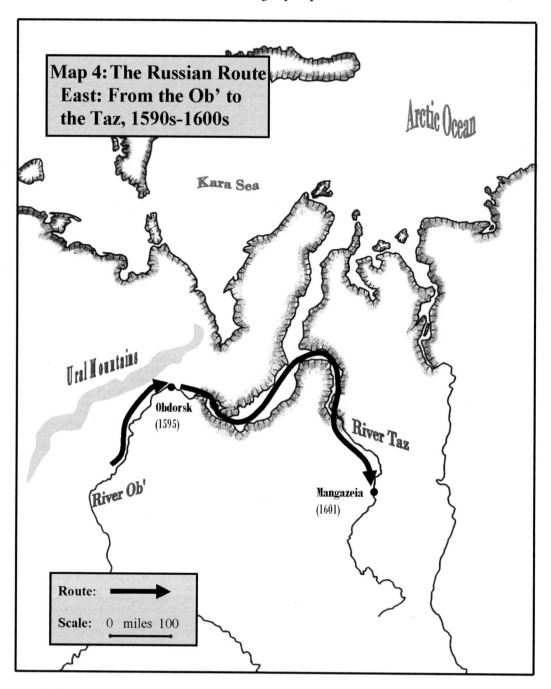

credit for the discovery. In the West, Bering has the great preponderance of support. Russian opinion is kinder to Dezhnev, though ultimately ambivalent.[26]

Little is known of Dezhnev's background.[27] He was born about 1605, probably by the river Pinega, close to the mouth of the Northern Dvina, not far from Arkhangel'sk — part of the world of the *Pomory*.[28] Moving generally south along the Dvina, he probably entered state military service in Ustiug in 1630, thereafter moving frequently to other nearby towns: Tot'ma, Vologda, Sol'vychegodsk, and so on. Around 1635 he was dispatched east across

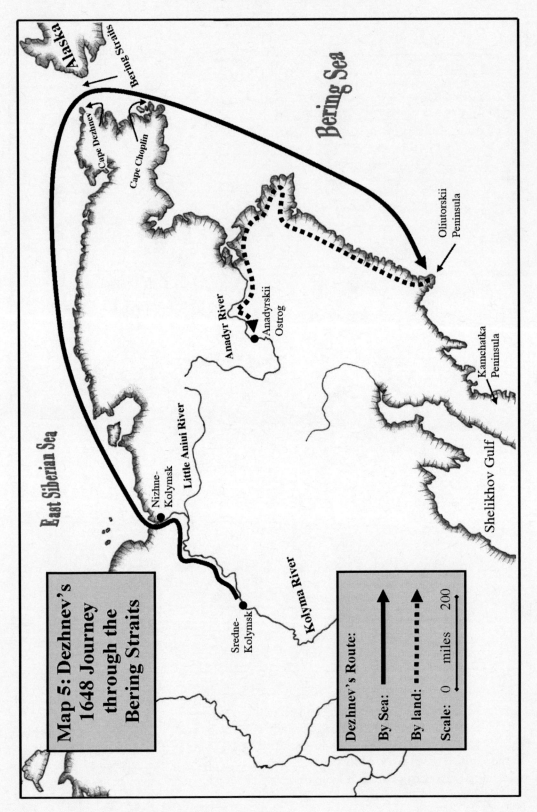

Map 5: Dezhnev's 1648 Journey through the Bering Straits

the Urals, first to the Siberian capital and gateway city of Tobol'sk, then quickly again to Eniseisk. By 1638 (in some later accounts) he was at Iakutsk, on the River Lena. Here he married a native woman named Abakaiada. Little is known of her, and it seems they did not remain together long. Under the command of Mikhail Stadukhin, during 1640–1642 Dezhnev traveled north and east in search of furs and tribute along the Iana and Indigirka river systems, serving for a time in Oimiakon, one of the coldest spots anywhere in the Northern Hemisphere, with winter lows near -90° F. After this—always moving east— came service (usually as a tribute-collector) on the Indigirka, the Alazeia, and the Kolyma. He arrived at this latter frontier in the summer of 1643.[29]

Along the Kolyma, in 1647, he met a Russian *promyshlennik* by the name of Fedot Alakseev (also known as Fedot Popov). Though the Kolyma had only been discovered in 1643, already it had attracted numbers of hunters and tribute collectors. With much of the best pickings already taken and many long years of service already behind him, Dezhnev was ready to pack up and head back to the Lena. Nearly at the last minute, Alakseev convinced him instead to join forces and pursue rumors of yet another great river system still further east. The river was the Anadyr (known to them at the time as the "Pogycha"). They set off in 1647 with four boats but were quickly forced back by ice. By the time they tried again in the summer of 1648, they had been joined by a third person — Gerasim Ankudinov, a runaway Cossack with a company of similar origins. Dezhnev and Alakseev appear neither to have liked nor trusted Ankudinov. They remained organizationally separate from him, even as they traveled together.

The expedition departed on June 20 — in most accounts from Nizhne-Kolymsk, near the coast, but more likely from Sredne-Kolymsk, much further inland.[30] At this point, there were seven vessels (all *koch*es), one belonging to Ankudinov, the rest to Dezhnev and Alakseev. The combined crew was between ninety and 120 persons. At least one woman was on board from the start, Alakseev's native wife.

Dezhnev had earlier been appointed a state representative and empowered to collect tribute from native peoples along the Anadyr. Ankudinov apparently also coveted this honor, and the two men argued — perhaps even fought — about it. Dezhnev retained his office, however. To smooth interaction with the natives, Dezhnev carried with him an impressive cargo of trade items and gifts: various English and Russian fabrics and skins, "shirts sewn with gold-colored thread, Moroccan leather boots and shoes (men's and women's), calf-leather shoes," coats, hats, mittens, belts, undersoles, along with "beads, bells, flints, firestarter, awls, axes, saws, drills, harpoons, copper cauldrons, tin saucers and plates," and much more.[31] They were also well armed.

Reaching the ocean, the boats turned east along the coast. The year 1648 was unusually warm across the Arctic. Ice conditions, consequently, were relatively benign. The payback, unfortunately, came in the form of unusually high winds and treacherous currents. Unfortunately for posterity, Dezhnev, though brave and resourceful, was not a particularly diligent record-keeper. Much of what we know about his adventure comes from a brief and rather vague official report he filed years later. The early part of the journey, during July and August, is a particular blank spot.

The expedition comes back into view, dramatically, at the start of September, when by various accounts three, four, or six boats — including those carrying Dezhnev, Alakseev, and Ankudinov — rounded the extreme easternmost tip of Eurasia and turned south. Apart from the number of boats, two larger unanswered questions attach to this moment. First, where were they, exactly? Ambiguities in Dezhnev's own descriptions complicate the search for answers. Most scholars believe Dezhnev was near what is now Cape Dezhnev — at the northern end of the Bering Straits. A plausible alternate view has him already through the straits, somewhere in the vicinity of modern-day Cape Chaplin.[32] The second question concerns the fate of the missing boats.[33] It is possible that adverse conditions drove some of them to return to the Lena. More likely, they were wrecked at sea or dashed on the coast.[34]

Then, suddenly, almost as soon as the remaining boats crossed from the Arctic to the Pacific, there was another wreck as Ankudinov was driven onto the rocks. But this time there were no further fatalities. Dezhnev and Alakseev were able to rescue their compatriots and bring them on board their own *koch*es. From this point on, Ankudinov sailed with Alakseev, with the latter's crew divided between both vessels.

The loss of Ankudinov's *koch* — and, presumably, of some of its supplies — made it all the more necessary for Alakseev and Dezhnev to attempt landings on the Asian mainland in search of water and food. One landing, made on September 20, perhaps near Cape Dezhnev, proved to have tragic consequences, however, as Dezhnev and some of his men fell into a fierce fight with the local Chukchis. Outnumbered, they were forced back to sea. Here matters deteriorated further. A storm blew up and the two boats were tossed violently. Then they lost sight of each other. Alekseev and Ankudinov subsequently were wrecked, leaving Dezhnev and his entourage alone to complete the epic voyage.

As with the other lost boats, alternative stories exist concerning the fate of Alekseev and Ankudinov's. One version — largely dismissed by modern scholars — derives from the eighteenth-century Russian explorer Stepan Petrovich Krasheninnikov (1711–1755) who in his *Opisanie zemli Kamchatskoi*[35] related rumors that he had heard while in Kamchatka: the two men and their company had not wrecked at all; they had made it all the way south to the Kamchatka River, where they wintered.[36] One version of this story has the Russians heading off again the following spring, around Cape Lopatka (the southern extremity of Kamchatka) and to the River Tigel' midway up Kamchatka's west coast, where they were finally killed in a conflict with the native Koriaks. Dating back to Dezhnev's own time, and resurfacing periodically to the present, come stories, and even serious (mostly Russian) scholarship, in service of another even more intriguing idea: that Alekseev and Ankudinov had been not been carried south at all, but east — all the way to Alaska itself.[37] Some historians also consider this a possible, though not enormously likely, fate for the other missing boats as well.[38] Evidence is scant: the remains of *possible* Russian camps in Alaska and various descriptions and rumors of "Russian-appearing" pottery, clothing, and even persons encountered by other expeditions to Alaska during the eighteenth century and after.[39] Some recent studies, on the other hand, firmly reject the idea of any of Dezhnev's lost boats reaching Alaska.[40] Even if it does one day turn out that there *were* Russians in Alaska during the 1600s, this would not prove they were from Dezhnev's expedition. A great many expeditions of all sizes, most mounted by the *promyshlenniki*, are lost to history.[41]

Dezhnev himself, along with twenty-four men, washed up on the Eurasian coast on 1 October 1648 — almost certainly on or near the Oliutorskii Peninsula. This area offered little in the way of suitable wintering, however. Their intended target and only real hope of salvation, the Anadyr River, they knew, lay to the north — but how far they could only guess. There was nothing for it but to set out overland along the coast. Winter was already hard upon them, making the journey particularly hazardous. They traveled on improvised skis, dragging on sleds what provisions they had been able to salvage from the *koch*. Where possible, they fished. After ten grueling weeks, Dezhnev reached the Anadyr without the loss of a single person — a remarkable achievement.

But here matters worsened again. At the Anadyr mouth they found no native peoples, and thus no one to trade with for vital supplies. Fish, fur, firewood, construction timber, and other necessities were in woefully short supply. In the intense cold, the party decided to split in two. Dezhnev remained at the coast, scavenging driftwood and improvising snow housing, while the others headed inland along the river in search of resources. It is unclear how long they were away. They found nothing of any use, however. Two men, Foma Semenov Permiak and Sidor Emel'ianov, later staggered back to Dezhnev's camp, half-dead from cold, hunger, and exhaustion. They had, they said, left their companions in a snowy dugout, promising to return with whatever food, furs, and other supplies Dezhnev could spare. But Dezhnev had nothing to offer. Each group's hopes in the other had been in vain. A return trip upriver found no trace of Foma and Sidor's party. Their fate remains unknown. Further fatalities in Dezhnev's camp over the long winter left only twelve men to meet the spring of 1649.

With the weather now improving Dezhnev took his men up the Anadyr on makeshift rafts. Remarkably, this depleted crew was able to "subdue the Anauls, a local subgroup of the Yukaghirs" and collect tribute. Dezhnev himself was injured in this effort. His party also charted a long section of the Anadyr and described its main natural features — a lasting contribution. At its headwaters the Anadyr closely approaches the Little Aniui River, part of which Dezhnev also navigated and charted. Having followed the Anadyr inland approximately 200 miles, and with the land finally becoming well forested, Dezhnev brought the expedition to a rest.[42] Near the confluence of the main river and a tributary named the Prorva, he and his men constructed the fortified settlement of Anadyrskii Ostrog. For Dezhnev, this was the start of eleven years' further service along the Anadyr.

Mikhail Stadukhin Arrives

Meanwhile, Mikhail Stadukhin — with whom Dezhnev had earlier served along the Indigirka and elsewhere — was conducting his own search for the Anadyr River, unaware of Dezhnev's success. Traveling east by river instead of along the Arctic Coast, he managed, with help from local Iukaghirs and a third party of Russians under Semen Motora, to open a useful route during 1649–1650, eventually accessing the Anadyr River at its headwaters by means of a relatively short portage from the Little Aniui River. A recent Russian reexamination of the evidence argues that Stadukhin traveled even further east on this journey than usually acknowledged, perhaps all the way to "Cape Serdtse-Kamen', very near the northeastern extremity of the Asian continent."[43] Though Stadukhin's was the more viable route to the Anadyr, he had been beaten onto the river by Dezhnev — a fact that he learned only upon encountering Dezhnev and his men shortly thereafter. The three Russian parties combined forces for a time. Although Motora and Dezhnev seem to have got along well enough, Stadukhin's envy of Dezhnev was palpable, especially since Dezhnev was the state's official tribute collector and had already established decent relations with the local indigenous people. Stadukhin, it seems, quickly spoiled these relations with his more brutal (and probably unauthorized) methods of tribute collection. After an open quarrel, Dezhnev and Motora decided to leave in search of furs, tribute, and another rumored river to the south, the Penzhina. Failing to find it, and with winter approaching, the two men and their company returned to camp. In their absence, Stadukhin had managed to further damage relations with the native Anauls — resulting in a rebellion that cost nine Russian lives before it could be suppressed. The following February, without waiting even for the end of winter, Stadukhin decided to cut his losses and try his own luck in search of the Penzhina.[44]

Though certainly the least appealing of the three Anadyr Russians, Stadukhin seems to have had some of the best luck.[45] He quickly found the river that had eluded his compatriots. Subsequently, he also attained the Gizhiga, Taui, and Okhota rivers. Motora, who remained behind, was killed by the Anauls. Dezhnev, despairing of ever reestablishing useful relations with the native people, resolved to return to the Kolyma settlement of Srednekolymsk. He and his men set to boat building then headed off downstream along the Anadyr.

In June 1652 Dezhnev's luck turned. Near the river's mouth he discovered a colony of walruses. To his amazement, the area was strewn with valuable tusks — the remains of earlier walrus generations. In times to come, Dezhnev was to consider *this*— not his rounding of the Chukchi Peninsula — his most important achievement. This, incidentally, convinces many scholars that Dezhnev was indeed unaware of exactly where he had traveled.

In 1654, following a return trip to the walrus colony, Dezhnev — exhausted from his travels and trials and anxious to cash out his winnings while he might still enjoy them — formally petitioned for release from his command and for a transfer. He would have to wait five more years before a replacement — Kurbat Ivanov, the discoverer of Lake Baikal — finally turned up, and one more year again for the season to permit travel. He finally left in 1660. (Ivanov, incidentally, added quickly to his own already-impressive portfolio of discoveries, heading that same year down the Anadyr then north along the Pacific coast, completing the first real survey of the Gulf of Anadyr and also discovering Provideniia Bay.[46])

Upon leaving, Dezhnev took with him 2½ tons of walrus tusks, a large cargo of fur tribute, and the prospect of a steady supply of the same so long as Russia should maintain tribute relations in the area. These he duly handed over to the state when he finally arrived at Iakutsk in the spring of 1662, asking in return only the back pay — nineteen years' worth!— that he was legally owed. This claim, unfortunately, could only be honored in Moscow. When he finally arrived there in September 1664 he was due twenty-one years of compensation. The Siberian Bureau received him and heard how he had been "scarred all over with wounds," had "collected tribute on several major rivers without 'salary in money and grain,'" and had "suffered all kinds of want and destitution, [eaten] larch and pine bark, and accepted filth for twenty one years." On the Anadyr especially, he told them, "I risked my head, shed my blood, suffered great cold and hunger, and all but died from starvation."[47]

Dezhnev's story has a happy ending. His service was properly recognized. He was promoted to Cossack commander and paid 625 rubles in cash and other items, a good sum for the day. In 1666 he returned to Iakutsk, his Iakut wife and young son, and Siberian service. He retired to Moscow in 1671 and died there one or two years later.

Dezhnev's *achievement*, however, has not fared so well. As noted, Vitus Bering, not Dezhnev, is widely recognized at the discoverer of the straits separating Asia and America — even though Bering was to sail eight decades later. What happened to Dezhnev's priority? Several factors need to be considered. First, it was not until later — specifically in connection with Bering's First Kamchatka Expedition of 1725–1730 — that ships were sent out charged more or less explicitly with finding out if America and Asia were separated or joined. Neither Dezhnev nor his contemporaries were focused on this question. Thus, they did not think of their travels in terms of an answer to it. Indeed, Dezhnev — in most ways a *promyshlennik* rather than a professional mariner — seems to have had no idea whatsoever of the geographical significance of his journey. Had seventeenth-century Moscow recognized and stated the value of the straits to, say, the China trade, Dezhnev's achievement might have been interpreted differently.[48] Second, Dezhnev's report was filed away and, so the story goes, lost in the Iakutsk archives, not to be found until 1736 — eight years after Bering's discovery. This fact alone has influenced several Western historians against claims on Dezhnev's behalf.[49] Based on discrepancies in his reports, it has even been asserted that Dezhnev did not sail round the Chukchi Peninsula at all.[50] This is an increasingly minority opinion, however. There is also the more philosophical question of what actually constitutes *discovery*: Is it enough "simply" to find something first? Must one be aware of the nature of the find? Or is it necessary, further, that others accept and act upon the discovery? (Consider the case of the Viking versus Columbian "discovery" of America, for example.) The debate is ongoing. Recent Russian-language scholarship, however, continues generally to advance Dezhnev's case on several fronts, claiming, for example, that his achievement — the discovery of the straits between the continents — *was* indeed understood and recognized at the time, quickly incorporated into maps and general knowledge (at least in Iakutsk and points east thereof).[51]

It is now claimed also that Dezhnev inspired numerous follow-up voyages. At least one appears to have been successful — that of Nikit Vorypaev and Ivan M. Rubets from the Lena all the way to the Kamchatka via the Bering Straits in 1661–1662.[52] At the end of the same decade a merchant named Taras Stadukhin also tried, unsuccessfully, to make a similar journey.[53] Many historians now believe that there were other attempts to follow part or all of Dezhnev's course through the Bering Straits (often in reverse direction, starting from the Anadyr). One Russian historian claims archival evidence for no fewer than 177 such attempts (mostly small, *promyshlenniki* affairs) between 1633 and 1689. It is speculated further that there must have been a great many other similar attempts of which no record was made or remains. Not a one of these many trips — aside from that of Vorypaev and Rubets — is known to have succeeded, however.[54] The difficulty of the route was so great, indeed, that it fell into disuse and was subsequently largely forgotten.[55] But not entirely. Bering apparently knew of some of these reports and even took them into account in his own epic voyage of 1725.[56] These facts, if facts they all are, drag heavily on the buoyancy of Bering's priority (see chapter 4)

Moskvitin and the Russian Discovery of the Pacific Ocean

Dezhnev and his companions were the first Russians (and Europeans) to sail into the Pacific from the Arctic. They were not, however, the first on the Pacific in general. This honor — in the form of the discovery of the Sea of Okhotsk — had already been taken in 1639 by Ivan Iur'ev Moskvitin, a Tomsk Cossack of obscure origins. In 1638, Moskvitin was at the newly founded Butal'skii fort on the Aldan — a major tributary east of the Lena. The following summer, chasing rumors of a great river (the Amur) and abundant silver deposits beyond the Stanovoi Mountains to the south, he set off along the Aldan with nineteen Tomsk Cossacks, eleven Krasnoiarsk Cossack runaways, and some native Tungus guides.[57] Moskvitin's plan was to avoid crossing the mountains by heading instead for the coast and sailing south to the mouth of the Amur (known to the Russians at first as the "Chirkola"). This was achieved by means of the Maia, the Iudoma,[58] and finally the Ul'ia rivers, following a route over and through the relatively unimposing Dzhugdzhur Mountains to the Okhotsk Sea, which Moskvitin entered about sixty-five miles south of the future Okhotsk (founded in 1649).

Here, in late August, they built a winter camp. Thus far the Cossacks had not ventured beyond the mouth of the river into the open sea. This changed at the beginning of October, when hunger drove a party of twenty into the sea and north along the coast. On the 4th, they discovered the Okhota River and found good fishing. Subsequently, working partly by rivers and land, partly by sea, Moskvitin's expedition explored the coast north to the westernmost part of the Tauiskaia guba and south to the mouth of the Amur itself. Among their other discoveries in the area were the Shantar and Langr Island groups.[59] It has also been speculated that Moskvitin discovered the much larger island of Sakhalin (see below). Four years later, in 1644, Moskvitin's compatriot Poiarkov found a land route to the Amur, and sailed it down to the Okhotsk Sea (see chapter 2). The next year, Poiarkov sailed north along the Okhotsk littoral to the Ul'ia River, adding handily to Russian familiarity with this coastline.

Exploration of the Okhotsk Basin and Kamchatka

Further, if basic, information about the geography of the Okhotsk basin quickly followed as fur-hungry *promyshlenniki* spread across the region beginning around 1650. Official Russian explorations over the course of the decade filled in many of the blanks. Mikhail Stadukhin, in particular, continued to carry out pioneering work — charting the Okhotsk coast north from Okhotsk itself to Penzhina Bay starting in 1656 and making in 1657 the first known *chertezha* (outline map) of the main part of the northern Okhotsk coast.

Russians moving along the shore eventually came also to Kamchatka — the peninsula boundary separating this sheltered sea from the open Pacific. (The first Okhotsk-Kamchatka round-trip by sea did not occur until 1716–1717, however.)[60] It has been suggested that Mikhail Stadukhin himself may have made the first sailing around Kamchatka, but this is almost certainly untrue, although he did gain some of the first information about select northern sections of the peninsula.[61] In 1695 Vladimir Atlasov, commandant of Anadyrsk (to the immediate north of the peninsula) sent an exploratory party into Kamchatka under the Cossack Luka Morozko. Over two summers, Morozko explored a portion of the northeast coast as far as the future settlement of Nizhne-Kamchatsk. In 1696, Atlasov went himself. Taking a crew of 120 men he explored and charted virtually the entire west coast and also crossed the peninsula by means of the Kamchatka River. (Atlasov was first to establish that Kamchatka *was* a peninsula.) He learned of the existence of the Kuriles, of other larger islands further south (perhaps Japan itself, Sakhalin, or both), and of the "hairy Ainu" (native inhabitants of the southern Kuriles and northern Japanese islands[62]). Atlasov also met on his travels a Japanese man by the name of Bembei. Brought back permanently to Moscow, Bembei became the apparently unwilling but indispensable nucleus of a Russian Japanese-language school.

In 1699, following a number of violent clashes with native Kamchadals, Atlasov (who is widely reputed to have been especially brutal among Russian conquerors), founded the fort of Verkhnekamchatsk (at present-day Mil'kovo). For his efforts and successes — particularly reports delivered to the capital of Kamchatka's great fur wealth and agricultural potential — Atlasov was made commandant of the whole peninsula. Unfortunately, this quasi-piratical man then wasted his appointment on a prison sentence earned for robbing a Russian commercial vessel along the Tunguska River, while on his way back to Kamchatka. Russian official business in the Far East being at this point essentially a matter of state piracy against the native peoples, Atlasov's abilities were eventually recognized and appreciated, however. He was set free in 1707 and sent back to continue the work of colonizing Kamchatka.

Incredibly, Atlasov soon got himself into even worse trouble. Violent and brutal to his own men almost as much as to the natives, the former mutinied and killed him in 1711 at the newly established settlement of Nizhnekamchatsk. The chief mutineers—Ivan Kozyrevskii and Danilo Antsiferov—went on to carry out further explorations of the southern tip of Kamchatka and into the nearer Kuriles, where they discovered and described the northernmost two islands (Shumshu and Paramushir). For these contributions they were pardoned of guilt in the mutiny, though Antsiferov was soon killed in any case by native Itel'mens. Over the following years, Russian settlements on Kamchatka remained forward positions on a wild frontier. Brutal suppression of the Kamchadals—and violent counterattacks—continued.

More serious efforts to map and explore the coasts of Kamchatka and the Kurile Chain followed beginning in 1719, when Peter the Great dispatched the geodesists I. M. Evreinov and F. F. Luzhin, instructing them among other things, to establish the relationship between these lands and the American coast. Though they were unable to do this, their expedition in some ways marks the beginning of serious efforts by the Russian state to reach America (see chapter 4).

The Kamchatka Expeditions

A greatly more detailed picture—not only of the Okhotsk[63] and Kamchatka regions, but of virtually all of Russia's coasts—was gained from the celebrated First and Second Kamchatka Expeditions (1725–1730 and 1733–1743) led by the Danish-born captain Vitus Bering. Remembered now primarily as journeys in search of the Bering Straits and Alaska, they were in fact far more ambitious efforts to chart great stretches of Siberia and its coastlines (map 6). The Second Expedition in particular—more appropriately known also as the Great Northern Expedition—was not a single exploration at all but rather a whole compendium of navigations, involving 600 academicians[64] and perhaps as many as 3,000 men in total, that added up to the single most ambitious undertaking of its type anywhere in the world in the eighteenth century. It involved a who's who of Russian and foreign expertise, more than a hundred boats and ships, and a staggering array of destinations all across Eurasia. Though ultimately stupendously successful, this epic adventure swallowed unheard-of quantities of money and other resources, and cost many, many lives, including that of the man who commanded it all.

Vitus Bering was born in Denmark, in the port town of Horsens halfway up the eastern coast, probably around 1 August 1681. His circumstances were comfortable. His great-uncle, Vitus Pederson Bering (after whom he was named), was a "royal historiographer and a poet known as 'the Danish Virgil.'"[65] His parents were Jonas Svendsen Bering, a customs official and churchwarden, and Anne Pedersdatter Bering. In search of adventure and opportunities lacking at home, Bering signed on as ship's boy at age fifteen in the company of a half brother bound for India. Over the following years he sailed widely under Dutch and Danish captains and trained in Amsterdam as an officer.[66]

The forces that would bring Bering to Russia were set in motion by Peter the Great. Early in his reign, this remarkable tsar determined to set the Russian Empire on a bold—but selective—path of modernization and Westernization. Uninterested in foreign devel-

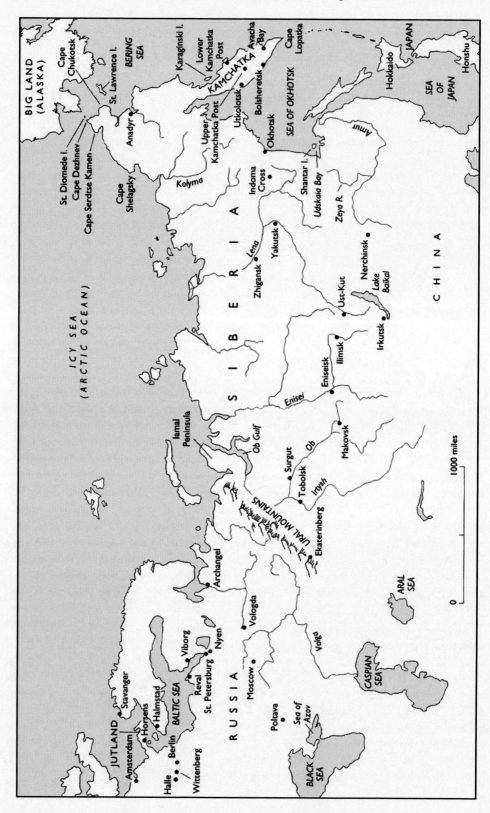

opments promoting popular sovereignty and natural rights, Peter focused instead on strengthening Russia by importing European advances connected with the military, commerce, and technical education. The centerpiece of this overall project was his founding of the Imperial Russian Navy, in support of which he invited numerous and varied specialists to live and work in Russia. One of these was Cornelius Ivanovich Cruys, also a Dane by birth, whom Peter had first met in 1697 during a stay in Amsterdam. In 1704 Cruys recruited his compatriot Bering—a veteran of both the East and West Indies—and made him a sub-lieutenant in the Russian Navy. Bering turned out to be a good choice, serving meritoriously on a variety of commissions in the White, Black, and Baltic Seas.

The new Russian navy offered capable persons opportunities for advancement and enrichment better than those available in their home countries. By 1720 Bering had risen to the rank of captain, second class. It appeared, however, that this might be the apogee. Three years later he was rejected for promotion to captain, first class (possibly a victim of biases against promoting non–Russians too far, too fast). Upset at the slight, Bering submitted his resignation, which was accepted. He received moving expenses but no pension. Interestingly, he was now given the promotion he had been denied, but only for use in retirement. Facing an uncertain future at age forty-two, he then left for Viborg, Denmark, where his wife's family maintained a small estate. Only five months later, however, he changed his mind, and requested and received a return to active service. He was also allowed to keep his promotion.

The First Kamchatka Expedition, 1725–1730

In December 1724, near the end of his life and reign, Tsar Peter began to consider more seriously the need for a basic reconnaissance of his Siberian domains, the full extent and basic geography of which still were poorly known.[67] The most important question seems obvious: whether the Siberian Far East was physically joined to the American continent or separated from it by a strait or sea. After all, the possibility of finding a Northeast Passage along Russia's Arctic coast and into the Pacific depended utterly on the answer to this question. Peter was concerned also about the British, Dutch, and French—all of which had interests of their own in the issue and were undertaking their own explorations. It would be advantageous to Peter at least to know whether or not his domains had a clear natural boundary in the east.

Thus it has been frequently assumed by historians that the primary goal of the expedition was indeed to seek exactly this answer—to find the Bering Straits. In fact, Peter's instructions were not so clear, leaving room for several alternative interpretations, including "expansion of trade with eastern Asia, extension of Russian dominion into and across the North Pacific, and concern for the security of Russia's far eastern territory."[68] The most recent major English-language study of Bering's life and work claims that Peter wanted him to carry out a more general reconnaissance of Siberia: to "map the [whole] way from Tobol'sk to Kamchatka, and from Kamchatka to the Icy Sea."[69] This was to be fully achieved: the expedition resulted in the "Bering Map," the most accurate of its kind at the time. If the disposition of Asia and America was *not* the overriding question on Peter's mind, then

Bering's limited success in this regard (he did not sail far enough north to completely rule out the possibility that Asia and America were connected by a land bridge) need not be seen as a failure. The matter remains a point of some controversy, however.[70]

Whatever the real background and ultimate goals of the First Kamchatka Expedition, Bering came to lead it by way of recommendation, being one of two captains suggested for the job by the Naval College (the other was a Dutchman named K. P. von Werd). Peter appointed Bering sole commander on December 29. The Dane accepted immediately. Bering was not motivated by scientific curiosity or the thrill of discovery, however. He and his wife Anna (who would travel with him as far as Okhotsk) saw the expedition as a means to a comfortable retirement and social advancement for their family and line.

To accompany Bering, Peter appointed two lieutenants: Martin Shpanberg and Aleksei Chirikov. These two men had little in common. Shpanberg, another Dane, was a highly experienced sailor but largely uneducated. He was reputed to be tough and hard. Chirikov, a Russian, was younger, with only a year at sea, but was far better educated. He had been a star student in navigation at the Naval Academy. Over the following few weeks, additional crewmembers were selected and the basic outlines of the expedition's route and goals were projected. Ultimately, however, these would remain unclear and contested, especially following the death of the primary sponsor, Peter the Great himself, on 28 January 1725. Before the official end of the Second Kamchatka Expedition in 1743 five more monarchs would occupy the throne. None of them would take quite the same interest as Peter had in Siberian and Pacific exploration.

Chirikov departed first, leaving St. Petersburg on January 24 with twenty-five men. Bering and Shpanberg followed on February 6 with a smaller party. The tsar's death came between these two departures. By December 14, Chirikov and Bering were both in Vologda. From here, in difficult weather, they traveled by horse and sledge along frozen rivers and across the Ural Mountains to Tobol'sk, arriving in the middle of March. Now they stopped for a time. With the warming weather, sledges became useless, so riverboats were built. Looking ahead Bering knew that much larger boats would be needed once Okhotsk was reached — ships that could sail the sea to Kamchatka and beyond. He knew also that very few Russians lived that far to the east. Accordingly, he spent time in Tobol'sk recruiting what labor he thought he would eventually need.

In mid–May, the swollen party pressed on by river, bound for the next great river system to the east, the Enisei. They traveled by the Irtysh-Ob'-Ket' route. At the end of June, they reached the upstream shallows of the latter river, pulled the boats and all their supplies ashore, and then dragged themselves and everything else forty-six miles across land. This brought them to a tributary of the Enisei and then, in short order, to the settlement of Eniseisk. Here they would remain until August 12.

Bering and his men spent the interim resupplying, repairing, and recruiting still more men for the next leg east. From Eniseisk, with winter already nearly upon them, they took the Angara River, which runs due east for about 300 miles before turning sharply south and emptying into the Ilim. Following this upstream brought the expedition into treacherously shallow waters. More suitable boats were eventually procured from a nearby Russian outpost, along with sleds to take some supplies overland. By now the expedition was approaching the celebrated Ilim portage, a pivot point in Russian eastward expansion where the Enisei and Lena river systems nearly meet. After several difficult portages and an overland trek of some eighty miles, Bering, Chirikov and their crews arrived at Ust'-Kut. This was an important destination. It sat astride the headwaters of the mighty Lena River, the major transport artery of eastern Siberia, just as the Enisei and Ob' are of central and western Siberia, respectively. It was thus another major milestone in the long journey east. Ahead lay the winter, much of which was to be spent constructing "fourteen lodkas [small boats] and eighteen good sized barges,"[71] and after that a comparatively easy 1,200 mile sail downstream to Iakutsk

Already, however, Bering's mind was fixed on what would come *after* Iakutsk, namely, the journey to the Pacific coast at Okhotsk. Though less than 700 miles, this promised to be particularly challenging. For the first time so far, Bering and his men would have to pioneer a new route — the area being relatively unexplored and lacking in Russian forts. Additionally, the region was reputed to have some of the shallowest and least navigable rivers in all Siberia, and its most forbidding climate. There were also mountains to cross. Acting with characteristic prudence, Bering opted to leave his men in two groups (some at Ust'-Kut, others at Ilimsk) and himself journey south to Irkutsk, on the shores of Lake Baikal where he hoped the governor might be able to give him useful advice on this daunting trek. All he got was a confirmation of the challenges ahead.

By mid–June 1726, Bering, Chirikov, Shpanberg, and all the men were in Iakutsk, the easy sail behind them and new problems already multiplying. Workers, horses, boats, supplies — virtually everything that should have been readied ahead of their arrival — were missing, insufficient, or delayed. Consequently, a month of good weather was wasted, the expedition leaving in dribs and drabs — some by land, some by river — during July and August. First out was Shpanberg, who "had the Herculean task of transporting seventy-six tons of anchors and cannon as well as fifty tons of flour ... [with] 205 men and thirteen flat-bottomed boats."[72] Bering, at the head of a party on horseback, finally departed in mid–August. Chirikov stayed behind until the following spring.

Conditions were as bad as Bering had feared: "The overland parties met staggering obstacles. Horses died for lack of grass. Rivers were forded as often as six times in a single day. Corduroy roads had to be built over boggy terrain. There were days ... [when the men] progressed slowly 'like pebbles' in the swift low water of a stream. Bering wrote, 'I cannot put into words how difficult this route is.'" Facing "wind, cold, and snow at higher elevations, three men in Bering's party died and forty-six deserted, stealing some of the remaining horses with the provisions they packed. Only a remnant of the overland parties reached Okhotsk in October. Then, for two months there was no news of Shpanberg's whereabouts."[73] He and a number of his party eventually made it to Okhotsk in January, but only after suffering conditions, including starvation, worse still than those Bering had experienced. Search parties were sent out over the rest of the winter. They found a mix of survivors and frozen corpses.

Bering's mission in Okhotsk was the construction of a new ship for the voyage across the Sea of Okhotsk to the Kamchatka Peninsula. This was no easy feat. Timber had to be selected, felled, shaped, and so on. As always, a short summer loomed, requiring a strict schedule and quick work. The resident population of the tiny Russian settlement of Okhotsk was greatly outnumbered by Bering's party. They took little interest in the explorer or his mission, seeing them primarily as unwelcome competitors for scarce food and other resources. The ship, to be called the *Fortuna*, was completed on schedule and put into the water on 8 June 1727. Another vessel, the *Lodiia* (which had earlier been put at Bering's disposal here), was repaired and refitted.[74] Together, the two ships, under Shpanberg's command, ferried ahead a large crew of carpenters, sailors, and others to Kamchatka before returning to Okhotsk for the rest of the expedition.

At about this time, Chirikov, who had earlier remained behind at Iakutsk, arrived at Okhotsk. He was a welcome sight. On horses and steers he had brought nearly 83,000 pounds of flour![75] And in contrast to the suffering and losses experienced by Bering's and Shpanberg's teams during the haul from Iakutsk to Okhotsk, Chirikov had taken only two months, and had lost only seventeen of 140 horses and no personnel at all.[76] Of course, Chirikov had traveled during the warmer months, a hugely easier undertaking. But it was not the last time Chirikov would have an easier run of things than his Danish captain.

From Okhotsk the entire party sailed on August 21–22 for Kamchatka, the jumping-off point for the final push to America. Significantly, however, they were bound for the west side of the peninsula, not the east side from which they would ultimately need to sail. This was Bering's choice. Rather than risk sailing unknown waters around the bottom of the peninsula, the captain had decided instead to take the better-known and shorter route to the nearside and then cross the peninsula on land. In fact, the other route (the future Cape Lopatka) would have been far easier, but Bering could not have known this. His trademark prudence showing through again, he chose the devil he knew over the unknown. The expedition thus arrived about a week after departure, without event, at the Bol'shaia River. It was September 1.

The first port of call was the fort of Bolsheretsk, near the southwestern tip of Kamchatka. Here, the expedition split again. Shpanberg took a party of men in small boats in search of shipbuilding timber and the peninsula's main river, the Kamchatka, which would take them part of the way across. Bering headed overland with the expedition's main baggage, drawn by dogs. Chirikov, again, was selected to remain behind and lead another baggage train the following spring. After nearly three years and 6,000 miles, the expedition was approaching its final and most important phase.

The parties recombined at the southeastern Kamchatka settlement of Ushka, some 125 miles upriver from the coast. Here, they completed construction of yet another new ship. This one was to be called the *Archangel Gabriel*. It was "60 feet long, 20 feet wide, and 7 feet tall, the largest ship yet built on Russia's pacific frontier. It had two masts and three cannon." It eventually departed Ushka on 13 July 1728, carrying 44 men (including two native Koriak interpreters) and "15 tons of flour, 3 tons of sea biscuit ... 20 barrels of fresh water ... 12 tons of fish oil, 760 pounds of dried salmon, and a fermented drink made from ... cow parsnip."[77]

Once in the sea, and after a short full loop, Bering took the *Gabriel* northeast, staying close to the Kamchatka coast and occasionally sending men ashore for water. On August 8, near what Bering christened Cape Chukotsk, the ship was approached by some natives (presumably Eskimo). Despite language difficulties Bering learned from them of an island to the east. Finding it easily on the 10th, he apparently dispatched a crew member named Petr Chaplin who landed once or perhaps twice, noted some built structures on the island, but found no people.[78] On the 11th Bering christened this place St. Lawrence Island, after the saint whose feast day it was.

On August 13 the expedition, continuing northeast, arrived at 65°35'N latitude,[79] at which point Peter's original instructions were again consulted. It was Bering's opinion that the mission had now been accomplished and the existence of a strait separating the two continents established. In fact, the ship was still south of the straits that now carry Bering's name. Bering asked Chirikov and Shpanberg for their opinions, which they gave in writing. Chirikov, sensing (rightly) that the question of the disposition of the two continents had not really been resolved, respectfully dissented. Instead, he urged that the expedition continue "until we are hindered by the ice, or the coast turns to the west"— in which case they should sail for the Kolyma.[80] This would essentially have recreated in reverse the route taken nearly a century earlier by Dezhnev. Toward this end Chirikov was willing to risk wintering over on whatever land they might find in these inhospitable latitudes. Shpanberg, on the other hand, considered this unacceptably foolhardy. He also contested that Peter's instructions were not so specific as to require this course. He was willing only to venture three days farther north. Bering agreed. The matter was closed.

This has become another of those decisions made during the two Kamchatka Expeditions that provide fuel for historians who consider Bering to have lacked the dauntlessness and determination needed for truly great achievements. Bering's critics, of course, are often also Chirikov's supporters, suggesting that better results would have followed had *their* man been in charge.[81] These arguments are moot, of course, since it cannot be known what would have resulted from different decisions. Chirikov's proposals would certainly have involved great risks, including being caught in the ice and wrecked. On the other hand, Bering's decision left doubts about the nature of his discovery and necessitated the Second Kamchatka Expedition, which ultimately led to his own death anyway (see chapter 4). Perhaps he would have been better off following Chirikov's advice after all.

Bering thus took the *Gabriel* through the Bering Straits and to 67°24'N. The most significant sighting during these days was an island that suddenly became visible in their wake on the 14th as a thick fog lifted. At about 3 o'clock on the 16th, there having been no indication of America or of any land bridge between the continents, Bering ordered the *Gabriel* to be turned around. The expedition was essentially over.

Later the same day, the recently sighted island came into view again. It was now given the name St. Diomede. The following day, they hugged the Asian shore, spying two Chukchi villages. The day after that took them past the Chukotsk Cape and toward St. Lawrence Island. Two days later still, the ship was approached by a group of forty natives, apparently looking to trade. Furs, pelts, and meat were exchanged for Russian needles and matches. Bering's interpreters, unfortunately, understood only dimly the rather vague comments of the natives about nearby lands and peoples. Nothing of value was learned and the expedition continued for home, reaching the mouth of the Kamchatka River on 2 September 1728, after having come through some rough seas and a dangerous storm just before. Ahead lay the winter, repairs, and some much-needed rest.

There is an important coda to the expedition. The following spring, acting on a tip he picked up at the Lower Kamchatka Post — that "on clear days land could be seen across the sea to the east,"[82] Bering took time out from the return trip west (around the bottom of Kamchatka rather than overland this time) to head back east in search of this land, which it had occurred to him might be America itself. Sailing for four days, part of the way in a heavy storm that damaged his sails, he reached 55°32'N and 166°25'E, close to the Commander (or Komandorskie) Islands, one of which would later be the site of his grave. Seeing nothing but sea and sky this time, however, he turned around and headed west, rounding Cape Lopatka in pursuit of his lieutenant, Chirikov, captaining the *Fortuna*. The ships reunited at Bolsheretsk on 3 July 1729 then sailed together for Okhotsk, arriving on the 24th. The return trip across Siberia requiring greatly less transport of supplies and men, Bering made good progress, arriving in St. Petersburg on 28 February 1730.

Evaluating the First Kamchatka Expedition

Bering was satisfied that he had proven the existence of the straits separating two continents: Asia and America. History largely concurs, as evidenced by the naming of the Bering

Straits. But not having traveled further north, his opinion could not be considered conclusive. Plans for a second expedition began almost immediately. The real prize of the First Kamchatka Expedition, perhaps, was the "Bering Map." This showed much of Siberia and contained "fairly precise latitude and longitude observations." Though named for Bering (and certainly a credit to his overall command), it was "chiefly the work of Chirikov and midshipman Petr Chaplin through their mastery of up-to-date Western European charting technology."[83]

In the meantime, other explorations of and beyond Russia's far eastern coasts continued. From 1738–1741, for example, Alexander Shel'ting and Mikhail Gvozdev, reconnoitered and described the "west and north coasts of the Okhotsk Sea and the [western] shores of Kamchatka," while Shpanberg and the Russianized Englishman Vilim Val'ton (William Walton, d. 1743) headed down the Kuriles to Japan.[84]

The Second Kamchatka — or Great Northern — Expedition

Both the failures and successes of the First Kamchatka Expedition demanded a follow-up undertaking. Bering's own suggestions and ambitions were greatly amplified by the Russian government, which desired to further understand, subdue, and expand its possessions across Siberia and beyond. By the time Bering set off again from St. Petersburg in April 1733 the Great Northern Expedition had been set a daunting and dizzying array of goals. They read more like a general plan of colonization than a geographical expedition: to survey and inventory the flora, fauna, peoples, and natural resources encountered throughout Siberia; where possible, to establish agriculture, mining, and metallurgical enterprises, along with a postal system from the Urals to the Pacific; to establish ports along the Pacific coast; and to find and chart the route from Kamchatka to Japan via the Kuriles. The great questions of the Northeast Passage were to be finally resolved — which meant nothing less than surveying the entire Arctic coast from Arkhangel'sk to the Chukchi Peninsula and properly certifying the existence of the straits separating Asia and America. America was to be searched for and found.

The Great Northern Expedition would end with Bering's famed and final voyage of 1741–1742 to Alaska. This is treated separately in chapter 4. During the earlier years of this expedition, however, Bering's primary responsibilities were to oversee and dispatch four detachments[85] to chart those sections of the Northeast Passage that were still poorly known.

The westernmost detachment started from Arkhangel'sk (on the Northern Dvina River) and headed east toward the Ob'. This was not entirely virgin territory: since at least the sixteenth century, the Pomory had traveled regularly between these two points. But the usual route combined sea travel with an overland river-and-portage trek across the enormous Iamal Peninsula. This time, the plan was to go north around it. The expedition was headed first by two poorly known figures named Murav'ev and Pavlov, then from 1736 by Stepan Gavrilovich Malygin (d. 1764) and A. Skuratov. During 1736–1737 Malygin and Skuratov succeeded completely, sailing to Dolgii Island, through Iugorskii Strait, and to the Kara River. After wintering here, they continued to the Ob' mouth and then round the Iamal Peninsula all the way to Berezov.[86] The Iamal portion of the journey was mirrored by V. M. Selifontov, who, starting from the Pechora River, made virtually the same trip on land, but in the opposite direction, following the coast. Together, these two journeys brought the Iamal into clearer focus.

The second detachment was based at Tobol'sk on the Irtysh (a tributary of the mighty

Ob') and commanded by Dmitri Ovtsyn, a hydrographer of obscure origins. Ordered to survey the coast as far as the Enisei, Ovtsyn set out in 1734. His route involved very little open ocean: the Ob' Gulf runs for some 450 miles, eventually almost merging with the gulf of the Enisei. Nonetheless, the expedition ran into severe weather and ice conditions. Brave and determined, Ovtsyn and his crew of about fifty tried again and again over several seasons. In 1737 they finally succeeded, adding another piece to the overall puzzle. Ovtsyn's route around the Gydanskii Peninsula (separating the mouths of the Ob' and Enisei) was tracked by an auxiliary detachment led by Prianishnikov and Vykhodtsev, which also investigated several sections of the Ob' itself. Later, in 1738–1742, under the leadership of F. A. Minin (c. 1709–?), a subdetachment explored the eastern bank of the Enisei and parts of the western Taimyr Peninsula, reaching a little over 75°N latitude in the vicinity of the Mamont Peninsula.[87]

The other two detachments headed into the Arctic from the Lena Delta. One, led at first by Vasilii M. Pronchishchev[88] and Semen Ivanovich Cheliuskin (c. 1700–c. 1760), was charged with heading west, over and around the imposing Taimyr Peninsula, to the Enisei. The other was to head east, following Dezhnev's route around the Chukchi Peninsula. Combined with the other detachments, this would represent an almost-complete survey of the Arctic coast. As it turned out, it would also provide some of the most storied parts of the entire expedition.

Some of the highest drama of all was provided by the voyage of Pronchishchev, chosen to make the westbound trip. A glance at the map shows this to have been in various ways a far more difficult and dangerous undertaking even than Ovtyn's commission. Though heading west may seem less truly "pioneering"—considering the general Russian drive to the east—in fact nothing could be further from the truth. To the west of the Lena Delta lay the single greatest blank spot in the entire Arctic coastal span, and also perhaps its most forbidding geographical obstacle—the enormous Taimyr Peninsula. Stretching more than 700 miles across (1,200 if one counts from the Lena to Enisei Deltas, which constitute the actual start and finishing points of such an effort), and extending to Eurasia's northernmost point (Cape Cheliuskin, at 77°43'N latitude), the peninsula had never been rounded. Its most famous previous challenger was Ivan Tolstoukhov who between 1686 and 1688 had tried unsuccessfully to circumnavigate it the other way, starting at the mouth of the Enisei and sailing east. One of the more poignant discoveries made during the Great Northern Expedition was a cross bearing Tolstoukhov's name, found at the mouth of Piasina river, near 108°E longitude. This meant Tolstoukhov had actually made it round Cape Cheliuskin when his luck ran out.[89]

The drama—and ultimate tragedy—of Pronchishchev's voyage is heightened by the decision of his wife, Mariia, to accompany her husband. The Pronchishchevs, who were still newlyweds when their journey began, seem an appealing—certainly an adventurous—couple, though little is known of them. Born in 1702, Vasilii excelled in studies at the School of Mathematical and Navigational Sciences in Moscow, graduating at age sixteen and earning at the same time the rank of garde marine. A highly capable seaman, he had by 1733 been made a lieutenant and was put at Bering's disposal. In choosing to accompany her husband, Mariia Pronchishcheva probably became the world's first female Arctic explorer.

The husband-and-wife team set off from Iakutsk in a gunboat of the same name on 29 June 1735 and followed the Lena north (downstream). They reached the Arctic in mid–August. Turning west they made for the mouth of the Olonek River. Here, on the inhospitable northern coast, they set up winter camp. For reasons that are unclear, the expedition waited until August 1 the following year before putting back to sea, bound for the Taimyr Peninsula. This they reached quickly enough. But as they turned north along the coast their late start caught up with them in the form of heavy ice and treacherous conditions. Nonetheless, the *Iakutsk* proceeded quickly, reaching over three-quarters of the way to the northernmost extension of the peninsula before being forced to turn back in mid–August. Now their luck turned as well. On the way back scurvy ravaged the crew. Though the Pronchishchevs made it back to their winter camp by the end of the same month, they were already very sick. Marooned on the bleak Arctic coast, within two weeks both were dead. They were buried together near the mouth of the Olenek River.

The expedition was not in vain, however. In addition to mapping the coastline from the Lena delta to the Cape of Faddei, the Pronchishchevs discovered the Peter and Eastern Samuil Islands and made the first really accurate survey of the Lena River all the way from Okhotsk to the Arctic. For this Vasilii Pronchishchev was honored in 1901 at the bicentennial of the founding of the Russian Naval Cadets Corps: "Great are the services of the graduates ... who heroically defended the fatherland ... [and] maintained the might of Russia; but no less glorious are their deeds for the benefit of science. In the history of it there will always remain the names of Chirikov, Pronchishchev, the Laptev brothers and other participants in the Great Siberian Expedition."[90] His wife has not been forgotten: one can still find Mariia Pronchishcheva Bay indicated on maps of the eastern Taimyr Peninsula. Overall, however, compared with many of their compatriots in the same set of expeditions, the name Pronchishchev remains obscure.

Pronchishchev's Taimyr commission was inherited by Khariton Prokof'evich Laptev, another Bering appointee. Like Vasilii Pronchishchev, Khariton Laptev started his career in 1718 as a garde marine. His destiny, however, was happier. During 1739–1742, he personally navigated the western two-thirds of the peninsula as far as the Taimyr River. Approaching from the Enisei, his lieutenant, S. I. Cheliuskin (a veteran of Pronchishchev's failed attempt), did the same for the eastern third. In the process, in 1742, he successfully rounded the northernmost point of Eurasia (on dog sled), which is now named Cape Cheliuskin in his honor (even though Tolstoukhov had been there before him). Along with coexpeditionists N. Chekin and G. Medvedev, Khariton Laptev's command surveyed the entire peninsula in detail from the Piasina River east to the Khatanga River, also discovering more islands en route. Khariton Laptev lived until 1763.

Fate, it seems, took a particular liking to the Laptev family. Khariton's brother, Dmitri Iakovlev Laptev (another garde marine from 1718), not only played an important role of his own in the Great Northern Expedition, but did so in a manner that eerily echoes Khariton's own — most particularly in that Dmitri too received his command and enjoyed his successes following the tragic death of his immediate predecessor. The unfortunate in this case was Peter Lassenius, head of the fourth detachment and a Swede by birth. Just as Bering had sent Pronchishchev — sailing in the *Iakutsk* — down the Lena to the Arctic in 1735, so did he send Lassenius in the sister ship the *Irkutsk*. Pronchishchev's commission had been to sail west toward Taimyr. Lassenius's was to head east. Scarcely out of the Lena delta, however, his ship was wrecked near the Kharaulakh River, taking the lives of Lassenius and thirtynine crew. Dmitri Laptev was quickly appointed to pick up the pieces. Between 1736 and 1742 he carried out a remarkable series of journeys — combining sea and land routes — resulting in the charting of the Arctic coast all the way from the mouth of the Lena east to Cape Bol'shoi Baranov, just past the mouth of the Kolyma. From this river, traveling by sled, he then turned south and east, charting the Anadyr and Bol'shoi Aniui river basins all the way to Penzhina Bay. Both Laptevs were subsequently honored by the naming of the Laptev Sea, upon which the bulk of their reputations were made.

Digesting Recent Discoveries

As geographical information continually poured in, Russians produced numerous new or updated maps of Siberia and its coasts.[91] Despite occasional efforts to keep the discoveries secret, much of the new knowledge also found its way into foreign maps. Unfortunately, most of the hundreds of outline maps (*chertezhi*) apparently made by various Russian explorers during the seventeenth century are lost. Among those remaining are one each from 1667 and 1668 attributed to the Tobol'sk military captain Petr Ivanovich Godunov and indicating in some opinions knowledge of Dezhnev's voyage through the Bering Straits.[92] The first Western maps to "reflect Russian concepts" of the strait of Anian (often considered synonymous with the Bering Straits) began appearing in the West a little over two decades later. One from 1690 by the Dutchman Nicolaas C. Witsen is sometimes considered the first such. The Russian chronicler, traveler, and cartographer Semen Ul'ianovich Remezov "produced a dazzling corpus of cartographic material in the 1690s and into the early eighteenth century."[93] Increasingly accurate depictions of the Bering Straits can be found on Russian maps dating from about 1700–1714.[94] After this time, a greater proportion of maps produced have survived to the present. The "Bering Map" of 1729 has already been noted. A more comprehensive "New General Map of the All-Russian Empire, and Borders Showing all the State's Forts" followed in 1731. It showed 140 settlements and was clearly designed to further Russian claims to the broad Eurasian expanse. Results of the First Kamchatka Expedition were incorporated into a new general map produced by I. K. Kirilov in 1734. Eleven years later, the "Russian Atlas" appeared — a collection of nineteen maps (thirteen of European Russia and six of Siberia) including information from the Great Northern Expedition.[95] A still more comprehensive map, incorporating material from the same expedition and worked on directly by many of its participants, was apparently compiled in 1746 but kept secret, eventually seeing print only in the twentieth century.[96]

Though many gaps and details remained to be filled in, with the Great Northern Expedition close to completion, a basic reconnaissance of most of Russia's coasts had now been achieved and a good sense acquired of the extent and disposition of Russian domains and limits. Further details would continue to be fleshed out, of course. A good chart of the Chukchi Peninsula's coasts, for example, had to wait until 1765, when Nikolai Daurkin, a Chukchi-Cossack in Russian state service, compiled one based in part on a journey of 1763–1764 to Saint Lawrence Island in the Bering Straits.[97] Beyond the wish simply to know Russian coasts, however, burned the desire to sail and conquer them. No challenge of this sort came close to that still presented by the Northeast Passage.

The Northeast Passage After Bering

Not just Russians, but people from many seafaring nations sought to sail this great northern coast. At the very least, the opportunities it offered — commercial and military — were too tantalizing and potentially profitable to pass up. For Russia, however, conquering the passage held extra significance and urgency. For one thing, it offered the hope of finally connecting Russia's far-flung cities and ports with each other and the capital to a degree that land and river routes could never achieve. (Potential alternative *oceanic* routes from European Russia to the Far East and North Pacific existed, but these were much longer and in any case were not sailed by Russians until the nineteenth century.[98]) Partly from pragmatic concerns such as these, partly from patriotism and scientific curiosity, Russia's pioneering scientist and a founder of Moscow University, Mikhail Lomonosov, evoked in an essay of 1747 the image of "'Russian Columbuses' sailing eastward among the ice."[99] Over the following couple of decades, Lomonosov became Russia's premier proponent of exploration in the Russian Arctic.

Russian (and foreign) efforts to open the new route continued during the second half of the eighteenth century. Difficulties encountered along the coast-hugging routes that had been tried so far led some to venture to higher latitudes, where the Northeast and Northwest Passage routes converge. One such effort was led by the Russian admiral Vasilii Iakovlevich Chichagov. In 1765 and again in 1766 Chichagov departed from Arkhangel'sk and headed for Alaska via a nearly due-north route. Both times he ran into ice and was forced home, having reached as far as 80°28'N on the second try (see chapter 7).[100]

In 1785, Russian empress Catherine the Great (r. 1762–1796) commissioned the Russianized Englishman Iosef (Joseph) Billings and his Russian deputy Gavril Sarychev for a nearly decade-long survey of the Russian Arctic and northern Pacific, with an emphasis on the Northeast Passage. Billings's expedition was early intended to be part of a much larger undertaking — the first Russian circumnavigation of the world, formally ordered by Catherine in December 1786 and to be commanded overall by Captain Grigorii Ivanovich Mulovskii. The planned great expedition, granted a generous budget and unusually well supplied, was intended primarily to assert Russia's claim to full possession of all its coasts. As such, it would have marked a major milestone in Russian expansion and European exploration. Concerned about foreign encroachments and potential claims — and spooked in particular by the Englishman James Cook's appearances in Unalaska in 1778 (with *Discovery* and *Resolution*) and in Petropavlovsk, Kamchatka, the following year — Catherine was motivated to act in defense of the coasts and borders of her enormous but unsecured empire. From this perspective, she authorized Mulovskii to destroy "shore installations," markers, or other manifestations of foreign presence on Russian territory. "Foreign shipping was to be ordered to leave Russian waters and force used against any vessels that refused to obey the order."[101] At the same time the expedition was charged with a large amount and diversity of scientific and navigational work.

But it was not to be. In the summer of 1787, Russia went to war with its old enemy Turkey, necessitating the redeployment of most of the expedition's ships. Only Billings's commission was maintained, to be known as the Northeastern Geographical and Astronomical Expedition. Like its predecessor, the Great Northern Expedition, Billings's outing was given a broad set of goals: to "search for new islands in the East Ocean, determine the precise latitude and longitude of the mouth of the Kolyma River, obtain the bearings 'for the shores of Chukotka Nos', mark on a map the islands of the Pacific Ocean which had been visited by the English, 'and even go to the shores of America' to collect information about the sea located between Siberia and America."[102] Further study of inland Siberia was also planned.

The Northeastern Geographical and Astronomical Expedition, at least that part of it aimed at the passage, proved something of a disappointment. Traveling overland, the main detachment left St. Petersburg 26 October 1785 and arrived the beginning of June the following year at Okhotsk, whence they traveled north to access the headwaters of the Kolyma River. With Billings sailing the *Pallas* and Sarychev the *Iasashna*, the expedition descended the river beginning 25 May 1787. On June 18 they passed Nizhnekolymsk, gateway to the Arctic, turned east, and headed along the coast. Quickly running into ice that was both impenetrably thick and dangerously mobile, the ships stopped for three days. Readings taken during this time confirmed that "all previous maps of the shore of the Arctic Ocean had ... an error of almost two degrees."[103] As the brief Arctic summer ripened, conditions improved marginally and the expedition proceeded slowly east. By July 19 they were only at Bol'shoi Baranov Rock Cape, less than a hundred miles east of the Kolyma River mouth from which they had begun. With ice conditions again perilous, Billings was forced to retreat. The expedition returned to Kolyma, pronouncing the route impassable. (One is reminded again of the unusually warm conditions that had allowed Dezhnev to pass back in 1648.) By 1789, Billings was back in Okhotsk, ready to sail for Alaska (see chapter 4). Though Billings also failed to open up a navigable path, his expedition overall did result in better charts of the coastal regions of the Chukchi Peninsula, Aleutian Islands, and parts of Alaska and the Okhotsk coast. These were published in 1826 as an "Atlas of the Northern Part of the East Ocean."

Sakhalin: Island or Peninsula?

Elsewhere, further holes in the puzzle of Russian coastal geography continued to be filled in throughout the eighteenth and nineteenth centuries. Though not strictly a "Russian coast," the case of the island of Sakhalin deserves mention here — in part because for many decades after the first documented landings had been made by the Japanese in 1635 and 1636, the area *was* mistakenly thought to be a peninsula, contiguous with the Eurasian landmass. The error was easily made, and was repeated by the Russians who arrived soon after, though exactly when is unclear. Ivan Moskvitin, the discoverer of the Okhotsk Sea, along with his companion Ivan Kolobov, may have been the first Russians to sight the island, passing by in 1640. One Russian account goes beyond speculation and specifically makes Moskvitin Sakhalin's discoverer, though this is still certainly controversial.[104] There are suggestions also that Vasilii Poiarkov glimpsed the island five years later on his homeward trip from the Amur, via the Sea of Okhotsk to the Ulia River (see chapter 2). Given the uncertainty of these events the honor of first European to see Sakhalin is usually given to Maerten Gerritzsoon Vries, a Dutchman who landed there on 15 July 1643.

The determination that Sakhalin was indeed an island, not a peninsula, was made in 1809 by the Japanese explorer Mamiya Rinzō who sailed through the narrow four-and-a-half-mile-wide strait separating the island from Eurasia. The Russians knew of this claim by 1834, and possibly earlier. It was not until 1849, however, that a Russian — Captain Gennadi Nevel'skoi — repeated Rinzō's feat. No doubt the Russians were disappointed by the truth. After all, a contiguous Eurasian peninsula was easier to claim as a legitimate part of Russia than was an island situated neatly in line with the Japanese Islands to its immediate south. In the event, Russia would come to dominate Sakhalin in any case.

In competition with the Japanese, Russians played a major role in explorations of the interior of the island, as well, especially between 1840–1870, when expeditions were dispatched under N. K. Boshniak, D. I. Orlov, V. A. Rimskii-Korsakov, N. V. Rudanovskii, and D. I. Samarin.[105] The "first scientific expedition to Sakhalin"—a joint venture of two

Imperial Russian organs: the Academy of Sciences and the Geographical Society — was carried out in 1854–1856 under the leadership of Leopold von Schrenk, who focused much of his energies on a study of the native Ainu people. Further Russian scientific expeditions during the 1860s and 1870s were carried out by M. M. Dobrotvorskii, I. Lopatin, and I. S. Poliakov. These focused particularly on archeology.[106]

The Final Conquest of the Northeast Passage

As Sakhalin slowly yielded its mysteries during the nineteenth century, efforts to sail the Northeast Passage continued. Otto Evstaf'evich Kotzebue, sailing in the *Riurik*, tried and failed to find a route from west to east during a grand Pacific expedition of 1815–1818 (see chapter 5). During the early 1820s, Fedor Petrovich Litke explored the coasts of Novaia Zemlia (work that was continued the following decade by A. K. Tsivol'ko, P. K. Pakhtusov, K. M. Ber, and others). Also in the 1820s, in the course of exploring east from the Indigirka to Koliuchin Bay, Ferdinand Petrovich Wrangel answered a lingering question from the days of the Great Northern Expedition: the possibility that the Eurasian coast in the vicinity of the Kolyma River might extend north into the East Siberian Sea beyond its actual extent of about 71°N. It did not. This, of course, was good news. At the same time Petr Fedorovich Anzhu (also Anjou) and others compiled more detailed charts of the region between the Olenek and Indigirka rivers and of the New Siberian Islands separating the Laptev and East Siberian Seas. Some of these islands are now named for Anzhu as a result.

Despite its efforts, Russia was ultimately beaten in the race to open the Northeast Passage by the Swedes. In 1878 N. A. E. Nordenskjöld completed the first complete voyage, traveling from west to east in the ship *Vega*, a "wooden vessel with a steam engine of only 69 [horsepower]."[107] Russians were not completely uninvolved, however. A Russian merchant, A. Sibiriakov, contributed to funding the Swedish expedition.

Nordenskjöld was well primed for his achievement. A veteran of Swedish Arctic exploration, he had during the 1860s and early 1870s already mapped and explored much of Spitsbergen as well as set the record for sailing north (to 81°42'N off Svalbard in 1868). Even so, the challenges of the Arctic were sufficient that Nordenskjöld took several seasons to achieve his goal. In 1875, approaching from the west, he successfully passed Novaia Zemlia and part of the Kara Sea before turning south up the Enisei River for a series of explorations. Not until 1878 did he resume the eastward Arctic journey, rounding Cape Cheliuskin and sailing all the way to the Bering Straits. Here, ice halted his progress again. The following year he proceeded through the straits and into the Bering Sea and North Pacific, eventually reaching China. The crossing thus took four years. In 1906, the Scandinavians made it two-for-two as the Norwegian R. Amundsen finished a four-year sea crossing (1903–1906) of the North*west* Passage.

The extreme rigors of the crossing meant that the Swedish conquest of the Northeast Passage in 1878 remained for some time an unrepeatable achievement of exploration rather than the beginning of more regular traffic. Yet the dream of eventually operating a navigable highway had clearly been given an enormous boost. Russia's own interest in the route was stimulated further by a disastrous and humiliating defeat during the Russo-Japanese War of 1904–1905, the severity of which was due in large part to the delays inherent in having to send the Baltic Fleet to the far eastern theater via the protracted North Sea–Atlantic–Indian Ocean route.[108]

The Russians finally completed a full crossing — only the second ever — in 1915. The achievement, made by two ships, the *Taimyr* and the *Vaigach* under the command of B. A. Vil'kitskii (1885–1961), beat the Swedes on speed, taking only two seasons (starting in 1914). It was also the first crossing from east to west. On these two accounts it was at least a little more than simply second place. This historic expedition, which also led to the discovery of Severnaia Zemlia, is discussed more fully in chapter 5.

Russia and the Development of the Northeast Passage After the Bolshevik Revolution

Russians became more serious still about the Northeast Passage after the Bolshevik Revolution of 1917. In addition to all the older considerations, the communists saw the Northeast Passage as critical in several new ways: to industrialization (via the exploitation of Siberian mineral riches), and to the spread of Soviet political and military power across the vast former tsarist Empire during an era of Civil War (1918–1920) and beyond. Improvements in shipping also made the region an increasingly vulnerable international border at a time when Soviet Russia's radical new political course was quickly earning it numerous and powerful enemies. Also worth considering were the propaganda and public relations benefits that conquering the north might bring to the communist system.[109]

In July 1918, Vladimir Lenin, head of the Soviet government, assigned one million rubles to found the Arctic Ocean Hydrographic Expedition, charged with investigating the Northeast Passage.[110] This began a trend. Over the following two decades the Soviet regime devoted ever-greater resources to Arctic exploration and development. Several important entities were established for this purpose, including the Northern Scientific-Commercial Expedition (*Sevekspeditsiia*, founded 1920), the Committee of the Northern Sea Route (*Komseveroput*, founded later the same year), an Arctic Commission within the Council of People's Commissars (1928), and, in particular, a high-level umbrella organization called the Main Administration of the Northern Sea Route (*Glavsevmorput*, 1932).[111] Though these developments were symptoms of Soviet commitment to a wide range of Arctic goals and programs, the abiding centrality of the Passage is clearly illustrated in *Glavsevmorput*'s motto: "Transform the Northern Sea Route into a normal and operational waterway!"[112]

During the first decade and a half after the Bolshevik Revolution, Russian and Soviet shipping technology and expertise increased dramatically, and was accompanied by the development of ports and other critical infrastructure along the Arctic coastal region. Beginning in 1921 — during a period of relative economic liberalism in Russia known as the New Economic Policy, or NEP — the Soviets became particularly active in international trade in the Kara Sea, with their vessels entering from the interior of Russia along the Ob' and Enisei rivers. Here, they met ships from Germany, Britain, Norway, and other countries, exchanged Russian timber, ores, cotton, and other commodities for foreign manufactured goods, and then returned upriver. There was a total of sixty-two Russian Kara Sea Expeditions during an eight-year period from 1921 to 1929. Though international trade of this sort stalled after 1930, the Soviets continued to develop the passage. When the Italian aviator Umberto Nobile and his crew crash-landed the dirigible *Italia* near the North Pole in 1928, Russians were able to use their expertise to lead a spectacular and successful international rescue from the icebreakers *Malygin* and *Krasin*. (An effort by the celebrated Norwegian explorer Roald Amundsen to reach the same crew by airplane ended tragically, costing the explorer his life.)[113] Events such as these set the scene for another series of great Russian expeditions and achievements — the first three single-season crossings of the entire Northeast Passage, carried out 1932–1934, to which we now turn.

The Voyage of the *Sibiriakov* (1932)

Still smarting, perhaps, from having been beaten across the Northeast Passage by the Swedes back in 1878, the Stalinist Soviet Union chose the occasion of the Second International Polar Year in 1932 to regain glory by attempting the first single-season crossing. (The trip was also planned in the shadow of a decision made the same year by the Soviet authorities to reject alternative proposals to connect Russia's northern territories by means of a great rail network.) The effort had already been two years in the planning, primarily under Otto Iul'evich Shmidt (1891–1956; a.k.a. Schmidt) — director of the Arctic Institute and a supremely versatile academician with a long resume in science, politics, and publishing — and Vladimir Vize, Arctic Institute member, climate scientist, and a seasoned Arctic explorer. The "ice-forcing" (as opposed to "icebreaking"[114]) ship *Sibiriakov* was provided for the trip. The *Sibiriakov* was diesel-powered and produced 2,000 horsepower. Built in 1909 it was not, in fact, a Russian ship at all, but a British hunting vessel constructed at Glasgow, Scotland,[115] originally named the *Bellaventure*, and purchased by the Russian government in 1916. It was put under the command of Vladimir Voronin with Shmidt as overall expedition leader.

Voronin and Shmidt set out on 28 July 1932 from Arkhangel'sk. On board were nearly fifty crew members and one-and-a-half-years' worth of food. Favorable conditions prevailed at first, and the *Sibiriakov* quickly reached Dikson Island at the mouth of the Enisei. From here, the route led northeast — well above Cape Cheliuskin — to a scheduled stop at the Soviet research station on Severnaia Zemlia. After swapping four crew members, the *Sibiriakov* headed south through the Laptev Sea around the Taimyr Peninsula, arriving at Tikso Bay by the delta of the Lena River on August 30.

The next stage took the expedition past the New Siberian Islands and into the East Siberian Sea. With the short Arctic summer already finished, conditions quickly grew worse. Chilling cold and storms provided serious challenges, but worse was the thickening ice. Several times the *Sibiriakov* became stuck fast. With his determination not to fail fortified by political pressures from Moscow, Voronin several times ordered detachments of crew members to disembark onto the ice, drill holes, and drop and detonate explosives to free the ship. The technique was risky in the extreme. Charges set too close to the ship risked sinking it. Setting them too far simply wasted explosives.

On September 10 a terrible noise was heard on board: the propeller had struck thick underwater ice. Half the blades were severed. Shmidt had the ship's coal supplies moved to the bow. This shifted the weight sufficiently to lift the stern clear and accessible, allowing repairs to be made and the *Sibiriakov* to proceed.

Unfortunately, the fix was not equal to the terrible conditions and continuing strains on the ship. A mere one hundred miles shy of the Bering Straits the propeller shaft again struck submerged ice. This time it completely snapped off. Repair was out of the question. In Stalin's Russia, so too was defeat, however. With a sail improvised from tarpaulin the *Sibiriakov* limped on, covering nine miles per day. On October 1 the ship entered the Bering Straits and the history books.

The Voyage of the *Cheliuskin* (1933–1934)

The combination of unusually mild conditions, the desperate, almost fluke-like nature of the final stretch, and the demands of the Soviet government that its country's achievements be beyond reproach set the stage for a follow-up attempt the very next year. Voronin and Shmidt were called up again as captain and expedition leader, respectively.

The ship — the *Cheliuskin* — was not the obvious choice for such a demanding and high-profile endeavor. Like its predecessor, it was not Soviet built but — in this case — Danish, completed in 1933. More curiously — the *Cheliuskin* was not an icebreaker, though the USSR now had several of these at its disposal. Consequently, it had to be custom fitted with an additional layer of steel plating — problems that would later complicate the trip. It is possible that at a time of breakneck industrialization (associated with the Stalin's first two Five-Year Plans) a more suitable vessel could not be spared. Otto Shmidt himself asserted later that "the Soviet authorities ... purposely chose ... to use an ordinary ship for the mission, on the grounds that the voyage would be more meaningful if a normal vessel proved able to sail freely through the Northern Sea Route."[116] Given that provision was made ahead of time for other icebreakers to clear the *Cheliuskin*'s route, this seems unconvincing.

The *Cheliuskin* embarked under fanfare and to a large crowd from Leningrad on 12 July 1933, bound for Vladivostok. On board were 112 people (soon to be swelled to 113 by the birth of a baby). Heading west across the Baltic, the ship soon encountered mechanical problems, forcing a stop en route at Copenhagen — ironically the port in which the *Cheliuskin* had been built. From here, it was out into the North Sea and round Scandinavia to Murmansk and across the White Sea to Novaia Zemlia and the Kara Sea. On September 1 the Taimyr Peninsula came into sight but did not present a major obstacle. The Laptev Sea crossing was also uneventful.

Then matters deteriorated. A Soviet Sh-2 airplane had been assigned to the mission to provide ice reconnaissance for the aforementioned icebreaking ships. Combined, the plane and icebreakers should have ensured a relatively smooth passage for the *Cheliuskin*. But the plane spent large amounts of valuable time grounded for repairs. Consequently, on many occasions the first information Shmidt's crew had about ice was upon directly encountering it in the East Siberian and Chukchi Seas. Worse — of the three icebreakers promised only one, the *Litke*, turned out to be functional and available, and even this only marginally. These were more than just disappointments or inconveniences. Lacking proper support, the *Cheliuskin* was forced to weave its way gingerly through the floes hoping for favorable conditions. On-board coal supplies ran low, requiring a strict system of rationing, keeping the ship's indoor temperature at a brisk 50° F. To preserve dwindling supplies, eight crew members were set down at Wellen.

Then came a bigger problem. In mid–October, again (as with the *Sibiriakov*) about one hundred miles from the Bering Straits, the *Cheliuskin* became icebound off Cape Serdtse-Kamen. The whole mission seemed in peril. But the ice, fascinatingly, cooperated — drifting east and carrying the frozen ship towards its destination. On November 4, encased in ice, the *Cheliuskin* entered the Pacific — a victory of sorts and the second single-season crossing. But the ice had one last trick to play. As if unimpressed with the Pacific Ocean, the ice floe suddenly reversed course — heading northwest and taking Voronin, Shmidt, and the rest of its human cargo back into the Arctic Ocean. The *Litke* was sent to help, but to no avail. Maddeningly, the ice was both too thick to break and too fissured and unstable to cross on foot and sled. With the Arctic winter worsening, fears rose that the *Litke* too would soon be hopelessly stuck. Consequently, on November 17, it left.

For the next three months the *Chekliuskin* and crew remained stuck fast as the drifting ice took them on a winter tour of the Chukchi Sea. In February the hull began to weaken and buckle. The crew and all supplies were readied in case an emergency evacuation might become necessary. On February 13 the hammer fell. Ice broke through the hull and the ship began to take on water and ice. Everything — and almost everyone — was evacuated successfully in two hours. But ship's quartermaster Boris Mogilevskii, the last man off, stumbled as he rushed to exit and hit his head badly on a beam. At that very moment the *Cheliuskin* reared, stern up, then slid into the waters — taking its one victim with it and leaving 104 others (including the recently born baby) stranded on a desolate island of ice currently 155 miles north of what is now Cape Shmidt.

The survivors quickly set up "Camp Shmidt" and began attending to the basics of Arctic survival. Their situation was unenviable but not hopeless. They had adequate supplies for the time being, including a radio, and more rescue attempts were already being planned. Given ice conditions, planes were the only viable option. But here too there were problems: bad weather, unsafe landing conditions, and even a paucity of aircraft in the region. Nonetheless, over the following weeks numerous aviators and planes took off for the camp, their exploits followed with bated breath by an entranced Soviet population. Despite the mounting number of failures, U.S. offers to supply rescue missions were turned down by the Soviet government, for whom the whole enterprise was still a point of national pride. After further trials the expedition members were eventually rescued by Soviet pilots A. V. Liapidevskii, S. A. Levanevskii, V. S. Molokov, N. P. Kamanin, M. T. Slepnev, M. V. Vodop'ianov, and I. V. Doronin. For their efforts these men were granted the title "Heroes of the Soviet Union" — the first use of the award.

The following year, the *Litke* completed the first relatively event-free single-season crossing of the passage, this time sailing east to west.

By now, the Northern Passage — the last of Russia's great coastal challenges — had been well and truly conquered. Soviet cargo ships began to ply its waters regularly beginning in 1935, taking advantage of a growing infrastructure of ports, stations, and icebreakers. In 1937 the Soviet ship *Mossovet* made the first roundtrip crossing of the entire passage in a single season. Exactly twenty years later, the Soviets launched the *Lenin*, the first of an eventual eight Soviet nuclear-powered icebreakers, making the journey easier still. By this time too, the remaining blank spots and errors on the region's map had been filled in by a series of early Soviet geographical and mapping expeditions. The centuries-old dream of a navigable passage had been realized completely — a fitting reward for the courage and sacrifice of generations of great Russian explorers.

These achievements are not without their unpleasant side, however. From the earliest times, Russians frequently built their successes on the misery of compatriots drummed into service, on the exploitation — sometimes brutal — of native peoples, and nearly always to the detriment of the latter's culture and independence.[117] This is to say nothing of the catastrophic impact of Russian coastal exploration and expansion on populations of fur-bearing animals — though many of these would eventually recover. Sadly, in these respects, the Russians were more ordinary than unique among European explorers and conquerors. More unusually, however, some of the most egregious Russian abuses carried out in the name of conquering the north came in the glory days of the 1930s (and continued at various levels up to the death of Stalin in 1953). Here, the victims were ordinary Soviet citizens. Caught up in the web of Stalin's political intrigues and paranoia, millions ended up as prison labor. Many toiled along the barren Arctic coasts building the infrastructure of the Northern Sea

Route. For others, the route became the "Middle Passage" of their own slavery — the frozen route to various outposts of what the Soviet dissident writer Alexander Solzhenitsyn later termed "the Gulag Archipelago." Nowhere was this intersection of national achievement and human bondage more poignantly illustrated than in the spring of 1934 when, as the rescue of the crew of the *Cheliuskin* was unfolding, another Soviet ship, the *Dzhurma*, also became stuck in the northern ice while en route to Magadan. The *Dzhurma* was a prison steamer. Crammed into its hold, allegedly, were thousands of Soviet convicts.[118]

Suggestions for Further Reading in English and Russian

Bagrow, Leo. *History of Cartography.* Revised and enlarged by R. A. Skelton. Cambridge, MA: Harvard University Press, 1964.

Belov, M. I. *Istoriia otkrytiia i osvoeniia Severnogo morskogo puti.* 3 vols. Moscow and Leningrad, 1956–1959.

_____. *Russians in the Bering Strait, 1648–1791.* Translated by Katerina Solovjova. Edited by and with an introduction by J. L. Smith. Anchorage, AK: Whitestone Press, 2000.

Black, Lydia T. *Russians in Alaska, 1732–1867.* Fairbanks: University of Alaska Press, 2004.

Bolkhovitinov, N. N., et al. *Istoriia russkoi Ameriki: 1732–1867.* 3 vols. Moscow: Mezhdunarodnye otnosheniia, 1997–99.

Bolkhovitinov, N. N., et al. eds. *Zarubezhnye issledovaniia po istorii russkoi ameriki (konets XVIII-seredina XIX v).* Seriia: Problemy vseobshchei istorii. Moscow: Akademiia nauk SSSR, 1987.

Burykin, A. A. "Pokhody Mikhaila Stadukhina i otkrytie Kamchatki." *Elektronnyi zhurnal "Sibirskaia Zaimka,"* no. 6 (2000). Viewed on-line at http://zaimka.ru/to_sun/burykin1.shtml.

Demin, L. M. *Semen Dezhnev. Zhizn' zamchatel'nykh liudei. Malaia seriia.* Moscow: Molodaia gvardia, 1990.

Divin, Vasilii A. *The Great Russian Navigator, A. I. Chirikov.* 1953. Translated by Raymond H. Fisher. The Rasmuson Library Historical Translation Series, vol. 6. Fairbanks: University of Alaska, 1993.

Dmytryshyn, Basil, E. A. P. Crownhart-Vaughan, and Thomas Vaughan. *To Siberia and Russian America: Three Centuries of Russian Eastward Expansion.* Vol. 2, *Russian penetration of the North Pacific Ocean, 1700–1797: A Documentary Record.* Portland: Oregon Historical Society Press, 1988.

Fisher, Raymond H. *Bering's Voyages: Whither and Why.* Seattle: University of Washington Press, 1977.

Frost, Orcutt. *Bering: The Russian Discovery of America.* New Haven, CT: Yale University Press, 2003.

Golder, F. A. *Russian Expansion on the Pacific, 1641–1850,* 1914. Reprint. Gloucester, MA: Peter Smith, 1960.

Gvozdetsky, N. A. *Soviet Geographical Explorations and Discoveries.* Translated by Anatoly Bratov. Moscow: Progress Publishers, 1974.

Istoriia Sibiri s drevneishikh vremen do nashikh dnei. Vol. 2. Akademiia nauk SSSR. Leningrad: Izdatel'stvo "Nauka," 1968.

Kivelson, Valerie. *Cartographies of Tsardom: The Land and Its Meanings in Seventeenth-Century Russia.* Ithaca, NY: Cornell University Press, 2006.

Krasheninnikov, Stepan Petrovich. *Opisanie zemli Kamchatskoi.* St. Petersburg, 1745. Available in translation as *The History of Kamtschatka and the Islands Adjacent; Illustrated with Maps and Cuts.* Translated by James Grieve. Glocester: R. Raikes, 1764. Reprinted 1962.

McCannon, John. *Red Arctic: Polar Exploration and the Myth of the North in the Soviet Union, 1932–1939.* New York: Oxford University Press, 1998.

Mitchell, Mairin. *The Maritime History of Russia, 848–1948.* London: Sidgwick and Jackson, 1949.

Nikitin, N. I. *Zemleprokhodets Semen Dezhnev i ego vremiia.* Moscow: Rosspen, 1999.

Okhotina-Lind, Natal'ia, and Peter Ulf Moller, eds. *Vtoraia Kamchatskaia ekspeditsiia: Dokumenty 1730-1733,* part 1, *Morskie otriady: Istochniki po istorii Sibiri i Aliaski iz Rossiiskikh arkhivov.* Moscow: Pamiatniki istoricheskoi mysli, 2001.

Pierce, R. A. *Russian America: A Biographical Dictionary.* Kingston, ON: Limestone Press, 1990.

Polevoi, B. P. "Zabytoe plavanie s Leny do r. Kamchatki v 1661–1662 gg." Itogi arkhivnykh izyskanii 1948–1991. *Izv. RGO* (1993): no. 2.

Postnikov, A. V. *Karty Zemel' Rossiiskikh: ocherk istorii geograficheskogo izucheniia I kartografirovaniia nashego Otechestva.* Moscow, 1996.

_____. "Outline of the History of Russian Cartography." In *Regions: A Prism to View the Slavic-Eurasian World. Towards a Discipline of "Regionology."* Edited by Kimitaka Matsuzato. Sapporo, Japan: Slavic Research Center, Hokkaido University, 2000.

Stephan, John J. *Sakhalin: A History.* Oxford: Clarendon Press, 1971.

Sverdlov, Leonid "Russian Naval Officers and Geographic Exploration in Northern Russia (18th through 20th Centuries)." *Arctic Voice* 11 (27 November 1996).

Chapter 4

To Alaska

At least three related factors encouraged Russians to push beyond the Eurasian coast and across the Bering Sea to Alaska: the promise of untouched, rich sources of fur; the proximity of China, whose markets, especially at Canton, offered some of the highest prices for these furs; and the desire to secure Russia's presence in the North Pacific against Spanish, British, and other possible challenges. One might add as a fourth reason a sort of geographical inertia: having come this far, the Russians were almost bound to carry on chasing down the eastern horizon — especially since Bering's voyage of 1728 had still not conclusively delineated natural boundaries in that direction.

As Russians did later begin to arrive in Alaska — bit-by-bit replacing their ignorance and questions with maps, charts, and real-life experiences — the enormous remoteness of these areas from sources of supply back in European Russia raised hard questions about the limits of expansion. Ultimately, Alaska would indeed prove a horizon too far for permanent Russian settlement and annexation. But through the eighteenth and well into the nineteenth century, the area's remoteness served instead as a powerful goad to further exploration. Seeking out alternative supply bases and a firmer presence in the North Pacific, Russians would eventually move on to California and Hawaii, and undertake numerous global circumnavigations. These broader movements are considered in later chapters. Here, we shall assess the Russian discovery and exploration of Alaska itself.

The Russian Discovery of Alaska

Especially in the West, priority for the discovery of Alaska is generally given to Vitus Bering, who arrived at the American coast in 1741. Like his discovery of the straits separating Asia and America, Bering's claim to Alaska remains a subject of some controversy: in this case because of competing assertions on behalf of several other "discoverers." The validity of these alternative claims varies from minimal to quite plausible. All of the rivals for Bering's honor in this regard, incidentally, are Russians, which Bering, of course, was not. Thus a certain amount of national pride has colored debate.

The earliest possible, though least likely, Russian "discoveries" of Alaska date back to the mid–1600s and are based on tantalizing but probably unfounded rumors (discussed in chapter 3) that members of Semen Dezhnev's voyage had sighted or even washed up on Alaska in 1648 or 1649. The possibility of Russian settlements dating from this time or shortly thereafter continues to be discussed, especially among Russians. A relatively new claim in this direction has been made by the Russian geographer L. M. Sverdlov, according to whom Taras Stadukhin (brother of the more famous Michael; see chapter 3) may have taken a crew of ninety to "Kozebue Sound in Alaska," then across the "Seward peninsula from the Buckland River to the Koyuk River, which empties into Norton Sound," during the late 1660s.[1]

Far better documented, in 1717 Peter the Great dispatched two geodesists, named Evreinov and Luzhin, to chart Kamchatka and the Kuriles. "Locating the American coasts in relation to Kamchatka was specifically mentioned in their instructions."[2] This, however, they could not do. Other abortive efforts to reach the American mainland were undertaken during the early 1720s from Anadyr.

A much stronger competitor to Bering is Mikhail Spiridonovich Gvozdev (birth and death dates unknown), a graduate of the Moscow Navigation School and Naval Academy. In July 1732 Gvozdev was aboard the *Saint Gabriel*, commissioned as geodesist (and thus responsible for charting and for scientific matters more generally), and sailing along the Chukchi coast under the command of the navigator Ivan Fedorov (d. 1733). The *Saint Gabriel* was in turn part of a larger expedition directed by Afanasii Shestakov and D. Pavlutskii, charged with mapping and studying the Okhotsk coast and the Chukchi Peninsula. The expedition was also a military effort designed to subdue the region's native peoples, especially the fierce Chukchi warriors.[3] Earlier and continuing confrontations between the Russians and the Chukchis had already stirred up great trouble and violence, with the Russians getting as good as they were giving. By the time Gvozdev and Fedorov arrived, the situation was fraught. Efforts at pacification had failed, resulting in the death of Shestakov on 14 March 1730 and a complete rout for the Russians, at least for the time being.

The troubles in Chukotka (as the region is known) sent Fedorov and Gvozdev back out to sea, where they undertook instead to fulfill contingent instructions bidding them to seek the "Big Land" (Alaska). After at least two false starts—occasioned by unfavorable winds—on or around August 19, Fedorov steered the *Saint Gabriel* east. They reached Big Diomede Island in a few hours and decided to land. As Gvozdev and his party approached the shore they immediately came under attack from a party of Chukchis—"relatives," they claimed, of warriors from recent battles against the Russians. "We responded," Gvozdev later reported, "by firing three flintlock guns over their heads."[4] After this inauspicious start, matters improved. Through an interpreter, Gvozdev learned from these men of other "Chukchi" living on the "Big Land" to the east. Gvozdev returned to the ship and sailed round to the south side of the island. Here, efforts to exact tribute failed. Though further conversations with the Chukchi yielded little useful information on the disposition of the geography to the east, Gvozdev and Fedorov nonetheless decided to continue in that direction, departing on the 20th.

They were already tantalizingly close. The Alaskan mainland—at the point now known as Cape Prince of Wales—came into view the very next day. Thus, and rather unspectacularly, Gvozdev and Fedorov had in fact become the first Europeans to see Alaska (Gvozdev alone, rather than both men, has typically been credited, because he did the surveying and authored the subsequent report). The crew headed south along the coast, where they quickly noticed Chukchi–style yurts at intervals of a mile or so. For the rest of the day and much of the next, Fedorov and Gvozdev sailed south along the Alaskan mainland, noting natural features, as well as indigenous tents and other signs of human habitation. It is unfortunate that at this point the weather quickly deteriorated, for it seems likely that the crew were at least considering a landing, which would have secured their fame. Instead, strong winds pushed the ship southwest and at one point forced the crew to stow all sails for a time. As

Alaska receded and conditions improved, Gvozdev and Fedorov encountered a lone Chukchi who paddled up in a one-man kayak. Unlike some earlier encounters, this one was peaceful and productive. The man volunteered information on the fauna of the "Big Land." There were valuable fur-bearing animals — including fox, marten, and beaver — and also deer. The people living on the mainland, the man said, were Chukchi like himself.

It must have become clear to the Russians at about this point that not only was the distance small between America and Russia, it was also easily navigable, evidently being constantly traversed by the Chukchi in their tiny if superbly adapted vessels. In retrospect, this encounter between one Chukchi and a small Russian vessel, was a historical tipping point. Combined with the partial picture established only four years earlier by Bering and Chirikov almost certainly linking the Arctic and Pacific Oceans at the Bering Straits, the whole region was now bound to become an area of intense interest to the imperial Russian state — with profound consequences also for the future of the area's indigenous peoples.

Whatever larger thoughts may or may not have been on Russian minds as the lone Chukchi departed, the crew had a more immediate and prosaic priority: supplies were low and the season late. It was time to return to Kamchatka. A course was set. The maybe- discoverers of Alaska headed home.

Ship's records indicate some tensions between Gvozdev, who seems to have resented not getting to record more scientific and geodesic observations, and Fedorov, whose priority was to return promptly and safely. Though the *Saint Gabriel* safely reached the Kamchatka River on September 28, Gvozdev did not have sufficient information for drafting a proper map. This he blamed on Fedorov, who he said had failed to keep sufficient records and even had withheld access to the ship's journal during critical parts of the journey. Consequently, when in 1743 Gvozdev finally did help draw a map of the region, it was of limited use.

This lack, and the scant nature of written observations made by the same expedition, are the main causes of the persistent obscurity of a man who has a strong claim, along with Fedorov, to be the discoverer of Alaska. Interestingly, there is no indication from ship's records of the kind of celebrations or remarks one might have expected to accompany a major discovery. This leads, reasonably, to the suggestion that no one on board knew what he was actually seeing.[5] If this was so at the time, minds appear to have changed shortly thereafter. Gvozdev's later report, along with notes made by the Okhotsk Chancellery, both indicate a sense that the "Big Land" had indeed been seen and, more importantly, that it could be reached from "the mouth of the Anadyr ... in five days and from Cape Chukchi within one and a half days."[6] Further, after 1732, "all Russian charts would carry an outline of a portion of the Alaskan coast with the notation 'Geodesist Gvozdev was here in the year 1732.'"[7]

The Official Discovery of Alaska: Bering, Chirikov, and Steller, 1741

Bering's First Kamchatka Expedition, it will be recalled, had fallen short of establishing with absolute certainty that Asia and America were separate continents. Nor had Bering sighted America itself. These unanswered questions, along with a myriad of new ones, had inspired the much more ambitious Great Northern Expedition discussed in the previous chapter. The planned capstone of this adventure, which is to be related here, involved a return to North Pacific waters in 1741 in order finally to locate the mythical "Big Land": Alaska. The setting off point was again Kamchatka — thus giving the whole Great Northern Expedition its alternative title of Second Kamchatka Expedition. And once again, it was Bering's show, with Chirikov captaining the sister ship.

There was an important new expedition member, however. Back in 1740, before leaving Okhotsk for Kamchatka, Bering had taken on a young German named Georg Steller. A Pietist with strong scientific credentials, Steller was to serve both as naturalist and unofficial ship's minister, ultimately earning lasting fame in the former field for his discovery of several plant and animal species in Kamchatka, Alaska, and in-between.[8] Well-known too is his somewhat antagonistic relationship with Bering, whom he sometimes found to be stubborn, ill-informed, and — worst of all in Steller's estimation — lacking real passion for exploration and adventure. Historians have often taken Steller's side, preferring the German's bold courage and devotion to science over the Dane's caution and careerism, and noting instances where Bering foolishly spurned Steller's advice on matters of navigation, diet, and so on. Emphasis has also been given many times to the interest and sympathy Steller showed toward native cultures he encountered on his travels — traits that set him apart from most of his coexpeditionists, including Bering. (Steller wrote letters to the Holy Synod and the Russian Senate complaining of extortionist priests, violence, and other Russian abuses visited upon Kamchatka's native Itelmens and Koriaks, for example.) Unlike most other members of the expedition — and to the irritation of many — Steller even had a penchant for "going native." Rather than preserve the aloof separateness "appropriate" to a European, he interacted with native peoples, befriended some, attempted to learn their languages, eat their foods, and so on. Not all historians have taken Steller's side, however. A recent, major American study more sympathetic to Bering calls the German "at first a highly biased and opinionated antagonist" and, while conceding that Bering did sometimes err in ignoring Steller's advice, notes several counterexamples.[9] No doubt both were imperfect men.

During May 1741 the expedition readied itself for departure. Two ships were to sail: the flagship *St. Peter*, under Bering's command, and the *St. Paul*, under Chirikov's. Both were packets — a Dutch design intended for hauling cargo and passengers in north European Seas. In preparation for possible confrontations — either with Spanish or other European vessels or with native peoples — each ship had been modified to carry a substantial array of larger and smaller cannons along with copious gunpowder supplies. On board, European decorum and protocol prevailed: Bering wore "splendid attire with accoutrements to match: gold watch, short silver sword with silver in-lined sword belt, gold cuff links, and silver shoe buckles. His immediate staff consisted of an adjutant, personal physician, two trumpeters, one drummer, and two personal servants."[10] Few of these things were to prove useful.

Beginning from Avacha Bay on the southwest corner of Kamchatka, they were, of course, setting themselves a far longer route to America than the one Gvozdev and Fedorov had taken when, thirteen years earlier, they had departed far to the north from the Chukchi coast. This was less a matter of intention than of geographical ignorance, of course.

A more serious mistake was about to be made as well. The expedition had been ordered by the Russian Senate and Admiralty College to take on board the French astronomer Louis Delisle de la Croyère and to heed his advice on the choice of route. Delisle, a man almost unanimously regarded — then and now — as incompetent and a drunk, insisted that the two ships head first in a southeasterly direction in search of what would turn out to be a phantom — Juan de Gama Land. This nonexistent island, supposedly occupying a line between 47° and 45°N latitude, was for Delisle something of a family project, featured on a map drawn by his brother, Joseph N. Though the expedition could not have known this at the time, Delisle's proposed route, heading southeast, led *away* from Alaska, directly into the immense emptiness of the Pacific. Delisle's plans were met from the start with a level of suspicion — an earlier mission to Japan headed by officer Shpanberg had already cast strong doubt upon the island's existence. Chirikov wisely urged that the "island" be ignored and the route toward it abandoned. Unfortunately he was overruled in the course of a Sea Council held on May 4. The ships were to head south until either they found the unfindable or reached 46°N latitude.[11]

Thus primed for hardship, the expedition set off around dawn, May 29. It was something of a false start, however. The lack of winds kept the two vessels stuck in the sheltered bay for several days. This was a blessing; on June 3 another Russian vessel, the *Nadezhda*, having rounded Cape Lopatka (the same southernmost point of the Kamchatka Peninsula that Bering had avoided on his previous expedition), entered the bay, bringing much-needed extra food supplies. Almost as soon as the supplies had been loaded, the winds grew favorable. The following afternoon Bering and Chirikov guided their ships out of the bay and into the unknown. The best of their good fortune was already behind them.

Despite intermittent, dense fogs the two ships were able to stay together on the southeasterly track, communicating periodically by means of flags, drums, bells, the speaking trumpet, cannon blasts, and lanterns. On June 12 they reached 46°N with no sign of Juan de Gama Land. Despite having agreed that this would be the southernmost limit of their detour, the ships nonetheless sailed still one degree further south before Bering finally decided to write the island off as a chimera. Ships' records show a considerable and understandable amount of resentment and bitterness among officers and crew who felt — correctly — that they had been placed in extra danger for nothing.

Over the next few days the two ships headed north, then northeast, into increasingly difficult and cold weather. On June 20, near 50°N and 180°E, the two ships lost sight of each other in thick fog. Following contingency plans, they returned, as best could be determined, to the area of last contact. For three days each searched for the other without luck. Finally, Bering and Chirikov resolved separately to push on alone toward Alaska. They would never meet again (map 7).

Chirikov's Voyage to Alaska

Chirikov's story is simpler and somewhat happier than Bering's. For three weeks he steered the *St. Paul* eastward in relatively uneventful seas. Though he did not know it, he was well ahead of Bering the whole time. On July 12 a duck was sighted — a sign that land might be near. On the 13th there were more signs: another duck, drifting trees, and a gull. On the 14th several shore birds were seen, along with a whale, driftwood, and schooling fish. In the early hours of the 15th, well before sunrise, land was finally sighted at 55°21': a "country of high mountains, the tops of which were covered with perpetual snow. At the foot of the mountain 'a forest of great growth was seen.'"[12] It was Baker Island (now also Point Baker). Chirikov was off the Alaskan coast. In fact, he had more or less sailed right past the whole of the subcontinent and arrived at the American West Coast near present-day Prince of Wales Island, well south of modern Juneau!

Finding no place to anchor, the ship moved on — heading generally north for the next three days before arriving on the 18th at Takanis Bay on Yakobi Island, located at 57°55'N. The bay was still too deep for anchoring, however. Not knowing what rocks or currents might lurk closer in, Chirikov kept the *St. Paul* a mile or so offshore. Remaining on board, he had one of the two landing boats lowered. Then he dispatched Fleet Master Avram Dement'ev and ten other men to the shore. Dement'ev was ordered to look for fresh water

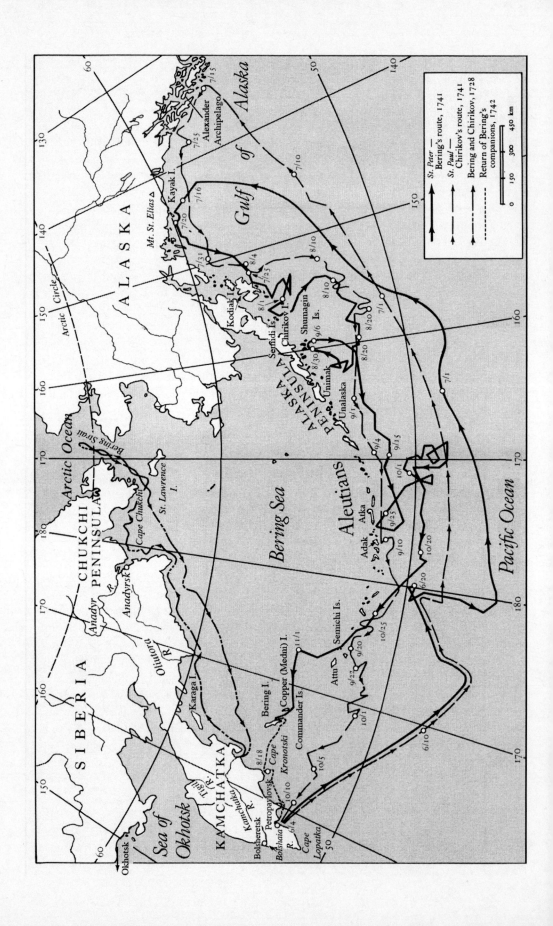

and to carry out a basic reconnaissance including potential harbors, precious minerals, and any signs of habitation. In order to smooth any encounters he was given "a copper kettle, an iron one, two hundred beads, pieces of Chinese materials, needles," and other items.[13] Just in case, the party was also well armed. Since the landing-boat would not be visible from the ship once it approached the shore, prior arrangements were made for Dement'ev to fire a rocket to signal that he had landed. The men boarded their boat and rowed off. After a while they rounded some rocks and were lost from sight. They would never be seen or heard from again.

Weather and fog conditions made a closer approach by the *St. Paul* impossible, and for several days Chirikov could only wait and wonder. Then on 23rd — five days after arriving at the bay — the crew of the *St. Paul* noticed smoke rising from the bay. Was it Dement'ev's party at last? Chirikov sent up several signals but got no reply.

Around noon on the 24th, in good weather and about nine miles from the coast, Chirikov ordered a second landing party. The only remaining boat, smaller than the first, was sent, this time with four men. The *St. Paul* followed it to a distance of about three miles from land before being forced back out by the currents. Sickeningly, the second landing attempt played out almost identically to the first. Visual contact was lost. Interminable silence followed. At nightfall signs of a fire on shore were seen again.

The following morning Chirikov brought the *St. Paul* as close to shore as he dared. Suddenly, two small boats were seen paddling toward the ship. But while still at a considerable distance, they stopped. It was not the missing sailors but two native Tlingit boats. One of them, carrying four men, came closer. The Tlingits[14] then stood up and began shouting. Their words, meaningless to the Russians, were described by crew members as "Agai! Agai!" — now taken to be the native word for "come." The Russians remained where they were. Similarly, the Tlingits declined Russian enticements to approach closer to the ship. Then they left. Chirikov spent one more day waiting in vain for news or other developments. With neither anchorage nor any further options for landing, and with water supplies precariously low, the heart-wrenching decision was made to abandon hope and compatriots and to head home to Kamchatka. It was now the 27th.

What had happened to the fifteen Russians? Chirikov and his crew at the time were in little doubt: the natives had attacked and killed them, or at least taken them prisoner. They based this conclusion partly on the reluctance of the natives to closely approach and no doubt partly on the accrued experience of decades of conflict between Russians and indigenous peoples across Siberia. The invitations of the Tlingits to "come" are in this interpretation invitations to a trap. Several modern writers agree.[15] Others, however, believe that the Russians simply drowned, victims of riptides, and that the natives' cries were either a warning or an invitation to see for themselves. It is unlikely the truth will ever be known.

On the way back to Kamchatka the *St. Paul* — several of its crew already coming down with scurvy — stopped at Adak Island. Here, during September 9–11, the first encounters occurred between Russians and Aleutian (rather than Tlingit[16]) native peoples (seven boats the first day, fourteen the second). It was a relatively harmonious affair. Initially timid, the

Aleuts accepted Russian trinkets in return for arrows, a piece of headwear, and sundry other items of anthropological interest. The Russians, who also got vital fresh water, expressed fascination at the Aleut habit of stuffing their noses with roots to the point of bleeding. Declining to spend time on further observations, Chirikov hastened home. On September 22 the *St. Paul* passed Agattu, the next to last island of the Aleutian chain. On October 9 Avacha was sighted. Wind conditions delayed the final landing until the 12th, by which time scurvy and other causes had claimed eight more lives. But despite its tragedies, Chirikov's voyage had been relatively successful. He had found Alaska, mapped 265 miles of its coast,[17] discovered the Alexander Archipelago (of which Baker Island is part), and made useful ethnological observations.

This was not quite journey's end, however. Concerned for the fate of the captain-commander and the *St. Peter*, the following May, more or less as soon as conditions allowed, Chirikov sailed back into the Bering Sea. He found nothing. In August, with all hope for Bering and his shipmates now abandoned, Chirikov and crew departed, soon arriving back in Petropavlovsk. Had they stayed a few more days they would have witnessed a remarkable sight: the arrival home of the remnants of Bering's expedition. They were sailing a makeshift vessel constructed from the corpse of the *St. Peter*. Bering, however, was not on board. He lay dead, not far distant, on a small island that now bears his name. Ironically, during his recent search for the *St. Peter*, Chirikov had sailed right past this island without seeing it. What, then, had happened to Bering and his crew following their separation from Chirikov that foggy June 20?

Bering's Voyage

Like Chirikov, Bering spent three days trying to reestablish contact and then sailed on. Unlike Chirikov, however, Bering may not have headed immediately for Alaska. Instead, at least according to one recent opinion, he sailed straight into yet another blunder, eerily reminiscent of the futile search for Juan de Gama Land.[18] Though less than conclusive evidence supports the claim, the fault appears this time to have lain with Bering's energetic guest, Georg Steller. Based on calculations of sea currents and sightings of plants and birds that he thought must be shore based, Steller asserted that land lay not far to the south of the *St. Peter*'s current bearing (about 46°N and 180°E). He was dead wrong. A thousand miles of empty ocean lay that way. Nonetheless, Bering steered the ship south for *four* days — all the time using up precious time and supplies — before finally giving it up and tacking east-northeast for the now longer-than-ever haul toward Alaska. The episode damned Steller in the eyes of the officers and crew — few of whom seem to have liked him much even beforehand. To Bering and others, Steller had always seemed conceited, brash, and idealistic. Almost from the start they had treated him shabbily, writing him off as a young pup whose expertise and intellectual authority, whatever they might be on land, did not extend to the sea — *their* domain. If Steller was indeed the cause of the *St. Peter*'s second disastrous detour (which is far from certain), his shipmates' responses certainly only compounded the expedition's problems. Good advice Steller gave thereafter would almost always be ignored. Stubborn and resentful crew and officers would henceforth condemn themselves to misery and death by refusing antiscorbutic plants Steller collected and prescribed, or by consuming water Steller correctly identified as tainted, and so on. Even the captain-commander was not immune to these self-destructive prejudices. And so the unhappy ship sailed on, trailing behind — but out of sight of— the *St. Paul*.

On June 25 the *St. Peter* entered the Aleutian Trench. For the next several weeks both ships sailed more or less parallel to the long chain of the Aleutian Islands, but always too far south to know it. Steller correctly suspected as much, but no one wanted to hear his ideas anymore. So Bering sailed on, seeing little but water and fog.

And then, suddenly, on July 16 at 1 P.M., land came into view. It was Alaska. They were near St. Elias Mountain (around 60°N, 141°W). Bering was still a day and a half behind Chirikov. But Chirikov had so far sighted only islands. Excepting Gvozdev and Fedorov, Bering's men were the first Europeans to see the mainland, but unlike these predecessors there is no doubt that Bering understood where he was. Bering, however, would never actually set foot on American soil. This final step in the long, slow Russian discovery of Alaska still lay far ahead, to be taken by Gavriil Pushkarev in 1761.

For the time being, however, the officers and crew were overjoyed at having finally found dry land. Only Bering demurred. Steller's diaries record the following, thoroughly remarkable, scene. "Everybody hastened to congratulate the Captain-Commander, to whom the fame of discovery would most redound. However, he not only reacted indifferently and without particular pleasure but in our very midst shrugged his shoulders while gazing at the land."[19]

Over the next days the differences in outlook between Bering and Steller became especially stark. Steller, never all that happy at sea, was finally in his element. He was a naturalist and ethnologist. And here was a whole new world to be explored. It was what he had been working toward for many years, and he was clearly thrilled with the prospects ahead. Bering's perspective and priorities were totally different. He was much older, seemed weary of the sea and of constant travel. He had come on this journey not for the thrill of discovery, but out of duty, and to achieve the rank and comfortable retirement that discovering Alaska would bring him and his family. These ambitions were now near fulfillment. Alaska had been found. Bering wanted his reward. Moreover, supplies were low and the season late already. For all these reasons Bering was anxious to head home. For him, the enterprise was over. Steller, conversely, felt it was just beginning. After the long sea trip he was finally ready to go out botanizing, to carry out basic research. He wanted to explore and was perfectly willing, perhaps even eager, to winter over. It was not possible that these diametrically opposed outlooks could lead to good relations.

Matters came to a head on July 20 as the *St. Peter* anchored a mile off what is now Kayak Island, near a spot Bering quickly named Cape St. Elias (after the day's patron saint). The captain-commander's sole interest in the island was to find fresh water in preparation for departure. This prompted Steller to his famous piece of exasperated sarcasm: "We have come [all the way from St. Petersburg to Alaska] only to take American water to Asia!" He then argued with Bering, urging that he be allowed off the ship. The tone of the confrontation, and perhaps some of the teasing Steller endured, can be inferred from the latter's diary notes: "I was then called a wild man who would not be kept from work even by a treat to chocolate, which was then being prepared."[20] Eventually Bering relented, allowing Steller to accompany the water carriers to the island. Steller requested men to assist him on the island but was allowed only to take one — Thomas Lepekhin, the Cossack personal assistant he had brought along. As Steller's boat pulled away from the *St. Peter*, Bering had trumpets sounded, a fine piece of sarcasm on Bering's part that has been variously interpreted as a mock salute and a funeral call.

Hardly looking back, Steller hastened toward the beckoning shore. He landed where a stream ran across the beach and into the sea. His head must have been buzzing with conflicted feelings. Here he was, an enthusiastic and well-qualified naturalist disembarking on an utterly unknown land. It was absolutely the opportunity of a lifetime. Months might be spent profitably here. But for reasons that made no sense to him he had only a few hours! Walking along the coast with Lepekhin his only company, he quickly encountered signs of human habitation: "Under a tree I found an old piece of log hewn as a trough in which a few hours earlier the savages, lacking kettles and dishes, had cooked meat with glowing stones according to Kamchatka ways." (Steller made several observations linking the culture of the natives of Kayak Island to those of Kamchatka, leading him to conclude, correctly, both that Asia and American came much closer together further north and that there was significant contact between the cultures.) "Where they had been sitting," he continued, "bones [apparently of reindeer] lay scattered, some with meat remaining, that had the appearance of having been roasted at the fires." Embers still glowed nearby. Steller also noted among the remains of the hastily abandoned meal giant mussels, dried fish, a drink made from boiled water and sweet grass, and other items. He also saw trees that had been felled and cut up with "stone or bone axes."[21] Presently, a boat carrying crew members arrived nearby, looking for water. Steller showed them his finds. When they returned to the ship he sent Lepekhin, carrying plant specimens, back with them. For a short while Steller was the only Russian on the island. Then the boat returned, bringing Lepekhin back, and the two men continued their explorations.

Almost everything around Steller spoke of the presence of people concealed very close by, startled by his and Lepekhin's presence. It is probable the two men were being watched constantly. Steller was aware of possible danger, yet not so much as to let it hinder his investigations. Of all the crew, he had been the quickest to trust and befriend native peoples in Siberia and Kamchatka, and he had never had cause to regret this. Besides, he was intoxicated with the thrill of discovery. He gave Lepekhin strict instructions not to fire his weapon, whatever the situation, unless ordered.

Steller's attention was soon drawn to a clumsy effort to conceal with plants a path into the forest. He and Lepekhin followed it. Soon it branched into multiple directions. Preferring to stick close to the coast, rather than risk becoming lost in an unknown forest and separated from the ship, they walked on for about thirty minutes. Then Steller came upon an even more remarkable find — a place "strewn with cut grass." He "immediately cleared the grass away and underneath found a covering of rocks." After moving these, he came to tree bark placed over poles in an oblong rectangle three fathoms long and two fathoms wide and found under it a dug-out cellar two fathoms deep."[22]

Steller's journal then relates a remarkable tale. With Lepekhin standing watch, Steller lowered himself into what turned out to be an underground storage room. At this point, he realized, he was taking an enormous risk. To any observer he would seem a thief. Worse, stuck in a pit, he would also be extremely easy to capture or kill. But he was too fascinated to leave. Waist-high containers made of bark stood filled to the brim with smoked fish of various sorts. Steller tried some and reported the taste to be superior to anything he had tasted on Kamchatka. He also noted sweet grass "from which liquor is distilled on Kamchatka," other grasses apparently for making nets, "larch or spruce bark" (a food of last resort), straps made of seaweed, "which by testing I found to be extraordinarily strong and firm," and arrows. Having searched the room thoroughly he climbed out, taking with him "for proof of having been there," "two bundles of fish, the arrows, a wooden fire starter, tinder, a bundle of straps from seaweed, bark, and grass." These he gave to Lepekhin, instructing him to return at once to "where the water was being loaded, with the command to take them to [Bering] and ask for two or three persons to assist me further in exploring the region." He covered the cellar up as best he could, then — "quite alone" — set off along the coast to "further investigate plants, animals, and minerals."[23]

Steller's request for research assistants was denied. Bering did send a small group to Steller, with Lepekhin at their head, but only in order that they should take a quantity of the natives' smoked fish for their own use. In return they left items including Chinese silk, knives, beads, kettles, and tobacco.

Steller's assumptions — that the island was alive with native people; that they had seen the boats coming and decided to hide themselves and cover their tracks; and that they were watching the Russians closely all the time — were corroborated nearly fifty years later when an elderly Tlingit man related to members of an expedition led by Captain Joseph Billings (see chapter 3) events he remembered from his childhood: A ship had come, and some men had put ashore in boats. The locals had hidden. After the visitors had left, the old man said, they had found their winter storage room opened, items taken, and other goods — specifically those Steller identified — given in exchange.

After walking northwest for about six kilometers, Steller found his way blocked by an escarpment and thick forests, forcing him to return to his starting point. Here he arrived just in time to catch the watering party, whom he bade to ask Bering for more time and, again, for some assistants. "Meanwhile on the beach, utterly exhausted, I described the rarest plants, which I was afraid would wilt, and revived myself by being able to check out the excellent water for tea." An hour later, with evening approaching, Steller got a disappointing response from Bering: "to get my butt on board pronto" or be left stranded.[24]

Determined to get as much as possible out of his maddeningly limited opportunities, Steller now pushed his luck. He did not return immediately, but spent a little further time exploring — mostly botanizing — and ordered Lepekhin to shoot "some rare birds." Only one was bagged, but it turned out to be a first — now known as Steller's Jay. With sunset approaching, Steller received a final word from the ship: return now or be abandoned forever. He could delay no more. The exploration was over.

In the space of a few hours, Steller had collected enough information and specimens — primarily on ethnology, botany, and zoology — to earn him a lasting place in the history books. Some of his samples were quickly thrown overboard at Bering's orders, from a lack of space, but otherwise Steller records being pleasantly surprised at the warmth of his reception by the captain-commander, the latter clearly pleased that the expedition was finally homeward bound. In his understandable haste Steller may have misidentified some plants. But by any measure it was a phenomenal day's work.

The following morning the *St. Peter* departed, bound, it would turn out, for a heart-breaking and deadly ordeal. With supplies low and time of the essence in the short Arctic summer, disagreement arose among the officers over the route to be taken. Bering, ever prudent, preferred the known way — the way they had come. His officers wished instead to follow and chart the land, which meant taking a more northerly, and ultimately a longer track. There is also indication the officers wanted to keep open the option of wintering over somewhere. In this instance Bering was overruled by Sea Council [meeting of the officers] and the northerly route was taken. Though for the first two weeks conditions were not unfavorable, significant time was lost negotiating constant surprises in the form of islands, the disposition of the mainland, unexpected and dangerous shallows, contrary winds, and so on. And there was often fog.

On August 2 the *St. Peter* was nearly wrecked off present-day Chirikof Island (named after Chirikov). Here, water was taken on and Steller again clashed with Bering — who refused to let him land. On the 10th, according to his journal, Steller spent two hours observing "a very unusual and new animal," which he described as "about two ells[25] long ... [with] a dog's head," whiskers he likened to a "Chinaman['s]," a "longish, round, and fat" body tapering toward its finned tail. The creature was covered in thick hair, colored gray and reddish-brown, and equipped with fins "just like on the sharks."[26] Dubbed a "sea ape" at the time, it has been identified in recent times as a fur seal.

On August 29, having made a huge circular detour away from the Aleutians and back, the *St. Peter* anchored off Nagai Island in the Shumagins. Though Steller was this time allowed to land, his useful advice was again spurned by the officers. His preferred sources of fresh water were rejected out of hand. Instead, the crew loaded brackish water — contributing mightily to subsequent mortality rates during the long trek home. And his request for men to help collect antiscorbutic plants — effective scurvy treatment — was also turned down, the utility of these plants not being understood by his companions. Steller, who was by now himself showing early signs of scurvy, managed to collect a supply anyway, and effectively treated himself over the following days. Not one to hoard for his own benefit, however, over the coming days and weeks Steller, at least in his own account, graciously shared what he had with some of the officers and crew, significantly improving their health. This, and growing realization that he had been right also about the water, marked the beginning of a change of heart about Steller among his companions, Bering included. Over the coming months Steller would prove invaluable to the survival of many of them.

But bad luck continued to dog the expedition. Poor weather hampered the return of crew members from island to ship. The wait was lightened by some more-or-less friendly encounters with Aleuts from a nearby island. These yielded significant ethnological information, about which Steller, in particular, wrote at length in his journal. Nonetheless, the *St. Peter* spent eight days at anchor before finally getting back in the water, further than ever behind schedule. For this reason in particular, Bering now steered into deeper waters, intent on getting home rather than charting the land any further.

For much of September, the ship headed west at a fair pace — but in a race with disaster. By now the benefits of Steller's plants had become obvious. So too had Bering's error in not organizing the collection of a bigger supply. Even though rationed only for the officers and a few others on a sick list — by the third week of the month the supply was nearly out. The scurvy attacked with renewed vigor. Consumption of the brackish water Steller had warned against worsened matters. On the 23rd a crew member died. Then, the next day, the ship nearly wrecked again as its course brought it unexpectedly back onto the then-unknown curve of the Aleutian chain near Atka Island. Avoiding disaster, the *St. Peter* was nonetheless no match for the fierce seas, furious storms, and contrary winds that now set in.

Over the next eighteen days the ship was blown in lines and circles, ending up on October 12 more than 300 hundred miles *east* of its position on September 25. By this time fully half the crew, Bering included, were seriously ill. The *St. Peter* was less a manned ship than a storm-tossed sick house. Stubbornly, Bering nonetheless refused to consider suggestions to find land on which to winter. Instead, falling back on prayers and determination, he took up a collection — to be delivered upon their safe return to the Orthodox and Lutheran churches. Later that day, as if in response, the weather improved. Bering rededicated his sails to Kamchatka. It was not to be, however. A few days later, the weather turned again, oblivious to all prayers. A second man succumbed to scurvy, then a third, a fourth, a fifth, a sixth. Men died directly of scurvy and indirectly from it: painful, swollen gums and utter exhaustion led to starvation and fatal dehydration. A sense of hopelessness set in. Some even welcomed the end of their suffering. Steller writes in his diary at this point of being one of only four relatively healthy men — a testament not only to his relative youth and constitution, but also to the more varied diet he had long kept up when possible, including on Kayak Island. There is no evidence for it, but it also cannot be ruled out that Steller may at this point have had access to a small personal supply of medicinal plants that he was no longer willing to share.

In this extreme condition, and though there were hardly any men well enough to sail her, the *St. Peter* moved steadily westward under now-favorable winds. On October 22, Avacha Bay — home — lay nearly 700 nautical miles off. By the 25th this was down to about 450. By now the ship's course had brought the men back up to the Aleutian chain, which they crossed without event from south to north near Kiska Island. Henceforth, they ran along the northern edge of the chain. On October 29, now less than 300 nautical miles from Avacha, the crew, falling in number nearly daily, passed the Semichi Islands. Then they trended north. By now not only the crew but the ship itself was ill, nearly a derelict, leaking, its sails and rigging badly damaged.

Then, on November 4, probably in the nick of time, an incredible sight finally came into view: dry land. The joy of crew and command was, in Steller's word, "indescribable." Everyone "spoke about how he intended to take care of his health and to take a rest after suffering such terrible hardships."[27] Brandy was produced. They had made it to Kamchatka!

But it was all delusion. As the crew would come gradually, sickeningly, to learn, the *St. Peter* was only at the Komandorskie Islands. Kamchatka was still several days' sail to the west. With both crew and ship close to complete collapse, it might as well have been several months' sail. The reality was appalling. There would be no homecoming this year. The expedition was stuck for the winter on what would come to be known as Bering Island — the tomb of the captain-commander.

As one of only a handful of men still healthy, Steller quickly became a leading force in the party's efforts to survive in their new environment. As the winter bit increasingly hard, he helped construct makeshift shelters, supervised the movement of supplies from ship to shore, tended and ministered to the sick, hunted and gathered food and medicinal plants, and helped lead the unending battle against the Arctic foxes that harassed their makeshift and minimal camp. These bold animals launched raid after raid of the men's food supplies; they attacked the sick where they lay, biting off noses and inflicting other wounds. At one point, foxes even partially ate the unburied corpses of four recently deceased crew members.

Several of the men responded positively to Steller's soups and other remedies. Others did not. Over the following weeks, more and more members of the crew — some ashore, others preferring the shelter of the anchored ship — succumbed to scurvy, malnutrition, exhaustion, and depression. Most were buried on the island. Bering, accommodated in a sailcloth tent on a ridge above the shore, lingered on — incapacitated by illness and utter exhaustion. Throughout all this, and despite his grueling schedule of duties and efforts for the crew, Steller continued to collect scientific specimens and to record observations about the island's flora, fauna, and geography.

Near the end of November, the ship, now almost completely dilapidated, was thrown by strong weather onto the beach. This was in fact a blessing. Efforts to haul it onto land, where it would be more secure, had all failed. Now the *St. Peter* was at least safe from total loss. Another surge, on February 1, would push it still further on land. Bering, however, was in much worse shape. On December 8, lying nearly immobile in a hollow that had been dug to keep him out of the wind, his legs already buried by drifting sand, he finally succumbed, most likely to heart failure. Official leadership of the expedition, which under current conditions had largely dissolved in any case, passed to Officer Sven Waxell.

Fatalities continued to accrue through the next month, but then stopped with the death in early January 1742 of Ivan Lagunov, an ensign. Steller took the opportunity to ply his first and favorite duties. With Thomas Lepekhin for company, he took several hikes about the island, botanizing, inventorying and studying birds and animals, at last carrying out the kind of exploring he had always craved — if not under these circumstances. On the other hand, he continued to play a leading role in the day-to-day affairs of the camp — from basic organizational affairs to hunting for sea otter and other meat. His and Lepekhin's near death in early April — when a sudden, fierce snowstorm cut them off from the camp and half buried them — would have been a severe blow to all those remaining.

In mid–April, with the weather improving, the survivors finally began to lay plans for escape from the island. The *St. Peter*, however, was beyond repair. It was decided instead to dismantle it and build from its remains a new, smaller vessel. Operating as de facto commander, Steller established a basic division of labor whereby a dozen men worked on construction while the others split into three food-supply teams — dedicated to hunting and transporting mostly sea otter. Serendipitous finds of fur seal and whale added mightily to caloric intake and stores, though not always to the general happiness: the crew unanimously found the meat of the fur seal so repulsive as to promote vomiting. By May 2 the *St. Peter* was no more. Construction began on the new boat — "to be thirty-six feet long with a twelve-foot beam and little more than five feet high."[28]

Spring floods and occasional shortages of palatable meat caused further hardships and delays. In May, with the weather improving rapidly, numerous efforts failed to hook and drag ashore one of the many huge sea cows (manatees) — some as heavy as four tons — that continually swam around just offshore. After nearly six weeks, however, one was successfully harpooned and slaughtered. To the crew's general astonishment and complete delight, both meat and fat smelled and tasted delicious. It was a good omen — but not for the sea cows. Now that a technique for catching them had been worked out, thirteen more were taken over the month of July. Within fifty years they would be hunted to extinction. The salmon now came into season, too. Work continued apace.

On August 8 the new ship, also named the *St. Peter*, was finally ready for the water. A day was spent overcoming problems with the hastily constructed launching-ramp — four more in loading, setting the mast, and making other final preparations. Being much smaller than its mother ship, there was not room for all the party's supplies. Hundreds of items had to be left behind and, as government property, were duly inventoried. On the night of August 13, a recently constructed longboat in tow, the reincarnated *St. Peter* was off. The weather was fair and the distance to Kamchatka not great. But it still was not an easy sail.

Almost immediately, the boat began to take on water. A leak was found and plugged, and some heavy items were dumped overboard. Still the crew had to bail water constantly. Then the longboat, proving a heavy tow, was abandoned to its fate. Though there were no storms or other severe conditions, neither were the winds particularly helpful. The crew supplemented by rowing periodically. Thus passed three days.

On August 17, almost anticlimactically, Kamchatka appeared. They were home — or nearly so: eight more days of hard rowing and sailing along the coast in a southwesterly direction finally brought the exhausted crew to Avacha Bay on the 25th. Here, they learned of Chirikov's recent unsuccessful efforts to find them; that they had been presumed dead; that their possessions had all been disposed of; and that Chirikov had already left for Okhotsk. It was hardly the heroes' welcome. Nonetheless the ordeal — and one of the more significant chapters in eighteenth-century exploration — was finally over. Of the *St. Peter's* original complement of seventy-seven, forty-six had returned.

Comparing and Evaluating Chirikov and Bering

The ghosts of Steller and Chirikov (and for that matter of Gvozdev and Fedorov) might concur with one twentieth-century opinion of Bering: that he was "a sixty-year old Dane, fatally ill of scurvy, who never set foot on Alaska's shores, who anchored but a few hours in the shadow of her towering mountains, yet, through the courtesy of historians, is credited with discovering the great land."[29] Certainly it is easy to see why Bering's priority has sometimes been challenged or impugned. Perhaps because Bering was Danish by birth, it is in Russia that his achievement has been questioned most frequently and vigorously. Several Russian writers have instead long championed their own Chirikov as the unsung hero and real discoverer of Alaska. The historian A. P. Sokolov, for example, wrote in 1851: "And so, discovering the American coast a day and a half before Bering[,] in longitude eleven degrees more distant, examining it for a distance of three degrees to the north and remaining five days later, Chirikov returned to Kamchatka, eight degrees farther west than Bering's refuge, a whole month earlier; making discoveries of the Aleutian Islands en route; suffering storms, hardships, disease, and death too, which fell more heavily, however, on his officers than his lower ranks. A striking superiority in all respects. For the times a genuine triumph of the nautical art."[30] Even more strident (if inaccurate) is the *Great Soviet Encyclopedia*, which notes that it is "customary to associate the discovery of Alaska only with A. Chirikov's expedition in 1741."[31] In this article, Bering is mentioned only among a list of persons whose earlier navigations (presumably the First Kamchatka Expedition) helped set the stage for Chirikov's achievement. These are minority and perhaps polemical opinions, however. Even among Russian scholars, Bering is still usually regarded as the legitimate discoverer of Alaska.

Recent scholarship has shed considerable new light on the Dane. In particular, during August 1991 the graves of Bering and several of his crew were finally found by the Danish contingent of a joint Russian-Danish expedition to Bering Island. The remains, subjected to rigorous scientific analysis, provided some more-or-less shocking revelations. Bering, rather than the corpulent man shown in his traditional official portrait, turns out to have been impressively muscular and powerful (casting doubt on the identity of the man in said portrait). The notion that Bering died not of scurvy but of a heart attack also derives from this new research, as does the claim that far from steadily sinking into depression, apathy, and chronic lassitude, Bering remained until near the end physically and mentally strong. Controversy persists on most of these issues, however.[32]

Post-Bering Explorations of Alaska

Though Bering was dead — and Steller and Chirikov were never to return to Alaska — their expedition quickly encouraged others to follow. For various reasons, however, no official state expedition was mounted for more than two decades. Consequently the interim period (and long after) was dominated by privateers — the *promyshlenniki*—whose nearly sole concern was to get rich quick through the fur trade. Steller, the richest of his comrades in this respect, had returned from Alaska with 300 specimens. "These pelts," one writer notes colorfully, "set Siberia on fire, and every merchant, nobleman, trader and freebooter who could buy, borrow or build a craft pushed off for the Komandorskies, the Aleutians, and finally the mainland of Alaska. For crews, the jails of Siberia were swept clean, and serfs and peasants were shanghaied aboard."[33] This claim, while exaggerated for literary effect, does gives a fair sense of the fur rush that Bering's voyage opened. *Promyshlenniki* arrived on the island of Bering's grave (now Bering Island) in 1743 — in other words, the very first season after the rebuilt *St. Peter*'s return to Avacha Bay. Thereafter, in their thousands, the hunters continued along the Aleutian Chain and the southern Alaskan coast, arriving at "Attu in 1745, Atka in 1747, Umnak in 1759, Unalaska in 1762, Kodiak in 1763, Kayak in 1783, [and] Sitka in 1799."[34] They left behind them a lengthening trail of devastated populations of sea otter and other fur- or ivory-bearing animals.

Bust of Vitus Bering (Anchorage Museum, B96.10.1. Forensic reconstruction of explorer Vitus Bering. Reconstruction by V. N. Zvyagin, Institute of Forensic Medicine, Moscow. 1992–1995? Photographer: Jan Oelker, Dresden).

Native Alaskans fared only somewhat better. Efforts to defend their lands and hunting grounds from the intruders resulted in brutal encounters; which the Russians almost always won. Among the particularly infamous — the *promyshlennik* Ivan Bechevin and his men killed a great number of Aleuts while wintering on Unimak Island and the Alaskan Peninsula during 1761–1762. This further poisoned already tense relations between the indigenous peoples and the newcomers, and also united, for a time, previously mutually hostile tribes into a single anti–Russian fighting force. Immediately thereafter, another Russian, Ivan Solov'ev, took up Bechevin's cause and launched a series of destructive raids along sections of the chain. Together, these violent campaigns successfully weakened Aleut resistance, opening the Aleutian chain and the peninsular beyond to further Russian penetration. Not all Russian-native interactions were bloody, however. A fur-hunting expedition of 1758–1762 carried out by Stepan G. Glotov (d. ca. 1769) aboard the *Saint Julian* (*Sv. Iulian*) is among several that reported generally friendly encounters with Aleuts.

During the later eighteenth century, the scramble for profits resulted in increasing organization and the decline of smaller, independent *promyshlenniki*. By the last quarter of the century "only four or five great merchant companies were left to compete for the American trade."[35] By 1799 there was only one — the monopolistic Russian-American Company, founded that year.[36] By then, the Russian state had long since abandoned its early post–Bering policy of neglecting Alaska in favor of efforts to develop an imperial presence in and beyond the region.

The Krenitsyn Voyage

The first official Russian expedition to Alaska after 1741 was that of Captain Petr Kuz'mich Krenitsyn (d. 1770), which ran officially from 1764 to 1769 and constituted (along with the journey of Vasilii Ia. Chichagov; see chapter 7) one-half of a major two-pronged Russian venture into Arctic waters, ordered by the empress Catherine the Great.

Krenitysn's commission was wide-ranging, comprising mapping, ethnography, astronomical observation, and a survey of the mineral, floral, and faunal resources of the Aleutian Chain and along the adjacent mainland. Since the Pacific Northwest was of interest also to the British, French, and Spanish governments, and to American traders, Krenitsyn was ordered to keep his commission, and his movements, secret. Sailing in the wake of the troubles stirred up by Bechevin and Solov'ev, Krenitsyn planned carefully, drawing heavily on the expertise of the growing cohort of *promyshlenniki* and other veterans in Kamchatka, many of whom he recruited.

He sailed from Nizhne-Kamchatsk on 21 July 1768 aboard the *St. Catherine (Sv. Ekaterina)*. His lieutenant, Mikhail Levashov, followed aboard the *St. Paul*. The pair arrived at Unalaska Bay a month later. Over the following months Krenitsyn and Levashov, relying heavily on the expertise of the Dudins, a father-son navigation team, explored the islands of Umnak, Unalaska, and Unimak, and charted the Pacific coast of the Alaska Peninsula as well as what are now called the Krenitzin (Krenitysn) Islands, located in the Fox group.

The winter was less glorious. With the season over, the two captains sought wintering sites. Krenitsyn decided on Unimak, where apparently his insistence on minimizing contact with the Aleutian natives (a safeguard against violent conflict) doomed a full half of the crew of seventy-one to death through malnutrition and scurvy. Levashov took a different approach — combining hostage taking with the giving of gifts to Aleut tribal leaders. In this manner he and his crew passed the winter in comparative security at Unalaska Bay, losing only three men. They also charted the bay in detail, carried out important ethnographic studies, collected specimens, made drawings, and so on.

On 23 June 1769, the two vessels joined again and headed for home. Krenitsyn soon fell behind, however, eventually arriving back at Nizhne-Kamchatsk on July 30, three days later than Levashov. Krenistyn's ill luck culminated the following summer, when his kayak capsized, drowning him in the Kamchatka River. His and Levashov's work proved of lasting importance, however, resulting in the publication in 1777 of a new, more accurate map of the Aleutians, published at St. Petersburg. By and large, however, the voyage was underappreciated at the time, and its results were neither publicized nor exploited as they might have been. Nonetheless, by now the Aleutian chain was crossing the threshold from undiscovered to discovered territory, and from unexploited to heavily impacted. The expedition also served, inadvertently, to alarm the Spanish, British, and French; all of whom wondered now more than ever about the intentions and limits of Russian expansion along Alaskan and American coasts and around the North Pacific more generally.

Early Russian Settlement of Alaska

Exploration led quickly enough to settlement. Although Unalaska Bay (or Illiuliuk) had been in more-or-less constant use by the Russians since the mid–1770s, the Russian colonial presence in Alaska is usually dated to 1784 and the establishment by the ambitious merchant-entrepreneur Gregorii I. Shelikhov (1747–1795) of a permanent settlement at Three Saints Bay on Kodiak Island. It was a bloody affair, involving one major and several minor confrontations with native Kodiak defenders, the latter ultimately suffering hundreds of casualties. This was not, of course, the first such episode between Russians and Alaskans; nor would it be the last. By the mid-nineteenth century, Russian colonization of the Aleutians and coastal Alaska in general may have resulted in the death or disappearance — through violence, disease, deportation, and other causes — of three-quarters of the original native population.

So far as the conquest of Kodiak is concerned, however, three ships led the charge, although one of them — the *St. Michael*, captained by a dimly known figure named Olesov — quickly went missing (by the time it reappeared, Russian Alaska was already a reality). The other two ships were the *Three Saints*[37] — after which the colony was named — and the *Sts. Simeon and Anna*. They were captained, respectively, by Gerasim Izmailov and Dmitrii Bocharov, highly respected navigators trained in Siberia. Departing in August 1783 from Urak (on the Okhotsk coast of the Russian far east), the expedition wintered at Mednoi Island before eventually arriving at Kodiak on 3 August 1784 where the battle for control of the bay was won by the Russians. Over the following two years, as Shelikhov's colony took shape, Izmailov in particular continued to explore and chart the coasts of Kodiak and several nearby islands. Further Russian outposts were established in the following years, including, most importantly, Novo-Arkhangel'sk, founded on the island of Sitka in 1799 by A. A. Baranov (1746–1819), head of the Russian-American Company, itself founded the same year. Novo-Arkhangel'sk henceforth became the "capital" of Russian America, whose settlements continued to grow in number. By the start of the nineteenth century, the list already included Pavlovsk/St. Paul's Harbor on Kodiak Island, Aleksandrovskoe/Alexander Redoubt on the Kenai Peninsula, Kenai Bay (comprising three separate settlements[38]), Chugatskii Bay (two settlements), Konstantine and Elena Redoubt, Delarov Harbor, Semenovskoe (at Cape of Saint Elias where Steller had explored), Iakutat Bay (two settlements), and Dobroe Soglasie/Unalaska.[39] These were all located along the Aleutian chain or the southern Alaskan coast (map 8). Russian outposts north of the chain followed in later decades, though they were not as numerous. Some Russian settlements lasted only a few years (Three Saints Bay, for example, founded in 1784 was destroyed by an earthquake in 1792), while others endured much longer. Several fine studies have been published on their history.[40]

Further Exploration of Coastal Alaska and Its Islands

Russian explorations of coastal Alaska continued to accrue through the eighteenth century and beyond. Only a few of the more important ones can be outlined here. The Rat, Andreanof, and Fox Islands (in the Aleutian chain) — as well as part of the Alaska Peninsula — were discovered separately during 1759–1764 by Andrean Tolstykh, Stepan Glotov, and S. Ponomarev. Following their pivotal roles in the Russian victory over native peoples at Kodiak in 1784, in 1788 Dmitrii Bocharov and Gerasim Izmailov explored parts of the

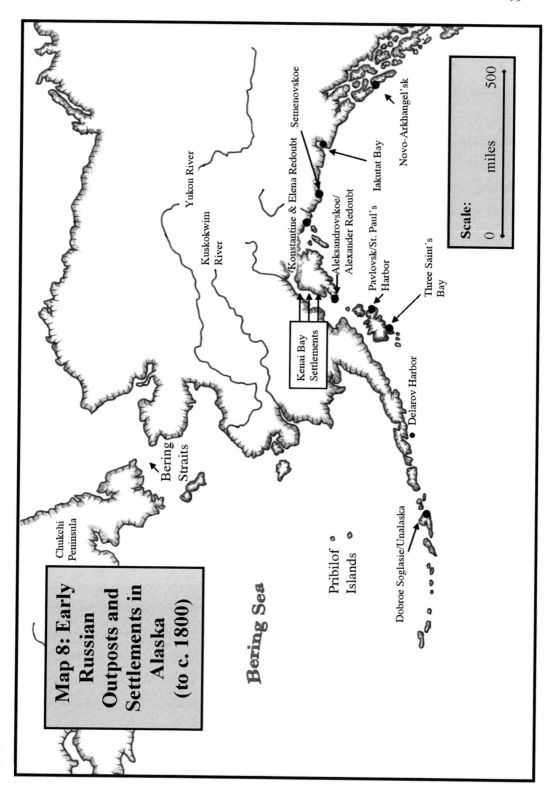

Map 8: Early Russian Outposts and Settlements in Alaska (to c. 1800)

Chukchi Peninsula

Bering Straits

Bering Sea

Pribilof Islands

Dobroe Soglasie/Unalaska

Yukon River

Kuskokwim River

Konstantine & Elena Redoubt

Aleksandrovskoe/ Alexander Redoubt

Kenai Bay Settlements

Pavlovsk/St. Paul's Harbor

Delarov Harbor

Three Saint's Bay

Semenovskoe

Iakutat Bay

Novo-Arkhangel'sk

Scale:

0   miles   500

northwest Alaskan coast "possibly as far as Glacier Bay."[41] The Pribilof Islands of St. George and St. Paul, which lie 200 miles due north of Umnak in the Aleutian chain, were discovered by Gavriil Loginovich Pribylov in the course of a two-year expedition (1786–1787) aboard the *St. George*. Pribylov reached them by sailing northwest from Unimak Island.[42] Over an extended period from 1791 to 1799 Alexander Andreevich Baranov, the future governor of Russian Alaska (as head of the Russian-American Company), traversed the southern edge of the Aleutians and the Alaska Peninsula from Unalaska to Kodiak,[43] adding greatly to knowledge of the region.

During the nineteenth century, exploration continued apace. Alaska's Kotzebue Sound — a major geographical feature of the Chukchi Sea north of the Seward Peninsula — was discovered in 1816 by Otto von Kotzebue (1787–1864) in the course of a four-year navigation (1815–1818) aboard the *Riurik*. Koztebue, a Baltic German in Russian service — as with so many mariners of the time — was searching primarily for the Northeast Passage, which he was unable to find. This lack was compensated for with other important discoveries besides Kotzebue Sound itself, including several islands in the warmer southern Pacific (see chapter 5). Following Kotzebue, during 1819–1820 M. N. Vasil'ev (1770–1847) and G. S. Shishmarev (1781–1835) sailing for the navy in search of a north*west* passage, charted parts of the coast north of the peninsula as far as Icy Cape on the Alaskan north slope. On behalf of the Russian-American Company, A. K. Etolen (a.k.a. A. A. Etholen) and Vasilii S. Khromchenko explored from Bristol Bay north to the Bering Straits during 1821–1822. Some of the areas they explored, due to their difficult currents and shoals, had been avoided by Cook and other non–Russian navigators who had passed this way beforehand.[44]

Another important nineteenth-century explorer of coastal Alaska was A. Kashevarov — a Russian born on Kodiak Island and educated at Kronstadt. He led an expedition in 1838 that charted a large section of the Alaskan northwest coast — from Kotzebue Sound north to near Point Barrow. His *Atlas of the Eastern Ocean* (1862) offered especially useful descriptions of the Okhotsk and Bering Seas.

Russians in the Alaskan Interior

The first Russian to land on the mainland of Alaska, rather than on an island, was Gavriil Pushkarev, who stepped onto the peninsula in 1761. Others, virtually all fur traders, quickly followed and surpassed him. In the late 1780s and early 1790s several separate Russian parties, many linked to the Lebedev-Lastochkin Company,[45] began to reconnoiter nearer parts of the Alaskan interior. One, under Dmitri Bocharov, completely crossed the peninsula in 1791, traveling north to south from near present Bristol Bay.[46] Further north the brothers Potap and Stepan Zaikov explored near Lake Clark. In the mid–1790s Vasilii Ivanov led an expedition toward the headwaters of the Kuskokwim River. He is believed to have reached an area near where either the Stony River or the Holitna River enters the Kuskokwim. Though his movements have not been fully established, several Russian scholars consider him the first European to reach the interior proper and the discoverer of the Kuskokwim River — Alaska's second longest.[47]

During 1818 Petr Korsakovskii, scouting out furs for the Russian-American Company, led an expedition deep into the Nushagak River region northwest of the peninsula — the territory Ivanov had earlier visited. From the Kvichak River, heading north, Korsakovskii crossed Iliamna Lake and Lake Clark. From here, traveling with a local trader named Eremy Rodionov, he reached the upper waters of the Mulchatna River and beyond that probably as far as the upper Kuskokwim. (The Kuskokwim empties into the Bering Sea at Kuskokwim Bay, north of Bristol Bay.) In late 1819 Korsakovskii planned — but did not undertake — an ascent of the river into the interior from this point. Unfortunately for posterity, no known map exists from these important travels.

Korsakovskii's work was continued by Ivan Ia. Vasil'ev — who also kept much better records. In 1829, Vasil'ev explored extensively in the region of the Nushagak, Wood, and Togiak rivers north of Bristol Bay. The following year he led a difficult expedition further north, reaching the Holitna and then the Kuskokwim. A search for the latter river's source was unsuccessful, however, partly due to the hostility of native peoples in the area. The accomplishments of both Korsakovskii and Ivan Vasil'ev — along with notes they made on native peoples they encountered — quickly fell into long-lasting obscurity, however. Materials from both expeditions were rediscovered in Russia only in the 1950s.[48]

Russian efforts to reach the Yukon, Alaska's greatest river, failed until 1833 when Andrei Glazunov — a Russian-American Company employee of mixed native and Russian background — entered it from the Anvik River. He sailed downstream to a point near modern-day Holy Cross (at about 62°N, 156°W), before moving on to explore parts of the Innoko, Kuskokwim, and Holitna rivers as well.

Also important is Lavrentii Alekseevich Zagoskin (1808–1890). Trained at the Naval Cadet School in St. Petersburg he joined the Russian-American Company in 1839, following early commissions in St. Petersburg and Astrakhan. His 1842–1844 expedition to Alaska focused on the Yukon and Kuskokwim rivers. He set out from Mikhailovskii Redoubt (modern St. Michael). Founded in 1833 by Mikhail Teben'kov, a Russian naval officer, this was at the time the northernmost Russian settlement in Alaska. Zagoskin eventually penetrated deep into the interior. His published account of his travels provided the first description of "the life and nature of the interior areas of this severe northern country."[49]

A more ambitious academic expedition, "to study the natural world of Russian America" and "make collections of plants and animals," took shape beginning in 1839 under the general leadership of Il'ia Gavrilovich Voznesenskii (1816–1871), a former printer's apprentice and taxidermist and a member of the Academy of Sciences.[50] Voznesenskii explored widely in California and coastal Alaska before setting off for sections of the near interior from bases at Nikolaevskii Redoubt (Fort St. Nicholas) and Mikhailovskii Redoubt. He also visited the Alaska Range before ending his expedition in 1849.

The Russian Withdrawal from Alaska

By now Russians had explored mainland Alaska considerably, being "well informed about the courses of the major rivers, the Yukon and the Kuskokwim"[51] at least as far inland as Fort Yukon. They had put most of the Southwest on the map as well. These various journeys, however, also represented the furthest advance of the Russians into the Alaskan interior. Though the region promised huge mineral and other forms of wealth, the distances and terrains were far from conducive to exploitation. Instead, Russians focused on the "soft gold" (furs) of the coastal and island regions. Ultimately, however, even these more accessible and profitable maritime regions would prove too remote from Russian population centers. Supply, always a problem, appeared intractably difficult, and the profit and benefit that Russia gained from its Alaskan possessions was not sufficient when measured against the great costs, political and economic, of their maintenance. These costs, moreover, escalated during the nineteenth century as the Russians faced growing competition for control of

Alaskan territory and waters. An agreement of 1812 by the United States recognizing Russia's claim to the fur trade north of 55° did not remain long in force. And from the 1830s the British Hudson's Bay Company increasingly encroached on Russian trade.[52] Finally, at the same time competition was increasing, populations of fur-bearing animals continued to fall from their earlier superabundance. Recognizing these various realities, the Russians sold Alaska to the United States in 1867.

In addition to these practical considerations, there are probably cultural factors to consider also when explaining Russia's eventual abandonment of its American possessions. Because it was not geographically contiguous with the Eurasian mainland, Alaska was more difficult to fit into the Russians' by now long-established mental framework for contiguous exploration and expansion proposed in the introduction to this book. The tandem fact that Alaska *was* entirely contiguous with the American landmass may also have helped nurture the sense that selling the territory to the United States government was not simply inevitable or the only realistic solution, but was also appropriate. Even the Russians' own use of the term "Russian *America*" seems to underscore this point.

Other interpretations, of course, are also possible. The Russian scholar Bolkhovitinov, for example, instead blames serfdom for the failure of Russian Alaska. Lacking freedom of mobility, Russians were not able to immigrate and settle the new land in useful numbers.[53] Lacking manpower, Russian America simply withered and died. (Against this, however, one might note that serfdom in no way prevented Russian settlement and permanent assimilation of the contiguous territories of Siberia and the Far East.) Further, one should not exaggerate the totality of Russians' acceptance of the loss of Alaska. It has sometimes been noted, for example, that Soviet-era writers generally displayed a notable partial silence about the whole topic. This, in turn, facilitated the spread of some peculiar (and possibly dangerous) ideas among the Russian and Soviet publics about the disposition of their erstwhile colony. Apparently, and until quite recently, many Russians believed, for example, that the United States had simply leased the area from the Russian government in 1867 and was due to return it in 2000. This irredentist myth has been promoted by some Russian nationalist politicians in post–Soviet times.[54]

Even if it is true that the Russian government had by the 1860s come to accept the need to sell Alaska, this was certainly not so at the beginning of the nineteenth century. At that time, in the early flush of profit and ambition, the Russians instead hatched other plans. If Alaska itself lay too distant to be supplied from European Russia, and if the climate and soils there were not conducive to self-sufficient agriculture and real population growth, then perhaps other territories, still farther to the south or southwest could provide what was lacking — could, in a sense, create a sort of workable contiguity among the ever more far-flung parts of the swollen Russian domain. Considerations such as these would drive Russians after about 1800 to still further explorations and adventures — in California, Hawaii, and across the Pacific and beyond. It is to these warmer waters that we turn in the next chapter.

Suggested Further Readings in English and Russian

Adamov, A. *Pervye russkie issledovateli Aliaski*. Moscow, 1950.

Al'perovich, M. S. *Rossiia i novyi svet (poslednaia chast' XVIII veka)*. Moscow: "Nauka," 1993.

Andreev, I. *The Destiny of Russian America, 1741–1867*. Edited by R. A. Pierce. Translated by M. Ramsey. Kingston, ON: Limestone Press, 1990.

Bagrow, L. "Ivan Kirilov, Compiler of the First Russian Atlas, 1689–1737." *Imago Mundi* 2 (1937).

Berhk, V. N. *A Chronological History of the Discovery of the Aleutian Islands.* Edited by R. A. Pierce. Translated by D. Krenov. Kingston, ON: Limestone Press, 1974.

Black, Lydia T. *Russians in Alaska: 1732–1867.* Fairbanks: University of Alaska Press, 2004.

Bolkhovitinov, N. N. *Rossiia otkryvaet Ameriku, 1732–1799.* Moscow, 1991.

_____. *Russia and the United States: An Analytical Survey of Archival Documents and Historical Studies.* Edited and translated by T. D. Hartgrove. Armonk, NY, 1986.

Bolkhovitinov, N. N. and Richard A. Pierce. *Russian-American Relations and the Sale of Alaska, 1834–1867.* Fairbanks: University of Alaska Press, 1996.

Bolkhovitinov, N. N., et al. *Istoriia russkoi Ameriki: 1732–1867.* 3 vols. Moscow: Mezhdunarodnye otnosheniia, 1997–99.

Bolkhovitinov, N. N. et al., eds. *Zarubezhnye issledovaniia po istorii russkoi ameriki (konets XVIII–seredina XIX v).* Seriia: Problemy vseobshchei istorii. Moscow: Akademiia nauk SSSR, 1987.

Breitfuss, L. "Early Maps of North-Eastern Asia and of the Lands around the North Pacific: Controversy Between G. F. Muller and N. Delisle." *Imago Mundi* 3 (1939): 87–99.

Chevigny, Hector. *Russian America: The Great Alaskan Adventure, 1741–1867.* New York: Viking Press, 1965.

Chistiakova, E. V. *Russkie stranitsy Ameriki.* Moscow: Izdatel'stvo Rossiiskogo universiteta druzhby narodov, 1993.

Coxe, W. *A Comparative View of the Russian Discoveries with those made by Captains Cook and Clerke.* London: J. Nichols, 1787.

Coxe, William. *The Russian Discoveries between Asia and America.* 2nd ed. T. Cadell, 1780. Reproduction by Readex Microprint, 1966.

Dall, William H. *A Critical Review of Bering's First Expedition, 1725–30: Together with a Translation of His Original Report upon It.* 1890 Reprint, Fairfield, WA: Ye Galleon Press, 2000.

_____. *Early Expeditions to the Region of Bering Sea and Strait: From the Reports and Journals of Vitus Ivanovich Bering, translated by William H. Dall, with a summary of the journal kept by Peter Chaplin.* U.S. Government Printing Office, 1891.

Divin, Vasilii A. *The Great Russian Navigator, A. I. Chirikov.* Translated by Raymond H. Fisher. Fairbanks: University of Alaska Press, 1993.

_____. *K beregam Ameriki. Plavaniia i issledovaniia M. S. Gvozdeva, pervootkryvatelia Severo-zapadnoi Ameriki.* Moscow: Geografgiz, 1956.

Dmytryshyn, Basil, E. A. P. Crownhart-Vaughan, and Thomas Vaughan, eds. *To Siberia and Russian America: Three centuries of Russian Eastward Expansion.* Vol. 2, *Russian Penetration of the North Pacific Ocean, 1700–1797: A Documentary Record.* Portland: Oregon Historical Society Press, 1988.

_____. *To Siberia and Russian America: Three centuries of Russian Eastward Expansion.* Vol. 3. *The Russian-American Colonies, 1798–1867. A Documentary Record.* Portland: Oregon Historical Society Press, 1989.

Fisher, R. H. *Bering's Voyages: Whither and Why.* Seattle: University of Washington Press, 1977.

_____. "The Early Cartography of the Bering Strait Region." *Arctic* 37, no. 4 (1984).

Frost, Orcutt. *Bering: The Russian Discovery of America.* New Haven: Yale University Press, 2003.

_____, ed. *Bering and Chirikov: The American Voyages and Their Impact.* Anchorage: Alaska Historical Society, 1992.

Goldenberg, L. A. "Geodesist Gvozdev was Here in 1732: Eighteenth Century Cartographic Traditions in the Representation of the Discovery of Bering Strait." *Polar Geography and Geology* 7 (1983): 214–23.

_____. *Gvozdev: The Russian Discovery of Alaska in 1732.* Edited by J. L. Smith. Translated by N. M. Phillips and A. M. Perminov. Anchorage, AK: Whitestone Press, 1990.

Golder, F. A. *Bering's Voyages.* New York: American Geographical Society, 1922; Octagon Books, 1968.

_____. *Russian Expansion on the Pacific, 1641–1850.* Cleveland: Arthur H. Clarke Company, 1914.

Grinov, A. V. *Indeitsy tlinkity v period Russkoi Ameriki (1741–1867 gg.)* Novosibirsk, 1991.

_____. "Tuzemtsy Aliaski, russkie promyshlenniki i Rossiisko-Amerikanskaia kompaniia: Sistema ekonomicheskykh otnoshenii." In *Etnograficheskoe obozrenie* 3 (2000): 74–88.

Heawood, E. A. *History of Geographical Discovery in the Seventeenth and Eighteenth Centuries.* 1912. New York: Octagon Books, 1969.

Hunt, W. R. *Arctic Passage: The Turbulent History of the Lands and People of the Bering Sea, 1697–1975.* New York: Scribner, 1975.

Krasheninnikov, S. P. *Explorations of Kamchatka, 1735–1741.* Translated by E. A. P. Crownhart-Vaughan, Portland: Oregon Historical Society, 1972.

Kurilla, I. I. *Zaokeanskye partnery: Amerika i Rossiia v 1830–1850e gody.* Volgograd: Izdatel'stvo Volgograd-skogo gosudarstvennogo universiteta, 2005.

Majors, H. M. "Early Russian Knowledge of Alaska, 1701–1730." *Northwest Discovery* 4, no. 2 (1983): 80–152.

Makarova, R. V. *Russians on the Pacific, 1743–1799.* Edited and translated by R. A. Pierce and A. S. Donnelly. Kingston, ON: Limestone Press, 1975.

Muller, G. F. *Bering's Voyages: The Reports from Russia.* Translated by C. L. Urness. Fairbanks: University of Alaska Press, 1986.

Okhotina-Lind, Natal'ia, and Peter Ulf Moller, eds. *Vtoraia Kamchatskaia ekspeditsiia: Dokumenty 1730–1733*, part 1, *Morskie otriady: Istochniki po istorii Sibiri i Aliaski iz Rossiiskikh arkhivov.* Moscow: Pamiatniki istoricheskoi mysli, 2001.

Petrov, A. Iu. *Obrazovanie Rossiiskoi-amerikanskoi kompanii.* Moscow, 2000.

Petrov, V. P. *Russkie v istorii Ameriki.* Moscow, 1991.

Polevoi/y, B. P. "The 250th Anniversary of the Discovery of Alaska." *Polar Geography and Geology* 7 (1983): 205–13.

Ray, D. J. *The Eskimos of Bering Strait, 1650–1898.* 1975. Seattle: University of Washington Press, 1992.

Russkoe otkrytie ameriki. Sbornik statei posviashchennykh 70-letiiu akademika Nikolaia Nikolaevich Bolkhovitinov. Moscow: Rospen, 2002.

Shur, L. A., ed. *K. beregam Novogo Sveta: Iz neopublikovannykh zapisok russkikh puteshestvennikov nachala XIX veka.* Moscow: "Nauka," 1989.

Starr, S. Frederick, ed. *Russia's American Colony.* A Special Study of the Kennan Institute for Advanced Russian Studies of the Woodrow Wilson International Center for Scholars. Durham, NC: Duke University Press, 1987.

Stejneger, Leonhard. *Georg Wilhelm Steller: The Pioneer of Alaskan Natural History.* Cambridge, MA: Harvard University Press, 1936.

Steller, Georg Wilhelm. *Journal of a Voyage with Bering, 1741–1742.* Edited by Orcutt Frost. Stanford, CA: Stanford University Press, 1988.

_____. *Steller's History of Kamchatka: Collected Information Concerning the History of Kamchatka, Its Peoples, Their Manners, Names, Lifestyle, and Various Customary Practices.* Translated by Margritt Engel and Karen Willmore. Edited by Marvin W. Falk. Rasmusson Library Historical Translation Series, vol. 12. Fairbanks: University of Alaska Press, 2003.

Svet, Y. M., and S. G. Fedorova. "Captain Cook and the Russians." *Pacific Studies* 6, no. 1 (1978): 1–19.

Urness, Carol Louise. *Bering's First Expedition.* New York: Garland, 1987.

VanStone, James, ed. *Russian Explorations in Southwest Alaska: The Travel Journals of Petr Korsakovskiy (1818) and Ivan Ya. Vasiliev (1829).* Translated by David H. Kraus. Rasmusson Library Translation Series. Fairbanks: University of Alaska Press, 1988.

Waxell, Sven. *The Russian Expedition to America.* Introduction and translation by M. A. Michael. New York: Collier Books, 1962.

Zagoskin, L. *Puteshestviia i issledovaniia v Russkoi Amerike v 1842–1844 gg.* Moscow, 1956.

Chapter 5

Warmer Climes: Russia Heads South

As the exploration and assimilation of the Aleutians and parts of Alaska proceeded apace, during the nineteenth century Russians also began to move beyond increasingly familiar coasts and out into the world's oceans. By midcentury they had left marks of varying importance and permanence on the exploration, study, and history of Hawaii, California, Brazil, Australia, New Zealand, and across parts of Polynesia, Micronesia, and Melanesia (map 9). (Far beyond these warmer regions, during 1819–1821, Russians also made some of the most important early contributions to the discovery and study of Antarctica; see chapter 7). By century's end, thanks largely to the frenetic peregrinations of one of Russia's more eccentric and compelling figures — a man named Nikolai Nikolaevich Miklukho-Maklai — to this list could be added also New Guinea, along with parts of Australasia and Indonesia. The primary impetus for all of these achievements was provided by the first Russian global circumnavigation, effected during 1803–1806 by Lieutenants Ivan Fedorovich Kruzenshtern (1770–1846; also known in the West as Johann-Anton von Kruzenshtern) and Iurii Fedorovich Lisianskii (1773–1839) sailing, respectively, the *Nadezhda* and the *Neva*.

Russia's First Global Circumnavigation, 1803–1806

Russians did not hurry to sail around the world. Nearly a century after the founding of the Imperial Russian Navy by Peter the Great in 1696 they still had hardly contemplated such a thing, preferring instead to pursue their traditional steady, contiguous outward movements. Matters began to change, however, during the reign of Catherine the Great (1762–1796) under whose patronage, as was seen in chapter 3, a circumnavigation was planned but then canceled, to have been commanded by G. I. Mulovskii.

Thus the honor of taking the Russian flag around the world fell instead to Kruzenshtern and Lisianskii, who departed in late spring 1803. Their voyage was conceived and undertaken against the background of the Napoleonic Wars and was from the start intended as an unambiguous public "Russian opening to the Pacific"[1] — an announcement of Russia's great power status and in service of imperial goals. Priority was accorded to establishing direct contact and commerce with Spanish and Portuguese America, to opening trade with the Chinese at Canton (and possibly with Japan also), and to scouting out strategic Pacific bases to support the Russian imperial enterprise in northern Pacific waters. In this latter regard, not only Alaska, but also Kamchatka and the rest of the Russian Far East were so remote from the populated areas of European Russia — and were separated from them by such difficult terrain and climate — as to make their supply and maintenance untenable *except* in the pres-

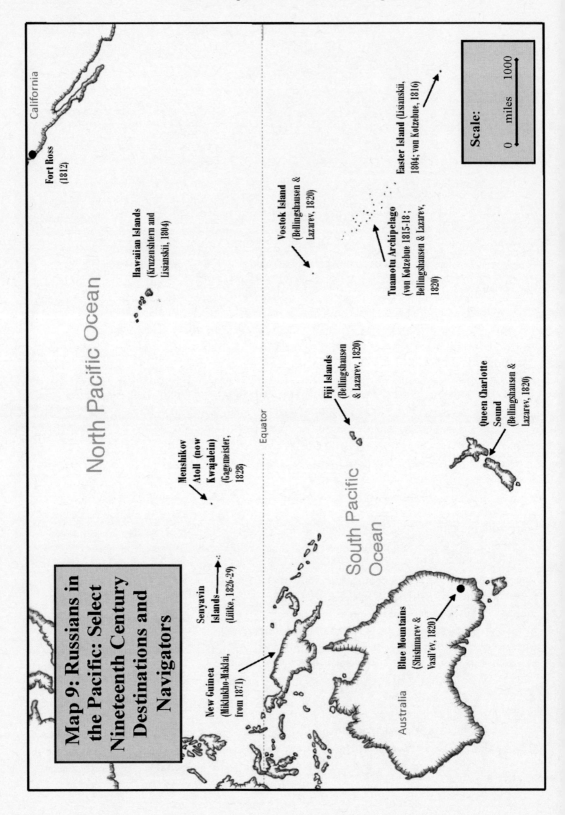

Map 9: Russians in the Pacific: Select Nineteenth Century Destinations and Navigators

California

Fort Ross (1812)

North Pacific Ocean

Hawaiian Islands (Kruzenshtern and Lisianskii, 1804)

Menshikov Atoll (now Kwajalein) (Gagemeister, 1828)

Equator

Vostok Island (Bellingshausen & Lazarev, 1820)

Easter Island (Lisianskii, 1804; von Kotzebue, 1816)

Tuamotu Archipelago (von Kotzebue 1815-18; Bellingshausen & Lazarev, 1820)

Fiji Islands (Bellingshausen & Lazarev, 1820)

South Pacific Ocean

Queen Charlotte Sound (Bellingshausen & Lazarev, 1820)

New Guinea (Miklukho-Maklai, from 1871)

Senyavin Islands (Lütke, 1826-29)

Australia

Blue Mountains (Shishmarev & Vasil'ev, 1820)

Scale:

0   miles   1000

ence of a larger Pacific footprint. These broad interests are reflected in the joint sponsorship of the voyage by the Russian crown and the private Russian-American Company.

Little real political or economic gain ensued directly from the voyage. Science, however, gained admirably: "geology and mineralogy, astronomy and physics, botany, cartography, even ethnology ... were systematically pursued by the savants and officers" of the two ships, and pioneering contributions were made to the study of the ocean depths.[2] The enterprise of Russian exploration benefited even more. Much of the route (from Europe west around Cape Horn) involved locations Russians had never before seen or contacted, but to which they would later return, including Brazil, Easter Island, the Marquesas Islands, and then the Hawaiian Islands. At this point the two ships parted company, with Lisianskii making for Russian Alaska and Kruzenshtern taking the *Nadezhda* to Kamchatka, the Kuriles, and

Portrait of Admiral Ivan F. Kruzenshtern. Unknown artist. Oil on canvas, 103cm × 77cm 19th century (The State Hermitage Museum, St. Petersburg. Photograph © The State Hermitage Museum. Photo by Vladimir Terebenin, Leonard Kheifets, Yuri Molodkovets).

Japan. Rejoining near the Luzon Strait, both vessels crossed the Indian Ocean and the Cape of Good Hope before heading again along separate northward tracks toward an eventual joint arrival at Kronstadt, whence they had originally set out. En route home, Lisianskii set a world distance record for nonstop sailing from Canton to Portsmouth.

As the first Russian trip south of the equator, the circumnavigation was also to have "far-reaching implications for the mental and cultural geography of the Russian Empire as it was seen from St. Petersburg."[3] For one thing, it made Russian America, and as-yet-unrealized other Pacific maritime destinations more accessible than were many landlocked Siberian locations, even though only the latter were contiguous with European Russia. This in turn increased Russia's interest in global destinations and affairs (as well as making the tsar's empire of greater concern to the other major maritime powers). Overall, then, the journey was a watershed in Russian perceptions of empire and expansion, chipping away at traditional adherences to contiguity and to incremental exploration and annexation. Eventually, however, the transformation would prove limited.

Returning to Kronstadt in 1806, Kruzenshtern, Lisianskii, and the rest of the Russians had, so far, made a good impression in the Pacific. It is, one historian notes, "the Russians' just boast that not one drop of blood was spilled as a result of their visits to the South Pacific Ocean, not one European sickness introduced, not one society destroyed."[4] For the moment, at least, this marked them out from their peers. Kruzenshtern and Lisianskii's voyage spawned several other important figures in nineteenth-century Russian exploration, including Fabian Gottlieb Bellingshausen (1778–1852; see chapter 7), Otto von Kotzebue (1787–1864), and Georg Ivanovich Langsdorf (1774–1852; also known outside Russia as Georg Heinrich Langsdorff). By midcentury the Russian Empire had completed forty-six more circumnavigations.[5]

Importantly — in a negative sense — Kruzenshtern and Lisianskii had also proved beyond much doubt the impracticability of supplying Russian America from European Russia — the distances and time involved simply being too great. It was this reality that would soon encourage the Russians to seek Pacific bases in the more-accessible and fertile Hawaiian Islands, in coastal California, and elsewhere.

Russians in California

One of the first Russians to express an interest in California was the entrepreneur Gregorii Shelikhov. During a trip back to the Russian mainland from Alaska during 1786 — and several years before he cofounded the Russian-American Company — Shelikhov had called repeatedly for official exploration and settlement in the region, though with no immediate results. Nonetheless, independent Russian fur traders — as usual in search of sea otters (typically in the company of American traders) — began to push ever further south along the American coast, reaching San Diego in the first years of the 1800s. One among them, a trader named Shvetsov, netted in the process more than 1,000 sea otter pelts — a real fortune at the time.

By now the Russian presence in America — long a source of tension with Britain — had become a major concern to other powers as well. Foremost were the Spanish, who since the 1770s had built settlements along the California coast, heading north from San Diego to San Francisco. French ships were also an occasional presence, and private trading vessels from New England regularly trawled the coast.

Then in April 1806, the *Juno*, an American schooner in Russian service and now bearing the Russified name *Iunona*, arrived at the Spanish outpost at San Francisco Bay. Captained by the American John de Wolf, the ship carried, among others, the aforementioned Langsdorf (later to make his name during the Russian exploration of Brazil; see below), Lieutenant Gavriil Davydov, and the primary initiator of the whole enterprise, Nicholas Rezanov.[6] Langsdorf's primary interest was the natural history of an area hitherto "so little known" to science. He devoted what time he could to botanical and zoological interests, including specimen collection.[7]

The rest of the officers were more concerned with commercial affairs. Rezanov's position in the Russian-American Company at that time has been aptly described as "lobbyist," charged with arguing "for the Company's interest before officialdom."[8] He and his entourage were received well enough by the Spanish and managed to secure ample supplies. The outlook for trade seemed good too: California had abundant grain and bread — which the Russians needed — but was lacking iron and cloth, which Russia could supply. On the other hand, Spanish law forbade commerce with foreign powers. Rezanov deployed his consummate diplomatic skills in search of an exemption, and made great progress. The possibility of Russo-Spanish commerce seemed even more secure following his successful — but apparently cynical — courtship of the California governor's fifteen-year-old daughter. Having secured a promise of marriage, Rezanov left for Russia, promising to return and marry. His untimely death in Siberia the following March ruined these plans. The revolts and subsequent independence of Spain's American colonies further ensured that Russo-Spanish trade would not develop very far.[9] Russian interest in California continued, however.

In 1808, under orders from Aleksandr Andreevich Baranov, who then was governor of Russian America, Nikolai I. Bulygin explored coastal Vancouver Island and parts of the Oregon coast. Plans for a settlement in the latter area failed when Bulygin's ship foundered at the approach to the Quillayute River, near the Olympic Peninsula of modern-day Washington State.[10]

Shortly thereafter, Ivan Kuskov, working for Baranov and sailing the *Kodiak*, pushed much further south, arriving at Bodega Bay (about sixty miles north of San Francisco) with forty Russians and a larger party of Aleuts. He raised the Russian flag and remained, mostly hunting, for about eight months, returning in the autumn of 1809 to Sitka. By now, Baranov had become committed to establishing a Russian settlement on the California coast and two years later sent Kuskov back to California for this purpose. Upon arrival, Kuskov purchased 1,000 acres of land from the local Pomo people, giving in exchange "three blankets, two axes, three hoes, and a miscellaneous assortment of beads." If it seems a paltry price, it was, apparently, the "only known occasion during the colonial period when the California Indians were given anything at all for their land."[11] Located twenty miles north of Bodega Bay, here the Russians built Fort Ross (from the word *Rossiia* or "Russia"). Construction began in March 1812. The population quickly swelled to about 200, including some two dozen Russians and more than a hundred Aleuts.

The founding and early growth of Fort Ross makes an interesting contrast with events unfolding at about the same time, half a world away, back in Europe. There, Napoleon Bonaparte, the already legendary French general and exporter of the great French Revolution, was getting ready to undertake his single greatest adventure — the invasion of Russia, which began in June. Seemingly unstoppable, Napoleon plunged confidently deep into Russian territory. By September he was at Moscow, the Russian army having failed to stop him at the bloody battle of Borodino to its west. The fate of the tsar's domains, and of the largest country in the world, hung in the balance.

But in the long run it was Moscow's fate to endure, Fort Ross's to wither and die. The Russian winter and the burning of Moscow began a rout of the French, reducing Napoleon's invading forces from about 600,000 to fewer than 50,000 and setting the stage for his total and final defeat. Russia thereafter emerged greater and more influential than ever, a primary force in the post–Napoleonic European order established in 1815 at the Congress of Vienna. But in Russian California, already by 1821 the all-important sea-otter stocks were collapsing. Then, in 1839, the Russian-American and the English Hudson's Bay Company negotiated a mutually beneficial trade agreement that made Fort Ross, as a supplier to Alaska, redundant. By 1841 the Russians were gone.

Russians in Hawaii: 1804–1817

Further west, strategic considerations also led Russians to a series of encounters — more often described as an "adventure" than as either exploration or expansion — with the

Hawaiian Islands (known in the West at the time as the Sandwich Islands).[12] Here too the foundation was laid by Kruzenshtern and Lisianskii who hove-to in 1804. They sought supplies not only for their own ships but, looking forward, had in mind also a more permanent relationship that might help the viability of Russian Alaska. They were hardly the first Westerners there, however. Similar considerations, and the lucrative sandalwood trade, had already attracted interest from the British navy and from independent American traders, with both of whom Kamehameha — the Hawaiian king of the recently unified islands — had established viable relations. The Russians thus had to insert themselves into a more-or-less triangular set of interactions.

Following the first Russian visit, in 1806 Kamehameha agreed in principle to trade with the Russian-American Company, accepting sea otter pelts in return for food, water, and other provisions necessary to the Russian outpost at Sitka. A Russian trader named Pavel Slobodchikov visited in 1807, making a similar exchange. Then, in 1808, Alexander Baranov sent the *Neva* back to the Hawaiian Islands. This time the ship was captained by the Russian Leonti Adrianovich Gagemeister (who would later succeed Baranov as Sitka's chief manager). It has been speculated that Baranov intended a cautious first step toward ultimate Russian colonization.[13] (It was at exactly this time that Baranov also sent out Russian-American Company ships to explore what is now the western coast of the United States, leading to the establishment of Fort Ross, as described above.) But Gagemeister was not well received. Consequently, having purchased salt, he left. Kamehameha, however, seems to have been spooked by the possibility of Russian ambitions, leading him to renew largely unsuccessful efforts to obtain official British protection. (George Vancouver had claimed the Hawaiian Islands for Britain back in 1794, but the British government had essentially ignored the gesture.)

For the next several years, no Russian ships returned. Then in 1814 the *Bering* arrived at Oahu. It took on supplies but was wrecked at Waimea Bay (on Kauai) and its cargo looted. To recover it (or to seek compensation), in October 1815 Baranov dispatched Georg Anton Sheffer (alternatively, Shaeffer or Shäffer), a German physician who had agreed to act on behalf of the Russian-American Company. Beyond recovering property, Baranov sought "friendly and mutually advantageous commercial relations."[14] He may also have had in mind to promote, gently, Russian influence on Oahu and around the Hawaiian islands more generally, though this is far from clear.

Sheffer, however, was not nearly so subtle and was overcome with grand dreams of empire almost from the moment he arrived in the islands. He made a good start of it, too. Success in curing Kamehameha of fever won him significant and valuable land grants near Honolulu. Over the following months Sheffer moved aggressively. He planted tobacco, pushed for more land, demanded a personal monopoly on the trade of local sandalwood, and began constructing a blockhouse, then a fort. Finally, and ominously, he raised the Russian flag. By now, Baranov had sent Sheffer reinforcements, including a thirty-strong Kodiak Indian bodyguard.[15] All this activity provoked Kamehameha, his British advisor John Young, and the Hawaiians more generally. They easily forced Sheffer from the island.

His colonial dream still burning, however, Sheffer merely removed to Kauai where he quickly forged an alliance of convenience with a local ruler and rival for Kamehameha's power named Kaumualii. By May 1816 Scheffer had leveraged offers of Russian support into a signed document establishing a virtual Russian protectorate over the islands of Kauai and Niihau, as well as a monopoly for the Russian-American Company over the islands' sandalwood trade. Sheffer, by now operating more-or-less on his own initiative, began to erect forts on Kauai at Waimea (Fort Elizabeth) and Hanalei (Forts Alexander and Barclay) with plans for others throughout the islands. Again the Russian flag was raised. Thereafter, "for nearly a year he was virtual ruler of Kauai, and as late as April 1817 he was sufficiently powerful to prevent the officers of a visiting vessel from having any communication with the shore."[16]

Scheffer's position remained precarious, however. American sandalwood traders pressured Kamehameha to act. For a while, the king held back, reluctant to provoke a wider confrontation with Imperial Russia. He need not have worried. There were no plans either on the part of the tsar or of the Russian-American Company to attempt (or even to back) colonization schemes in Hawaii. Nor was there any interest in risking conflict with the British over the islands. Scheffer was acting independently and reprehensibly. The Russian explorer Otto von Kotzebue told King Kamehameha as much during a brief visit late in 1816. Relieved suddenly of any legitimate fears of Russian reprisals, the Hawaiian monarch quickly set his forces against Scheffer who retreated temporarily to Oahu then left the islands forever, settling eventually in Brazil where he died in 1836. The possibility of Russian annexation of the islands lingered for a few more years before being finally and authoritatively ruled out in 1819 by Tsar Alexander I. The Russians, incidentally, never received either their looted property or any compensation.

The Langsdorf Expedition to Brazil (1821–1828)

As Hawaii faded from the Russian imperial horizon and Fort Ross struggled on, other New World destinations beckoned. Brazil, conveniently located along the Russian sea route from Kronstadt to Alaska via Cape Horn, held a particular fascination. A largely closed Portuguese colony prior to the beginning of the nineteenth century, the region's ports had quickly opened to the world beginning in 1808 following the arrival in Rio de Janeiro of the Portuguese government — chased from their home country by Napoleon's invasion of Iberia. Brazil's opening attracted visitors from numerous countries, including traders, diplomats, naturalists, and explorers. The most important Russian among them — Georg Ivanovich Langsdorf[7] — was all four of these things.

Langsdorf was an energetic and accomplished man who impressed with his dedication, ability, and amiability. (Countervailing opinions of him as petty, dry, weak, or even "slipper-nosed[!]" are no longer much accepted — written off nowadays to the mistranslations and misrepresentations of earlier biographers.[18]) He was born into a noble family in southwest Germany and educated in medicine and surgery at Göttingen. From 1797–1802 he lived in Portugal, where he practiced medicine and, with greater enthusiasm, studied natural history.[19] It was at this time that he became deeply interested in the Brazilian colony. In Portugal too, Langsdorf began his connections with Russia, primarily in the form of correspondence with some of its leading scientific figures and the dispatch of scientific specimens from Portugal to the St. Petersburg Academy of Sciences. In 1803 he became a corresponding member of the academy (elevated to full rank in 1812). These connections helped him secure a place the same year as ship's naturalist and physician under the command of Kruzenshtern aboard the sloop *Nadezhda*, at that point about to embark in the company of the *Neva* on the pioneering first Russian circumnavigation noted earlier.

Langsdorf sailed for much but not all the route: from Copenhagen, round Cape Horn, to Hawaii, getting off in Russian America. Early in the voyage, en route to the cape, the

Nadezhda stopped at Santa Catarina Island off the coast of southern Brazil, allowing Langsdorf his first visit to this new land. From Russian America he traveled to Japan, eventually completing his own circumnavigation by way of Siberia to St. Petersburg, arriving with a trove of natural history specimens.[20]

There now followed a protracted period in Russia itself. Unable to forget the majesty and beauty of Brazil, however, Langsdorf was delighted to accept appointment in 1812 as Russian consul general in Rio de Janeiro. He arrived at the colony in 1813. His light duties allowed plenty of time for research. A man of broad learning and great energy, Langsdorf spent much of his time on farming (using slave labor for a time), immigration and settlement schemes, and pursuing interests in botany, zoology, and geography. He made a number of scientific forays into the nearby interior, one with the celebrated French naturalist Auguste de Saint-Hilaire to the Minas Gerais province. He shipped back to St. Petersburg many more crates of specimens collected during these travels and also from research on his own expansive estate.

This was only a prelude, however, to the great expedition for which he is best known: a hugely ambitious and arduous trek during the second half of the 1820s through the heart of the Brazilian interior from São Paulo on the southeast coast to the Amazon River in the northern province of Pará.

In the spring of 1821, Langsdorf visited St. Petersburg to promote the expedition and lobby for funds. He construed the project broadly, promising dividends for Russia in geographical, ethnographical, botanical, zoological, mineralogical terms, as well as for commerce and trade. At the time, Brazil — its interior especially — was almost entirely unknown, its flora and fauna especially so. Three centuries of Portuguese presence and rule had in fact contributed to the ignorance: the monarchy, intent on keeping secret the nature and location of their colony's resources, had actively discouraged exploration, inquiry, and all contact; and they had aggressively censored relevant publications, where it was within their power to do so.[21] All this, as has been noted, changed after 1808 and the arrival of the Portuguese monarchy (which returned home only in 1821). It was in this context that Langsdorf had been appointed Russian consul general in Rio de Janeiro in 1812. Langsdorf also painted Brazil as an emerging economy and power with whom it would benefit Russia to have familiarity and relations. He noted also that other European powers were undertaking similar work. The tsar was favorably impressed and in June personally authorized the expedition.

Although amply funded, Langsdorf opted to organize a relatively small outing, comprising only eight men overall, and even fewer at expedition's start. The original core featured Ludwig Riedel (1790/1791–1861), a Prussian-born naturalist and polyglot in Russian service, to be responsible for specimen collections; Édouard Ménétriès (1802–1861), a French zoologist trained by the great Cuvier; Johann Moritz Rugendas (1802–1858), a German-born painter and the first of a small cadre of artists ultimately to join the expedition[22]; and naval officer Nester Gavrilovich Rubtsov (1799–1874), the only true Russian among them and a man qualified in geography, geology, and astronomy. All were around the age of twenty, except Langsdorf, who was forty-seven.

The expedition began modestly, focusing on the province of Rio de Janeiro, where Langsdorf resided. During it, Brazil declared its independence, which Russia refused for several years to recognize. Langsdorf's considerable diplomatic skills helped assure the expedition's smooth continuance. In May 1824 the expedition kicked into high gear. Langsdorf moved northwest, across the Paraíba River, to explore the landlocked province of Minas Gerais. Rich in gold, diamond, and other mineral deposits, the area had been kept strictly off-limits to exploration until 1808. Thereafter, prospectors and their slaves had begun moving in. Nonetheless, almost nothing was known of the region's flora and fauna, giving the Russian expedition a nearly blank canvas. Toward year's end, lack of funds and an excess of baggage persuaded Langsdorf to turn back temporarily for Rio de Janeiro.

There were also personnel problems. Rugendas and Ménétriès chose this moment to quit—the latter quickly heading to Russia and a career in the St. Petersburg Academy of Sciences. Replacements were Christian Hasse (1792–1830)—a Prussian doctor and naturalist—and Aimé Adrien Taunay (1802/1803–1828)—a French-born artist. Hasse turned out to be of little use, departing the expedition in its early stages to pursue a local Brazilian beauty in Porto Feliz. The others stayed on to the bitter end. Langsdorf also recruited an extra artist, the young Frenchman Hércules Florence (1804–1879).

In late August 1825 the expedition set out again, heading first by boat south from Rio along the coast to the port of Santos in fair weather. The vessel—named the *Aurora*—was not the expedition's own, but a Brazilian transport on private business. As Langsdorf quickly learned, this business was the slave trade. In the hold lay a writhing cargo of sixty-five slaves recently brought from Africa. Most, apparently, were in poor condition. It is unlikely Langsdorf thought too much about the matter, however. Brazil at the time was awash in slaves, and Langsdorf himself had recently owned several. He would make use of still others (and of free Brazilian laborers) in the journeys that lay ahead, primarily as porters. At least in his attitudes toward slavery and race, Langsdorf appears to have been a man of his times—assured of the superiority of Europeans and untroubled about the morality of the "peculiar institution." He criticized it only for its inefficiencies, or when unusual cruelty was involved.[23]

Langsdorf's intention was first to establish a base of operations in São Paolo, then to set out on a great circle through the largely unknown Brazilian interior: northwest toward Cuiabá, then north to the Amazon, and east to Belem do Pará. Even under the best of conditions it promised to be an extraordinarily arduous route.

The first leg, from September 1825 to June 1826, was spent productively enough on research in São Paolo province. Thereafter, the real journey began, as the expedition departed from Porto Feliz, some one hundred miles inland along the Tietê River, bound for Cuiabá in Mato Grosso province. Unaware of alternatives, Langsdorf had at first intended to travel primarily by land but now chose the river route instead as it promised to ease greatly the burden of hauling equipment and supplies. On the other hand, travel by river also involved the constant possibility of attack from hostile indigenous peoples.

Canoes made of hollowed-out tree trunks fifty feet long were constructed, along with a variety of smaller vessels. The Tietê proved a more difficult highway than anticipated—not because of the feared attacks, which never came, but from the great many cataracts and whitewaters that punctuated its length. The Paraná and Pardo rivers were more accommodating, but still difficult. After these, a major portage was required to bridge the distance to the Paraguay River system, one of whose tributaries would take them close to Cuiabá. Adding to the difficulty, most of the travel was upstream. The weather had now turned stiflingly hot and humid, encouraging the clouds of relentless mosquitoes.[24] Nonetheless, Cuiabá was reached at the end of January 1827. A settlement of some 3,000 persons, it provided a welcome respite, serving for nearly a year as the expedition's base for productive natural history and anthropological studies in the Mato Grosso region.

In December of the same year, Langsdorf and his companions finally quit the area and embarked on the last—and by far the most ambitious—part of the journey: an enormous slog through dense rainforest and punishing equatorial latitudes to the far north of Brazil. Their goal was the mighty Amazon — discovered back in 1494 by the Spanish conquistador Vicente Yáñez Pinzón, but still little explored after all that time. To increase the expedition's coverage, and also to reduce the chances of running into a dead end, Langsdorf split his expedition into two parties. Langsdorf, Rubtsov, and Florence headed for the Arinos, Juruena, and Tapajos rivers, while Riedel and Taunay set off on a parallel route further west, along the rivers Guaporé, Mamoré, and Madeira. If all went well, they were to meet at Santarém.

It was a tall order. The difficult terrain, oppressive heat and humidity, ubiquitous mosquitoes, and torrential rains slowed progress painfully. Swamps, snakes, and other venomous creatures added to the danger. Both parties suffered horribly from persistent and unfamiliar fevers. Various expedition members had sometimes to be carried for days on stretchers. So too did some of the porters. When the number of sick, or the severity of illness, became too much, as happened on several occasions (to both wings of the expedition), a general halt was called. Sometimes these lasted for weeks. But whether moving or camped there was always much of interest to see. Exotic plants, birds, and other specimens were taken in great quantity. Natural features were noted and charted. Paintings and sketches were made.

But the suffering and setbacks continued nearly unabated. In early 1828 Taunay drowned while attempting to cross a fast-flowing river near the Bolivian border. Then, on May 8 of the same year, at the Juruena River in Mato Grosso, after a long struggle with fever and hunger, Langsdorf made the following entry in his notebook: "Torrential rains ruined everyone's peace. We are intending now to make for Santarém. Our provisions are disappearing before our eyes. We must make effort to speed up our progress. We have still to cross waterfalls and many other dangerous places along the river. If God wishes it, we will today continue along our route."[25] It was his last diary entry.

Not death, however, but some kind of fever-induced madness — probably malarial — was about to overcome Langsdorf, leaving him, by most accounts, permanently deranged.[26] Rubtsov and Florence now took over, dragging the ruined expedition leader with them. They managed with great effort to arrive on 1 July 1828 at their goal — the Amazon River by Santarém (map 10). Given the miserable conditions in which they arrived, it was a bittersweet victory. From here the expedition detachment sailed to Belem do Pará. Langsdorf himself, his career over, was subsequently shipped back home to Germany and granted a generous pension by the Russian government. He lived another two-and-a-half decades before finally expiring in 1852. Conflicting reports exist regarding the degree to which he ever recovered any measure of health or sanity.

Riedel's detachment fared better. Though sick and depleted, they eventually completed their more westerly tack, suffering no deaths or permanent disabilities. They joined Langsdorf and companions at Belem do Pará six months after the first party's arrival there.

Langsdorf's illness had cut the expedition short. Ambitious plans to carry on and explore the Brazilian coast and what are now the states of Venezuela, Guyana, Surinam, French Guiana, and perhaps also Peru and Chile, were set aside. Instead, the expedition returned to Rio de Janeiro. Thereafter, however, Riedel reestablished it with some new personnel and returned to the field. The Russian government continued to provide financial support until 1836, after which time Riedel ended relations with Moscow and found other sponsors. Langsdorf's original expedition thus metamorphosed into a continuing series of explorations of South America, but no longer under Russian auspices.

Langsdorf's original party had covered more than 9,000 miles and acquired a great amount of knowledge and materials pertaining to various Brazilian native peoples, as well as stores of natural history specimens. The richness of the environment, contrasting with the small scale and huge difficulties of the expedition, meant that much had to be left behind. But a large collection, along with copious written and illustrative material, was nonetheless brought back to Russia primarily by Riedel and Rubtsov (separately) and

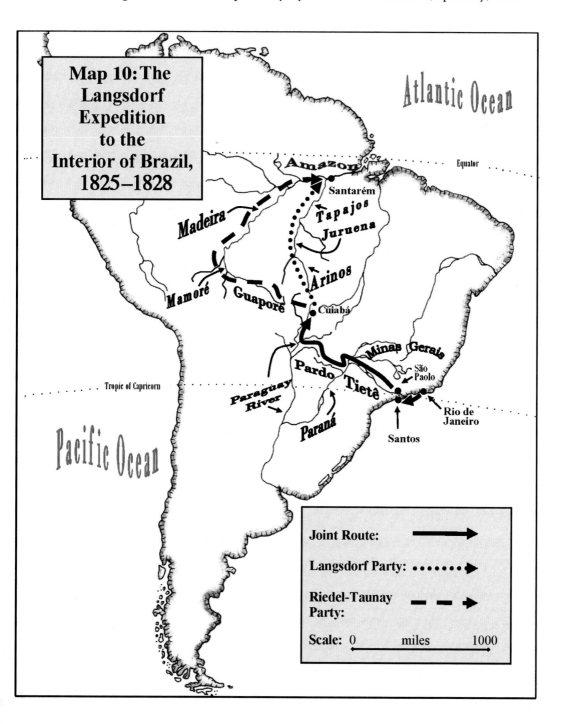

Map 10: The Langsdorf Expedition to the Interior of Brazil, 1825–1828

deposited, mostly in St. Petersburg. Combined, these materials filled close to a hundred crates. With Langsdorf incapacitated, however, and amid disputes over ownership and access to expedition materials, efforts to organize and study these materials quickly stalled. Florence's diary was published in 1875–1876 in Brazil by the traveler's nephew, followed by a few further aspects of the expedition, mostly in Portuguese, over the following several decades. Serious engagement with Langsdorf's materials and legacy had to wait until the late 1920s, however, when Soviet scholars began to dust off files and crack open specimen cases. The first Russian-language book-length biography was published in 1948.[27] The first full treatment of expedition materials — in any language — appeared only in 1973.[28] This facilitated a surge of evaluations and publications thereafter in Russian, Portuguese, and English — many of them inspired partly by the arrival in 1974 of the bicentenary of Langsdorf's birth.[29] It seems, however, that full use has still to be made of many materials, including notes, drawings, and vocabularies the expedition compiled of "Indian tribes now long extinct."[30] Obscure until recent times, Langsdorf is these days increasingly well known to educated persons in both Russia and Brazil, though less so elsewhere.

The South Pacific

Among all the Russian contributions to world exploration, the most completely forgotten, at least in the English language, seem to be those concerning the vast southern Pacific Ocean — including Australia and New Zealand, Polynesia, Melanesia, and Micronesia.[31] As with all Pacific destinations Russian involvement and interest in the South Pacific again arose largely out of Kruzenshtern and Lisianskii's circumnavigation and against a backdrop of increased official Russian concern to secure coastlines and establish a global maritime presence. Scientific interests — the study both of nature and of native peoples — were also pursued by the Russians across the region.

Australia

The first Russian ship to arrive in Australia — the Russian-American Company's vessel *Neva*, recently returned to Kronstadt from the first Russian circumnavigation but now under the command of the aforementioned Lieutenant L. A. Gagemeister — did so back in 1807, stopping for two weeks at Port Jackson, Sydney. Before departing Russia in October, Gagemeister's brief had been to waste no time on science or exploration, but rather to carry supplies as quickly as possible to Petropavlovsk-in-Kamchatka, taking the same route Kruzenshtern and Lisianskii had — that is, round Cape Horn and then northwest across the Pacific. Delays and adverse weather conditions during the first part of the voyage, however, convinced Gagemeister, already at sea, to avoid the treacherous cape and try the opposite route instead — heading east via the Cape of Good Hope and the Indian Ocean with a resupply stop at Sydney, Australia. The route was already well-known, having been sailed many times by other countries' ships. But this was the first time a Russian vessel had tried it. It proved an important precedent, kicking off a series of sixteen Russian visits to Australia in the period 1807–1835.[32] Although Gagemeister and his entourage did little in the way of exploring, they did learn that the Australian interior remained almost completely unknown, even to the English settlers. Over the following years, Gagemeister's compatriots would rise to the opportunity, playing a significant (and to this day an underappreciated) role in helping fill in that enormous blank. "Completely lacking," in the words of a recent Russian account, "any political or economic interest" in Australia, Russian observations and accounts are, moreover, "quite objective."[33]

During 1820, for example, a detachment under the general command of G. S. Shishmarev and M. N. Vasil'ev traveled into the Blue Mountains — some seventy miles west of Sydney — during March, returning with important new information on the area's mineralogy, geology, flora, and fauna.[34] Other Russians, or sometimes Germans in Russian service, made significant contributions from this time forward in areas as diverse as geology, meteorology, surveying and charting, botany, ornithology and zoology, and ethnology. They also brought back to Russia many specimens, helping to establish new, or fill existing, university and academy collections.[35] Particularly important Russian contributions were made, and have since languished, in the study of the Australian aboriginal peoples[36] and also of the English settlements during the early nineteenth century.[37]

New Zealand

The first and most important Russian visit to New Zealand was made in 1820 by Faddei Faddeevich Bellingshausen (a.k.a. Fabian Gottlieb von Bellingshausen) and his lieutenant Mikhail Petrovich Lazarev, and was carried out in-between two austral summers spent — more famously — circumnavigating Antarctica (see chapter 7). Their ships, respectively, were the *Vostok* and the *Mirnyi*. Heading north in the early southern autumn, Bellingshausen and Lazarev repaired to Sydney, arriving in April. From here they steered for the north island of New Zealand, but were forced by contrary winds to anchor instead in Queen Charlotte Sound, between the two main islands, on May 28. They stayed until June 9, spending much of their first five days observing the local "Hapu" Maoris. It was a fortunate diversion. Though they could not know it at the time, Bellingshausen and his expedition were to be the first and last Europeans ever to encounter this particular people. Shortly after the Russians' departure — but in no way connected with it — the Hapu were all killed by another Maori group, the invading "Atiawas, allies of chief Te Rauparaha."[38] The memory of the earlier clan thus owes to the Russians, who left several short written accounts and a small collection of artifacts. No further Russian visits to New Zealand occurred until 1881.

Smaller Pacific Islands

In the southern winter of 1820, after their stay in Queen Charlotte Sound, New Zealand, Bellingshausen and Lazarev sailed north into a counter-clockwise loop that took them out to the Tuamotu Archipelago and back. En route they visited Oparo (now Rapa, in the Bass Islands of French Polynesia). Discovered by Vancouver back in 1791, little enough was known of the island that the Russians were able to leave an "unusually rich" published series of accounts of Rapa, its nature, and peoples, including valuable information on their canoes — much of which remains underutilized to this day.[39] Arriving thereafter in the Tuamotu Archipelago on July 10, the Russians came upon Angatau, previously sighted but never formally recorded. Thereafter, several more islands, these completely unknown — and hence legitimate Russian discoveries — were encountered and charted: on July 13, Nihiru; on the 15th, the Raevskii Islands and Katiu; on the 16th, Fakarava; Niau on the 18th; and Matahiva on the 30th. In-between these last two noted encounters, Bellingshausen and Lazarev completed a six-day stay and study of people, flora, and fauna at Tahiti's Matavai

Bay (July 22–27). On August 1, Bellingshausen made the "first solid report" of Vostok Island.[40] Doubling back toward Australia, the expedition sailed past the Fiji Islands where, on August 19, they discovered Tuvana-i-Tholo and Tuvana-i-Ra. Oni-i-Lau, which may earlier have been found by the *Bounty* mutineers, was also sighted and recorded, and a landing made. Thus, within a few weeks, "seventeen islands were meticulously charted."[41] Over the course of their travels, Bellingshausen and Lazarev amassed a rich collection of ethnographic and natural historical specimens and notes.

Easter Island, discovered in 1722 by the Dutch sailor Jacob Roggeveen, was another early Russian Pacific destination. First to arrive here was Lisianskii, aboard the *Neva* in 1804. He spent five days at anchor, but did not land. In March 1816, Otto von Kotzebue made the first Russian landing, arriving in the 180-ton brig *Riurik*. He was met with a hail of stones from locals who had been angered by an episode of mistreatment and kidnapping at the hands of other recent white visitors. Kotzebue remained only a day before resuming his larger mission of finding a northern route from the Pacific to the Atlantic. Between them, however, Lisianskii and Kotzebue, though less important in this respect than James Cook and some others, clearly made worthwhile contributions to early Western knowledge of Easter Island, its people, geography, and natural resources.

Koztebue himself made several other important contributions in the southern seas, mostly during 1815–1818 as captain of the *Riurik* charged with finding the elusive Northeast Passage. His discoveries here include — in the Tuamotus: the Romanzov Islands (now the King George Islands) and the Kruzenshtern Islands (now the Tikehau Atoll); and the Riurik Islands (or Riurik's Chain, now Arutua).[42] He surveyed Tahiti and described the Coral Islands in greater detail than anyone hitherto. The published accounts of his travels also include much of ethnographic interest. Indeed, Kotzebue's expedition — which benefited greatly from the participation of Ludovik Khoris[43] (1795–1828; a German-Russian artist), Adelbert von Chamisso (1781–1838; a French-German botanist and poet), Morten Worm-skiöld (1783–1845; a Danish naturalist), and Johann Friedrich Eschscholtz (1793–1831; an Estonian-born German naturalist and physician) — carried out some of the first such work in the Wotje, Maloelap, and Aur Atolls in the Marshall Islands, as well as making significant original contributions in botany, hydrography, and other fields. Further north, in the summer of 1816, Kotzebue also discovered Kotzebue Sound and Cape Kruzenshtern, both in Alaska. In the course of a later circumnavigation, aboard the sloop *Predpriiatie* in 1823–1826, he added further discoveries of small islands and atolls in the Tuamotu Archipelago and in Samoa (known in his time as the Navigator Islands).[44]

Another notable Russian discovery in the South Pacific is the Menshikov Atoll in the Marshall Islands, first observed in 1828 by L. A. Gagemeister during the course of a two-year circumnavigation aboard the *Krotkii*. The same year, F. P. Lütke (a.k.a. Litke) discovered the Senyavin Islands[45] — one of many proud achievements during a highly productive four-year sailing (1826–1829), much of which focused on the Marshalls and the Carolines.

Nikolai Nikolaevich Miklukho-Maklai: Russian Explorer of Papua New Guinea

One of Russia's greatest explorers, and almost certainly its single most eccentric, was born Nikolai Nikolaevich Miklukho, into the noble Miklukho family, on 17 July 1846, not far from Novgorod. He is also known by the family names *Miklukho-Maklai* (variously spelled in English), and in the West often just as *Maclay* (an Anglicization of the last part of his name). Though he traveled widely in Indonesia, the South Pacific, and Australasia, he is best remembered in connection with Papua New Guinea. Miklukho-Maklai was the first white man to study the island in any detail; in fact he lived there, almost Robinson Crusoe–style, on-and-off over several years beginning in 1871. In many respects, he is the odd-man-out among Russian explorers, most of whom — after the great age of the *promysh-lennik*— relied heavily on official support and funding, worked closely with geographical institutions at home, and were closely connected, both officially and in their hearts, to the incremental expansion or consolidation of Russian boundaries and influence. Miklukho-Maklai, by contrast, received little funding from any official Russian sources (at least until late in life), took a dim view of Russian (or any Western) imperialism, operated almost entirely on his own, and in some respects seems not even to have been particularly fond of his home country. He is, nonetheless, a genuine Russian national treasure.

The name *Miklukho* is of Zaporozhe Cossack origin; *Maklai* is almost certainly the Scottish *Maclay*. Although sometimes traced to a putative Scot among the explorer's maternal ancestry, the name was likely pure whim. The future explorer was the only member of his family to use it — adopting it at the start of his career and henceforth wearing it as a badge of pride that marked him out from his family and native country. Throughout his life, Miklukho-Maklai always seemed most at home in foreign places and among foreign peoples, and he was given to rather idealized views about the corrupting influences of Russian (and all Western) society and the purity and moral superiority of "unspoiled" native peoples, especially the Papuans with whom he spent many years.

Miklukho's father died young in 1857, pushing the family into slow financial decline. He had been an engineer, and this was the career toward which the son was first and long urged by his mother. Under circumstances that remain obscure, Miklukho — who had never in any case been inclined to follow his family's wishes — was early derailed when after only two months of study he was expelled from St. Petersburg University and officially barred from ever again entering *any* Russian university. Apparently he had participated in student unrest. This seems odd: Miklukho had little sympathy for the radical political winds blowing about the capital at the time. It is possible he deliberately sabotaged himself so as to break decisively with all that he hated about Russian society, its accomplishments, and vanities. With his bridges burned, he was free to leave the country. Though he returned often (but for limited times only), the die was cast. Never again would he live permanently in Russia. He was, however, fated to die there.

Miklukho-Maklai began his post-expulsion life in Germany. During 1865–1866 he studied in several universities before gravitating to Jena. Here he began to find his calling. He studied zoology with Ernst Haeckel, the famous Darwinist and pioneer of the science of ecology. Under Carl Gegenbauer he learned anatomy. And in the winter of 1866–1867 he undertook his first expedition, traveling with Haeckel and the cell biologist Hermann Fol (1845–1892) west across France, Spain, Portugal, the Madeiras, and the Canaries, and then to Morocco. Mainly he divided his attention between sponges and fish, combining anatomical studies with observations on environment and distribution. His first published scientific papers on these subjects quickly followed.

Anxious to continue traveling and studying, Miklukho-Maklai now encountered a problem that would plague him his whole life — lack of money. For the time being, he found what he needed in his mother. Over the following years he would write to her frequently — mixing pleas for support with affectionate pronouncements and lofty statements about the scientific importance and urgency of his work. Over time, also, he would make repeated, vague promises on behalf of some future day when the family (usually meaning Miklukho-Maklai, his mother, and his beloved sister, Olga[46]) might settle down on a Russian estate — or perhaps in some Italian villa. Later letters suggested that perhaps they might all retire together one day in the tropics. It is hard to know whether these were fantasies seriously entertained or just so much filial manipulation. For a while his mother duly sent what was asked, but over time her patience grew thin. Early in the explorer's career the maternal source of funds slowed then stopped. Though the two never entirely broke off contact, they became increasingly distant.

While still in his mother's good graces, and at her expense, Miklukho-Maklai made several trips during 1868–1869, most notably to Sicily, Egypt, and Syria. He spent time at the Red Sea frantically studying sponges and other marine life, convinced that the imminent opening of the Suez Canal would sweep this ecosystem away forever. (In fact it had only a limited effect.) Collecting destinations almost as enthusiastically as he acquired specimens, Miklukho-Maklai made a series of stops on the way to and from the Red Sea, including Alexandria, Cairo, Jeddah, Massawa, Beirut, Smyrna, and Istanbul. Back in Russia he began the spring of 1869 studying fish anatomy in the Crimea and at the Don and Volga rivers. Then he headed to Moscow to present at the Second Congress of Nature Enthusiasts (*S"ezd estestvoispitatelei*), and to St. Petersburg where he spent September working in the Zoological Museum of the Russian Academy of Sciences and also presented to the Russian Geographical Society on his Red Sea studies.

By fall 1869, Miklukho-Maklai had begun planning a much more ambitious and lengthy expedition focusing broadly on the western Pacific — from the equator north to the Bering Straits. His program of intended study was nearly universal: marine and land zoology, botany, meteorology, ethnology, anthropology, and so on. He imagined, more realistically, that the enterprise might need seven or eight years. No amount of filial persuasion or motherly love could possibly fund such a thing. He contacted the Russian Geographical Society. Drawing on his family's aristocratic connections, he also ingratiated himself as best he could with the Naval Ministry. Both proved sympathetic, but both also took much more interest in the northernmost parts of the proposed itinerary — specifically the Okhotsk region of Russia. Miklukho-Maklai's interests, in contrast, lay in the south (a fact he prudently kept to himself for the time being).

New Guinea in particular fascinated him. Alfred Russell Wallace had lately called the island "the greatest terra incognita that still remains for the naturalist to explore."[47] Only its coasts had been investigated, and even these minimally, patchily, and almost entirely from the sea. Its native Papuan peoples had been variously proposed by several "experts" as the original settlers of the whole Pacific and Southeast Asia; conversely, as recent invaders who had displaced the original people; and as still other things besides. The interior of the island, it was rumored, hosted completely unknown peoples and other natural wonders. Ernst Haeckel had been particularly optimistic, anticipating the discovery there, perhaps, of modern man's direct evolutionary ancestors and of evidence for the earlier existence of a lost or sunken continent, first proposed by the English zoologist-lawyer Philip Sclater (1829–1913) and known as Lemuria. Miklukho-Maklai was determined to replace these uncertainties with real knowledge.

By spring 1870 he had secured a modest subsidy from the Russian Geographical Society (primarily thanks to Petr Petrovich Semenov-Tian-Shanskii — the famous explorer and now a rising star in the Society's leadership; see chapter 6). He also had permission from the tsar himself to travel to New Guinea aboard the *Vitiaz*, a Russian corvette. His long-suffering mother provided additional money. Even so, his resources were still far short of his ambitions. But it was time to begin. Further funds could be found later.

April and May Miklukho spent journeying to several European capitals in search of scientific contacts and soliciting scientific questions (he received sufficient of the latter to fill a lifetime of research!). During summer and early fall he finalized travel arrangements. Finally, on 27 October 1870 the *Vitiaz* departed from Krondstadt. Miklukho-Maklai, packing about a hundred cases of supplies, sailed only as far as Copenhagen, however, before setting off on a tour of major northwestern European cities in search of further contacts, instruments, and advice. He rejoined the ship at Plymouth, England. The next several months were passed at sea on a route leading around West Africa, with stops at the Madeiras and the Cape Verde Islands, then across the Atlantic to Rio de Janeiro. From here ship's captain Nazimov steered south and then west through the Strait of Magellan. During a stop at Punta-Arenas, Miklukho-Maklai encountered the native Tehuelche who had so fascinated Darwin four decades earlier. The Russian thought them degraded and alcoholic, ruined by contact with civilization. He longed all the more for the imagined "uncorrupted" natives of New Guinea.

After stopping at Valparaiso, the *Vitiaz* headed west across the Pacific. Over the next weeks the ship made close passes or stops at several islands — Easter, Mangareva, Tahiti, and others. At each, Miklukho-Maklai found to his disappointment what seemed to him only the remnants of native civilizations ruined or struggling amid a growing European presence. Throughout the long voyage the explorer made various scientific observations and kept up his journals. For much of the time he also nursed a fever — something he would become expert at over the coming years.

Then, on September 12 the *Vitiaz*, having now nearly crossed the entire Pacific, arrived at Port Praslin, New Ireland. The local people, for the first time, were Papuan — closely related to those Miklukho-Maklai expected to encounter on New Guinea, now only a few hundred miles further west. The Papuans of New Ireland pierced their ears and noses with bone and wood; their teeth were black from betel; and their hair was dyed white or red. Although these people had obviously met Europeans before, Miklukho-Maklai imagined them more authentic and culturally intact than the other Pacific peoples he had met so far.

While crossing the Pacific, Miklukho-Maklai had picked up what he had been unable to procure in Europe or South America — two servants: a Swede named Olsen and a twelve-year-old Polynesian boy named Boy. Unfortunately, both would turn out to be more a hindrance than a help. They, in turn, would have their own reasons for regretting having ever met the Russian.

Finally, on 8 September 1871[48], the northeastern coast of New Guinea came into sight. Passing this way back in 1827 the French explorer Jules Dumont d'Urville (1790–1842) had spotted a broad, deep inlet stretching south of modern-day Madang. He had named it Astrolabe Bay. Although he had mapped the bay's northern and southern ends, he had refrained from sailing far enough into it to form a proper impression of the land it washed or to discover what kind of harbor it might offer. Scanning the approaching shore Miklukho-Maklai noticed a spit of low-lying land near the middle of the bay. Here and there native people could be seen — running, hiding, reappearing — obviously alarmed by what the sea was bringing in. They gestured in ways that no one on board could interpret for sure as either friendly or hostile. While still a good distance out, the crew watched a lone Papuan — his associates now obscured in the jungle immediately behind — lay a coconut on the beach. What did this mean? Miklukho-Maklai was as puzzled as anyone. He was determined to land. As the *Vitiaz* maneuvered along the coast, more Papuans, and then several villages, were seen. Taking a small crew in a landing boat, the Russian struggled against the surf, only to find himself at first repulsed. But then, late in the day he made a final, successful effort, attaining the shallows at a point subsequently to be called Cape Konstantin, after the current Russian admiral of the fleet. Approaching the shore Miklukho-Maklai noticed a jungle track. Leaving his companions to beach and tie the boat, he jumped into the water, waded ashore, and started down the path.

Then, all of a sudden he was on New Guinea—and completely alone. If the possible dangers of the situation occurred to him, he seems to have paid them no mind. He came quickly to a clearing. Before him stood a small, neat village: "a dozen huts around a small 'square' of beaten earth. Dark jungle and groves of fruit trees set off palm-leaf thatch silvered by time and sunlight, crimson hibiscus flowers and the leaves of multicolored shrubs."[49] The place was deserted. Yet all around lay signs that it had become so only moments before: a still-burning cooking-fire, hut doors flung open, freshly split coconuts.

His circumstances were in many respects eerily similar to those in which Georg Steller had found himself thirteen decades earlier (see chapter 4). Back then, the young German had stood similarly alone in an equally strange new world, had followed a comparable trail, and had also come upon a hastily abandoned camp. Both men, too, had been tracked at a distance by uncomprehending eyes.

Fascinated, Miklukho-Maklai came to the doorway of one of the huts. Inside he noticed beds made of bamboo, assortments of shells and feathers, a human skull. Then a sound broke his reverie. He wheeled round to behold a man—a Papuan. He had appeared, seemingly, from nowhere. The Papuan stood for a moment, half-frozen in fear or wonder; then he turned and ran into the bushes. The Russian gave chase. After a short while the Papuan, who had almost certainly never before seen a white man, slowed and looked back at his pursuer. Seeing the latter was unarmed he lost some of his fear and stopped.

"I slowly approached the savage," Miklukho-Maklai later wrote, "and, making no sound, gave him a piece of red cloth, which he accepted with visible satisfaction and tied about his head." Of "average build and a dark chocolate color" with "short, tightly-curled matt-black hair" the man had, he fancied, "a rather pleasant ... face."[50] And then the European touched the Papuan's arm.

Moments later, combining gestures, incomprehensible words, and some physical pressure, Miklukho-Maklai persuaded the reluctant man—his name would turn out to be Tui—to walk with him back to the village. It was deserted no more. Boy and Olsen had arrived. And around the periphery of the main square "seven or eight" more Papuans could now be seen. At first unwilling to come out of the jungle, they slowly yielded to the white man's entreaties and gifts—more pieces of red cloth, nails, and fish hooks. Presently the Papuans reciprocated with "coconuts, bananas, and two squealing piglets."[51]

After a while, Miklukho-Maklai, Olsen, and Boy managed to persuade the Papuans to come and visit the *Vitiaz*. As they rowed out, some of the Papuans suddenly took fright and jumped from one of the landing boats. The rest were brought successfully on board where they were amazed at many things, but above all mirrors. After a short time they were allowed to return to their village. Miklukho-Maklai remained on the ship, exhausted and exhilarated. By any standards it had been a remarkable encounter for all involved.

Over the next several days, more than a hundred men from the *Vitiaz* worked to clear a patch of land not far from the same Papuan village to construct a home for the three men—Miklukho-Maklai and his two servants—who would be staying. The end product included a two-room cabin set on stilts and a small storeroom-cum-kitchen. The Russian's minimal furniture and more generous baggage and food-supplies nearly filled them completely. The whole was shaded by several enormous trees. For his protection, the approach to Miklukho-Maklai's compound was ringed with land mines (not the sort that explode when stood upon, but which he might detonate from within his hut if he so desired). He also stocked himself amply with guns and ammunition. These devices were, he claims, partly forced upon him by his concerned compatriots. Miklukho-Maklai was determined not to use any of them against his new neighbors. Instead he resolved either to win their trust or at least to subdue them with the authority and fear he felt he, as a European, might expect to command from "savages"—even if of the "noble" sort. On September 15 the *Vitiaz* and its crew departed. Miklukho-Maklai intended to spend at least a year on New Guinea. Hardly anyone expected him or his servants to survive even half that long.

And so began a remarkable and pioneering effort in modern anthropological research. For the first few days, Miklukho-Maklai settled in as best he could. For a while his health was good, but then fever returned. It would plague him on and off thereafter. Early experiences with the Papuans were both exciting and frustrating. Although they visited and shared gifts, in general Miklukho-Maklai's new neighbors avoided close contact and appeared unhappy with their visitor, refusing to look him in the eye or stay in his presence for long. Even Tui seemed uncomfortable. Several times he made gestures and pointed to the distance, seemingly—the explorer fancied—to warn of impending dangers or a possible attack. Miklukho-Maklai resolved to stay and face whatever came. For several days he stayed around his camp with Olsen and Boy. They, for their part, quickly found their new life uncongenial and unhealthy. They wished to leave, but could not. Miklukho-Maklai soon began to regret having brought them.

After four days, the Russian set out—alone, unarmed, and before dawn—for Tui's village. "I really want to get better acquainted with the locals," he wrote of this decision in his journal.[52] On the way he lost the path, but found another. This led to a slightly more distant village with which he had so far had no contact whatsoever. Nonetheless, armed only with his notebook and pencil, he resolved to try his luck. He was met by two flying arrows that narrowly missed him, and then by armed and clearly unamused warriors. These spoke sternly and, in one case, waved a spear so close to his face that it nearly took out an eye. The women and children, Miklukho-Maklai noticed, were all gone. But the warriors remained, calmly implacable. If the situation seems surreal, the Russian's next action was even odder. With the half-standoff dragging on, and neither side seeming to know what to do, Miklukho-Maklai appropriated a nearby woven mat and, under constant gaze, positioned it under a tree. Then he took off his shoes, lay down, closed his eyes and tried to sleep! One can only guess what the Papuans must have thought. But the tactic had an effect. Soon Miklukho-Maklai was alone again.

The Russian stayed fifteen months in his new island home. He would try many times again to visit nearby settlements. He also became something of a tourist attraction in his own right, a must-see for curious Papuans from along what came to be known until the 1930s as the Maclay Coast, and then from nearby islands as well. Over time, his hosts came to regard Miklukho-Maklai as something supernatural, a magician, a "moon-man"—even, perhaps, a god.[53] Not just the visitor's utter foreignness convinced them of this, but also his ability to treat and heal sores and some minor illnesses. Success in treating a head wound sustained by his first Papuan contact, Tui, won him considerable respect. Even more spectacularly, the white visitor could burn "water" (actually alcohol), banish night (a flare), and so on.

And yet he was also a curiously powerless and disappointing god—unable or unwilling to lead the locals into war with their neighbors or protect them from invasion by others. Nor could he cure more serious illnesses, bring rain, or do other things he was sometimes asked. And he himself seemed nearly constantly to be unwell, alternating between nursing a manageable fever or leg sores and more prolonged bouts of real debilitation.

Though he made progress, even after more than a year Miklukho-Maklai still found the islanders uneasy in his presence. Despite endless efforts, his understanding of the local language remained rudimentary—limited mainly to nouns and adjectives. And in some anthropological version of the Heisenberg uncertainty principle, his subjects never acted normally in his presence, making it impossible for him to gain real insight into their cultural ways. The rituals surrounding such basics as birth, marriage, and death remained largely hidden from him. At home and in the field he also struggled against the island itself—ants, wasps, mosquitoes, rains, winds, funguses all conspired to eat away at his resolve, his health, his collections and notes, his cabin, the expedition itself. When his food supplies ran out after about five months he was still unable to feed himself either from his garden of imported seeds (which mostly failed to grow) or by hunting (there being very few large animals). He got by on a haphazard combination of involuntary fasting, irregular Papuan hospitality, and whatever he could catch or forage. Over time he grew thin and malnourished.

The servants, Boy and Olsen, turned out to be as little suited to the castaway life as their master was fascinated with it. They shared neither his interests in science nor his natural inclination toward solitude. They became depressed. They complained. Miklukho-Maklai soon came to regard them as a curse and regretted having taken them on. They ate up food, time, precious quinine, and contributed nothing. Tending to them tied him to his camp, when he would have preferred to explore further afield.

But if truth be told, the Russian was merely inconvenienced by these circumstances. The real victims were the hapless Swede and—especially—Boy, neither of whom was at liberty to pursue his own best interests; both of whom became much more ill than their master. Miklukho-Maklai's contempt for them grew daily. Even the Papuans relegated them to inferior status—they were servants of no consequence, not other demigods. Nearly from the time of his arrival Boy had lingered at death's door inside the little cabin. But even after several months, release had not come. Eventually, Miklukho-Maklai, with help from Olsen, put the child out of his misery with a hefty dose of chloroform. Then he cut up the body and removed some organs—ostensibly for science—before weighting the corpse with stones and dropping it into the sea. Olsen fared better, surviving long enough to leave forever on a passing boat.

Seemingly untroubled by Boy's miserable fate, or about his own part in shaping it, Miklukho-Maklai returned to his anthropology. He visited villages, watched what he could of local life, interacted to the extent possible with his often-gracious—but always artificially formal—hosts, reveled in the beauty of his environment, enjoyed his own company, and tended to his scientific collections. Mostly, he viewed the Papuans favorably, seeing in them, perhaps, his own image of that European figment, the "noble savage." Compared to Europeans he found them free, kind, unconflicted, and functional. Though they discussed and practiced sexuality in ways that might have scandalized polite society in St. Petersburg, he thought them, especially their women, morally superior to Europeans. He noted, but completely accepted, a clear division of status along gender lines: "While the men ate the best food, seated on their platforms, the women sat on the ground among dogs and pigs, consuming what their husbands discarded." The men were despots, but benevolent ones. Women were "seldom beaten or required to work beyond their strength." Invalided wives were generally kept and cared for rather than discarded.[54] The children seemed well loved and contented.

In early December 1872 Miklukho-Maklai was rescued from a probable early, slow death by the arrival of a Russian steam clipper, the *Izumrud*, sent from Vladivostok by order of Grand Duke Konstantin specifically to find the by-now increasingly famous explorer — or failing that, his traces. After fifteen months without contact or any news, there was considerable surprise among the crew and command to find their compatriot in reasonable shape. The Papuans, however, were reluctant to lose their protecting spirit. Miklukho-Maklai, sensing that he had only scratched the surface when it came to understanding his hosts' culture, felt similarly.

LATER CAREER

Miklukho-Maklai subsequently returned several more times to New Guinea — twice for extended periods. From December 1873 to July 1874 he lived on the other side of the island, based at Cape Aiva in a region known as Papua-Koviai. The area was more ethnically mixed than the Maclay coast: Malays, Arabs, and a now defunct Dutch fort had all left their marks. Gin was in demand. And from his first day Miklukho-Maklai found the area plagued with violence and strife (for which he especially blamed Malays). Examples included a local ruler who had recently been dispossessed of his island, and his people scattered, by mercenaries; tribal wars between coastal and inland groups; piracy, raids, and murders. More than once, these things touched Miklukho-Maklai himself. His cabin was raided, his property stolen, and Papuan acquaintances murdered. He managed to capture one of the presumed culprits — later turning him over to the Dutch authorities. More happily, from his base on Cape Aiva, this time he succeeded in penetrating a little further into the interior — though not nearly to the center. The discovery of Lake Kamaka-Vallar offered some compensation and stands as perhaps his main geographical contribution.

He finally returned to his beloved Maclay coast, and to the

Photograph of Nikolai Nikolaevich Miklukho Maklai, c. 1880. Photographer Unknown (John Oxley Library, the State Library of Queensland, Australia).

villagers he had earlier known, in June 1876, remaining this time for more than sixteen months, and establishing himself a short distance from his previous residence. Earthquakes had altered parts of the landscape and killed or displaced villagers. Many of his old acquaintances were gone. Though he explored widely along his namesake coast, he was again unsuccessful in penetrating either the island's interior or the profound linguistic and cultural barriers forever separating him from his hosts.

Although best known for his stays on New Guinea, from the time of his first visit, Miklukho-Maklai had repeatedly indulged his inner peripatetic, traveling to an astonishing array of tropical destinations throughout Indonesia, Malaysia, the Philippines, western Micronesia, northern Melanesia, and Australia. Especially on the smaller islands, he hoped and searched time and again for "pure" and uncontacted peoples, especially Papuan. Mostly, however, he instead found himself lamenting corruption and decline in the face of growing European encroachment and rapine. He was scarcely less critical of Malaysian migrations and influence.

There were, as well, relatively sedentary periods. During protracted stays in Java, Singapore, and elsewhere he worked on his collections, prepared travel notes for publication, and wrote popular and scientific articles. He struggled with recurring health problems, sometimes spending weeks and even months in hospital or convalescing. And he remained desperately short of funds. With nothing forthcoming from his mother, and his expenses in any case far too much for her to properly defray even had she wished, he survived into the early 1880s on the only currencies he possessed — personal celebrity, powerful connections, noble background, and appeals to the interests of science. These he converted repeatedly into loans from various creditors or into free accommodation with persons such as the governor-general of the Dutch East Indies. For the most part he was in no position to repay with anything but gratitude or reflected glory. A rare subsidy from the Russian Geographical Society, paid out in early 1878, canceled some of his older debts, but he immediately incurred more and larger ones on new travel plans.

In June 1878, Miklukho-Maklai arrived for the first time in Australia. He had set out partly on the advice of doctors in Singapore. His health, they had argued, was by now so fragile — fevers, sores, chronic fatigue, and who knew what else? — that only the southern continent's more congenial climate and better medical facilities could stave off an early death. Preferring other justifications for travel, Miklukho-Maklai noted that he had in any case always been interested in studying this vast continent and its aboriginal peoples.

His arrival down under, though it did not end his illnesses, marked the beginning of a new phase of his life — the closest he ever came, in fact, to settling down. Though many further travels lay ahead (including a nine-month odyssey around Melanesia during March 1879–January 1880), Australia, and especially Sydney, was henceforth to become his new home and primary base of operations. He worked here almost without cease, forging a close relationship with the Linnean Society in Sydney, among other connections. It was in Sydney, too, in 1882, that Miklukho-Maklai met Margaret Clark (née Robertson). Widowed, attractive, educated, and fascinated with stories of travel, she quickly fell for the Russian, and he for her. Her family, though of modest background, was politically important. Her father, Sir John Robertson, was a fixture in New South Wales politics.

Though love was blooming, Miklukho-Maklai was committed, for professional reasons, also to making a trip back to Russia. He departed, alone, in February 1882, traveling on a series of Russian warships to Kronstadt via Adelaide, Singapore, Alexandria, and numerous European ports. At one of these ports, during the long six-month sail, he mailed a proposal of marriage to Margaret — "Rita" as he affectionately called her. She accepted. Other letters mailed from other ports brought him closer at last to another goal — significant financial support from the Russian government or the Russian Geographical Society.

Upon arrival in Russia, Miklukho-Maklai was given a hero's reception. During September and October he gave numerous interviews, exhibited some of his collections, and gave lectures at the Geographical Society in St. Petersburg and at the Society of Natural History Enthusiasts (*Obshchestvo liubetelei estestvoznanie*) in Moscow. He was granted an audience with Tsar Alexander III. One might wonder if he should not have paid the visit years earlier. Along with the recognition, he finally received state funds: 20,000 rubles to settle all his debts and 6,000 more — personally from the tsar — to fund publication of his journals; and further support for two years in Australia, to be spent preparing the manuscripts. (In fact, although Miklukho-Maklai was to live another six years, the manuscripts were never finished.) A full-blown celebrity, he headed on November 28 for Western Europe with stops at Berlin, Antwerp, Leiden, Paris (where he met the novelist Turgenev), London, Greenock (Scotland), Genoa, and Naples.

The following January (1883) he departed from Australia, arriving in June. Following a brief return visit to the Maclay coast, there then followed the closest thing Miklukho-Maklai was ever to know, since childhood, to a settled existence. From June 1883 to February 1886 he remained in Australia. On 27 February 1884 he and Margaret were married. Two sons were born soon after: Alexander Niels on 18 November 1884 and Vladimir-Alan on 29 December 1885.

This was to be no retirement, however. Aside from the never-to-be-completed manuscript and other scientific work, Miklukho-Maklai devoted more and more time to a project he had become interested in years earlier and for which he would ultimately be best and most fondly remembered: a campaign for native peoples' rights — particularly those of his beloved Papuans. Like his contemporary, the Russian explorer of Central Asia, Nikolai Przheval'skii (see chapter 6), Miklukho-Maklai operated during the "high tide" of European Imperialism. Unlike Przheval'skii, who was an uncomplicated Great Russian chauvinist and imperialist (sometimes scathingly critical of the non–Russians he encountered) Miklukho-Maklai reacted viscerally against the steady and corrupting march of European power into his idealized tropical Edens, New Guinea especially. Already by the 1870s this large island — with its possibilities for trade, settlement, naval bases, extractive industries, and the rest — had attracted interest from Dutch, French, German, Italian, and British sources. By the early 1880s annexation appeared possible at short notice from almost any of these. Appalled at such prospects, but aware of the march of history and of the vulnerability of native peoples in an industrial-imperial age, Miklukho-Maklai pondered the options.

His preferences were for programs that would allow Papuans to retain much of their lifestyle and all of their dignity and independence while introducing them slowly to selective Westernization. He sought to protect Papuans from the worst the West had to offer — alcohol, individualism and personal greed, forced conversion, relocation, confinement, and extermination — while exposing them incrementally to its best: trade, education, "civilization," and the rest. He toyed from the late 1870s on with a variety of schemes: a Papuan Union under Russian or British protection; a Russian settlement program that would bring to New Guinea Russian homesteaders and farmers — persons of some wealth and education committed to developing the region's agriculture in ways that respected native traditions. (He eventually received some 2,000 statements of interest from prospective colonists.) During his Australian years in particular, Miklukho-Maklai devoted more and more time to these projects, to the partial detriment of his scientific work and efforts to organize and publish his travel accounts. He raised awareness of the problems of slavery and human trafficking in the Pacific, published open letters in the Russian and international press, and contacted numerous major Western statesmen.

Miklukho-Maklai's most audacious plan was his "Maclay Coast Scheme." It involved a trading company, tropical agricultural plantations, extraction of guano and other minerals, with the profits to be distributed fairly among Western shareholders and the Papuans. His ideas were not always realistic. He envisioned uniting the various Papuan tribes and villages, even though their history thus far had been marked only by mutual isolation, mistrust, or war. He imagined a hierarchical and expanding web of political and economic cooperation, even though the pivotal concepts of political authority and private property were alien to the Papuans. Financial support, he hoped, would be supplied by international philanthropy, while overall political authority — and vital military protection — might come from the Russian Empire, but without annexation or undue interference. When the tsar categorically refused any official Russian involvement at all, Miklukho-Maklai quickly refocused his hopes on the British as the best substitute (earning in the process some short-lived cries of treachery from Russian patriots). Above all, he feared German annexation or unregulated settlement and encroachment from Australia.

Another common element to these various visions of New Guinea's future was Miklukho-Maklai's own position in it — invariably that of benevolent despot. He considered himself at once his people's brother — a "white Papuan" and their natural representative — but also their superior and autocrat. Though many of his plans were carefully considered — and enjoyed support from such luminaries as the celebrated Russian novelist Leo Tolstoy — they were all unrealistic, relying on highly unlikely forms of European-Papuan cooperation, unworkable reinventions of Papuan culture and tradition, and an almost oxymoronic formula of major-power involvement and noninvolvement. Unsurprisingly, little came of them. Instead, at the end of 1884, one of Miklukho-Maklai's two worst-case scenarios began to unfold as Imperial Germany took its opportunity and annexed the northeastern part of New Guinea. In desperation the white Papuan cabled Bismarck himself, urging the Iron Chancellor to reject or abnegate all German claims. Around the same time, the British halfheartedly claimed parts of the south. In fact, neither the German government nor the British was very serious about settling or exploiting New Guinea. The island remained divided, under loose German and British administration until the First World War, after which time it came increasingly under Australian control, Maklai's other great fear. (The island is now divided between Indonesia in the east and independent Papua New Guinea in the west.) One can only guess to what degree Miklukho-Maklai, were he still around, would assess the results of these events.

Death

In February 1886 Miklukho-Maklai sailed again for Russia, hoping to promote interest in his latest Russian settlement and protection plans. By now he was broke once again. Unable to pay for four tickets, he left his family behind. In Russia he was again well received, gave lectures, and staged an exhibition of Papuan artifacts and culture. It was on this visit that the tsar finally ruled out any hope for a Russian protectorate over the island. At the same time, Miklukho-Maklai's health was deteriorating dramatically. He was plagued with rheumatism, toothaches, and headaches. His face swelled. In this condition he dragged himself onto a boat back to Australia. To pay his way he resorted again to borrowing. He also signed on as reporter for a lowbrow Russian newspaper, though he was too ill to write much.

Once in Russia he collected his family and, despite his health and woeful finances, quickly set out yet again for his homeland. His primary intention this time was to deposit materials from his rich collections of natural history specimens and Papuan artifacts. En route he and Margaret were married again, this time according to the rite of the Orthodox Church at Vienna. He made it to St. Petersburg in extremely poor condition, requiring hospitalization. On April 2, his wife's arms about him, he died. A large tumor was later found in his brain.

Miklukho-Maklai's last wish was that his wife should burn all of his papers. For what purpose is not entirely clear. Was it a vain attempt to somehow preserve his beloved Papuans' independence, by returning them to the obscurity from which he perhaps felt he had raised them? Perhaps the tumor had clouded his judgment? One can only guess. In any case, after burning some items, Margaret changed her mind and kept the rest. Nonetheless, the partial destruction, combined with her husband's lifelong inattention to proper organization left a great deal of difficult work for future scholars and editors. Margaret and her children returned to Australia. Miklukho-Maklai was buried in St. Petersburg.

LEGACY

Miklukho-Maklai's place in history is hard to sum up simply. In the Anglo-American world he is not especially well known outside of academic circles. This has been the fate of many Russian explorers, of course. He is better known in the areas where he lived and worked. Undercurrents of criticism among Australians — based on the Russian's opposition to Australian settlement of New Guinea — have long since given way to a greater appreciation of this remarkable man who in many ways stands also at the forefront of the southern continent's journey toward Aboriginal rights and compensation. In recent decades, consequently, there have been several efforts to raise his profile there. In New Guinea, in the years after 1888, his legend grew into a minor religion for a short time. Nowadays, reduced to human scale, he is the historical pivot point about which swings New Guinea's journey from tradition and isolation into the modern world. Among Russians Miklukho-Maklai has never become obscure. A small current of opinion — focusing either on his willingness to hand New Guinea over to British protection or on his reluctance to champion unlimited Russian annexation — has questioned his patriotism. But for the most part he has been a source of great pride and is warmly regarded.

Miklukho-Maklai's legacy can be considered in at least three categories: scientific research, geographical exploration, and political activism and humanitarianism. He rates lowest in the first regard. Whether studying human or nonhuman subjects he is now judged a dilettante, a man who ranged widely across many subjects — from marine anatomy to Papuan anthropology — but whose work, though far from useless, failed to make a real or lasting imprint. He did not, his critics say, ever develop a clear theoretical framework or apply a consistent methodology. His scientific papers, though numerous, are of limited value, scattered, and occasionally error-prone. Though he recorded much, he was not a meticulous record-keeper. And there were important gaps in his interests — especially geology and botany — that limited the use others could make of his work. On the other hand, his more-or-less complete immersion in Papuan life clearly did break new ground, establishing a model for anthropological study that, directly or indirectly, has inspired countless others to approach their human subjects in a similar manner — by throwing off at least some aspects of one's own culture and assimilating into the one under study.[55] This is no small achievement or contribution.

Although he failed to reach far into the interior of New Guinea, Miklukho-Maklai nonetheless added greatly to knowledge of his namesake coast and some other parts of the island, as well as surrounding islands. As noted, he is the discoverer of Kamaka-Walla lake. He also was first to chart parts of the interior of Johor on the Malay Peninsula.

Miklukho-Maklai's greatest achievement, however, was raising awareness of the plight of native peoples during the most frenzied years of the Age of Imperialism. At a time when Western governments and populations often acted as if the entire world belonged by right to them, Miklukho-Maklai was in the vanguard of contrary opinion and effort. In many respects he can be placed legitimately in the line of nineteenth-century campaigners for human dignity and freedom — including abolitionists, feminists, and the various champions of the working class. It is somewhat in this tradition, incidentally, that Soviet-era historiography placed him, downplaying his noble background and emphasizing instead his solidarity with the common man, his anti-imperialism, and so forth.

It is worth noting, of course, that despite his rages and writings against the depredations of the White Man, Miklukho-Maklai himself was not immune from imperialist sentiment or action. He clearly enjoyed his elevated status among people he considered "savages." Nor did he refrain from construing and volunteering himself as their natural leader. He introduced them to Western goods and trade trinkets — mirrors, cloth, fishhooks, bottles, knives, and the like. More than any other single person he brought his Papuans to the world's attention, raising the possibility of further, quicker contact. On maps he marked the island's natural features with Russian, not Papuan names: Port Konstantin, Izumrud Strait, Vitiaz Strait, and so on. He was an "ecological imperialist" as well, introducing a variety of foreign plant seeds, and (on his later trips) new animals, such as goats and cows. And, of course, he promoted Russian settlement and called for Russian or British protection. These are perhaps anachronistic criticisms, however. With or without Miklukho-Maklai, Europe would soon enough have collided with New Guinea. With him, the impact was perhaps softened ever so slightly.

* * *

The travels related in this chapter mark a high point in Russian explorations far beyond traditional Russian boundaries and across vast oceans. Even as Miklukho-Maklai journeyed frenetically in the western Pacific, however, other Russians were reexamining the possibilities of contiguous exploration and expansion, of once again pressing outward on existing land-based Russian boundaries. This time, they would look not east, but south, into the great spaces of Central Asia.

Suggested Further Readings in Russian and English

Alakseev, A. I. *Osvoenie russkimi liudmi dal'nego vostoka i russkoi ameriki, do kontsa XIX veka*. Moscow: Izdatel'stvo "Nauka," 1982.

Aleksandrova, K. V., et al. *Akademik G. I. Langsdorf i russkaia ekspeditsiia v Braziliiu v 1821–1836*. Bibliograficheskii ukazatel'. Leningrad: Akademiia nauk, SSSR, 1979.

Barman, Roderick J. "The Forgotten Journey: Georg Heinrich Langsdorff and the Russian Imperial Scientific Expedition to Brazil, 1821–1829." *Terrae Incognitae* 3 (1971): 67–96.

Barratt, Glynn. *Russia and the South Pacific, 1696–1840*. Vol. 1, *The Russians and Australia*. Vancouver: University of British Columbia Press, 1988.

_____. *Russia and the South Pacific, 1696–1840.* Vol. 2, *Southern and Eastern Polynesia.* Vancouver: University of British Columbia Press, 1988.

_____. *Russia and the South Pacific, 1696–1840.* Vol. 3, *Melanesia and the Western Pacific Fringe.* Vancouver: University of British Columbia Press, 1990.

_____. *Russia and the South Pacific, 1696–1840.* Vol. 4, *The Tuamotu Islands and Tahiti.* Vancouver: University of British Columbia Press, 1992.

_____. *The Russian Discovery of Hawaii: The Ethnographic and Historical Record.* Honolulu: Editions, Ltd., 1987.

_____. *Russian Exploration in the Mariana Islands 1817–1828: Accounts by Otto von Kotzebue, Ludovik Choris, Adelbert von Chamisso, Fedor Lutke, V. M. Golovnin, Friedrich Heinrich von Kittlitz.* Saipan: Historic Preservation Office, Office of the High Commissioner, Trust Territory of the Pacific, 1984.

_____. "Russian Naval Visits of Tahiti and Mo'orea, 1823–1829: An Overview." *Journal de la Société des océanistes* 98 (1994).

Beidelman, Richard G. *California's Frontier Naturalists.* Los Angeles: University of California Press, 2006.

Bolkhovitinov, N. N. "Russkie na Gavaiakh (1804–1825)." In *Istoriia Russkoi Ameriki,* vol. 2. Edited by N. N. Bolkhovitinov. Moscow: Mezhdunarodnye otnosheniia, 1999, 275–302.

Brower, Daniel. "Imperial Russia and Its Orient: The Renown of Nikolai Przhevalsky." *The Russian Review* 53 (July 1994): 367–81.

Govor, E. V., and A. Ia. Massov, comp. *Rossiiskie moriaki i puteshestvenniki v Avstralii.* Moscow: Nauka, 1993.

Hussey, J. A., comp. *Notes Toward a Bibliography of Sources Relating to Fort Ross State Historic Park, California.* Sacramento: State of California, Resources Agency, Department of Parks and Recreation, 1979.

Istomin, A. A. "Osnovanie kreposti Ross v Kalifornii v 1812 g. i otnosheniia s Ispaniei." In *Istoriia Russkoi Ameriki,* vol. 2. Edited by N. N. Bolkhovitinov. Moscow: Mezhdunarodnye otnosheniia, 1999, 190–274.

Ivashintsov, N. A. *Russian Round-the-World Voyages, 1803–1849 with a Summary of Later Voyages to 1867.* Materials for the Study of Alaska History, no. 14. Kingston, ON: Limestone Press, 1980.

Kotsebu (Kotzebue), Otto von. *Puteshestvie v Iuzhnyi okean i v Beringov proliv dlia otyskaniia severovostochnogo morskogo prokhoda, predpriniatoe v 1815, 1816, 1817 i 1818 godakh na korable "Riurike,"* parts 1–3. St. Petersburg, 1821–23.

_____. *Puteshestvie vokrug sveta na voennom shliupe "Predpriatie" v 1823, 24, 25, i 26 godakh pod nachal'stvom flota kapitan-leitenanta Kotsebu.* St. Petersburg, 1828. 2nd ed., Moscow, 1948.

Komissarov, B. N., and C. G. Bozhkova. *Pervyi rossiiskii poslannik v Braziliiu, F. F. Borel'.* St. Petersburg: St. Petersburg University, 2000.

Langsdorff, Georg Heinrich von, *Remarks and Observations on a Voyage around the World from 1803 to 1807,* ed. Richard A. Pierce, trans. Victoria Joan Moessner. Kingston, ON, and Fairbanks, AK: Limestone Press, 1993.

Makarova, R. V. *Russians in the Pacific, 1743–1799.* Edited and translated by R. A. Pierce and A. S. Donnelly. Kingston, ON: Limestone Press, 1975.

Manizer, G. G. *Ekspeditsiia akademika G. I. Langsdorfa v Braziliiu, 1821–1828.* Edited by N. G. Shprintsin. Moscow: Geografgiz, 1948.

Miklouho-Maclay, N. N. *Travels to New Guinea: Diaries, Letters, Documents.* Edited by D. Tumarkin. Moscow: Progress Publishers, 1982.

Miklukho-Maklai, N. N. *Sobranie sochinenii v shesti tomakh.* Vol. 1: *Puteshestviia 1870–1874 gg. Dnevniki putevye zametki, otchety.* Moscow: Nauka, 1990.

Mills, Peter R. *Hawaii's Russian Adventure: A New Look at Old History.* Honolulu: University of Hawaii Press, 2004.

Ogloblin, A. K. "Commemorating N. N. Miklukho-Maklai (Recent Russian publications)." In *Perspectives on the Bird's Head of Irian Jaya, Indonesia: Proceedings of the Conference.* Edited by Jelle Miedema et al., Amsterdam: Rodopi, 1998, 487–502.

Pierce, Richard A., *Russia's Hawaiian Adventure, 1815–1817.* Berkeley: University of California Press, 1965.

Putilov, Boris Nikolaevich. *Nikolai Miklouho-Maclay: Traveller, Scientist and Humanist.* Moscow: Progress Publishers, 1982.

Shur, L. A., ed. *Materialy ekpeditsii akademika Grigoriia Ivanovicha Langsdorfa v Braziliiu v 1821–1929 gg. Nauchnoe opisanie.* Leningrad: Nauka, 1973.

Vinkovetsky, Ilya. "Circumnavigation, Empire, Modernity, Race: The Impact of Round-the-World Voyages on Russia's Imperial Consciousness." *Meeting of Frontiers/Vstrecha na granitsakh.* http://www.loc.gov/rr/european/mofc/vinkovetsky.html.

Chapter 6

Russian Journeys into Central Asia

Not all of Russia's expeditions during the eighteenth and nineteenth centuries led to Alaska or the various other maritime destinations central to the previous two chapters. Coeval with these navigations, Russians also pressed by land into and across the huge spaces of Central Asia and Mongolia. Well south of the Siberian forest-belt, these lands — variously flat and mountainous, fertile and arid — promised neither great fur wealth nor the promise of supply for Russian America or the Russian Far East. They attracted for different reasons. Perhaps most important was the absence of clear national boundaries. With the exception of the Chinese-Russian dividing line established in 1689 at Nerchinsk, Russia's southern borderlands — stretching from the Caspian Sea, through Central Asia, and on to Mongolia — remained relatively amorphous, both in a political and geographical sense. Consequently, if contiguous eastward (Siberian) expansion had by Bering's time been essentially completed, the same could not be said looking south. Here, instead, the imperial mind could freely imagine whole new vistas: a second stage of "manifest destiny," the further spread of Russian culture, and — ultimately — those elusive natural boundaries. Moreover, taking up this challenge was a matter of the traditional land-based and contiguous exploration and expansion the Russians had long practiced and which had already delivered the massive Siberian dividend. To these considerations may be added other lures: the promise of huge new stores of natural resources and the opportunity to further spread Russian culture, for example. In the middle and later nineteenth century in particular, Central Asia also attracted numerous expeditions focused on natural science — including questions of geography, zoology, botany, geology — and on ethnography and archeology (the regions along and beyond the southern borderlands having hosted some of history's great, especially nomadic, cultures). As with the Pacific, of course, the vast spaces of Central Asia captivated the imperial imaginations of other western powers, too. Consequently, Russian moves in the area were often conceived or shaped in competition (or limited by concerns of conflict) with these rivals — the British in particular.

Russian Explorations in Central Asia

Like the word *Siberia*— which depending on the time frame and context can refer to a single Mongol successor state, a much larger administrative unit in contemporary Russia, or the entirety of Russia east of the Urals — the term *Central Asia* also has multiple meanings. In post–Soviet studies it usually refers only to the five former Soviet republics of Kazakhstan, Kirghizstan, Tajikistan, Turkmenistan, and Uzbekistan. In other settings, including when used by nineteenth-century Russian explorers, it refers to a much larger territory, comprehending the area of the five states noted *plus* Mongolia (inner and outer), all of western China, Tibet, and the broad stretch of southern Russia bordering these regions. It is this larger unit — also known as Inner or Middle Asia — that is referred to throughout this chapter.

From ancient to early modern times, Central Asia was almost entirely unknown to Europeans, even Russians, except through occasional secondhand information. It was, nonetheless, a critically important region. Across its flat plains and through mountain passes ran the famous Silk Road — one of the world's great trade routes, for centuries bringing eastern luxuries and commodities to Russia, Europe, and elsewhere. Also from and across Central Asia came periodic waves of nomadic horse-riding invaders, culminating with the nearly invincible Mongol armies of the thirteenth and fourteenth centuries, whose effects on Russia have already been noted (chapter 1). Of the few Europeans who ventured into Central Asia before modern times the most famous is Marco Polo, who in the late 13th century traveled across the region as far as the ancient Mongol capital of Karakorum and on to Peking. Russia's most famous and well-traveled voyager of the early modern period, the merchant Afanasii Nikitin (d. 1472), largely skirted the region to the south, crossing the Caspian Sea before moving on to Persia and India.

Russian familiarity and interaction with Central Asia increased during the time of Ivan the Terrible and Ermak, whose actions (see chapter 2) increasingly brought the northern periphery of Central Asia, if not under Russian control, at least within sight. Contact with the Chinese, begun around the start of the seventeenth century, served as an important conduit for some of the first Russian forays into more eastern parts of Central Asia, particularly Mongolia. Ivan Petlin, Russia's first ambassador to China, visited Mongolia and China during 1618–1619, for example. Thereafter, a small but growing number of Russian ambassadors, missionaries, and others followed. Though most focused their sights and studies on the Chinese capital and Far East, their routes sometimes led through Mongolia, about which sporadic information began to accrue. Examples include N. G. Spafarii (Russian ambassador to Peking, 1675–1678) and A. Trushnikov, a noble from Tobol'sk who in 1713 traveled across Mongolia and western China — visiting Lake Koko Nor ("Blue Lake," now known as Qinghai Lake) and the headwaters of the Yellow River. Through the late eighteenth century, however, Russians were at best a fleeting and slight presence — and only in a few areas of Central Asia.

This began to change as the decline of Ottoman Turkey and Imperial China during the late-eighteenth and nineteenth centuries facilitated a major push south by the Russian Empire along a broad front stretching in the west from the Ural River and the Caspian Sea east to the Altai and western Dzungaria. In these changed circumstances, a small but growing number of Russian explorers pushed beyond even these spreading boundaries — deep into the heart of Middle Asia. In the Far East, still using China as a base and primary focus, a few pioneers crossed into Mongolia, studying its resources, peoples, and ways. N. Ia. Bichurin (1777–1853), a Russian monk and pioneering Sinologist sent in 1802 on a fourteen-year mission to China, was also perhaps the first Russian to publish in depth on Mongolian language and culture. Similarly, during 1820–1821 Egor Fedorovich Timkovskii (1790–1875), a longtime diplomat in the Russian Ministry of Foreign Affairs, also traveled through Mongolia to China, making and subsequently publishing careful observations of local culture, customs, and religion.[1] At the start of the following decade, Aleksandr Andreevich Bunge (1803–1890) brought the eyes and skill of the botanist and taxonomist to parts of Mongolia.

The Sinologist P. I. Kafarov used a protracted stay in China from 1840 to 1859 as a platform for studying Mongolian history and made the first translation into a Western language of the *Secret History of the Mongols*— that culture's earliest work of literature and a hugely important source.

Further west, during 1820–1821— the same years Timkovskii was in Mongolia and western China — Eduard Aleksandrovich Eversmann (1794–1860), a transplanted German, took part in the first official Russian expedition to Bukhara (in present-day Uzbekistan). During 1825–1826 he explored the Ustiurt plateau west of the Aral Sea. Eversmann collected and described a great number of bird, insect, and mammal specimens, including several new species.

By midcentury a growing number of Russian explorers were pushing their way around the uncharted vastnesses of Central Asia. Study of the Aral Sea and its tributary rivers, the Syr Dariia and Amu Dariia, was pioneered during 1848–1863 by I. A. Butakov (1816–1869; discoverer of Vozrozhdenie Island and other smaller Aral Sea islands), and subsequently by L. S. Berg (1876–1950).

Kazakhstan was placed on the map in large part through the pioneering efforts of Grigorii Silych (1801–1872), a naturalist and explorer who turned banishment to Orenburg (for criticizing the reactionary Russian statesman Count Arakcheev) into an opportunity for travel and study during 1827–1829. Silych went on during the 1830s also to place the northern, eastern, and southeastern Caspian shores on the map, and in 1840–1842, he and the cartographer-geographer I. P. Kirilov reconnoitered the Semirech'e region south of Lake Balkhash and the upper basin of the Irtysh River. Early Russian studies of the Altai region were carried out before midcentury by Petr Aleksandrovich Chikhachev (1808–1890), a geographer and geologist, and by Aleksandr Andreevich Bunge. The scale and remoteness of these vast areas ensured that these travels constituted only the most preliminary sketches, however, leaving room for a host of further investigations over the following decades.

Although especially well represented, Russians were not the only ones exploring Central Asia during the eighteenth and nineteenth centuries. The Hungarian scholar S. Kőrősi traveled through in the 1820s, subsequently publishing on Tibetan linguistics. Further south, and at a similar time, the study of Tibet was given another important fillip by the French missionaries E. Huk and J. Gabet. The great German naturalist-geographers Karl Ritter (1779–1859) and Alexander von Humboldt also passed through northern Central Asia, focusing their studies primarily on orography.

Petr Petrovich Semenov-Tian-Shanskii (1827–1914)

One of the early giants among Russian explorers of Central Asia is Petr Petrovich Semenov-Tian-Shanskii. He was born Petr Petrovich Semenov — the "Tian-Shanskii" sobriquet was conferred late in life by Tsar Nicholas II in honor of Semenov's having opened to science the great Tian Shan (also *Tien* Shan) Mountains dividing Semirech'e in the north from the Tarim Basin to the south. An active explorer for only a short portion of his long life, Semenov-Tian-Shanskii nonetheless continued to contribute hugely to the field through his dominating role in the pre–Revolutionary history of the Russian Imperial Geographic Society (founded 1845). From this institution he functioned well into the twentieth century as an unofficial "patriarch" of Russian exploration and natural science, sponsoring and mentoring many other Russian explorers, including N. M. Przheval'skii (see below) and N. N. Miklukho-Maklai (chapter 5).

Born into an established and prosperous noble family, Semenov started life swathed in prosperity and security at his parents' estate near Riazan. Like most of his peers, he seemed headed for a short military career followed by a long, comfortable, and respectable retirement. When he was just five, however, twin disasters struck. First, his father died suddenly. Then his mother fell into depression and a lifelong battle with serious mental illness. The family's financial fortunes declined accordingly. The youngest of three children, Semenov took refuge in his late father's library, immersing himself in Russian and European literature, poetry, philosophy, and science. By the time he was enrolled at age fourteen in military school in St. Petersburg he was already a promising, broadly trained intellectual. Less than four years later he graduated with high honors and a sterling reputation for scholarship — for which he was rewarded with a grant of noble status (at the ninth rank) and easy entrance in 1845 to St. Petersburg University. Here he focused on natural sciences. In 1849, a year after earning his degree, Semenov joined the fledgling Russian Imperial Geographical Society. It was the beginning of a lifelong association. Starting out as a secretary and librarian in the Physical Geography Section he served in a variety of posts, most importantly as vice president of the entire Society from 1872 until his death in 1914.

Semenov's career as an explorer began in Berlin where he studied geology and geography during 1853–1855 under the geographer-explorer Karl Ritter. Here also, he came into close contact with Alexander von Humboldt. Semenov could scarcely have had finer instructors. Ritter and Humboldt are together considered to this day the founders of modern geographical science. With both men's encouragement, and the support of his own Geographical Society, Semenov returned to Russia in 1855 to organize the two-year expedition (1856–57) for which he is best known — toward the Tian Shan Mountains. At the time, no European had visited them. Asian accounts offered only the slightest information. They were, Humboldt supposedly remarked, as unknown to science as the surface of the moon.

Ongoing Russian imperial expansion into western Central Asia was bringing the distant mountains closer, however. By the 1850s the military had made forays as far as the Syr-Dariia River and the approaches to the Zailiisk Ala Tau Mountains, immediately north of the Tian Shan range. Semenov supported further Russian influence and even annexations in the area, and, when it seemed appropriate, couched his proposed travels in the area accordingly. There was, however, reluctance in some official corners about allowing Semenov to travel all the way to the Tian Shan. What might the response of local peoples be? Or of the British, who had their own imperial interests in the region? Semenov answered with an itinerary that went close to — but stopped just short of— the mountains.

Taking only 1,000 rubles from the Geographic Society he set off from St. Petersburg in the spring of 1856. At Omsk the governor of Western Siberia provided topographers and a generous military guard. Semenov's expedition spent most of the summer surveying and collecting in the Russian Altai. In early August they moved on to Semipalatinsk. Here, Semenov was stunned to meet an old friend — the novelist Fedor Dostoyevsky. Dostoyevsky was not in the area to explore, however. Rather, he was waiting for permission to return home after serving a four-year sentence (mostly in Omsk) for his involvement in meetings of a supposedly seditious group of intellectuals named the Petrashevtsy. The group, which had in fact been relatively harmless, had famously been broken up by the tsarist police. Dostoyevsky and other members had not only been sentenced to death but marched to the firing range and hooded for execution. But at the last, terrifying moment his sentence had been commuted to exile. And here he was now, in Semipalatinsk. Semenov might have had reason to shudder, or to thank his deity. He himself had been involved, if only marginally, in the exact same circle.

Semenov continued south to Vernyi (a.k.a. Alma-Ata or Almaty)—his primary base of operations for the push south — arriving in late August. Here he picked up another military escort and two local guides. His first goal, the mountain lake Issyk Kul, he reached on September 9. The lake itself was spectacular. And Semenov, arriving on the north side, was the first European here. He tested the water, finding it salty, and he marveled at its gorgeous dark blue color. He remarked on the huge size of the lake —"five times greater" than Lake Geneva. But most of all his eye — and his heart — were captured by what rose *beyond* its distant southern shore: the glorious Tian Shan Mountains: an "unbroken, snowy chain ... stretch[ing] away for at least 200 miles of the length" of Issyk Kul. "The sharp outlines of the spurs and the dark furrows of the valleys in the front of the range," he wrote wistfully after his return, "are softened by a thin, transparent mist which hangs over the lake but which heightens the clear, sharp outlines of the white heads of the Tian Shan giants as they rise above it and glisten in the sunlight on the azure-blue canopy of the Central Asian sky."[2]

For now, Semenov — lacking permission to head to these "giants"— had to content himself with taking the expedition along the north shore of the lake to its western extremity. Wary of hostile locals, he first returned briefly to Vernyi for reinforcements. He traveled for the rest of the season with some fifty Cossacks and was rewarded with an important discovery: that the Chu River, a major waterway, does not reach Lake Issyk Kul. This overturned notions held by Ritter and Humboldt that they were part of the same system.

The following May, after wintering at Barnaul (in the Russian Altai), Semenov headed back to the region of Issyk Kul, determined to press into the Tian Shan. This time he brought with him an artist, "fifty-eight soldiers, twelve camels, and seventeen horses."[3] Perhaps even more important for his security, and for the eventual success of the expedition, he also took the time to ingratiate himself with the Kirghiz sultan Tezek, through whose domain he was to pass and whose protection he would need against the depredations of the various warring tribal peoples in the region. Tezek, it seems, took quickly to Semenov and gave him every possible assistance. This boded well for reaching the mountains. But there was another problem. The Russian governor of Western Siberia — whom he had visited earlier, during a winter trip to Omsk — was still unwilling to authorize the expedition to head further into Kirghiz lands than it had penetrated the previous year. Rather than risk a clear order not to proceed to the Tian Shan, Semenov kept his intentions to himself. If there were political consequences to be faced, he would deal with them later. He had to reach the mountains.

Thus, in June, taking advantage of Tezek's cooperation, Semenov pressed quickly south past Issyk Kul and upstream along the Dzuku River basin. Soon he was climbing into the Tian Shan range itself. As the land rose and oxygen levels fell, progress slowed. The animals became exhausted, and on the rocky inclines they could not find proper footing. At one point a horse slipped, fell on the jagged rocks, and rapidly bled to death. Semenov's ultimate goal was to cross the Zaukinsk Pass, peaking at well over 10,000 feet, in the shadow of the great mountain Khan-Tengri, itself around 23,000 feet high. As the expedition ascended, breathing became ever harder. Men and beasts suffered alike. As the peak of the pass neared, Semenov ordered exhausted detachments to remain behind. Thus by June 13, with the top of the pass in sight, his company had dropped — by measures — from more than fifty to just three men. Four horses accompanied them on the final leg up. But on that memorable day Semenov achieved what he had set out to do. He later wrote of the moment: "Our guide warned us that, at the summit of the pass, breathing would become so difficult that one could not survive for more than half an hour. At last we attained our goal and found ourselves at the summit ... where an unexpectedly beautiful panorama spread out before our eyes.... Here I found myself at last in the very heart of Asia, somewhat nearer to Kashmir than to Semipalatinsk."[4] Satisfied, Semenov turned around and began the return descent, but this time taking a more easterly route north from Arasan — skirting Lake Sasykkol (near the present Kazakhstan-Chinese border).

By expedition's end the Russian had made several major discoveries, including five Alpine glaciers (unexpected given the aridity of the region); the mountains' unusually elevated snow line, averaging around 11,500 feet; and, fascinatingly, many of the mountain passes that had obviously served in the past as routes from Asia to Europe for waves of nomadic peoples, including the Huns. Perhaps most important for science: Humboldt had believed the Tian Shan Mountains to be volcanic, but Semenov had clear evidence that this was false, at least in the areas where he had been. He also recorded copious new information about the range's dimensions, altitude, position, features, and orography. And there was information about local flora and fauna, and specimens.

Back in St. Petersburg, Semenov quickly proposed to lead a second expedition to the region. He was rebuffed. Although feted for his great achievements and contributions, his unauthorized visit to lands beyond Issyk Kul was also noted. Segments of the government were still opposed at this point to exploration much beyond the state's current Central Asian borders, and Semenov, though respected as an explorer, had revealed himself as untrustworthy in this regard.

In fact, the best of Semenov's exploring career was already behind him. Though still in his prime he would soon trade in the wilderness for more urban and sedentary pursuits. Over the following years he consulted for the government on its planned peasant emancipation, enacted in 1861. Thereafter, an interest in statistics led him to important positions on the Central Statistical Committee and the Statistical Council. He later played a major role in organizing the first Russian census (1897) and in dividing European Russia into economic regions.

Exploration, of course, remained at the center of his life, but henceforth he would mostly travel vicariously — through his aforementioned career at the Russian Geographical Society, his sponsorship of others' journeys, his writings, organizing specimen collections for the Society and other institutions, and so on. His own peregrinations he confined primarily to frequent trips to western European cities on behalf of another abiding passion: art collecting, which his considerable wealth allowed him to indulge significantly. He died in 1914, shortly before the outbreak of war, one of Russia's most celebrated and beloved scientists and public figures of the late Imperial Era.

Nikolai Mikhailovich Przheval'skii[5] (1839–1888)

Among the many Russian explorers whose names and achievements have fallen into unwarranted obscurity, few are so underrated — at least in the West — as Nikolai Mikhailovich Przheval'skii. Among the general public in the Anglo-American world he is remembered today, if at all, primarily as the scientific discoverer of the breed of wild horse that bears his name. And yet, surveying his four epic journeys across the vast and forbidding expanses of western China, Mongolia, and Tibet, one recent author has dubbed Przheval'skii "Russia's greatest explorer, a man who traveled further and accomplished more than America's Lewis and Clark or England's Livingston."[6] There is much truth in this evaluation (map 11).

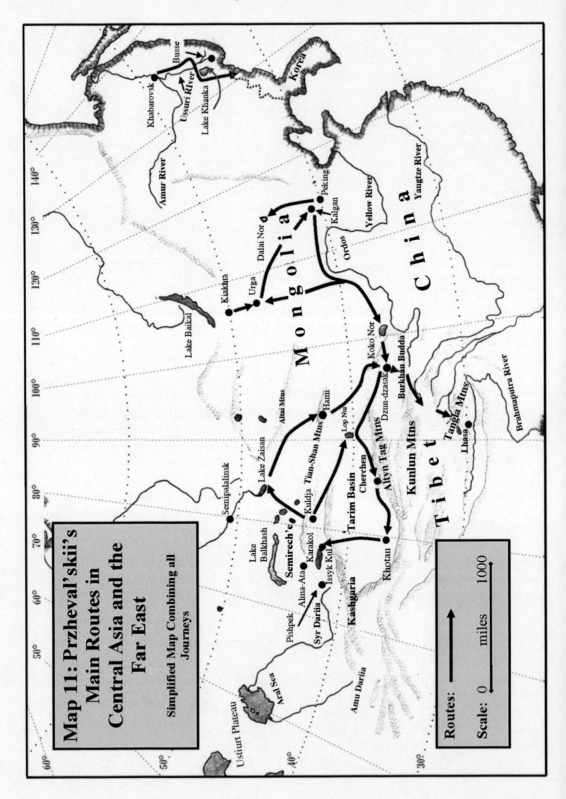

Map 11: Przheval'skii's Main Routes in Central Asia and the Far East

Simplified Map Combining all Journeys

Often misidentified as a Pole, Przheval'skii was a Russian with mixed Zaporozhe Cossack, Polish, and Russian roots. Born and raised in a minor gentry family in the countryside outside Smolensk, his childhood has been described as "free, almost savage ... in unspoilt country." He spent "the summer days in the woods, cut off from human contact."[7] Though he learned academics well enough — at first partly from an uncle, partly from his own reading, and later formally in Smolensk grammar school and the St. Petersburg Military Academy — Przheval'skii did so without enthusiasm. Indoor and urban pursuits bored him, though a supposedly photographic memory got him successfully through his exams. As a grown man he found city life so uncongenial that on several occasions it literally made him ill. Instead, he craved adventure and the harsh solitude of the wilderness — and spent most of his adult life experiencing it. From an early age he became passionate about guns and hunting; in later life his prowess with the rifle was legendary and his appetite for the thrill of the kill insatiable. Among his other traits Przheval'skii was a strict disciplinarian (but a huge eater) who thrived on physical hardship; a capable planner and organizer; a keen student of nature; brave but rarely reckless; resourceful, intelligent, and indefatigable: all qualities that served him well on his journeys. He could also be highly judgmental, inclined to pour scorn on any who did not live up to his personal standards. Devoted to his mother and to his childhood nurse, Przheval'skii nonetheless supposedly held women in contempt. He never showed any interest in marriage or children. He did, however, both demand and inspire a kind of familial — if subservient — loyalty from his closest travel companions.

Przheval'skii spent 1855–1860 in the military, posted variously, but rarely happy: he regretted having missed real action in the Crimean War; he condemned the moral degradation of soldiers, with their womanizing and drunkenness. Refusing to participate in such things, he instead hunted, studied (mostly geography, history, and statistics), and wrote. In 1861 he combined these interests in his first publication — *Memoirs of a Sportsman*. He also became particularly interested in the Russian Empire's acquisition during 1858–1860 of formerly Chinese far eastern territories north of the Amur. In lieu of pursuing a dream to go and explore these lands personally, and working entirely from available sources, he compiled and published *A Military and Statistical Review of the Amur Region*. The book found favor among his military and political superiors and would eventually help open the doors to real exploration. After a brief military adventure helping the Russian Empire suppress a Polish uprising in 1863, Przheval'skii was posted in 1864 to Warsaw to teach geography and history. His formal education, the hated "squalor" of St. Petersburg, and the years of frustrating military service were now behind him. But the adventure he craved was still slow in coming.

Prezhval'skii nonetheless made good use of his time in Warsaw. In the early morning hours he worked on writing a geography textbook. From eight to twelve he taught. In the afternoon he studied. The combination of these three activities provided a rigorous education. This, the reputation he earned as a first-rate teacher, and the royalty income from the book (and a greater amount still from disciplined card-playing) all brought his dreams of becoming a great explorer closer to reality. At the end of 1866, he happily accepted reassignment 5,000 miles east to the East Siberian military district to work as a surveyor-explorer.

The Ussuri River — most of which had only recently been brought under Russian control[8] — was to be his first focus. Before leaving, Przheval'skii traveled briefly to St. Petersburg where he impressed and won important support for his proposed travels and work from the Imperial Geographical Society, and in particular from the president of its Physical Geography Section (and future general president), the aforementioned Petr Petrovich Semenov.

The expedition set out from Irkutsk toward the end of May 1867. It was a modest affair: Prezhval'skii took only two assistants, a sixteen-year-old topography student name Nikolai Iagunov and a Cossack named Nikolaev. His supplies too were spartan: in the way of scientific aids he took only "a thermometer, a compass and maps."[9] Planning to feed himself primarily by hunting, he took a dog, a large amount of gunpowder and shot, and little else. Traveling relatively light would remain one of Przheval'skii's standard operating procedures, even on his more ambitious and better-supported later travels. Until relatively late in life, for example, he eschewed the use of photographic materials in favor of hiring an artist.

Przheval'skii entered the Ussuri River from the Amur and headed upstream (south), eventually covering the 300-mile route from Khabarovsk to Busse. He was not the first European on the river, however. Jesuits mapping for the Chinese had been this way back in 1709. More recently, he had been preceded by other Russians — L. I. Shrenk and K. I. Maksimovich (respectively, an ethnographer and a botanist) had been in the area in 1854–1856, followed in 1857–1859 by the ethnographer M. I. Veniukov and the naturalist R. K. Maak; while the governor-general of Eastern Siberia, N. N. Murav'ev-Amurskii (1809–1881), had earned his sobriquet heading or dispatching expeditions to the region, including along the Ussuri, during 1858–1860. Przheval'skii, however, would be the first to carry out a comprehensive survey and description of the region's ethnography, geography, flora, and fauna.[10]

Along the Ussuri, there were also small Cossack settlements, founded by the Russian government essentially by a process of deportation. One of Przheval'skii's commissions was to collect information on them. He found the settlements in poor shape, struggling for survival in damp and unfamiliar conditions in a world of summer gnats and mosquitoes, bitter winters, and year-round alcoholism. Przheval'skii, also finding the insects insufferable, was forced to spend most of the twenty-three nights of this part of his journey staying with the Cossacks, some of whom he also hired as porters. His official report treated them poorly, emphasizing their "filth, hunger, and paupery."[11] More to his liking was the extraordinary natural diversity of the river basin, especially its curious blend of northern and southern species, for example the "sight of grapes twined around fir-trees."[12]

Perhaps the most important destination on this expedition was Lake Khanka, located in the headwaters of the Ussuri system, straddling the new Chinese-Russian border at about 45°N latitude. Apart from a few hundred Cossacks and a much smaller Tungus presence (and one lone Chinese), the huge lake was undisturbed and teeming with migratory birds. The hunter in Przheval'skii found it impossible to turn down such sport. He and Iagunov spent August 1867 shooting, collecting, and surveying, ending the month with an impressive and varied collection. In September they traveled to Novgorodskaia (nowadays Pos'et), a small Russian settlement near the point where Russia, China, and Korea intersect. En route Przheval'skii discovered an abandoned Manchu Nü-Chen fortress, encountered local Chinese (for whom Przheval'skii had only contempt), and at considerable personal risk, illegally crossed briefly into Korea.

Though the journey was technically over, Przheval'skii's wanderlust was not. Toward the end of October, with the winter now setting in, he opted to resupply and walk (with horses and Cossack soldiers following) north along the coast, eventually reaching a point midway between modern-day Ol'ga and Rudnaia Pristan', before heading west via the Tazusha (Tadusha) Valley, over the mountains and back to the Ussuri basin, which he reached in January. Along the difficult route, Przheval'skii continued to collect animal, bird, and plant specimens. Efforts to shoot an example of the magnificent Ussuri tiger failed, however. Przheval'skii spent most of the spring back at Lake Khanka, watching the annual migration and shooting relentlessly.

Przheval'skii's Ussuri journey, though not inconsequential, was only a warm-up for what was subsequently to make him one of history's great explorers: four major expeditions into the largely unknown expanses of Central Asia, focusing on western China, Mongolia, and — his most important goal — Tibet. Various factors led Przheval'skii to these regions. His own curiosity about the geography, flora, and fauna of these hardly trodden lands was certainly critical. But so were external political and military factors. In an age of Great Power Imperialism the lands in question — at the crossroads of Chinese, Mongolian, and nomadic Tibetan (or Tangut) civilizations — were fast becoming critical squares on the chessboard of the so-called "Great Game," the ongoing competition for decisive influence over the vast spaces and strategic routes between the growing Russian, British, and (to a lesser extent) French Empires in Asia. Przheval'skii, consequently, was able to draw on support for his travels not only from the Imperial Geographical Society, but also — at times — from the Ministries of Foreign Affairs and, especially, of War. His own Great Russian chauvinism made him a willing agent and enthusiastic proponent of Russian conquest of the areas he explored.

In August 1870, some three years after his time on the Ussuri, Przheval'skii set off on his first Central Asian expedition. His brief was to survey as comprehensively as possible the nature and geography of parts of Mongolia, north and western China, and — if possible — Tibet. The Ordos Plateau and Koko Nor — both essentially blank spots to Western science — were priority destinations. He left Kiakhta, near the Russian-Chinese border on 17 November 1870. With the young Iagunov now studying in Warsaw, Przheval'skii found a replacement in Mikhail Pyl'tsov, a sublieutenant and former student in Przheval'skii's history classes. He also took a dog (a setter named Faust), a small caravan of camels, and a Cossack guard. Travel permissions from the Chinese were arranged ahead of time. Once across the Russian frontier Przheval'skii headed, along an established route, for the Mongolian capital of Ulan Bator, then known as Urga. He covered the distance in comfort — in a two-wheeled Chinese cart beneath the relatively benign skies of a Mongolian autumn. The next stage promised real hardship, however — a winter crossing of the formidable Gobi Desert bound for the Chinese city of Kalgan (now Zhangjiakou), just north of Peking. Przheval'skii attached himself to a Mongolian caravan headed the same way. December brought harsh cold, below -30° C.; but by the start of January he was in Peking. From here he made a number of side trips, most notably one to the northeast, to the beautiful and bird-rich Dalai Nor ("The Great Lake," now Hulun Lake).

Over the next two years or so his route (much of which he backtracked and then retrod) took him on a great southwestward arc, much of it along a track to the north of the Yellow River: to the Ordos Desert, Gansu, and beyond. Koko Nor (now known as Qinghai Lake) was a special highlight — "the dream of my life" Przheval'skii called it upon arriving at its shore on 13 September 1872.[13] Both on the way west and returning, Przheval'skii and his companions struggled through unforgiving terrain in murderous heat and cold; they suffered from lack of— or contaminated — water, and from altitude sickness; they were troubled by crows so aggressive they literally tore open the humps of the camels as they walked or rested. Pyl'tsov nearly died from typhus. Faust, Przheval'skii's beloved setter, expired from heat and thirst.

But not only nature presented dangers. On this and subsequent journeys, Przheval'skii sometimes had to hide his surveying activities from locals who distrusted his motives. Worse, in remote parts of western China where no or few Europeans had ever visited, he had to make his way through lands devastated — and sometimes still terrorized — by a violent anti-Chinese rebellion (1862–1877) of the Muslim Dungans. Poisoned wells and scattered human skeletons attested to the ferocity of the ongoing troubles.

The expedition eventually reached northern Tibet and came within 528 miles of the capital of Lhasa. But here, at the headwaters of the Yangtse River system (near the confluence of the Mur Usu and the Do Chu [or Dza Chu]) Przheval'skii was forced to turn back. His few remaining camels were in poor condition, and he no longer had any funds with which to buy or bargain for replacements. The "dream of Lhasa," however, was now firmly fixed in his heart. He would variously nurture and pursue it over three more great expeditions to Central Asia during the following decade.

By the time Przheval'skii headed out in 1876 on his second Central Asian expedition his published account of the first journey had made him an internationally celebrated explorer. He was now also a lieutenant colonel. The changes affected him hardly at all, however; nor did they much alter the manner in which he traveled. Though a grander affair than his previous journey, still it was by the standards of contemporary explorers a lean and inexpensive operation. He took a single primary companion, an eighteen-year-old boy named Fedor Leont'evich Eklon,[14] a two-man Cossack guard, and minimal baggage. To this he added two translators, twenty-four camels, and four horses. They set out on August 12, this time from Kuldja (modern Yining in western Xinjiang Province).

Przheval'skii's intention was to cross Mongolia on a more westerly track than before and then penetrate deeper into Tibet — all the way to Lhasa. En route he would seek out Lop Nur, the enigmatic lake that no European since Marco Polo had visited. The tortuous two-year journey provided a rich mix of success and failure, of triumph and heartbreak. On the positive side, Przheval'skii reached, studied, and charted Lop Nur (triggering dispute among geographers for some years thereafter[15]); encountered and described the area's native Khara Khoshun people (described as the most primitive of all Turkic peoples in Central Asia); greatly improved cartographical knowledge of the Altyn Tag range to the lake's south — including ascertaining that the border of geographical Tibet was some 200 miles further north than previously thought; and collected a wealth of important specimens. Additionally, he was promoted again during the expedition, to the rank of colonel. On the other hand, he failed again to penetrate Tibet, this time due to the sudden outbreak of war as the Qing Chinese moved in en masse to reassert control of Kashgaria following the death of its upstart Muslim ruler, Yaqub Beg, in 1877.

Though circumstances were entirely beyond his control, Przheval'skii nonetheless bitterly and long regretted being forced away from his goal. Other issues troubled him deeply too. During the journey Przhehval'skii had become seriously sick, troubled especially by a debilitating skin condition that responded poorly to the various treatments he tried and which necessitated a lengthy period of post-expedition convalescence. And while still in the field news reached him of his mother's death, a blow that knocked the wind out of his sails for a time.

Przheval'skii's third Central Asian jaunt (1879–1880) is sometimes known as the First Tibetan Expedition, since Tibet — and particularly Lhasa — was its explicit goal. Eschewing earlier approaches from Kiakhta and Kuldja, the expedition this time left from Zaisan (on the shores of Lake Zaisan). It was April 1879. This was also a somewhat larger expedition than the first two, consisting at the outset of fourteen people, thirty-five camels, and five horses. Among the men were F. L. Eklon, who had accompanied Przheval'skii on his previous journey, and Vsevolod Ivanovich Roborovskii (1856–1910), a naturalist and explorer who would go on to great achievements of his own. The intended route led southeast, across eastern Dzungaria, via Bulun Tokhoi (Fu-Hai), and then south via Hami (Kumul) and K'u-fi (K'u Shui), across the Pei Shan, along the western extremity of the Nan Shan, and to Dzun-dzasak, the staging post for a push further south onto the Tibetan plateau, hopefully all the way to Lhasa.

Almost immediately out of Zaisan, Przheval'skii made the discovery for which he is still best remembered — the short, donkey-like Mongolian horse that now bears his name. He had heard earlier of the existence of the animal and had made finding it a minor priority. He was denied the full thrill of real discovery, however: in fact, he was simply approached with a skull and complete skin by some Kirghiz hunters who had heard of the expedition's interest. Przheval'skii immediately understood that he was looking at the rumored beast, and that it was new to science. Sending the specimen on to St. Petersburg he redoubled his efforts to find a living herd and was later rewarded with sightings in the Dzungar Desert. The horses proved extraordinarily wary, however, and despite great effort he was not able to shoot a single one.

In late May, after passing through terrible and persistent sandstorms, Przheval'skii reached Hami, a third of the way to Lhasa from Zaisan. From here a long, hard summer slog took him across the Pei Shan and along the western end of a previously unknown range — the Nan Shan. Passing this, he named some of its peaks for Humboldt and Ritter. Once, while in the mountains surrounding the salty marshes of the Syrtyn plain, Przheval'skii lost sight of one of his critically important Cossacks, a man named Egorov. Days of searches yielded nothing and Egorov was reluctantly given up for dead — only to reappear, dressed in rags and half dead from exhaustion, thirst, and starvation — sixteen miles farther down the road. It turned out that he had become lost while searching for a yak he had shot. It was a near miracle that Egorov's desperate wanderings and the expedition's departing path had crossed.

It was only August, but already the winter frosts were upon the expedition as it moved across the Tsaidam Basin. By the middle of September, they were at Dzun-dzasak, ready to push onto the Tibetan plateau. These 200,000 square miles "were still a virtual blank on the map. An area never lower than 14,000 feet, of arid, freezing winters and cool, wet summers, eroded and made uninhabitable by perpetual gales, its waters undrained except for those that broke through to the eastern gorges, the plateau was the largest and most hostile unexplored region outside the polar circles."[16] Geography and climate were not the only obstacles in Przheval'skii's way at this point, however. Relations between Russia and China (whose territory Tibet officially was) were at a low ebb, with the outbreak of war a distinct possibility. In Dzun-dzasak and elsewhere, consequently, Chinese assistance with guides, supplies, permissions, and other indispensables (most of which had been arranged well ahead of time) were either entirely withheld, sabotaged, or given only under duress. The possibility of outright Chinese hostility, and even of military action against Przhaval'skii, could also not be ruled out for the time being.

Nonetheless, the Russians, now numbering twelve, pressed on and up, crossing the Burkhan Budda range. As they entered onto the plateau the temperature dropped punishingly. Snow, hail, and the thin air added their own miseries, especially during repeated crossings of the many ridges rising above the plateau itself. The stony ground provided little food for the horses and camels, who suffered accordingly — the latter also from the damp. The altitude hampered efforts to burn wood and boil water.

But there were also great rewards. Passing over the Shuga Range—at an altitude of more than 15,000 feet—they descended into the Shuga River valley, where Przheval'skii marveled both at the richness of the fauna—"hundreds of herds of yaks ... many antelope," and other creatures in abundance. But even more fascinating to Przheval'skii was these animals' extraordinary tameness, a consequence of their isolation from human contact. "One can hardly believe," he remarked, "that these can be wild animals," so close did they allow one to approach. They did not yet know that man was their "most malicious enemy."[17] Przheval'skii, unfortunately, did not refrain from teaching this lesson over and over in the manner he knew best, killing greatly higher numbers than anything remotely necessary for food or skin—or reconcilable with any reasonable definition of sport.

Pressing further into Tibet, the expedition crossed the Koko Shili range and descended into the Mur Usu River valley. This was the same river—one of the sources of the mighty Yangtse River—that had marked the southern extent of Przheval'skii's first Central Asian journey. This time, however, Przheval'skii was about one hundred miles upstream of his previous location. He followed the river uphill for another hundred miles, whereupon it turned nearly due south into the Tangla Mountains, almost directly in the direction of Lhasa. By now the conditions were killing the camels—requiring Przheval'skii to cast off specimens and other nonvital supplies as he transferred some of the baggage to the remaining animals. Rising eventually to nearly 17,000 feet, the expedition arrived first at the Toktonai River, then at the A-k'o-ta-mu River, tributaries of the Yangtse.[18] From this point, things began to go seriously awry.

On November 7 (1879), a mere 150 miles short of Lhasa, Przheval'skii and his men were attacked by a group of armed bandits. Only the Russians' military training and superior firearms saved them. Over the course of two encounters at least a half-dozen bandits were killed and several more injured, while Przheval'skii and his men escaped unscathed. They pressed on.

Shortly thereafter, at the San-Chu (Sonchu) Valley, a mere seven-days' march from Lhasa, the expedition was again approached, this time by a peaceful threesome of Mongol-Buddhist pilgrims. They bore disheartening news, however. Tibetan lamas had become increasingly uncomfortable with the expedition's movements. Rumors were abroad that the Russian's real goal was to harm or kidnap the Dalai Lama. Przheval'skii must turn back. A little while later two Tibetan officials arrived to deliver a similar message. They added that should he not comply Przheval'skii would meet armed force. It was a devastating blow. Even if he had been willing (and one suspects he might have been), Przheval'skii knew full well that he could not shoot his way through to Lhasa. Diplomacy was his last hope. He spent the next two-and-a-half weeks meeting with Tibetan officials, waiting for news, and hoping for a change of mood. He argued passionately that his party was intent only on scientific research and that it was in any case far too small to pose any kind of realistic threat. He even tried lecturing his interlocutors on the appropriate manner in which one should receive a foreign guest. Nothing worked. On December 3, miserable and furious, Przheval'skii turned away from his goal yet again. Once more he resolved to return.

Despite his disappointment, Przheval'skii did not waste his retreat. During the ten months or so it took the expedition to return to Kiakhta, he explored and mapped a variety of more-or-less uncharted places, including three months in the upper basin of the Yellow River and the nearby spine of the eastern Kunlun Mountains, followed by a month in the "Tetungskie" mountains. By the end, Przheval'skii had covered and mapped some 4,750 miles, mostly hitherto unknown. He throughout had carried on a rigorous regime of meteorological measurements and discovered several new ranges in the Nan Shan (naming them after Marco Polo, Humboldt, Ritter, and other explorers). This is to say nothing of the enormous botanical and zoological collections he had amassed and, of course, the horse he had discovered for science.[19]

During the interlude between this and his next Central Asian expedition Przheval'skii spent some time back home at Otradnoe. But with his mother now dead, the place held less attraction for him. Since his last visit, also, a railroad line had been laid nearby bringing in its wake major forest clearings and reducing the amount of game in the area. Both of these circumstances inspired Przehval'skii to move, in June 1881, to a large new estate in the northwest Smolensk region called Sloboda. Here he relaxed, entertained, hunted, wrote, and — especially — planned his fourth Central Asian expedition.

Here, too, he met an eighteen-year-old boy named Peter Kuzmich Kozlov (1863–1935), a distillery worker and herdsman's son. Attracted to the boy's simple honesty and enthusiasm for travel, Przheval'skii took him on as a new protégé, much in the manner of Iagunov and Pyl'tsov beforehand. Przheval'skii taught the boy to hunt, prepare specimens, survey, and so on. Kozlov, for his part, threw himself wholeheartedly into this wonderful and unexpected apprenticeship with Russia's great explorer — even completing a short stint of military service in Moscow in order to qualify for formal employment under Przheval'skii. When Eklon suddenly pulled out of the fourth expedition shortly before departure in 1883, Kozlov replaced him eagerly — joining Roborovskii as one of Przheval'skii's two main assistants.

Though Lhasa continued to exert a powerful fascination, Przheval'skii did not make it the primary goal of this new expedition. Indeed, once out, he opted for a route through northern Tibet, with its closest approach to Lhasa being a point on the northern edge of the Yangtse River, some 350 miles north of the Tibetan capital. He kept in mind, however, the possibility of a detour south should conditions permit. The planned journey overall followed a great arc running from the headwaters of the Brahmaputra River, across northern Tibet from northeast to southwest, then west toward the Karakorum range, lake Lop Nur, and Khotan, then north across the western Takla-Makan Desert and the Tian-Shan Mountains, finishing back in the Russian Empire at Lake Issyk-Kul'.[20]

Compared to previous outings, this one was large — twenty-one people, fifty-seven camels, and seven horses. It was also richly financed — at 43,500 rubles, nearly twice the amount of the third expedition (the first two had cost even less). Departing from Kiakhta on 21 October 1883, the expedition traveled for many months along the by-now familiar southern route to and just beyond the Alashan Desert and then west past Lake Koko Nor. In mid–May 1884, not far from Dzun-dzasak, Przheval'skii left the road he knew and headed south. His route took him again across the Burkhan-Budda range and onto the Tibetan plateau, but in a region never before trodden by Europeans and hardly known even to the Chinese. Przheval'skii's goal at this point was the source of the Yellow River, something he had come close to on his previous trip but had not been able to devote time to pinning down. Happily, finding it proved relatively easy, and just over a week later, on May 17, it was on the map — and on the already impressive list of Przheval'skii's achievements. "Our joy was without end," he noted in his later published account of the journey.[21] Not far away, Prezhval'skii also discovered two large (and other smaller) lakes. Known now as Dzharin-nur and Oring-nor, he called them, respectively, Russkoe and Ekpeditsii.[22]

The headwaters of the Yellow River are not far from those of China's other great river, the Yangtse (they are divided by the Baian-Khara-Ula range, Przheval'skii remained throughout much of the summer to study and chart the region. Despite the season, the elevation and the incessant dampness kept the weather bitterly cold. Here too, the expedition had to fight off another ambush by Tibetan bandits. In August Przheval'skii moved on, heading first north and then west along the southern edge of the Tsaidam. During November he crossed and began surveying the Kunlun Mountains at the northern edge of geographical Tibet. This proved among the most important parts of the expedition, yielding over the following months several previously unknown ranges and mountain lakes, all of which Przheval'skii charted and named, including Mount Shapka Monomakha, the Columbus Range, Lake Nezamerzaiushchee, and the Zagadochnyi Range — the latter renamed the Przheval'skii Range by decision of the Russian Geographical Society.[23]

Toward the end of January 1885, still in the shadow of the mountains, the expedition arrived at Lop Nur, which Przheval'skii had rediscovered eight years earlier. The locals remembered him fondly and welcomed him warmly. Mindful of the controversy over the lake's position, Przheval'skii took the time to resurvey parts of it, confirming his earlier readings. Roborovskii added to the record by taking a series of photographs (Prezheval'skii presumably having overcome by now his earlier objections to the new technology!). The party stayed here until late March, when they headed southwest along the bottom of the Takla-Makan toward Keriia. En route, west of Cherchen (Qiemo), they came upon the foot of a large range, part of the western Kunlun chain and reaching over 21,600 feet, but unmapped and — apparently — unnamed even by the locals. Przheval'skii called it "Russkii" (Russian). This was in April. By late August the expedition had skirted the southern edge of the Takla-Makan all the way to Khotan. From here the journey led north, across the desert, and toward the Tarim River, over the Tian Shan, and back into Russia. The final stops were at Lake Issuk-Kul and the city of Karakol on its eastern edge. This latter destination Przheval'skii reached on 29 October 1885, where he and his expedition were deservedly received as great and triumphant returning explorers.

In several respects this had been Przheval'skii's greatest expedition. He had covered 4,856 miles, discovered, mapped, and named numerous ranges and peaks, as well as the source of the Yellow River. He had amassed an even greater number of botanical and zoological specimens than on previous journeys, collected vast quantities of meteorological data, made many ethnographical notes, and much more. He was rewarded, more lavishly than ever, with medals, pensions, acclamations, and honorary memberships of various scientific societies, both in Russia and across Europe. He was promoted to major-general, received by the royal family, consulted by the Cabinet on foreign policy, and so on. Roborovskii and Kozlov, and even the Cossack guards, shared in the glory and rewards.

During the first part of 1886, Przheval'skii remained tied to St. Petersburg, receiving honors and making speeches. It suited his disposition poorly. Only toward the end of March was he able to tear himself away to his estate at Sloboda. Here he quickly shook off the dust of the city and immersed himself again in his beloved outdoors. He camped and hunted, hiked, and set about directing the construction of a new house. Somewhat less enthusiastically he also began work on a written account of his latest travels. Over the next two years he struggled to balance the demands of his fame with a burning desire — stronger than ever — to escape again to the solitude of the wilds. He had been living outdoors too long now ever to be able to feel entirely comfortable anywhere else. Thus, while writing up an account of his fourth expedition he was already busily planning a fifth one.

Time was no longer on his side, however. Nor was his health. By now he was in his late forties. Over the past twenty-eight years he had traveled more than 20,500 miles —

mostly on foot. He had spent ten years in some of the harshest climates and most forbidding terrains anywhere in the world — to say nothing of the years of hiking, hunting, and outdoors living at or near his homes. He had exposed himself constantly to conditions that would have long ago sickened, beaten, or killed most men. Though he accepted the toll these years had taken, still the thought of retirement was unacceptable, even terrifying. And so he submitted his plans for the fifth expedition. They were quickly accepted. The new journey was to last two years, at first retracing his steps south from Karakol, across the Tian Shan to Khotan, Keriia, and Tibet. This time, however, he resolved to achieve what he had been denied previously. He planned to push further south — by force if necessary — all the way to Lhasa, his great and still-unrealized dream. Roborovskii and Kozlov again signed on, and in early fall the main party headed east toward the intended starting-off point at Karakol.

But it was not to be. On 4 October 1888, while hunting near Pishpek (now Bishkek), Przheval'skii several times drank unboiled water from a source which the previous winter had been at the center of an outbreak of typhoid. It seems an odd slip for a man so experienced in the outdoors. Is it possible Prezheval'skii deliberately risked his life? The idea is intriguing, and not entirely implausible. Przheval'skii was no longer at the height of his powers. He would soon be too old for the kind of travel he craved. Yet the thought of retirement appalled, even frightened him. Marriage, suggested by friends, he had firmly rejected as "not my profession." As for children, "Lop Nur, Koko Nor, Tibet, and so on — these are my children," he had said.[24] Some time after returning from his fourth expedition he confided to his sister-in-law that he could not "get on with 'civilization.'"[25] Did he opt, then, to die doing what he loved? One can only guess.

Przheval'skii arrived at Karakol on the 14th — already too sick to travel further. On the 20th he was dead. In accordance with his wishes, he was buried on the southern bank of Lake Issyk Kul. His funeral, held in Karakol, was a stately affair that attracted "more than half the population" of the town.[26] His passing was widely mourned in Russia and beyond.

Przheval'skii's accomplishments are legion: new species discovered (including the wild horse, wild camel, innumerable fish, birds, trees, bushes, and so on); a collection of specimens so large and significant that it is still being studied today[27]; the discovery of mountains, ranges, lakes, and other landforms. He mapped thousands of square miles of territory previously known only dimly to science or not at all. And he amassed an overwhelming quantity of other data: meteorological, geographical, topographical, and ethnographical. In short, his life's work "radically changed the map of Central Asia" and was a "turning point in the whole history of research of this region."[28] The enormity of his contributions is matched only by the injustice of his growing obscurity in the Western popular imagination.

Although Przheval'skii was an undeniably brilliant, successful, and important explorer, he was not without his shortcomings, nor has he lacked critics. During his lifetime and later (somewhat like his contemporary Miklukho-Miklai), he has been considered a scientific amateur — reasonably knowledgeable but improperly trained, especially in geology, and thus unable fully to appreciate or evaluate all that he saw. Prezheval'skii himself apparently reacted defensively to suggestions to this effect, often misinterpreting good advice as efforts to impugn his character or undermine his leadership. Efforts gingerly made by the Imperial Geographical Society to have the explorer tutored, or his expeditions accompanied by more formally trained personnel, were unsuccessful. In the end, his enormous reputation and other positive personal qualities kept him in official favor. And ultimately, the scale of his achievements render any carping incidental.

More significantly, from his own time to the present, Przheval'skii has also been repeatedly taken to task for his unbridled imperialistic enthusiasm and Russian-chauvinistic views — manifested, for example, in his violently anti–Chinese rhetoric, in frequent calls for Russian annexation of areas he traveled in, and even — perhaps — in the relatively small amount of attention he gave to ethnographic studies of the many native peoples he encountered. (In these regards he could hardly be more different from Miklukho-Miklai.) Some of his comments about Asians were crude enough to make even the Russian foreign minister of his day wince (and politely ignore his recommendations for war and conquest against the Chinese).

It would be unfair, however, not to offer a countervailing view. Przheval'skii was, after all, equally scathing in his opinion of "debauched" Russian soldiers, the "drunken" and "idle" Russian peasants near his home, "wretched" Cossack settlers in Ussuria, and anyone else who did not live up to his rather puritan — even misanthropic — standards. On the other hand, he lavished praise on anyone — Russian and non–Russian alike — who *did* live up to them, including most of the men with whom he shared the wilderness, and also the "friendly" native peoples of Lop Nur, whom he held in especially high regard. Any realistic evaluation of Przheval'skii must take into account both sides of this remarkable and imperfect man.

Portrait of Nikolai Mikhailovich Przheval'skii (Ria Novosti/Photo Researchers, Inc. SPL Reference Number: C009/749. Copyright © 2011 Photo Researchers, Inc. All Rights Reserved).

Post-Przheval'skii

Despite the loss of its leader, Przheval'skii's planned fifth expedition went out anyway, delayed until the following year, with Colonel (later Major-General) Mikhail Vasil'evich Pevtsov (1843–1902) in command. Roborovskii and Kozlov accompanied him (both would subsequently lead their own expeditions in the region). Also on board was K. I. Bogdanovich, a geologist — one of a number of individuals who went on to help remedy Przheval'skii's above-noted deficiencies.[29]

Pevtsov, like Przheval'skii, was a military man and erstwhile geography teacher. And he had also already undertaken Central Asian exploration of his own: in Dzungaria in 1876, and across the Gobi Desert to Kalgan, but by a different route from Przheval'skii, in 1877–1878. In other ways, however, he was quite unlike the man he had replaced. When the authorities — concerned about the international and diplomatic implications of a drive into southern Tibet — directed him to forget about Lhasa and focus instead on mapping further north, Pevtsov accepted ungrudgingly. He took Przheval'skii's expedition to Kashgaria and the Kunlun, covered more than 6,000 miles, and eventually delivered a greatly more accurate and detailed map than any hitherto of eastern Turkestan and extreme northern Tibet, including the discovery of the Toksun basin in northwest China. Pevtsov lived until 1902.[30]

Roborovskii also went on to enjoy great fame and achievement, leading his own Central Asian expedition beginning in 1892. He was the "first European to reach the Great Yuldus [and] discovered the Lükchun depression, a hole in the Central Asian plateau that descends down to 154 feet below sea level." He "revealed the Turfan inscriptions which were to open up the closed book of ancient Turkestan's history."[31] Roborovskii paid dearly for his achievements, however. In January 1895, his body rebelled against the constant oxygen starvation at high altitudes, causing a devastating attack of paralysis. His comrades dragged him home, but he never recovered. Nor did he quickly pass away. Instead he deteriorated and lingered for fifteen miserable years before finally expiring in 1905. The similarity of this fate to Georg Langsdorf's is notable (see chapter 5).

Fate was far kinder to Kozlov. The young boy whom Przheval'skii had plucked out of complete obscurity and trained for exploration turned out to be his dead master's single greatest successor. Pevtsov's retirement and Roborovskii's sudden incapacitation left Kozlov the preeminent Russian explorer of Central Asia. Already in 1899 he set out to retrace Przheval'skii's steps from Mongolia to Chörtentang, Kansu and on through the highlands of the Yellow, Yangtse, and Mekong rivers. Ultimately, he got as far as Chamdo (Qamdo) in eastern Tibet, some 400 miles northeast of Lhasa.

In the end, despite Kozlov's efforts, not Russians but the British first got to Lhasa. In 1904 a military detachment under Colonel Francis Younghusband finally breached the city's veil of secrecy and occupied it. Nonetheless, the following year, Kozlov was able to realize one of Przheval'skii's greatest dreams when he met the Dalai Lama. Unfortunately, the meeting occurred not in Lhasa but in the Mongolian capital of Urga (now Ulan Bator), where the Tibetan spiritual leader had recently fled, following the British incursion. The two men got along well, and Kozlov received a formal invitation to visit Lhasa itself. For the time being, however, Kozlov was otherwise engaged. During 1907–1909 he led another expedition into the Gobi Desert, headed for the far northeastern region of Tibet known as Amdo. This area had been crossed many times by Russians and others, but remained relatively little studied. This time Kozlov scored a stunning success when he uncovered the ruins of the Tangut city of Khara-Khoto, sacked in 1227 by Chingiss Khan. A protracted archaeological dig at the site made the trip to Lhasa impossible but yielded some 2,000 Tangut writings.

By 1914 Kozlov turned his attention yet again to Lhasa. This time he was foiled by the outbreak of the First World War. Operating under Soviet auspices in 1924, Kozlov tried once again. In Urga an emissary from Lhasa handed him a piece of silk — the Dalai Lama's coveted personal invitation and authorization to visit Lhasa. Kozlov noticed that the precious permit had been cut in half. The other half, he was told, was in the possession of the Dalai Lama's guards at Lhasa. But Kozlov reached only as far as Gashun Nor, Mongolia.[32] Though he never would reach Lhasa, he had unearthed numerous Xiongnu royal burial sites dating back to the first century and collected a quantity of Bactrian textiles of even older provenance. He returned permanently to Moscow in 1926. Unlike his mentor, Kozlov enjoyed and indulged in the urban lecture circuit. Unlike him too, he was able to enjoy retirement from exploring. He died in 1935.

G. N. Potanin

Another important explorer of Central Asia was Grigorii Nikolaevich Potanin (1835–1920), whose reputation, then and now, has been obscured by Przheval'skii's. The two men, who explored similar parts of the world, also began on similar tracks — both serving in the military as young men during the 1850s. Their careers diverged for a time thereafter, however, as Potanin became involved in liberal political causes. In 1861, the year of the serf emancipation, he was exiled to Siberia for having participated in student riots in St. Petersburg. In exile he further upset the authorities with his advocacy of Siberian independence — for which he was rewarded with a decade of imprisonment, hard labor, and further exile from 1865 to 1874. Two years prior to this second sentence, however, and despite his other troubles, he participated in an important expedition to Lake Zaisan and the Tarbagatai Range (which crosses from northwestern Xinjiang into eastern Kazakhstan). This was led by Karl Struve, a celebrated Russian-born astronomer of German heritage, and sponsored by the Russian Geographical Society. It was to a life of exploring that Potanin returned once freed from his obligations to the state after 1874.

During 1876–1877 he traveled in northwest Mongolia and to Tuva (on the Russian-Mongolian border east of Altai). In 1879–1880 he explored parts of eastern Tibet and the north of China. The years 1884–1886 he spent in the Tangut-Tibetan region. He returned to central Mongolia during 1892–1893. In 1899 he visited the Greater Khingan Mountains, a volcanic range in the Chinese northeast. His wife, A. V. Potanina, shared almost all of these journeys. She died near Chung-king in 1863.

Although Potanin's early Central Asian expeditions overlapped with Przheval'skii's, his later ones are usually grouped along with those of the many other Russians who "continued" Przheval'skii's work. Overall, Potanin's efforts both complemented and expanded upon Przheval'skii's. In one of Przheval'skii's weaker areas — ethnography — Potanin was particularly distinguished, collecting vast amounts of data and offering important insights into the culture, mores, art, and history of the Dungans, Tanguts, and various Mongolic and Turkic nations he encountered. He published prodigiously until some years before his death in Tomsk in 1920.

Other Russian Explorers of Central Asia

In Przheval'skii's day, and for several decades thereafter, Central Asia and western China drew many other brilliant and dedicated Russian naturalists besides those surveyed here. Among the many names and expeditions worthy of note, and of further study, but which can only be listed here, are P. A. Kropotkin (travels during 1863–1866), A. L. Chekanovskii (1869–1875), I. D. Cherskii (1873–1876, 1891), V. F. Oshanin (1876–1878), G. E. Grum-Grzhimailo (1884–1914), V. A. Obruchev (1886–1888), D. A. Klements (1891–1898), V. A. Obruchev (1892–1894, 1905–1906, 1909), V. V. Sapozhnikov (1895–1915), and G. Ts. Tsybikov (1899–1902). Geological and metallurgical studies of the region were pioneered beginning in the 1870s by Grigorii Petrovich Gel'mersen, while N. M. Iadrintsev discovered the ruins of Genghis Khan's ancient capital at Karakorum during an expedition in 1878–1891. During 1866–1878, Nikolai Alekseevich Severtsov carried out the first in-depth study of the fauna of Turkestan — a field to which major contributions were made also (especially in ornithology) by the aforementioned Roborovskii, Kozlov, and others.

In 1868–1871, while Przheval'skii was just planning and then embarking on his first Central Asian expedition, Aleksei Pavlovich Fedchenko journeyed through Turkestan, exploring in particular the lower portions of the Syr-Dariia River (the northernmost of the Aral Sea's two tributaries) and hitherto unknown regions in the vicinity of Kokand. Fedchenko also carried out the first Russian exploration of the Alai Valley at the western end of the Tian Shan. He discovered the Zaalai Range in Kirghizia and drew "the first orographical map of the Gissar-Alai mountain system."[33] His account was published posthumously in five volumes as *The Journey to Turkestan of A. P. Fedchenko* (1872–1877).[34]

* * *

Given the mystery and alluring beauty of Central Asia, Tibet especially, it is perhaps not surprising to hear a Soviet-era author note a curious irony: that by the end of the nineteenth century, thanks to the men listed above, more was known of these distant lands than of some of the parts of Russia bordering them. Drawn to distant targets, Semenov Tian-Shanskii, Przheval'skii, and others had "passed through [south and eastern Russia's largely uncharted] border regions without paying them any attention."[35] These regions, consequently, constituted a focus of attention for a new generation of Russian explorers beginning around 1895 and continuing far beyond. The construction of the Trans-Siberian railroad between 1891 and 1916 and the advent of Soviet power in 1917 would only intensify these trends. By this time, however, new and even more forbidding frontiers were beckoning Russian explorers: the North and South Polar regions.

Further Reading in Russian and English

Website

The Komarov Botanical Institute (Collections of Przheval'skii and many other Russian naturalists-explorers). http://www.mobot.org/MOBOT/Research/LEguide/index.html.

Books and Articles

Andreyev, Alexandre. *Soviet Russia and Tibet: The Debacle of Secret Diplomacy, 1918–1930s*. Leiden: Brill Academic Publishers, 2003.
Bassin, Mark, *Imperial Visions: Nationalist Imagination and Geographical Expansion in the Russian Far East, 1840–1865*. Cambridge: Cambridge University Press, 2006.
Breyfogle, Nicholas B., Abby Schrader, and Willard Sunderland, eds. *Peopling the Russian Periphery: Borderland Colonization in Eurasian History*. London: Routledge Publishers, 2007.
Dubrovin, N. F. *Nikolai Mikhailovich Przheval'skii: Biograficheskii ocherk*. St. Petersburg: Berezovsky, 1890.
Izvestiia Vsesoiuznogo Geograficheskogo Obshchestva, 72/4[–]5 (1940): 456[–]705. (This is a special issue of the *Proceedings of the Geographical Society of the USSR* dedicated to Przheval'skii. It contains a full annotated bibliography of nearly 1,000 publications relating to him (including his own works).
Karataev, N. M. *Nikolai Mikhailovich Przheval'skii, pervyi issledovatel' prirody Tsentral'noi Azii*. Moscow: Academy of Sciences of the USSR, 1948.
Kozlov, I. V. *Velikii puteshestvennik: Zhizn' i deiatel'nost' N. M. Przheval'skogo, pervogo issledovatelia prirody Tsentral'noi Azii*. Moscow: Mysl', 1985.
Kozlov, P. K. *V aziatskikh prostorakh. Kniga o zhizni i puteshestviiakh N. M. Przheval'skogo*. Khabarovsk, 1971.
Lincoln, W. Bruce. *Petr Petrovich Semenov-Tian-Shanskii: The Life of a Russian Geographer*. Newtonville, MA: Oriental Research Partners, 1980.
Murzaev, E. M. "Nikolai Mikhailovich Przheval'skii (1839[–]1888)." In *Tvortsy otechestvennoi nauki: geografi*. Edited by V.A. Esakov. Moscow: Agar, 1996.

_____, A. V. Postnikov, and G. V. Sdasiuk. *N. M. Przheval'skii i sovremennaia geografiia (k 150-letiiu so dnia rozhdeniia).* Moscow: Znanie, 1989.

Palace, Wendy. *The British Empire and Tibet, 1900–1922.* London: Routledge-Curzon, 2005.

Przheval'skii, N. M. *Ot Kiakhty na istoki zheltoi reki: Issledovanie severnoi okrainy Tibeta i put' cherez Lob-Nor po basseinu Tarima.* Moscow: OGIZ, 1948.

Rayfield, Donald. *The Dream of Lhasa: The Life of Nikolay Przhevalsky, Explorer of Central Asia.* Columbus: Ohio University Press, 1976, 3.

Sapozhnikov, V. V. *Po Russkomu i Mongol'skomu altaiu.* Moscow: Gosudarstvennoe Izdatel'stvo, 1949.

Semenov-Tian-Shanskii, Petr Petrovich. *Travels in the Tian'-Shan': 1856–57.* Edited by Colin Thomas. Translated by Liudmila Gilmour, Colin Thomas, and Marcus Wheeler. London: Hakluyt Society, 1998.

Stockwell, Foster. *Westerners in China: A History of Exploration and Trade, Ancient Times through the Present.* Jefferson, NC: McFarland, 2003.

Zelenin, A.V.. *Puteshestviia N.M. Przheval'skago.* 2 vols. St. Petersburg: Soykin, 1900.

Chapter 7

To the Ends of the Earth: Russians in the North and South Polar Regions

North of the Russian-Arctic littoral lie several islands or island groups, many of substantial size (map 12). Those located close to the Eurasian mainland include Kolguev, Vaigach and Novaia Zemlia, Severnaia Zemlia, the Novosibirskye (or New Siberian) Islands, and Wrangel Island; together they comprise a total land area of about 70,000 square miles. Russians played important roles in the discovery or exploration of all of them. The Russian role diminishes, however, for Arctic destinations more distant from the home mainland. The Franz Josef Land archipelago, for example, is only slightly farther north than Severnaia Zemlia, but is separated from Russia by hundreds of miles of ocean. Though now a Russian possession, it was discovered by an Austro-Hungarian expedition in 1873.[1] Farther north still, particularly in the race to reach the Pole itself, Russians played a negligible role until after the Bolshevik Revolution of 1917, by which time the main prizes had already been won by other nations' explorers.[2] Nonetheless — and remarkably, given its late start — the Soviet Union managed to make an indelible mark on exploration of the region after 1917, as will be seen.

At the opposite end of the earth, Russians, although ultimately overshadowed by British, American, and Scandinavian explorers, in the early nineteenth century assured themselves a coveted, early place in the history of Antarctic discovery and exploration with the hugely successful but rather forgotten voyage made by F. F. Bellingshausen during 1819–1821. After a lengthy interlude, the Soviets followed his lead, making important contributions in explorations toward and at the South Pole.

Northward Bound: Russians in the High Arctic

Easy Discoveries: Small Offshore Islands

No great leap was needed for the Russians to make their first discoveries beyond their own northern coastline. Several islands lie so close to the Eurasian mainland that they can be seen from it in clear weather. Vaigach, for example (located just north of the Iugorskii Peninsula), was, according to some Russian accounts, discovered in the 1600s by an obscure Russian mariner of the same name. In fact, the Englishman Steven Barrow had already landed there in 1556, though it is unclear if he was aware he was on an island. Neither the Russian nor the Englishman was the first person there in any case. Since at least the four-

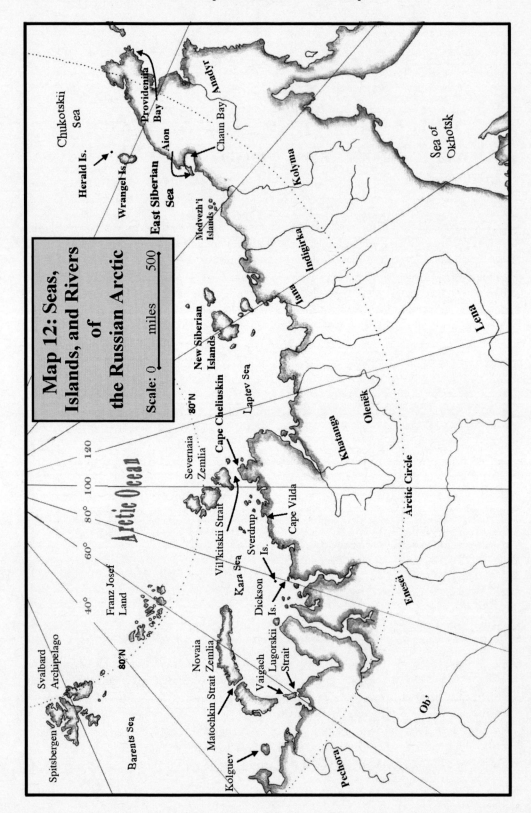

Map 12: Seas, Islands, and Rivers of the Russian Arctic

teenth century the island had been visited frequently, but never settled, by the Nentsy, indigenes of the Russian mainland to the south. Little is known of the discovery of other minor offshore islands, including Bol'shoi Begichev (at the mouth of the Khatanga River) and Aion (at the mouth of Chaun Bay). Slightly more remote (at fifty miles from land), Kolguev Island (located in the Barents Sea near the Kanin Peninsula) was known probably from the eleventh century to the Pomory. Though these and other islands close to the mainland were discovered early, many long remained only vaguely known and improperly charted. Kolguev and Vaigach, for example, were properly surveyed only during the 1920s, by A. I. Tolmachev and I. A. Perfil'ev.[3]

Novaia Zemlia

The discovery of Novaia Zemlia ("New Land"), the largest island north of Eurasia, is also lost to history. Russians — the Pomory and Novgorod traders — were already visiting by the eleventh century. The Englishman Hugh Willoughby made the first officially recorded landing in 1553. And in 1596 the Dutchman Willem Barents mapped the west coast and then wintered near the island's northeast extremity. Until much later, however, no one managed to circumnavigate the *whole* of Novaia Zemlia, leading to the perpetuation of serious errors about its basic geography. Many seventeenth-century Russian navigators, for example, believed it to be much bigger than it actually is, extending perhaps all the way along the north Eurasian coast even to America. And it was long mistaken for a single island when in fact it is two.

Some of the first detailed information about Novaia Zemlia came from an expedition of 1768–1769 led by the Russian Fedor Rozmyslov (d. 1771). Failing in his primary goal of navigating the Northeast Passage, he arrived at Matochkin Strait — the narrow strip of water separating Novaia Zemlia's two main islands — and made an important survey of the area. Fedor Petrovich Litke (1797–1882) mapped the west coast of the islands in 1821–1824, but still questions remained, especially about their northeastern stretches. These were answered only in the 1920s, as detailed surveys of the area were made by Soviet ships, especially the *Taimyr*.

Severnaia Zemlia

Looking at a modern map of the Arctic, it is easy to imagine Novaia Zemlia — with its northeastern-slanting orientation — pointing directly to a group of islands just north of the Taimyr Peninsula. These are the islands of Severnaia Zemlia ("Northern Land"). In fact, Severnaia Zemlia would prove to be one of the most elusive land masses on the face of the earth — finally discovered only in 1913 by the Russian Northern Arctic Ocean Hydrographic Expedition under the command of Boris Andreevich Vil'kitskii (1885–1961). This was certainly a major event. Severnaia Zemlia was the "last [discovered] big tract of land in the world." Finding it, in one Russian opinion, was "the greatest geographical discovery of the first quarter of the 20th century."[4]

It is possible, though not very likely, that 1913 may have represented only a *re*-discovery. In the late 1600s the Dutch mariner Nicolaas Witsen (1641–1717) noted reports "from Russian sources" about the existence of rich walrus-hunting lands, called the Sobach'ye ("Dog") Islands, located east of Novaia Zemlia. Some Russian historians have wondered if this was not a reference to Severnaia Zemlia itself, and even suggest the possibility that the islands were well known to seventeenth-century Russians, then became completely forgotten.[5] So far, however, the evidence is scant for such a claim.

Still, it is surprising that the islands should have remained unknown so long. At its closest, near Cape Cheliuskin, Severnaia Zemlia is only thirty-six miles from the Russian mainland. Yet somehow all earlier passers-by managed to miss it — from Tolstoukhov in the 1680s to Nordenskjöld in 1878 (see chapter 3). Nordenskjöld's expedition, however, did at least raise suspicions of the existence of land to the north. Crew members aboard the *Vega*'s companion ship, the *Lena*, while trying unsuccessfully to skirt north around heavy ice, noted flocks of geese coming from the north. Nordenskjöld soon saw similar signs, including large numbers of pharlaropes and brant geese on a similar southward track.[6] The land itself remained unseen, however. Other famous passers-by also missed the discovery, including the Norwegian polar explorer Fridtjof Nansen in 1893, and the Russian Baron Eduard Vasil'evich Toll in 1901. The area's trademark fogs no doubt played a major role.

THE RUSSIAN ARCTIC OCEAN HYDROGRAPHIC EXPEDITION OF 1910–1915 AND THE DISCOVERY OF SEVERNAIA ZEMLIA

This expedition was intended by the Russian government as a major effort toward turning the Northeast Passage into a regularly navigable Northern Sea Route. Its primary task sounded deceptively mundane: a comprehensive survey of the coastal waters between the Chukotskii and Kara Seas (including extensive underwater soundings). Should the opportunity present itself, the expedition was also charged with a more compelling mission: completing what would be only the second ever crossing of the route — following Nordenskjöld's pioneering achievement of 1878 — and the first ever from east to west. Not only was all this achieved but the expedition also made humanity's very last discovery of a major piece of new land: that of Severnaia Zemlia.

Officially begun in 1910, the Russian Arctic Ocean Hydrographic Expedition comprised two purpose-built vessels, the *Taimyr* and the *Vaigach*. Both were icebreakers, fifty-four meters in length, displacing 1,200 tons, and producing 1,220 horsepower. Their double-steel hulls were relatively flat profiled, offering good protection against ice crushes — but at a significant cost in stability (and seasickness!). The ships departed from St. Petersburg in November 1909, headed for the expedition's starting point, Vladivostok. For now, the *Taimyr* was commanded by naval officer F. A. Matisen and the *Vaigach* by A. V. Kolchak (the later counter-revolutionary general). The man remembered by history as expedition commander, captain of the *Taimyr*, and discoverer of Severnaia Zemlia — B. A. Vil'kitskii — was at this point unassociated with the operation. He would take command only in 1913, just in time to reap the credit for the main discovery. Already on board in 1909, however, was L. M. Starokadomskii, ship's doctor and the author of an important published narrative of the expedition.[7]

It is interesting to compare, briefly, the experiences of this expedition to those of earlier times, such as Bering's, in terms of the preliminary journey from St. Petersburg to the Russian Far East. What had in the eighteenth century required several years of unimaginable hardship — the trudge overland and along rivers across Siberia by foot, animal, and sled — was now, thanks to the opening up of maritime routes and improved shipping, a comparatively leisurely, if long, sail — in this case from Kronstadt (near St. Petersburg) to Vladivostok (on the Pacific coast) via the Suez Canal and Indian Ocean. While there were certainly hardships — bad weather, on-board illness, boiler repairs and regular maintenance, and so on — there was also time for sightseeing, at least for the officers, as Starokadomskii's engaging account makes clear. A two-and-a-half month repair stop in Le Havre near year's end, for example, facilitated trips to Rouen, Paris, and London.

At Port Said, the captain of the *Taimyr* was recalled and replaced by one A. Makalinskii. The crew passed the layover with trips to the Sphinx and pyramids at Giza. Then it was through the Suez Canal, with quick pauses at Ismailia and Suez itself. After this, calls were made at the ports of Perim (near the Red Sea mouth) and Djibouti. From the latter, some of the officers managed to visit Addis-Ababa. For some of those left behind, the beach beckoned. But here, Starokadomskii reports, things soon turned for the worse. A number of crew members, enjoying the seashore and fine weather, accidentally "trod on, and one man even stumbled and sat on sea urchins. These animals bristle with spines, which are not very numerous, but are up to ten cm in length. The brittle spines break off after entering the body and cause a burning pain. Fortunately, the pain soon passes after the pieces of spine have been removed." Suitably chastened, the Russians headed into the Indian Ocean and on to Colombo, Ceylon.[8] Here, there were parades to be enjoyed, as well as brightly dressed locals, botanical gardens, and fresh coconut milk, which the Russians found a particular delight. After a stop at Sabang in western Indonesia the expedition pulled into Singapore. Here they encountered an unpleasant reminder of their country's defeat nearly a decade earlier in the Russo-Japanese War of 1904–1905: a ship called the *Azami*, which the Russians quickly recognized as their own sunken vessel, the *Variag*, now raised, restored, and flying the Japanese flag. The intriguing delights of breadfruit, pineapples, mangoes, and so on, helped take away some of the bitterness before the next port, Saigon, was reached. After this the route led to Cam Ranh Bay, Vietnam, then to Shanghai, and —finally— Vladivostok, which was reached on 16 July 1910 after eight months at sea. Here, the crews were changed and one new captain installed: B. V. Davidov on the *Taimyr*. Kolchak remained as captain of the *Vaigach* for one more season. He was replaced in 1911 by K. V. Loman. Only Starokadomskii and a handful of others stayed on throughout. I. S. Sergeev, the new overall expedition leader (through to 1913), arrived in August. The beaches and fresh coconuts lay far behind; spiny urchins would be replaced with other dangers.

The ships' first foray north was only a teaser. With the season already late (departure occurred August 30), there was time only to carry out surveying work as far as Provideniia Bay, at the south end of the Bering Straits, before heading back to Zolotoi Rog Harbor in Vladivostok. The next year was almost the same. Time was spent replacing Kolchak with Loman. Then there were mechanical troubles. Only on August 4 did the expedition finally get out of port. Setting a good pace, they passed Provideniia Bay, the previous season's turnaround point, on the 18th. On the 24th they entered the Arctic. By September 3, according to Starokadomskii, the "first goal of our voyage had been achieved. The coast from Bering Strait to the Kolyma [River] had been accurately re-plotted on the map. We had recorded the depths along uninterrupted traverses, and several marine navigation beacons had been set up along the coast and on islands. The data gathered by the expedition would allow the compilation of a pilot, i.e. sailing directions, from Vladivostok to the Kolyma."[9] On September 8, the vessels turned back for Vladivostok, separating en route to allow the *Vaigach* to explore Wrangel Island.

The following two years followed a similar pattern. As Starokadomskii tells it, each year, beginning in 1911, he and many coexpeditionists hoped that *this* would be the year they would not turn around, that *this time* they would finally push all the way west to Arkhangel'sk. But each year the rigorous schedule of surveying, the treacherous ice conditions off the Taimyr Peninsula, and "cautious" and "indecisive" leadership conspired to send them back to Vladivostok for the winter. It was far from a total loss, of course. Every year stretches of coast and many islands were surveyed, thousands of soundings were taken, and a clearer picture of the Arctic geography, above and below water, was forged.

The 1913 sailing season brought several important personnel changes. The ships' captains, Loman and Davidov, were both recalled. Their replacements, respectively, were B. A. Vil'kitskii and P. A. Novopashennyi. Two weeks after departure from Vladivostok on July 9, there was yet another change at the top. Expedition commander Sergeev suffered a debilitating brain hemorrhage. Vil'kitskii, new captain of the *Taimyr*, succeeded him.

The ships again headed for the Arctic, this time largely following separate courses toward a rendezvous at Mariia Pronchishcheva Bay on the eastern Taimyr Peninsula. According to Starokadomskii, the crew reacted with mixed feelings to the leadership changes. On the one hand, Vil'kitskii "was spoiled, fickle, and impatient" and "got along badly with his subordinates." On the other, he "showed himself as a bold, inquisitive explorer," and— unlike Sergeev—a "resolute and decisive commander" who would "not be restricted to the known route" but intended making new discoveries.[10]

There was not long to wait. On August 20, at about 5 A.M., the *Taimyr* arrived at a previously unknown, if tiny, island now known as A. I. Vil'kitskii Island, after the discoverer's father, and located at about 155°E and 76°N. A modest discovery, but it was only the beginning of a remarkable season. On September 2, reunited after a spell of separate sailing, the *Taimyr* and *Vaigach* arrived at the great obstacle: Cape Cheliuskin. Even at this late date in history, only a few navigators had managed to round it fully, including, in recent memory, Nordenskjöld in 1878, Nansen in 1893, and Toll in 1901. The ice conditions this year were far from favorable. Determined to find a way through, and assuming that the ice in his way was attached to the Asian coast, Vil'kitskii directed his ships north in search of open water. Suddenly, and unexpectedly, land appeared—a second island discovery, now known as Malyi ("Little") Taimyr. Vil'kitskii led a survey of the island's east coast, while Novopashennyi tried and failed to steer the *Vaigach* through the ice to the south. While waiting for its sister ship to catch up, the *Taimyr* anchored, allowing a few crew members to spend three hours on what Starokadomskii described as a "lifeless" and "dreary" rock.[11] And then it was back to the business of finding a route west through the ice.

Heading north of Malyi Taimyr the ships quickly ran into another surprise—icebergs. In all the records of Russian or other navigations this was perhaps the first time icebergs— a by-product of glacial or ice-shelf breakup, and an indicator of land—had been encountered anywhere along the Arctic coast between the Bering Straits and the Taimyr Peninsula. Their origins mystified the crew: had the icebergs drifted here all the way from Franz-Josef Land or Novaia Zemlia?[12] The answer, hidden for the moment in the early morning Arctic twilight, lay just ahead. Let Starokadomskii pick up the narrative:

> [The night of September 2–3] was overcast.... [T]he nights, while still short, have ceased to be light. The consolidated ice edge, along which we were steaming, was powdered with snow, which smoothed out the irregularities in the ice. To port and starboard of our course, dark patches could be seen in the cloudy sky—indications that there was open water somewhere over there. The edge of the fast ice was gently deviating off to the west.
>
> I did not feel like sleeping. I was standing on the bridge and gazing at the scattered, broken ice through which *Taimyr* was forging. At 0400 hours ... [the] Warrant Officer ... came on watch ...[,] stood near me, and leaning on the rail, fell deep in thought about something. The expedition leader [Vil'kitskii] was sitting dozing in the charthouse, wrapped in an enormous sheepskin coat.
>
> Dawn was breaking, but the horizon was still hidden in the haze. And suddenly, ahead

and a little to starboard of our source, I began to make out the vague outlines of a high coastline....

Was I the victim of ... an optical illusion? No, there could be no mistake: I could definitely see land....

Restraining my excitement, I stepped into the charthouse and woke the expedition leader.[13]

The watch on the *Vaigach* made the discovery almost simultaneously. Vil'kitskii, to whom — as commander — the honor of discovery redounded, divided up surveying labors in the same manner as he had done with Malyi Taimyr: the *Vaigach* was sent west along the south shore, the *Taimyr* north along the east shore. As with the previous island, the *Vaigach* found its course blocked by ice while the *Taimyr* sailed on unhindered. The *Vaigach*, however, took the opportunity to anchor. Within an hour a landing party had scrambled across the ice and onto the unknown land. Later, the Russian flag was hoisted and the following proclamation read out: "While fulfilling our instructions ... to travel ... west in search of the Great Northern route from the Pacific Ocean to the Atlantic, we were able to reach a place where man has never been before, and to discover land of which no one has ever imagined."[14]

They returned to ship a few hours later with rock and other samples, but were still unable to proceed west. On the 4th, the *Vaigach* headed north after its twin. The *Taimyr*, meanwhile, reconnoitered the east coast northwards until the land trended west, a little above 81°N. But then the ice blocked their way, too. Stymied at all points north, but buoyed by the great discovery, the expedition resolved to head south again and look for a westward opening near the mainland coast.

On September 8 the *Taimyr* anchored off the recently discovered Malyi Taimyr. Starokadomskii and others went on land. While walking, Starokadomskii happened to glance beyond the north end of the island where he saw — the word *discovered* seems almost too grand for such an easy catch — the island that now bears his name.

Yet for all these exciting developments, the officers and crew quickly understood that the discovery of Severnaia Zemlia was in fact a mixed blessing. Though the new land was obviously a major acquisition for the Russian Empire, it also immediately changed the status of the waters north of Cape Cheliuskin from open sea to narrow straits. This in turn meant a perpetually greater tendency towards icing (and also explained the mystery of the icebergs). As if to confirm these fears, all further efforts at westward progress ran into impassable ice. On the 13th — with the great prize, the Northern Sea Route, appearing more unattainable than ever, the expedition gave it up and turned yet again toward Vladivostok, which they reached on November 25.

The clouds of World War I were fast gathering as the expedition set out again on 7 June 1914 from Zolotoi Rog, through Tsugaru Strait (separating Honshu from Hokkaido) and into the Pacific. Three weeks later, Archduke Franz Ferdinand — and with him the prospects for peace — lay dead. For a time it seemed that the expedition might be called off too. Several of the crew and officers expressed a desire to head to the front. But the expedition was ordered instead to continue. (In fact, several officers and crew went on to fight — and some to die — in the war, after the expedition's end in the fall of 1915.) The arrival of war underscored the long-acknowledged potential role a viable Northern Sea Route might eventually come to play in Russian military affairs. Consequently, along with the usual surveying duties, greater emphasis was placed on pushing through to Arkhangel'sk.

The ships rounded Provideniia Bay on July 28. By mid–August they were in the area of Wrangel Island where the expedition offered assistance to members of a stranded Canadian expedition (on the ship *Karluk*). On August 27 the crew of *Vaigach* discovered another new island, this one north of Vil'kitskii Island and now called Zhokhov Island. These were all interesting and worthy achievements. But ahead, as it had every year since 1911, lay the real test — the Taimyr Peninsula, which the ships reached at the start of September. With the weather already turning and Vladivostok dangerously far behind — and with the more adventurous Vil'kitskii in command — it looked this time as if the through route would be a go. The peninsula, however, had other ideas.

On the 3rd, the two ships entered Vil'kitskii Strait (named after the captain) and immediately ran into heavy fog and treacherous ice. On the 5th, moving west past the Firnlaias, one among the many small island groups dotting the region close to its namesake coast, the *Taimyr* suddenly became trapped between two enormous — and converging — ice sheets. The vise closed quickly, causing extensive damage to the ship's port side. Frigid water gushed in. The *Vaigach* tried to help but got frozen in too, damaged its propeller, and sprang a minor leak. But just when things seemed at their most desperate, a radio signal was unexpectedly received. The unknown caller turned out to be Harald Sverdrup, a Norwegian oceanographer aboard the *Eclipse*. Sverdrup and a mostly Norwegian crew were currently participating in a Russian-commissioned search for missing Russian explorers Brusilov and Rusanov.[15] The *Eclipse* remained in radio contact from a distance of some 160 miles as it wintered at Mys Vil'da. It was not able to provide a rescue, however. Although the *Vaigach* and the *Taimyr* were able to escape the worst of the ice clutches, they remained hemmed in — "the *Taimyr* at 76°40'N; 100°30'E and *Vaigach* sixteen miles north-northwest of her."[16] Wintering over was now inevitable.

Though the ships were able to avoid being crushed in the ice, new dangers lurked in the long, frigid, and dark season now setting in. Depression and other psychological disorders were kept at bay as best as possible by a rigorous schedule of busy work and exercising. But crowded conditions, gnawing boredom, and a constant diet of the same old tinned meat raised stress levels. By October, with the light nearly gone altogether for the next few months, it became very hard indeed to keep spirits up. Great efforts were made to enjoy Christmas and New Year, which were celebrated with as much gusto and provisions as could be mustered.

Radio technology at the time allowed for reception and transmission only within a radius of several hundred miles — enough to keep the two ships in contact with each other and with Sverdrup's *Eclipse*, but not enough for contact with loved ones back in Russia. By relaying messages via Sverdrup the two Russian ships were, however, able eventually to establish and irregularly maintain indirect contact with a Russia station at Iugorskii Strait, a thousand miles to the west. Although this greatly lessened the crew's sense of isolation, radio contact was no substitute for mobility. Even the ship's decks and the surrounding ice provided little respite from monotony and crowding. For four months, from November to March, the temperature rarely rose above minus 30° C., making excursions difficult.

Then on February 14 there appeared a wonderful sight, no less inspiring for its predictability: the sun. Although it rose only slightly, creating a short noon time brightening on the horizon before sinking into the blackness again, it spelled the end of eternal night. Spirits improved. Light, even in short doses, made possible surveying and other work. Even the prospects for hunting looked up. What still remained unclear, however, was whether or not the summer, once it came, would be long and warm enough to melt the ice sufficiently to allow escape. For several more months the possibility could not be ruled out of a second winter sentence. In the spring, as the days lengthened, forty men were sent overland to the

Eclipse, primarily to hunt, reconnoiter food supplies, and plan for just such an undesirable outcome.

It was not to prove necessary. On July 21 both the *Taimyr* and *Vaigach* began to move. Though neither ship was yet free from the ice, the floes in which they were (independently) stuck had now broken free of their surrounding sheets. But there was also bad news. Unable still to break free entirely, the two ships were drifting with the ice toward shallows. Then, on August 8, with little time to spare, both suddenly broke completely free. By now the *Eclipse* too was sailing freely, making the expedition a trio. Troubles still lay ahead, however. On the 11th the *Taimyr* grounded off the mouth of the Taimyr River, sustaining damage to the hull. To lighten the vessel, more than 100 tons of drinking water were dumped. Even so, the *Taimyr* remained stuck until the *Vaigach* arrived and towed her out of the shallows.

The worst was now over. With the *Vaigach* in the lead, the expedition continued west. The winter had been faced and beaten. The forty who had earlier overlanded to meet Sverdrup were picked up on September 6 by the *Vaigach* at the mouth of the Enisei. In late August, with the Taimyr Peninsula and the worst of the ice behind them, the three ships took on supplies not far from modern-day Sverdrup Island before landing on August 30 at Dikson Island.

Leaving here on September 8, Vil'kitskii and the rest — now virtually assured of a successful first crossing of the Northern Sea Route from east to west — faced little more than a simple westward victory lap. All three ships arrived around midday, September 16, at Arkhangel'sk. Considering the dangers they had faced, they had all come through remarkably well — although not unscathed: uraemia and peritonitis, the isolated conditions of the winter ice, and a winching accident had taken a handful of lives. Vil'kitskii's great geographical discovery was at first named Nicholas II Land, in honor of the tsar. In 1926 a decree of the USSR's Central Executive Committee changed this to Severnaia Zemlia, its current designation.[17]

Fundamental questions remained about the nature of Vil'kitskii's discovery, however. Was it a single landmass or a group of islands? What did its interior look like? What minerals and other resources might it offer? These questions were largely resolved by Soviet expeditions in the 1930s, especially one of 1930–1932 — led by G. A. Ushakov and N. N. Urvantsev under the auspices of the Arctic Institute — which in addition to mapping and exploring much of the archipelago also discovered further territory in the area: Schmit Island, Dlinnyi Island, and the Sedov Archipelago. An evocative description of the area's scenic attractions was given by Ushakov, writing of the vicinity of the Soviet base on Severnaia Zemlia: "I have seen God-forsaken Chukotka Peninsula, blizzard-ridden Wrangel Island, twice visited fog enshrouded Novaya Zemlya, and I have seen Franz Josef Land with its enamel sky and proud cliffs garbed in blue, hardened glacial streams, but nowhere did I witness such grimness or such depressing, lifeless relief as on our little island."[18]

There is a twist to the story of the discovery of Severnaia Zemlia. In July 1947, a skeleton was found on Bolshevik Island (the southernmost major island in the group), along with the badly rotted remains of a small boat and campfire. These are believed to be the remains of Rusanov's expedition of 1912 in the *Gerkules* (*Hercules*). The possibility that Rusanov might have been the discoverer of Servernaia Zemlia thus cannot be ruled out.

The New Siberian (Novosibirskye) Islands

The discovery of land in the New Siberian Islands has sometimes been attributed to one Maksim Mukhoplev, about whom nearly nothing is known.[19] The attribution seems apocryphal, however. It is likely that some of the islands were visited even earlier by native peoples from the mainland, but this too is uncertain.

The first reliable information on the islands probably derives from the early-eighteenth-century Cossacks Ia. Permiakov and M. Vagin, both whom sighted one or more of the nearer islands but do not seem to have landed. Vagin in particular is considered to have sighted Bol'shoi Liakhovskii, one of the smallest islands of the group and close to the mainland, in 1712. The first landings, about which little is known, probably occurred between 1759 and 1773.

In 1770 a Russian merchant named Ivan Liakhov (d. 1800) explored in the same area, passing among some of the southernmost of the New Siberian Islands. These now bear his name. During 1773–1774 Liakhov explored further and discovered Kotel'nyi Island, the largest of the entire group. A little closer to the mainland, in 1775, with S. Khvoinov, he surveyed his earlier discovery, Bol'shoi Liakhovskii. During 1808–1810, Matvei Matveevich Gedenshtrom (c. 1780–1845) led an expedition to the New Siberian Islands. One member of his team, Ia. Sannikov, subsequently claimed to have seen land northwest of Kotel'nyi Island, where there is, in fact, nothing but sea and ice. This putative "Sannikov Land," however, long remained a phantom fixture in the Russian imagination, not being fully put to rest until well into the twentieth century. In all other respects, however, Sannikov provided relatively accurate and useful information on the disposition of the main New Siberian Islands. During 1821–1823 the Russian explorer P. F. Anzhu added further to knowledge of the area. Detailed surveys were carried out by the Soviets beginning in the 1920s.

Wrangel Island

Wrangel is the easternmost of the major islands north of the Russian Arctic coast. The first information on its existence was given to the Russians during the early 1700s by Chukchi natives on the peninsula south of the island and on the Medvezh'i ("Bear") Islands several hundred miles to the west.[20] It was finally and officially discovered in 1849 by the British captain Henry Kellet. But between these times, Russians tried long and hard to find it themselves and came tantalizingly close. As well as native reports, Russian belief in the island's existence was fired in the later eighteenth century by evidence from tide and ice movements in the region. (Opinions also existed in the eighteenth century that the land might be a far westward extension of the American continent.)

A Russian Cossack, Sergeant Stepan Andreev, traveled in 1763 "north from the mouth of the Krestvaia" river to the Medvezh'i Islands. From here he reported having seen a larger landmass to the east. Six years later, however, the Russian surveyors Leontev, Lisev and Pushkarev, sailed in this same region and "established the fact that there is no land east of the [Medvezh'i] Islands near enough to be seen from them" and that what Andreev had seen was in fact part of the Eurasian mainland itself.[21] Nonetheless, rumors persisted long thereafter that Andreev had seen Wrangel Island. In 1820 the Russian government sent Baron Ferdinand von Wrangel (for whom the island was eventually named) and Admiral Fedor Fedorovich Matiushchkin (1799–1872) on a four-year expedition to resolve the matter once and for all. Some sources argue that the expedition sighted the island, and even tried unsuccessfully to reach it across the ice. More likely, they got within about fifty miles or so, but never within sight, of the island.[22]

The island finally and definitively yielded itself to the aforementioned Kellet, sailing on HMS *Herald*, in search of another lost expedition.[23] On August 6 by the western calendar, Kellet discovered, named, and landed on Herald Island, from which Wrangel (first dubbed

Kellet's Land) was visible to the west. Over the following decades the island was visited only rarely, and passed from British to American formal possession, though neither power made much effort to secure its claim. Though the first Russian visit came only in 1911 as part of the grand itinerary of the Russian Arctic Ocean Hydrographic Expedition of 1910–1915 discussed above, the Russian explorer Wrangel's name was attached forever to the island in 1867 as a gesture of respect from the American whaler Thomas Long (who, unaware of Kellett's priority, at first thought *he* had discovered the island himself) to the man who had spent four years seeking it out. Not without contest or incident, the island eventually (and gradually) became an internationally accepted Russian possession during 1916–1926. In fact, in 1926 the USSR laid official claim to *all* lands and islands not yet claimed by other powers — including any yet to be discovered — between her existing frontiers and the North Pole (within a sweep running from 32°4' 35"E and 168°49' 36"W).

The North Pole and Nearby

During the nineteenth and early twentieth centuries the North Pole (like the South) became one the great "holy grails" of travel and the inspiration for countless heroic and tragic adventures. In early modern times, however, it was viewed simply as a point of some interest along the far more crucial (because potentially profitable) Northeast Passage. The frustrating experiences of Barents and Hudson between 1594 and 1608 (see chapter 3), which had strongly suggested the impossibility of sailing the latter, also brought down the curtain on serious efforts toward the Pole until the eighteenth century, when three were launched. To one degree or another, all were influenced by a peculiar (and surprisingly tenacious) theory holding that the Polar Sea, despite so much evidence to the contrary, was actually unfrozen and navigable — at least once one had crossed a ring of much colder water and ice circling the warmer pole.[24] Constantine John Phipps of the British Royal Navy tried this idea out in 1773 but ran into impenetrable ice and turned back after reaching 81°52'N. The other two expeditions, which preceded Phipps's by nearly a decade, were Russian ones — led by Vasilii Iakovlevich Chichagov (1726–1869).

Chichagov's interest in the Pole itself was very much in the pre-nineteenth-century tradition — as a means to finally conquer the Northeast Passage, rather than as a goal in and of itself. Following a Russian version of the same, incorrect, Polar Sea theory to which Phipps had subscribed — Chichagov hypothesized that a ship would encounter less ice if it avoided the more coast-hugging routes traditionally favored by would-be navigators of the passage and instead headed much farther north. In other words, he planned to sail between the Atlantic and Pacific Oceans not by wending his way east or west, but by sailing right across the top of the world!

Sailing with three ships (the *Chichagov*, the *Panov*, and the *Babaiev*) Chichagov departed from Arkhangel'sk headed for Alaska via a nearly due-north route in the summer of 1765. Northwest of Spitsbergen (at 80°26'N) the ice defeated him. Back in Arkhangel'sk, Chichagov, souring on ideas of relatively warm polar waters, reported that the route was impassable. He cited not only his own experience but also that of a Dutch sealing captain who had fifteen years' experience in the area and with whom he had conferred. The Russian Admiralty was not so easily convinced, however, and sent him back along a similar route the following summer, this time with instructions to winter at Klok Bay on Spitsbergen.[25] This second attempt, which technically set a record for furthest north ever sailed (reaching two degrees further north than the previous season), also failed, however.[26]

Official Russian interest in the North Polar region fell nearly to zero after Chichagov. Even the breaking of the Chichagov's latitude record in 1806 by the Brit William Scoresby, Sr.—who sailed the *Resolution* to 81°30'N[27]—had no effect. In fact, Russian maritime and exploration efforts by this time had begun to refocus instead on the Pacific, following the first successful Russian global circumnavigation, completed the very same year (see chapter 5). Thus, the history of North Polar exploration in the nineteenth century is dominated by British, American, and Scandinavian teams. Although at the century's end, all of these countries would find themselves temporarily trumped by an Italian expedition of 1899–1900 that suddenly seized the record for coming closest to the Pole,[28] the ultimate prize itself went—though not without considerable controversy–to the American Robert Edwin Peary in 1909.[29]

In this same year, Russia reentered North Polar exploration, though only modestly, when a "daring and clever young Russian" by the name of Nicholas Popov (Popoff) copiloted the *America II* airship used by U.S. journalist and explorer Walter Wellman on his fifth (and final) attempt to reach the Pole. Popov was at the helm when mechanical problems forced the expedition to give up and turn around.[30]

The first modern, fully Russian effort to reach the Pole was launched in 1912, led by navy lieutenant Georgi Iakovlevich Sedov (1877–1914). Sedov chose to sail, rather than fly. He left Arkhangel'sk late summer 1912 in the *St. Foka* (*Sviatoi Foka*) and steered for Franz Josef Land but was iced in near Pankrat'ev Island off Novaia Zemlia's west coast and forced to winter. He spent the dark season usefully, carrying out a variety of scientific work. The following summer, freed from the ice, he got as far as Hooker Island, just above 80°N in the southern stretches of Franz Josef Land. On February 2 he and two companions set off over the ice with sledges and three dog-teams. It was a foolhardy venture. Sedov was already suffering from scurvy when he set off and conditions were bleak. "While waiting out a blizzard ... just south of [Rudolf Island], he died, on March 5, 1914."[31] The two others made it safely back south to their ship and home.

By now Russian involvement in the high Arctic had begun to gain momentum. In August 1914, the Polish-Russian navigator I. I. Nagurskii (or Jan Nagórski) entered the record books when in the course of a search for the missing expeditions of Sedov, Brusilov, and Rusanov he became the first person to fly a plane north of the Arctic Circle.

The Bolshevik Revolution of 1917 greatly accelerated Russian interest and efforts in the Arctic, especially from the 1930s forward, when the Stalinist USSR purposefully and loudly pursued a policy of taming and colonizing the far north. Although the main prize — first to the Pole — had been achieved more than two decades earlier by Peary, many other prizes were still up for grabs, and new ones could always be invented. Thus several nations continued to compete for other polar firsts.[32] Soviet prestige was boosted in 1928 when Russians aboard the icebreaker *Krasin* swept elegantly towards the Pole in mid–July to effect a well-publicized rescue of the members of an Italian team led by Umberto Nobile — whose airship *Italia* had crash-landed during an unsuccessful shot at the Pole. (Nobile himself had already been evacuated on a Swedish plane long before the Russians arrived.)

Thereafter, the Soviets poured huge resources into exploration of the region, primarily in search of high-profile firsts and their propaganda value. In 1937, at the height of the Stalinist Terror, Soviet explorers undertook three separate efforts to fly nonstop from the USSR to the U.S., crossing the North Pole. The most celebrated of them was Valerii Pavlovich Chkalov (1904–1938) who, with copilots G. F. Baidukov and A. V. Beliakov, departed Moscow on the morning of June 18. Flying a Tupelov ANT-25, they crossed Franz Josef Land that same evening and passed over the Pole at 4:15 the following morning. They finally touched down triumphantly in Vancouver, Washington, on June 20, having flown 5,288 miles,[33] a new world record and the first nonstop flight between Russia and the United States. On July 12 pilots Mikhail Mikhailovich Gromov and Andrei Iumashev, and navigator Sergei Danilin set out to outdo Chkalov, flying a similar aircraft from Moscow bound for California via the Pole. Sixty-two hours later they landed successfully in San Jacinto, having set a new record of just over 6,300 miles. The new record lasted over a year, until in November 1938 Englishman Richard Kellet and crew flew 7,158 miles from Egypt to Australia.

More than in any other country, perhaps, women participated fully in many of these efforts and achievements. During 1937–1938, for example, Soviet women set numerous flying distance records. Of particular note were the flights of Valentina Grizodubova (1909/1910–1993) and Marina Raskova (1912–1943). In October 1937 the pair covered a record-breaking 898 miles. Thereafter, Raskova upped her own record twice more before sharing honors again with Grizodubova and a third copilot named Polina Osipenko, all of whom flew an ANT-37 all the way from Moscow to Khabarovsk in September 1938, covering a total of 4,001 miles. During these two years the Soviets suffered tragedies too. On 12 August 1937 Sigismund Aleksandrovich Levanevskii and four crew members disappeared over the high Arctic while chasing yet another long-distance record across the Pole from Moscow to California. No trace of Levanevskii or his crew of five was ever found, despite an eight-month search involving Soviet, American, and Canadian teams. The much-loved Chkalov himself crashed and died on December 15 the same year while test-flying a Polikarpov I-180. Considering the nature of Chkalov's earlier record, his immense popularity with the Soviet people, and the manner of his death, one is hard pressed not to see strong parallels with the life, achievement, and death of Soviet cosmonaut Iurii Gagarin two-and-a-half decades later (see chapter 8).

Despite the losses, "between 1932 and 1938, the USSR broke no fewer than sixty-two worldwide flying records [many but not all connected with Arctic routes] and made much of the fact. Aviation Day, celebrated yearly on 18 August, became one of the key holidays in the Stalinist calendar." The authenticity at least of some of these records has been challenged, however.[34]

Shmidt, the Papaninites, and the First Drifting Polar Research Station

One of the early USSR's most ambitious and successful polar exploits began as a dream to land a plane on the North Pole. Undertaken, again, in 1937, plans began to take shape during 1934–1935 under the leadership of Otto Iul'evich Shmidt (1891–1956; a.k.a. Schmidt) — director of the Arctic Institute and soon to be one of the USSR's more celebrated explorers. To make the achievement more meaningful, Shmidt planned from the start to make it a *double*-first, using the event to set up what would be the world's first North Polar research base[35] — a drifting station set on the ice.

The idea for a drifting station dates to 1884, when wreckage from the *Jeanette*, vessel of the American De Long expedition, having come to its end near Bennet Island in the De Long group (in the northern New Siberian Islands), was found subsequently on southwest Greenland. This provided some of the first direct evidence of a western-running trans–Polar current, the first real use of which was made by the Norwegian Fridtjof Nansen. Rather than avoid the ice, as all previous polar sailors had tried, in 1893 Nansen deliberately got his specially built ship, the *Fram*, frozen in, hoping in this manner simply to drift to the

Pole in an ice floe. His reasoning was generally sound, though the current actually took his ship across the Arctic well south of the Pole. The slow pace of the ice eventually got the better of Nansen, who the following year left the *Fram* and its crew, took one companion and set out, unsuccessfully, for the Pole by sledge and foot. The idea of a floating station — to study polar currents and conditions rather than to reach any particular place — impressed the Soviets, who devoted considerable resources to it and enjoyed great success, eventually launching at least thirty. The hardest part of the operation, as Shmidt saw it, was getting *to* the Pole. Getting home would simply involve letting the ice one had landed on drift away from the Pole. Eventually it could be met by ships. The project came to be called the "North-Pole-1" Expedition (*Severnyi polius-1* or SP-1).

Shmidt's first assistant on the project was academician and Arctic specialist Vladimir Iul'evich Vize (1886–1954). Ill health forced Vize out of his intended position as head of the on-site research team in favor of Ivan Dmitreevich Papanin (1894–1986). Plans called for a team of forty-four people to make all or part of the journey in a combination of planes and ships, and for a small nucleus of four to stay (for an intended nine months) at the drifting polar station itself. The four — Ernst Krenkel, Petr Shirshov, Evgeny Fedorov, and Ivan Papanin — subsequently became known fondly as the "Papaninites." Proposals were approved by the Soviet authorities in early 1936.

In March of the same year, pilots Mikhail Vodopianov and V. M. Makhotkin, took a plane north to reconnoiter likely routes. Rudolf Island, the northernmost point in Franz Josef Land, was chosen as the base from which to launch the final flight to the Pole — some 336 miles away. Construction of a facility began shortly thereafter, under the supervision of Papanin. *North Pole-1*— the Papaninites intended home at the Pole itself— was a strikingly modest affair, however: a black tent 6½ feet tall, 9 feet wide, and 12½ feet long. Back in Moscow, some elderly nuns (!) were assigned the task of stitching together the tent's three separate layers of tarpaulin, rubberized cloth, and silk. This was hung on an aluminum frame and weighed eighty pounds in total.[36] All equipment and supplies were ready by late January 1937. Most aspects of life in the USSR during the 1930s were under strict government inspection, but few more so than this highly visible expedition loaded with potential propaganda value. Consequently, on February 13, Shmidt and Papanin were summoned before Stalin and a bevy of other Soviet bigwigs, including Prime Minister Viacheslav Molotov, Commissar of Defense Kliment Voroshilov, Commissar for Heavy Industry Sergo Ordzhonikidze, and the chief of secret police, Nikolai Ezhov. With these men satisfied (Stalin, most importantly), permission was given to go ahead.

On March 22 six bright-orange Tupelov TB-3 bombers, specially outfitted for the expedition, took off under escort from Moscow. Over the next few weeks, flying via a variety of Arctic stopovers, they made their way to Rudolf Island, which they reached on April 12. At Rudolf the expedition made final preparations and waited for appropriate weather. Some three weeks later, on May 5, a reconnaissance flight reported favorable ice conditions for a landing at the Pole. Local conditions on Rudolf ruled it out, however. More than two weeks later, on May 21, both local and polar conditions finally cooperated allowing the final stage to get under way. A single N-170 plane, flown by Vodopianov, took off, bound for the Pole, carrying Shmidt, the Papaninites, and a partial crew. The flight was uneventful and the expedition safely landed at the Pole a little while later. Moscow was duly informed and sent back its congratulations. Over the next five days the other planes followed from Rudolf Island. By the 26th thirty-five men stood at the Pole. Two days later camp had been set up. On the June 6 it was opened officially with festivities. Back home, the Papaninites' early successes kicked off a spectacular month for Soviet exploration and endurance, added to mightily on the 20th by the successful trans–Polar flight of Chkalov noted above. Decorations and medals flowed.

With the "easy" part over, and camp set up, most of the Russians, Shmidt included, bade their comrades farewell and departed the Pole, leaving the four Papaninites alone at the top of the world. Though the four men remained in their tiny, claustrophobic camp for nine long months, they were not long at the Pole — their drift almost immediately took them south, though not towards the USSR as earlier calculations had indicated. Instead, by the end of 1937 *North Pole-1* was far to the west, sitting in the Greenland Sea not far to the east of Greenland itself, some 930 miles from its starting point. By now the surrounding ice floe was melting quickly, prompting the Soviets to undertake to pick up their men. The rescue, done in February, involved several ships (the icebreaker *Ermak* and the steamers *Taimyr* and *Murman*), three submarines, and a dirigible. Tragically, the dirigible crashed en route killing all thirteen on board. But on February 19 the two steamers converged on the camp and the Papaninites came on board. It was none too soon. By now their ice floe measured just thirty by fifty yards. They had been on it for 275 days.

Coinciding with some of the worst years of mass arrests and political repression in the Soviet Union, the years 1937–1938 represented an early peak of Soviet aviation-based exploration and endurance. In fact, repression and achievement went hand-in-hand, as the Soviets relentlessly pushed and used their pilots, explorers, and other brave men and women for political and propaganda purposes, hoping through their achievements to prove to the world the superiority of the Soviet socialist system. Over the following several years, however, the USSR would find itself forced instead to spend its energies on the massive trials of the Second World War. Well before the Nazis invaded in June 1941, however, other clouds had also begun to gather over the polar enterprise. Test pilot Vladimir Kokkinaki's 1939 attempt to fly directly from Moscow to the World's Fair in New York City via the Arctic, for example, ended in embarrassment when he crash-landed in Canada — a humiliation the Soviet government neither appreciated nor felt inclined to risk easily again. The political stresses of the Stalin years also took their toll on many fine explorers, including the aforementioned Chkalov, who some believe was essentially sacrificed (for becoming too popular) at Stalin's orders by being forced to fly an unready plane.[37] The purges of the middle and late 1930s senselessly ruined countless Soviet citizens' careers and lives, including those of many Arctic and Polar explorers. Papanin, for example, used the atmosphere of fear and denunciation for his own purposes and against Shmidt, whom he succeeded in 1939 as head of *Glavsevmorput* (the chief administrative body for Soviet Arctic affairs). In this instance, however, Shmidt was able ultimately to save his scientific career and life.

In the years following the end of the war, the USSR would return to the business of combining solid exploration with carefully constructed propaganda coups on behalf of Soviet socialism. By then, however, propellers were increasingly being replaced with rockets, and terrestrial routes with the goals of early space flight. This story is told in chapter 8.

Nonetheless, in the postwar era the USSR also continued to push into the front rank of nations pursuing North Polar exploration. With the Northern Sea Route now a vital economic and military supply line, little expense was spared in developing the world's best fleet of icebreakers, culminating in 1959 with the development of the nuclear-powered *Lenin*. The investment yielded an important dividend for exploration when, on 17 August 1977, another nuclear-powered icebreaker, the *Arktika*, became the first ship to sit at the Pole, after an eight-day journey from Murmansk. The Soviets repeated the feat with a different icebreaker in 1987, and numerous times thereafter.[38] Nowadays, Russian icebreakers make the journey routinely.

There is a final, possible, irony to contemplate in the history of Russian and Soviet Arctic exploration. Although an American, Peary, is traditionally granted priority as conqueror of the North Pole, and though several other non–Russians followed him thereafter before any Russian did, the first person actually to stand *exactly* at 90°N (the precise location of the geographic pole) may have been a Russian after all: the pilot P. A. Gordienko, who flew in on 23 April 1948. The claim is plausible, at least technically, since all previous explorers appear in fact to have only *approximately* reached the exact Pole (or merely flown over). This is due to the relative inaccuracy of earlier methods of geographical measurement.[39]

Southward Bound: Russians in the Antarctic Region

Prior to the early nineteenth century, the southern polar regions constituted the largest blank spot left on the face of the earth. As late as 1819, says one estimate, 37,000,000 square kilometers were completely unknown, an area larger than the whole of Africa.[40] Some of the earliest incursions into the region were made by French explorers. In 1739 Jean Baptiste Charles Bouvet de Lozier sailed to 55°S and discovered Bouvet Island. In 1772 his compatriot Marc-Joseph Marion du Fresne added the Prince Edward Islands and Crozet Island, while still another Frenchman, Yves-Joseph de Kerguelen Trémarec, discovered Kurguelen the same year. French contributions were soon eclipsed by the navigations of one of history's greatest sailors, the Englishman James Cook who during an expedition of 1772–1775 completely circumnavigated the globe in Antarctic waters (reaching as far as 71°10'S), discovering the South Sandwich Islands in the process. Cook, who was the first person to cross the Antarctic Circle, came close to discovering Antarctica itself, but turned north just short of sighting the continent.

Antarctic exploration following Cook's voyages was slight and yielded only modest discoveries, including Macquarie Island in 1810 by the Australian Frederick Hasselborough. Things took off again, however, in 1819 as sailors from two nations — Britain and Russia — made major strides south, headed, it would turn out for a nearly neck-and-neck discovery of Antarctica. First, the British: In February 1819, Englishman William Smith's ship, the *Williams*, struggling to round Cape Horn to Valparaiso, was blown off course to below 62°S at about 60°W. Smith thought he saw land here, but had no time to stop. Returning to the same place in October of the same year, he was rewarded with the discovery of the first of the South Shetland Islands. Smith, a British *promyshlennik*, if we may use the term for a non–Russian, found here rich pickings of seal fur and blubber. News of his discovery quickly leaked. Within weeks the *Williams* had been hired at Valparaiso by the British Navy, given a new commander (Edward Bransfield), and sent back to better reconnoiter the Shetlands. On January 30 (New Style) Bransfield sighted the continent at Trinity Peninsula. Unknown to him, however, a Russian — Fabian Gottlieb (in Russian usually Faddei Faddeevich) von Bellingshausen — had beaten him to it, spying the icy continent at a different point just three days previously.

Bellingshausen's Antarctic Travels

Bellingshausen is one of history's great forgotten explorers. Along with Columbus and Willem Janzsoon (the discoverer of Australia) he is one of only three men credited with the discovery not just of a new land but an entire *continent*. Yet, his discoveries were underappreciated by his contemporaries and compatriots and remain so today. Part of the problem, no doubt, is the nature of the continent he discovered. Unlike the New Worlds of the Americas and Australia, Antarctica is an uninhabitable frozen desert — in the early nineteenth century a mere geographical curiosity. Bellingshausen's fame has suffered accordingly. Also the man's journeys, though interesting and important, lack the high drama and tragedy of many better-known polar explorations, and his journals are considered a tedious read, weighted with basic facts about weather, temperature, and position. Often, one has to tease out the adventures from the monotony.

Bellingshausen's journal was not published at all until 1831, and then only 600 copies in Russian. This reflected the lack of official interest in the area, as well as the expansion of Russian maritime activities in warmer portions of the Pacific (see chapter 5). Bellingshausen's expedition also came to be tainted by association, due to the subsequent participation of a crew member named Torson, with an attempted political coup in 1825.[41] The first translation of the journal (into German) came only in 1902. The first English translation was made in 1945 by the Hakluyt Society.[42] There are relatively few secondary treatments of his life and travels. Even the Soviets, rarely ones to shy away from glorifying the geographical achievements of Russians, produced little on this man. Oddly, even the *Great Soviet Encyclopedia* gave him only the briefest of glosses. Finally, not only Bellingshausen's journal but his *discovery* is itself somewhat anticlimactic. There is no first, clearly unambiguous sighting of the continent; no triumphant moment; no pioneering step onto a new world of unforgettable sights, sounds, or smells. In fact, there is no obviously great moment at all, only an important discovery understood in retrospect from analysis of the journal. Indeed, even the basic proposition *that* Bellingshausen (rather than Bransfield) discovered Antarctica merits qualification, since it is still possible (though difficult) to question legitimately whether he really even saw the Antarctic continent at all.

Bellingshausen was born in 1778 on Ösel Island (now Saaremaa), Estonia, then part of the Russian Empire. He was of Baltic German ancestry. At age ten he entered the Russian Navy and later studied at the Naval Cadet Corps in Kronstadt. Although a bright student and a highly capable mariner, he was throughout his life a man of very few words, reputed to be awkward socially, stiff and formal in conversation. He sailed as fifth lieutenant on Kruzenstern's first Russian global circumnavigation of 1803–1806, after which time he served mostly on the Black and Baltic Seas until 1819 when he received his Antarctic commission (he was the Admiralty's second choice). As a captain he modeled himself on James Cook. He was relatively strict, but highly organized and efficient. On his Antarctic ventures he paid great attention to details of hygiene, lost only three crew (none at all to scurvy), and was well regarded by his men.

Russia at the end of the 1810s was at a relative peak of international reputation. Its armies (along with the country's climate and sheer size) had recently defeated Napoleon, and in the ensuing reorganization of European power politics, Russia had become Europe's primary gendarme, committed to preserving a conservative status quo internationally. It was against this background of national glory that the emperor Alexander I authorized two major Russian naval expeditions: one each towards the North and South Polar regions. The northbound venture, undertaken during 1819–1820, involved two navy ships, the *Otkrytie* and *Blagonamerennyi*, commanded, respectively, by M. N. Vasil'ev (1770–1847) and G. S. Shishmarev (1781–1835). The expedition's brief was to scout out a northern passage connecting the Atlantic and Pacific Oceans. Beginning in the Bering Straits, the expedition tried both easterly and westerly routes without success. Nonetheless, the two men charted much land, including — for the first time — parts of the Alaska coast north of the peninsula and as far as Icy Cape. The southern expedition, Bellingshausen's, was the first major effort toward the conjectured southern continent by any power since James Cook's celebrated second voyage of 1772–1775. Bellingshausen aimed to sail in waters Cook had missed.

Commissioned in April 1819, Bellingshausen was given two ships. The *Vostok* was a 129-foot frigate of some 500 tons, carrying 117 crew and officers. On it sailed also Ivan Zavadovskii, the expedition's overall second-in-command. The *Mirnyi*, captained by M. P. Lazarev (1788–1851), was a sloop, of similar weight, but some ten feet shorter. It would be home to seventy-three men. Though both ships were made of pine with copper-plated hulls, only the *Mirnyi* was ice-strengthened (and partly in consequence was also the slower ship).[43]

Bellingshausen was ordered to sail as far south as possible in search of Antarctic islands, and of the postulated southern continent itself. The Ministry of Naval Affairs outlined a compendium of scientific experiments, readings, specimen collections, drawings, and so on, to be undertaken. Nonetheless, and surprisingly, only one "civilian scientist" was assigned to the expedition — an astronomer named Simonov.[44] Efforts to make up the deficit en route, by recruiting in England, failed.

The ships left Kronstadt 4 July 1819. After stops at Copenhagen, Portsmouth, and Tenerife they passed the equator on October 18. During a rest at Rio de Janeiro during November the ships took on large quantities of food and other supplies. While ashore, Bellingshausen also took the opportunity to visit one of the "shops here for the sale of negroes, grown-up men, women, and children." His account of these "abominable" places with their "inhuman proprietors" is one of the few emotional — and thus one of the most engaging — parts of his whole journal.[45]

From Rio the expedition made a course for South Georgia, arriving in mid–December without major event. Here they met British whalers, carried out a rigorous survey of the southwest side of the main island, and on the 15th made what is still sometimes considered the expedition's first discovery — Annenkov Island (Bellingshausen himself thought so).[46] In fact, Cook's second expedition had already sighted it.

A week later they were at the South Sandwich Islands where the expedition made uncontestable new finds: Leskov Island on December 22 and on the following day Vysokoi (literally "high") and Zavadovski Islands.[47] The three together were dubbed the Traversay Islands in honor of the French-born current Russian minister of naval affairs.

Zavadovski Island, named (as Leskov) after expedition officers, made a particular impression. For one thing, it was volcanically active, emitting "an unbroken dense cloud" that reminded Bellingshausen of "thick smoke from the funnel of a steamer." The warmth attracted penguins; "from the base [of the island] midway up the hill every spot was covered with them." The next day, Christmas Eve, the officer Zavadovskii, in the company of two other men, was allowed to set foot on his namesake island. The place impressed the nose more than the eye. The combination of "thick stinking [volcanic] vapor" and "a particularly bad smell from the great quantity of guano from the penguins" forced the landing party to cut the visit short.[48] The modern names of many of the island's features tell a similar story: "Acrid Point, Stench Point, Fume Point, Reek Point, Pungent Point, and Noxious Bluff."[49]

Over the next few days, as the expedition moved through and beyond the South Sandwich Islands, Bellingshausen theorized that the Sandwich Island Group (also Cook's discovery) and his own Traversay Islands were geologically related, consisting "of the summits of a mountain range." This range, he speculated was in turn connected (by the Clerke rocks[50]) "with South Georgia and by the Aurora Islands with the Falkland Islands."[51] Later investigations proved this to be accurate.

The Discovery of Antarctica?

Making good progress in mostly fine weather, the expedition during the first part of January headed east in search of an opening to the south and "higher latitudes" (map 13).

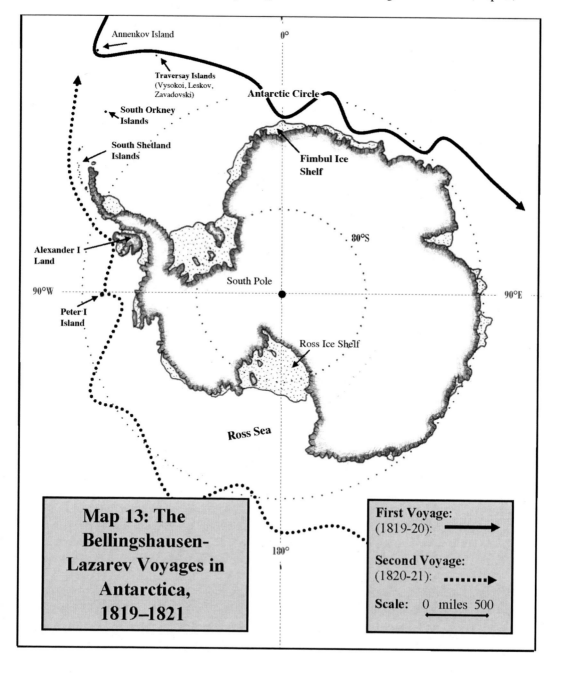

Map 13: The Bellingshausen-Lazarev Voyages in Antarctica, 1819–1821

First Voyage: (1819-20):
Second Voyage: (1820-21):
Scale: 0 miles 500

On the 8th, at about 60°S and 18°40'W, the ships encountered and shot at "a sea animal"—probably a leopard seal—some twelve feet in length. "May one conclude," Bellingshausen wrote, "on encountering such animals in the polar seas, that there is land near or not?" In fact, there was none. No islands were in the immediate vicinity and Antarctica itself lay unknown hundreds of miles south. Finally, on the 11th, at about 59°44'S and 8°11'W, Bellingshausen found an opening in the ice. The expedition turned nearly due south and progressed rapidly, crossing the Antarctic Circle on the 15th. The next day, at 69°21'28"S and 2°14'50"W he encountered impenetrable ice blocking any further southward movement. In his journal that day he noted "a solid stretch of ice running from east through south to west ... covered with hillocks."[52]

At this point Bellingshausen was off the Fimbul Ice Shelf surrounding the Crown Princess Martha Coast. It is the critical moment in our narrative: the discovery of Antarctica. Or is it? Here are the facts. First, Bellingshausen was indeed very close to the Antarctic coast, but it is not known exactly how far (from thirty down to "a few" miles, in the varied opinions of scholars[53]). Second, the ice he was looking at was not a floe but the aforementioned ice shelf, joined solidly and permanently to the Antarctic coast (the shelf does expand and contract from year to year, however). But now come the questions: is the ice shelf to be considered part of Antarctica itself? The majority opinion seems to be *yes*. The English writer Alan Gurney, for example, notes of Bellingshausen's priority that "ice shelves can be considered an integral part of the continent—not quite so obvious as [the continent itself] ... but still Antarctica."[54] Not all opinions concur, however.

Another question concerns how *far* Bellingshausen saw that day—just to the ice shelf or beyond it to indisputable solid land? The question is complicated by the fact that there is no obvious visible boundary marking the transition from ice that is covering the sea to ice that is covering the Antarctic landmass. Looking south from Bellingshausen's probable vantage point, one would simply see ice stretching out to the horizon and perhaps sloping gently up with the underlying land. But notes in his journal that day speak of poor visibility occasionally lightened by an appearance of the sun. Was he able to see far enough to be looking at land? We cannot know.

A final question concerns Bellingshausen himself. What did *he* think he had seen? His journal entries strongly suggest he thought little of the view. He makes no mention at all of a landmass or gives any sense of discovery, noting (as already quoted) only "a solid stretch of ice running from east through south to west ... covered with hillocks."[55] But perhaps he was already nurturing suspicions. In a subsequent letter to the Marquis de Traversay, dated 8 March 1820 (about six weeks later), Bellingshausen revisited the moment. This time, however, he wrote of the obstacle in his path as "continental ice." Perhaps Bellingshausen was now following the opinion of Lieutenant-Commander Zavadovskii, who immediately upon encountering it back on January 16, had used exactly the same words. Unfortunately, Bellingshausen's more recent biographers and students have not been able to agree on the meaning of the term "continental ice." For some the phrase is evidence that Bellingshausen clearly understood the ice to have been attached to a major landmass.[56] Others suspect the term is merely a vague superlative, as in "a very large amount of ice," or "stock from which smaller pieces break off."[57]

Also worthy of consideration is the claim that Bellingshausen's original narrative—long since lost without a trace—was "edited in the Russian Admiralty before publication" by "General L. I. Golenishchev-Kutuzov, a Cook enthusiast, who cut out controversial new ideas, especially if they appeared to contradict Cook."[58] The possibility thus arises that

Bellingshausen may have thought — and written — more about his discovery than we will ever know. The Russian historian M. I. Belov has argued in this direction.[59]

Bellingshausen's indistinct encounter with the continent was repeated on the 21st when at 69°25'S and 2°14'W his ships ran into "precisely an extension of [the ice] which we had seen ... on the 16th."[60] With visibility much better than on the previous date, Bellingshausen again gives no indication of an awareness of discovery, again recording simply that the ice ran east, west, and south as far as the eye could see. At this point he was perhaps thirty miles from the Antarctic coast. Given the good conditions he was almost certainly looking upon Antarctica itself. But by this time, he was no longer the first. Two days earlier, on January 19 (which was 30 January by the Western calendar at the time,[61] and thus three days after Bellingshausen's first, ambiguous, Antarctic encounter) the aforementioned Captain Edward Bransfield and William Smith, sailing on the *Williams*, a chartered vessel of the British Admiralty, had seen and charted "continuous land" south of the South Shetlands and called it Trinity Land. This was Antarctica without a doubt.[62]

Generally heading east, Bellingshausen made a third and final push south for the season. His journal entries for February 5 and 6 are tantalizing — clues of land abound and are clearly described. But never, it seems, is Bellingshausen either certain of his discovery or willing even to speculate openly. Instead he describes "floating ice [that] resembles that found in bays," "ice-covered mountains," and, perhaps most intriguing of all, a mass of ice whose "edge was perpendicular and formed into little coves, whilst the surface sloped upwards towards the south to a distance so far that its end was out of sight even from the mast-head." Was this the upward slope of the ice-covered continent itself?[63]

These descriptions have been interpreted as unrealized sightings of ice both contiguous with the continent and covering the coastal regions of the continent itself and, thus, as "the first discovery of the main Antarctic continent by man" (since Bransfield had only seen the peninsula), though with the proviso that Bellingshausen, again, seems to have been unaware what he was seeing. At this point, Bellingshausen was almost certainly off the Princess Ragnhild Coast, perhaps at a distance of fifty miles, though perhaps much closer.[64] There is no serious doubt at this point that Bellingshausen knew he was near land.

Whatever his suspicions, on March 4, changes in the weather and shortages of fuel and food provisions inspired Bellingshausen to call it a season. He ordered the ships by separate courses back to Australia. The *Vostok* arrived in Port Jackson, Sydney, in late March. The *Mirnyi* pulled in a week behind it. After a short rest the ships headed off again for a variety of South Pacific destinations, themselves of considerable interest and import (see chapter 5). In early September they returned to Sydney. On October 31, Bellingshausen took his two ships out for stage two of the Antarctic survey.

The Russians must have found Australia — at least its wildlife — fascinating. As well as livestock (for food), they had taken on board the two ships a kangaroo and eighty-four birds (mostly of the parrot family), all as pets. It is not recorded what these creatures made of the un–Australian cold that lay ahead.

A week out, the *Vostok* sprang a serious leak that could only be improperly repaired at sea and necessitated continuous pumping for the rest of the expedition. Though over 1,200 miles south of Sydney and at about the same latitude as South Georgia, Macquarie — their first port of call — presented a very different aspect: not icy white, but green and lush. This pleasant aspect, however was countered by sealers, who having recently and completely exterminated the island's fur seals, were at that moment doing the same with the remaining elephant seals. On November 20 Bellingshausen pressed south again over difficult and stormy seas.

On November 28, at 62°18'S in what is now named the Ross Sea, the ice sheet again forced Bellingshausen to start heading east, a course he eventually pursued for some 145 degrees of longitude. On this same day, however, looking south, officer Zavadovskii claimed to see land. None exists within the viewing range of this point, however.

Six weeks later, on January 10, shortly after having turned back from his furthest point south (69°53'S and 92°19'W) Bellingshausen and his crew noticed "a black patch through the haze to the east-north-east." This time, with the visibility favorable, there was no doubt, and Bellingshausen — consistent with the argument that he had indeed *not* realized his earlier probable discovery of Antarctica — wrote it up accordingly: "Words cannot describe the delight which appeared on all our faces at the cry of 'Land! Land!'" The land was "250 nautical miles farther south than any other land yet discovered." But Bellingshausen realized at once that it was not the continent. Immediately naming it Peter I Island, he nonetheless felt that "there must surely be other land in the vicinity."[65] Sure enough, a week later, at 11:00 A.M. on January 17, at approximately 68°29'S and 75°40'W, with the day "as beautiful ... [as] could have been desired in high southern latitudes," Bellingshausen sighted another shore. This time, however — as if in compensation for his earlier uncharacteristically emotional outburst of "Land! Land!" — Bellingshausen returned to his usual taciturnity, noting: "We sighted land." He followed this with a brief description of its position and main features. Bellingshausen named the discovery Alexander I Land, after his tsar. "I call this discovery 'land' [rather than an island] because its southern extent disappeared beyond the range of our vision," he wrote.[66] At this point, indeed, there was no obvious reason not to suspect it was part of the Antarctic continent itself. For reasons that can only be guessed at, Bellingshausen declined to investigate his discoveries at any length, or to search the area for still more land — decisions for which some historians have since faulted him. Not only Bellingshausen failed to take a greater interest in the islands, however. Not a single ship from any country visited either of them again for ninety years.

Turning his back on these discoveries, Bellingshausen instead set course for the South Shetlands (discovered in February 1819 by Smith) "to ascertain whether this recently discovered land belongs to the supposed Southern Continent."[67] After charting a number of islands in the group (and giving them Russian names) the expedition headed north to warmer waters, rest, and repair, arriving February 27 at Rio de Janeiro. Three months later Bellingshausen and Lazarev sailed for Russia, arriving at Kronstadt in July 1821. They had been away 751 days and sailed more than 57,000 miles.

Bellingshausen Assessed

"Provided that shelf ice attached to the ice cap of the continent can be accepted as 'land' itself, there is no doubt that Bellingshausen was the first to sight the Antarctic continent, on 16/27 January, 1820, three days before Captain William Smith and Edward Bransfield did so at Trinity Land." So says A. G. E. Jones in a detailed analysis, published two-and-a-half decades ago, of the various claims to the discovery of Antarctica.[68] This remains the dominant opinion internationally, though almost always with the caveat that Bellingshausen probably failed to understand at the time what he was looking at.

It is likely that this is the correct view. It cannot be entirely ruled out, however, that Bellingshausen may have thought more of his first encounter with the Antarctic landmass than he let on. This is suggested by the events of 15 January 1820. On this date — the day before his discovery of Antarctica — Bellingshausen crossed the Antarctic Circle: another important and memorable event. And yet he made absolutely no mention of it in his journal. There can be no doubt that he did indeed cross this line on this day. So why did he not note it down? Perhaps the answer lies in his personal character. Throughout his journal, and in life more generally, Bellingshausen comes across as a man driven by duty (and perhaps a little by curiosity), but never by ambitions for personal glory. As much as any man can be, he seems to have been immune to the stuff. Another captain might easily have written a more speculative and hopeful account of his encounters with the continent, and thereby might have fashioned a greater reputation for himself. But this was not Bellingshausen's style.

The man is certainly deserving of greater repute, however. Like Cook, Bellingshausen sailed all the way round the world at high southern latitudes — indeed, on average, at *higher* latitudes than Cook. He also made detailed and useful preliminary surveys of parts of the South Shetlands and discovered several islands, including the large one he named for Alexander I. And, of course, even if indistinctly, he discovered a whole new continent.

The Soviets in Antarctica

After Bellingshausen and Lazarev's expedition, Russian interest in the South Polar region went dormant. Unlike in the north, even the transition to Soviet authority for several decades made little difference. Partly it was a question of geography (the distance to Antarctica), but even more so of other priorities, including the huge emphasis placed on the more realistic, if still hubris-laden, matter of conquering the nearer (and contiguous) Arctic — an epic affair combing political and scientific goals, and so well treated recently by John McCannon.[69]

Significant Soviet activities in the far south began only in 1946, when the Antarctic Whaling Flotilla *Slava* began annual operations.[70] By this time, most of the important firsts had already fallen to other countries.[71] Then, along with nearly a dozen other countries, the USSR hugely ramped up Antarctic activities in preparation for International Geophysical Year (beginning 1 July 1957). During 1955–1957 the explorer-scientist M. M. Somov led the first of numerous Soviet Antarctic expeditions, a highlight of which was the establishment of the first of many Soviet Antarctic research stations. The expedition also managed to complete a trek across the continent's interior from Mirnyi to Pionerskaia, two newly established stations. The second expedition, headed by A. F. Treshnikov, was first to the geomagnetic South Pole, a significant (and constantly mobile) destination, but not nearly so much so as the far more romantic *geographical* South Pole reached back in 1911 by the Norwegian Roald Amundsen. Currently the Russian Republic maintains three permanent stations in Antarctica: Mirnyi and Vostok, which date from 1956 and 1957, respectively, and Bellingshausen, built in 1968.

Although the Russian and Soviet role in the Antarctic is perhaps not as great as that of some of the English-speaking and Scandinavian countries, a Soviet writer could reasonably assert in the mid–1970s that his people's achievements in the region were "reflected in the Russian names on the map of Antarctica: Alexander I Land; Peter I Island; Bellingshausen Sea; Bellingshausen Island (in the South Sandwich Islands); the Bellingshausen Island Arc (Weddell Sea); Smolensk, Mordvinov and Shishkov Islands (in the South Shetland Islands); Shokalsky Strait; Annenkov Island (Scotia Sea); Zavadovsky, Leskov, Vysoky islands (in the South Sandwich Islands)" along with "over 200" more minor geographical features.[72] No doubt the Russians will add further to this record going forward.

Further Readings in English and Russian

Armstrong, Terence. "Bellingshausen and the Discovery of Antarctica." *Polar Record* 15 (1971): 887–89.

Baldwin E. B. *The Franz Josef Land Archipelago: E. B. Baldwin's Journal of the Wellman Polar Expedition, 1898–1899.* Edited by P. J. Capelotti. Jefferson, NC: McFarland, 2004.

Barr, Susan, ed. *Franz Josef Land.* Oslo: Norsk Polarinstitutt, 1995.

Barr, William, "The 'Discovery' and Exploration of Ostrov Bol'shoy Begichev 1908." *Terrae Incognitae* 16 (1984): 15–24.

Bellingshausen, F. F. *The Voyage of Captain Bellingshausen to the Antarctic Sea, 1819–21.* Edited by Frank Debenham. 2 vols. 1945. Hakluyt Society, 2nd series, nos. 91–92. Nendeln, Liechtenstein, 1967.

Belov, M. I. *Pervaia russkaia Antarkticheskaia ekspeditsiia, 1819–1821 gg. i otchetnaia karta.* Leningrad: "Morskoi transport," 1963.

Berton, Pierre. *The Arctic Grail: The Quest for the North West Passage and the North Pole, 1818–1909.* New York: Viking, 1988.

Brontman, L. *On Top of the World: The Soviet Expedition to the North Pole, 1937.* Edited by O. J. Schmidt 1938. New York: Greenwood Press, 1968.

Gvozdetsky, N. A. *Soviet Geographical Explorations and Discoveries.* Translated by Anatoly Bratov. Moscow: Progress Publishers, 1974.

Hayes, Derek. *Historical Atlas of the Arctic.* Seattle: University of Washington Press, 2003.

Holland, Clive, ed. *Farthest North: The Quest for the North Pole.* London: Robinson, 1994.

Jones, A. G. E. *Antarctica Observed: Who Discovered the Antarctic Continent?* Whitby, UK: Caedmon of Whitby, 1982.

McCannon, John. *Red Arctic: Polar Exploration and the Myth of the North in the Soviet Union, 1932–1939.* New York: Oxford University Press, 1998.

Rosove, Michael H. *Let Heroes Speak: Antarctic Explorers, 1772–1922.* Annapolis, MD: Naval Institute Press, 2000.

Starokamdomskiy, L. M. *Charting the Russian Northern Sea Route: The Arctic Ocean Hydrographic Expedition, 1910–1915.* Edited and translated by William Barr. Montreal: McGill-Queen's University Press, 1976.

Stefansson, Vilhjalmur, et al. *The Adventure of Wrangel Island.* New York: Macmillan, 1925.

Ushakov, G. A. *Po nekhozhenoi zemle.* Moscow: Izdatle'stvo "Mysl'," 1974.

Chapter 8

A New Frontier: Russians[1] the USSR and Space

More than perhaps any other area of Russian exploration, the Soviet space program, especially during its heyday in the late 1950s and 1960s, has presented problems to specialists who have tried to write its history. Secretive in virtually all their affairs, in missile and space technologies the Soviets' behavior verged on paranoia. Work was carried out under conditions of extraordinary security within secret programs in hidden facilities and closed towns. The flow of information was, at best, strictly on a need-to-know basis. People involved at the highest levels often had little knowledge of what was going on beyond their own immediate domains, or even within them. Would-be cosmonauts trained rigorously for missions the nature of which they could only guess at. Iurii Gagarin, the famous first person in space, learned only days beforehand of the flight he was to make. His wife learned at the same time as the rest of the Soviet public — when Gagarin was already in orbit! Failed tests and launches were covered up for years and successful ones selectively described only after the fact.

Even when crowing loudly about their greatest achievements, the Soviet authorities remained vague and evasive, fudging on questions such as how or where its cosmonauts had landed, the nature of the technology involved, and so on. The identities of key space personnel were closely guarded secrets — ostensibly to prevent "enemy agents" from getting to them. And in some cases persons and events seem to have been fabricated out of whole cloth.[2] Not surprisingly, in the West and in Russia, conspiracy theories still plague aspects of the program. (One of the more enduring has it that Gagarin was actually not the first man in space but either the second or even third — and that the first two either died in space, landed in China, or suffered some other fate the Soviets successfully covered up.[3])

In recent times, taking advantage of relatively improved access to Soviet archives, several important new studies have been undertaken, especially by Russians.[4] These have filled in many blanks and corrected earlier errors. They stand in stark contrast to some of the Soviet-era hagiographies written about the program — and particularly about its chief architect, Sergei Pavlovich Korolev.[5] But it seems clear that much remains to be done. (A recent review article claims that even recent Russian scholarship, including work done by the Russian Academy of Sciences, still "glosses over" some "unpleasant episodes" in the Space Race.[6]) This is a field still very much in its infancy.

Russians and Space: Dreams and Dreamers

In the realm of space travel Russians are pioneers twice over. Long before the celebrated launch of *Sputnik* in 1957, the flight of Iurii Gagarin aboard *Vostok*-1 in 1961, or any of the other great milestones of the Soviet space program, nineteenth-century Russians invented or dreamed up many of the foundations of those achievements. The very first person to promote realistically the possibility of developing a jet engine — powered by explosives and designed to propel a flying machine — was almost certainly Nikolai Kilbachich (1853–1881). Unfortunately, Kilbachich is far better known for his role in another explosives-based "achievement"— the bombing-assassination of Tsar Alexander II in 1881, which he helped carry out and for which he was quickly executed. During his last days, however, while locked in the Peter and Paul Fortress in St. Petersburg, Kilbachich drafted a design for a rocket — a simple tube, open at one end, powered by a slow-burning explosive, and steered by alterations to the direction of the thrust. His plans were presented to the State Police Department a year later. Had they come from someone else they might have fared better. Kilbachich's status as political radical and executed terrorist tainted them fatally, however. They were filed and forgotten. (This reminds, perhaps, of another instance in which the Russian government reacted to the political crimes of an individual by burying his positive contributions as well — that of Torson, whose involvement with the Decembrists helped stifle official interest not only in this one man's work in the Pacific, but in the whole expedition of Bellingshausen, with which he had been involved [see chapter 5].) The demise of the Russian Empire and the rise of the Soviet Union changed the situation, however. Kilbachich's ideas were finally published in 1918 by Nikolai Rynin (1877–1942), a Russian space-enthusiast and the author of a remarkable nine-volume Russian encyclopedia about space travel (published long before its subject became a reality, of course).[7]

Kilbachich envisioned rockets for use on the earth. The first person to explore seriously their potential for *space* travel was Konstantin Edvardovich Tsiolkovskii (1857–1935). Though the American Robert Goddard and the German Hermann Oberth are also important in this regard, Tsiolkovskii has the best claim to be considered the father of space travel. This is due both to the priority of his ideas over those of the other two men and to the importance thereof. Deaf from the age of ten and largely self-tutored, Tsiolkovskii first wrote on the subject in 1883. His earliest publication was an essay entitled "Exploration of the Universe with Reactive Machines," which appeared in 1903. Over the next half-century Tsiolkovksii produced some 500 further works, mostly short papers, in which he proposed and developed many of the concepts basic to subsequent rocket and space programs: the use of liquid fuels (including oxygen and hydrogen), rocket nozzle designs, multi stage rockets, steering rockets, space stations, air locks, space suits, regenerative cooling, using a centrifuge to create artificial gravity, and so on. Not just a visionary, Tsiolkovskii grounded his ideas in solid science. As early as 1903, he worked out the necessary velocity for putting an object into earth orbit (about seven miles per second or 25,000 miles per hour). Later, he pondered the possibilities of atomic and solar-powered drives and a permanent human presence in space.[8]

Following the October Revolution the Soviet authorities offered support to domestic rocket-development initiatives, primarily by establishing a laboratory in Moscow in 1921. It was run first by N. I. Tikhomirov. Government interest lay, of course, in the military uses of rockets, not space travel. But this was simply a case of applications: the ongoing development of rocket boosters inexorably brought Tsiolkovskii's dream ever closer. In 1924 Tikhomirov's facility was renamed the Gas Dynamics Laboratory (GDL) and relocated to the newly named city of Leningrad (the former and current St. Petersburg). By 1929 the GDL had been joined (and would soon be led) by another talented young engineer — a rocket-engine specialist named Valentin Petrovich Glushko. Both men, but especially Glushko, would go on to great success in the Soviet Space Program. For now, however, their experiments with various liquid and electrical jet engines were dedicated to weapons applications.

Another important player at this stage, one who like Tsiolkovskii envisioned rockets as merely a means to the great end of space travel, was Friedrikh Arturovich Tsandr (or Tsander). Back in 1908 Tsandr had written up some of the first-ever ideas about life-support systems for future cosmonauts, including the possibility of providing oxygen and food by means of space-based greenhouses. Throughout the 1920s he worked on designs for rockets and spacecraft, even patenting at least one blueprint. Along with fellow space-fanatic Iurii Kondratiuk he founded in 1924 a Society for the Study of Interplanetary Travel. Tsiolkovskii was also a member. Tsandr spent most of his life working without any state support. Nonetheless, in 1933 he would launch Russia's first ever liquid-fueled rocket (several years after Goddard had done much the same in the United States).

Though these men played great roles in the early history of Russian and Soviet space exploration, all are eclipsed by one other — the primary architect and eventual "Chief Designer" of the entire Soviet Space Program and of its greatest successes from the launching of the first artificial satellite in 1957 to the first spacewalk in 1965. His name was Sergei Pavlovich Korolev.

Sergei Pavlovich Korolev

Korolev was born 30 December 1907 (Old Style) in Zhitomir, Ukraine. His parents separated when he was three and Korolev was raised partly by his often-absent mother (and later also by her second husband), but mostly by his maternal grandparents. From adolescence Korolev nurtured an interest in aviation, which he began aggressively to pursue beginning in 1923 at age sixteen. The newly formed Soviet Union provided him with various opportunities — starting that year with the Society of Aviation and Aerial Navigation of Ukraine and the Crimea (OAVUK) and the Odessa hydroplane squadron. The following year he enrolled in the aviation-mechanics school of the Kiev Polytechnic Institute. Here he studied theory, designed and flew gliders, crashed one of his own designs (fortunately suffering only broken ribs), and generally consummated what would become a lifelong infatuation with the science and adventure of flight. From 1926 he studied at the N. E. Bauman Higher Technical School under the guidance of celebrated aircraft designer Andrei Tupolev. Here, in 1929, Korolev earned his diploma by submitting and successfully defending a design for a light-engine aircraft. At about the same time he finally awoke to the idea of space travel, apparently from the works of Tsiolkovskii. Soon the thought of breaking the bonds of the earth and exploring other planets grew from an intriguing thought into a full-blown obsession. It would grip him for the rest of his life. For the while, however, his days were taken up on practical work designing aircraft for the state. One of his creations, the SK-3 glider, became in 1930 the first such craft of Soviet provenance to fly loops. Around the same time he won his pilot's license. And in 1931 he married his longtime girlfriend, Zhenia Vincentini.[9]

In 1926 the American Robert H. Goddard successfully launched the world's first liquid-fueled rocket. Though it flew for only 2½ seconds and to an altitude of just 41 feet, it proved the technology's viability and was a major stride forward. The Leningrad GDL redoubled its efforts in response, but progress was slow. Then in 1931 a Russian competitor to GDL appeared. Based in Moscow, it was known as the "Group for the Study of Reactive Motion," or GIRD (by its Russian acronym). Founded by Tsandr, GIRD quickly attracted several talented individuals, most notably Korolev, who leapt at the chance to work on rockets. Compared to GDL, GIRD was a strictly amateur affair, begun in a residential basement and lacking official support or funds. But within only a year or so the group had attracted the attention of no lesser a person than Deputy People's Commissar for Military and Naval Affairs Mikhail N. Tukhachevskii. In the fall of 1933, at Tukhachevskii's recommendation, GDL and GIRD were merged into a new and relatively well-funded entity within the Soviet military — the Reaction Propulsion Institute (RNII), based in Moscow. Sadly, Tsandr had died a few months earlier of typhus while only in his mid-forties.

Korolev now found himself deputy chief of the new organization (under chief engineer Ivan Kleimenov) and organizationally ahead of Glushko. In August 1933, immediately prior to the merger, Korolev's GIRD team also managed to beat Glushko's GDL by launching the USSR's very first rocket, designed by Tsandr. Known as GIRD-09, this was a forty-pound liquid-fueled device that attained 1,300 feet in eighteen seconds.[10] These were, perhaps, the first in a long series of events that would strain — and eventually poison — relations between Glushko and Korolev. For now, however, Korolev was moving ahead quickly. The following year, he and another engineer — E. S. Shchetinkov — jointly developed and began testing the first Soviet winged-rocket.[11] Though Goddard in the United States was still ahead, the Soviets were at least in the rocketry game now. As it would turn out, throughout much of the 1930s Goddard, distracted by other related projects and unable to secure appropriate government support for his work, made relatively little progress, allowing the Soviets to gain ground.

In popular Soviet and Russian accounts, GIRD, although it lasted only from 1931 to 1933, has acquired semimythical status as the "forge of cadres" — that is, as the nursery of the personnel that would dominate the Soviet Space Program thereafter. More sober opinions point out that only a few dozen people ever labored there, and that though some became giants, many others among the USSR's eventual cohort of great rocket and space designers were not among them. There is little doubt, however, about the importance of GIRD for Korolev himself: it transformed him from "a glider pilot with dreams of adapting an unknown type of engine to glider use" into "the greatest specialist in the area of rocket technology, a specialist with a broad vision, who clearly saw the long-range possibilities and the road toward [achieving these]."[12]

Although Korolev remained absorbed in his work throughout the 1930s, external circumstances intruded. In the spring of 1937, during the worst of several terrible years of Stalinist purges, the Soviet state security organ, the NKVD, arrested and soon thereafter executed Tukhachevskii on trumped-up charges as an "enemy of the people." In the warped logic of the Stalinist purges, suspicion quickly fell on virtually everyone and everything associated with Tukhachevskii. Over the following year most of the personnel at RNII, from Kleimenov on down, were also rounded up. Each new arrest produced forced "confessions" that led, in turn, to further arrests, and so on. Korolev's turn came on 27 June 1938.[13] Glushko, already arrested, was one of his main accusers. The two men would never enjoy each other's company again. Within a month the NKVD had forced Korolev to "confess" to economic sabotage and wrecking of industry, terms applied liberally to large numbers of arrestees at the time. More specifically, he was charged with the deliberate and treasonous manufacture of faulty engines. The charge was not only baseless, but absurd. Engines were Glushko's field. Korolev — who as first Chief Designer was responsible not for component parts but for the overall rocket system — had never even worked on them. But it made no difference.[14] Nor did any of the subsequent retractions of his confession or the statements of his complete innocence Korolev would later write. He received ten years' hard labor.

Recent scholarship has provided new details about the conditions and places of Korolev's detention. But some parts of the story remain unclear. He was held first in Moscow. From October to the following June, he was in a prison in Novocherkassk in southwest Russia. After this he was moved east. By October, if not earlier, he was in one of the USSR's most notorious labor camp complexes at Kolyma, in the far northeast. The place was a virtual death factory. Prisoners were routinely beaten, starved, and worked to oblivion in temperatures as low as -50° C. Korolev had his jaw broken here (perhaps multiple times), lost all his teeth, developed kidney and heart ailments that would plague him periodically thereafter, and suffered many other miseries.[15] It was a brutal and utterly undeserved ordeal, yet it could have been even worse. Most members of RNII had already been shot or would soon be. Ironically, it was around this time, on 28 February 1940, that the first successful test flight of a Soviet jet plane took place — one based significantly on Korolev's own designs.[16]

In or around November 1939, Korolev was released and recalled to Moscow for reconsideration of his case. Left to make his own travel arrangements, he found himself stranded for the winter pending the resumption of shipping during the spring thaw. Surviving cold and hardships only somewhat less murderous than camp conditions, he passed several months as a virtual vagrant. Once back in Moscow his sentence was reduced, but only by two years. Return to Kolyma loomed. He was rescued indirectly by the outbreak of the Second World War in Western Europe (which increased the value of a skilled weapons engineer like Korolev). In this context, more specific help came from his old advisor — Tupolev, also incarcerated but working on rocket design for the state and in need of Korolev's expertise. Thus, beginning in September 1940 — as Hitler's forces battled unsuccessfully for air supremacy in Britain — Korolev began work near Moscow on rocketry for military aircraft design in a uniquely Soviet institution — a combination prison camp and workplace for scientists, technologists, and other intellectuals useful to the state. They were known as *sharaga*s and run by the NKVD — the much-feared state security apparatus and forerunner to the KGB. In June 1941, the Nazis invaded the Soviet Union and quickly advanced on Moscow and other cities. Accordingly, Korolev and his team were transferred several times to various locations. Finally, in late 1942 he was assigned to a *sharaga* in Kazan, much further east, where he found himself working again, uneasily, with Glushko. He remained here until August 1945 (despite being "officially released" a year earlier).[17]

Whatever the specifics of his arrest and subsequent treatment, it seems clear that these experiences constituted a profound personal test. In the words of a Russian biographer: "During these harsh years [Korolev] managed to preserve his sense of self-worth. If he had [instead] allowed fear into his soul — a desire to adapt, to compromise — then he could never have been the same Korolev who during the postwar years set about work [involving] such incredible difficulties and responsibilities. The problems which he had to resolve could be shouldered only by a man with a strong spirit. The years of repression did not break him. In all probability this was the greatest victory in S. P. Korolev's life."[18]

The German Windfall and the Development of Soviet R-Series Rockets

By the end of World War II, the most advanced rocket technology on earth was neither American nor Soviet, but the German V-2 program based in Peenemünde on the Baltic coast. Standing 14.3 meters high and weighing 12½ tons, the V-2 could carry a one-ton warhead 150 to 200 miles. By war's end more than 3,000 had been deployed, nearly half against London, the rest against a variety of targets in Allied Europe. They had killed 12,685 persons and destroyed 33,700 structures.[19] As Nazi Germany collapsed, the incoming Soviet and U.S. militaries raced to capture what they could: rockets, plans, and personnel. The Americans fared better, netting most of the hardware and — the greatest prize — the German mastermind behind it all (and the eventual architect of the U.S. space program) Werner von Braun.[20] In the rush, however, much was left behind for the Soviets, including as many as 7,000 Germans — rocket experts, related workers, and family members — who were brought back to the USSR.[21] Among the Russians sent to evaluate and appropriate German technology was Korolev himself, newly promoted to colonel in the Red Army. Beginning in the fall of 1945, he spent more than a year in Germany.

Once everything had been brought back home, the Soviets undertook to combine the German windfall with their own expertise. The main result was a new rocket institute named NII-88, founded in 1946 in Podlipki, near Moscow, and run by Commissar of Armaments Dmitri Ustinov. It served as the central hub of a much larger new military rocket industrial complex decreed the same year by Stalin. Work was divided among a number of chief designers, each in charge of his own specialization and working on a part of the overall puzzle, such as engine design, auto-guidance systems, and so on. The designers included Valentin Glushko, Nikolai Piliugin, Vladimir Barmin, Mikhail Ryzanskii, and Viktor Kuznetsov. Many others entered the picture thereafter.

Officially, these men were organized as a collective — a council of chief designers — which Korolev chaired from early 1947 until his death in 1966. Most of his biographers emphasize that here Korolev was — at the very least — first among equals. More often he is depicted as the undisputed and absolute center of the whole enterprise. This did not mean he had unlimited power or resources at his call, however. The Soviet economy lagged far behind its U.S. counterpart, greatly limiting what was possible. And from the start, a considerable amount of overlap and redundancy was built into the Soviet space program, fostering competing designs and projects, as well as direct competition for financial and political support (more so, ironically, than in NASA). Korolev spent the rest of his life fighting for every scrap of money, permission, or support.

Remarkably, neither Korolev nor any of his council of designers had an advanced scientific degree. These men were essentially amateurs — skilled, experienced, practical engineers. In their ability to deliver spectacular results in the face of difficult conditions they may remind us somewhat of the venerable *promyshlenniki* from the days of Siberian conquest. (They did not, of course, enjoy the freedoms of the old hunter-entrepreneurs.) Korolev, did not lament his lack of advanced theoretical training, but more or less reveled in it, always preferring hands-on experience to book and university-laboratory learning. Under Korolev and his council of designers labored thousands, and eventually hundreds of thousands, of other technicians, workers, and administrators spread across a vast complex of scientific organizations, government ministries, factories, and educational institutions. At its peak in the 1970s, years after Korolev's death, the Soviet space program may have involved as many as 500,000 persons and sucked up 1.5 percent of the entire Soviet gross national product.

This was all far in the future, however, as Korolev and his designers began work in 1947 reverse engineering the V-2. The first successful launch occurred 18 October 1947 at Kapustin Iar in Astrakhan oblast'. A year later Korolev successfully tested a modified V-2 called the R-1. It had a similar range to the German original, but could not carry quite so heavy a payload. By the end of 1949, Korolev moved beyond mere copies and developed the R-2 — the first truly Soviet long-range missile and a significant improvement on the German device. The first successful test flew 370 miles, twice the R-1's range. By this time Korolev had been officially appointed head not only of the council of chief designers but also of his own NII-88 bureau titled OKB-1, dedicated to further development of R-series rockets. Over the following years huge improvements were made in range, reliability, accuracy, and stability. As Soviet rocketry moved far beyond the capabilities of the German V-2, German personnel were retired and repatriated. By 1954 they had all gone home.

But Korolev dreamed of space, not of the intercontinental ballistic missiles his political and military bosses demanded. As early as 1953, he had begun to make suggestions in this direction to the authorities. At the time neither he nor anyone else possessed a rocket nearly powerful enough to achieve escape velocity. Nor was there political support for such an adventure: the Soviet leadership was interested in rockets solely as weapons.

The first of these obstacles began to recede in the mid–1950s with development of the R-7. The primary innovations involved joining together multiple rocket clusters in two stages. The result was a 220-ton, thirty-four meter high behemoth powered by five thrusters of four rockets each (four of which were designed to fall away soon after liftoff) and providing some nine times the thrust of early R-series rockets. There were also important new developments in guidance systems, including small radio-controlled steering rockets. In January 1956, long before he had fully developed the R-7, Korolev proposed to the government to use it to send up an artificial satellite. Again he received little encouragement.

Things changed fairly suddenly in the spring of 1957, due to at least three new considerations. First, International Geophysical Year (IGY) was looming.[22] Under its aegis numerous scientific projects had been proposed by states around the world. Among these, the United States, as early as 1955, had publicly mooted the idea of launching an artificial satellite into orbit — officially for scientific purposes, but clearly also intended as a spy satellite. Though official support in the United States for such an undertaking was lukewarm at best, the possibility that it might happen caught the imagination of the Soviet leadership, especially Khrushchev, who decided almost at the last moment that the USSR must beat its rival. Domestic Soviet politics were a second determining factor. In June 1957 Khrushchev, a relative moderate in Soviet politics, defeated a coup attempt by the Stalinist old guard (primarily Molotov, Kaganovich, and Malenkov). A successful space launch seemed ideal to cement his new ascendancy.

Finally, technological developments also underlay the sudden Soviet interest in a satellite launch. In August 1957 Korolev's new R-7 rocket was ready. Following a heartbreaking series of unsuccessful tests during the spring, on August 21 one flew perfectly from the recently built missile-testing facility at "Baikonur"[23] to the Kamchatka Peninsula, a distance not far short of 4,000 miles. This made the R-7 the world's first intercontinental ballistic missile and put the USSR more than a year ahead of the United States.[24] It also provided a realistic satellite launch vehicle. As it would turn out, the R-7 design would provide the basic platform behind all of the USSR's great successes during the height of the Space Race. It is rightly considered "the chief result of all Korolev's earthly labors."[25]

Suddenly, after years of foot dragging, the goal of placing an artificial satellite — a *Sputnik*[26] — in orbit became a frantic rush. Around the beginning of September, Korolev found himself being pushed hard to get something — anything — into orbit in the absolute shortest possible time. This turned out to be about four weeks! Unfortunately for Korolev and his team, Khrushchev's interest was in a splashy propaganda coup, not useful science. With time and resources scarce, and failure unacceptable, Korolev was forced to scale back earlier plans for a sophisticated orbiting science-lab in favor of the "simplest possible device" — a small, polished sphere not quite two feet in diameter and weighing about 185 pounds. Apart from basic heat sensing apparatus, it was equipped only with a transmitter and batteries — so that the world, especially America, could pick up the craft's beeping signal and satisfy itself of the Soviet achievement. *If* it all worked.

During the month prior to launch, Korolev, never one to take things easy, outdid himself in sheer hard work, spending endless hours intensely micromanaging every stage and facet of the program. Supposedly, he even obsessed about the need to polish to perfection both the actual *Sputnik* and its duplicate — the former bound, hopefully, for heavenly glory, the latter for high-profile tours and museum displays. By the beginning of October, everything was ready.

The actual launch took place at the Baikonur facility on the night of October 4. By all accounts, it was both spectacular and textbook perfect. Some among those watching at first became alarmed to see the rocket tilt shortly after take-off, expecting it instead to head straight up. This, however, was merely a necessary trajectory adjustment in order to achieve orbit — a sign of success, not of failure. Within minutes the little satellite was sweeping around the globe, beeping loud and clear for all to hear.

To this day, for many Russians the launch of *Sputnik* constitutes the critical pivot point that Americans and other Westerners might more readily ascribe to Neil Armstrong's "one small step ... one giant leap" onto the surface of the moon — that is, it marks the beginning of the Space Age and humanity's first arrival beyond earth. A sense of the Russian perspective can be gleaned from comments made shortly after the event by A. N. Nesmeianov, then-president of the Academy of Sciences of the USSR: "The orbital flight of the radio-controlled metallic sphere has outdone everything else — the discoveries of Columbus and Magellan, mankind's first use of steam and electricity to drive machinery, the conquest of the skies by the first aircraft, and [even] the epochal liberation of the power of the atom.... All these were mere steps on the earthly ladder of progress — victories in mankind's unending battle to tame terrestrial nature."[27]

It was in something like this spirit that the world's media first greeted the announcement of *Sputnik*'s successful launch back in October 1957. Around the globe, reports, whether in newspapers, on radio or television, verged on hysteria. Korolev later described the month following the launch as the happiest time of his life, a time of vindication for his science and a glimpse of incredible possibilities ahead. But if Korolev and his team were feeling good, Khrushchev was ecstatic. Like nothing before it, *Sputnik* seemed to confirm everything he had ever claimed and wished for about the supposed superiority of the Soviet system over capitalism and the West. Almost immediately he demanded a follow-up — a second *Sputnik*, timed to coincide with the fortieth anniversary of the Bolshevik Revolution on November 7. This, again, gave Korolev only about four weeks.

In fact, *Sputnik*-2 was launched ahead of even this crazy schedule, on the 3rd. This time a dog, Laika, was on board. As the first living creature in space,[28] she provided invaluable — and highly encouraging — information about the prospects for human life in space and under conditions of weightlessness. Unfortunately, no provision was made for bringing *Sputnik*-2 or its lonely occupant back, and so poor Laika also became the first earthling to die in space, succumbing to heat exhaustion after less than six hours. For five months her corpse orbited the earth inside Korolev's tiny capsule (to the dismay of animal welfare activists, especially in the UK). Then, on 14 April 1958, Laika and *Sputnik*-2 fell into the earth's atmosphere and burned up in a blaze of light in the night sky over Barbados.[29]

Sputnik-2 was basically the same device as its predecessor, but by arranging for the first *and* second stages to go into orbit, the Soviets were able to claim a total orbiting weight of more than 1,100 pounds — six times that of the first *Sputnik*.[30] The failure of the first U.S. satellite launch, named *Vanguard TV3*, on December 6 added to Khrushchev's glee and further convinced millions of people in the USSR and around the world, even in the United States, of the superiority of Soviet space technology. The successful launching the following January of *Explorer*-1, the first U.S. satellite, did little to change this perception, even though the craft made an important discovery missed by Korolev's *Sputnik*s: the Van Allen radiation belts.

For his great achievements with *Sputnik*s-1 and -2 Korolev received absolutely no publicity whatsoever. Instead, his name was kept a strict secret — and not only at this time but for the rest of his life. Over the coming years, as the number of his achievements accrued — the first man in space, the first woman, the first spacewalk, and so on — the world, including the Soviet public, knew the architect of it all only by the vague appellation the "Chief Designer." At public gatherings and ceremonies, Korolev was kept to the side, out of the limelight — a silent spectator to his own achievements. Adding insult to injury, until about 1960 the Soviet authorities sometimes even explicitly credited Korolev's work to a minor colleague — the physicist L. I. Sedov. Other times the pseudonym "K. Sergeev" (nearly his real name backwards) was used instead. Officially, Korolev's anonymity was for his own protection — and that of the Soviet space program. Unable to compete fairly, the logic went, "enemy agents" would no doubt seek to find and kill him. (One might see some irony in this situation, since it could be seen to suggest the Soviets' own sense that their space successes were the result *not* of a superior system but of the towering genius and colossal efforts of one fragile individual.) Korolev resented the secrecy but carried on undeterred. What else could he do? Space rocketry was his lifelong dream and obsession. He was now making it a reality. On 15 May 1958 he and his team put into orbit the 2,920-pound *Sputnik*-3. It stayed up for nearly two years. The United States responded two-and-a-half months later with the creation of NASA.

By now, the United States had also scored three successful launches, following *Explorer*-1 with *Vanguard*-1 and *Explorer*-3 (*Explorer*-2 did not reach orbit). Nonetheless, world opinion remained convinced America was behind. In fact, the Soviet lead was partly illusory. Designed primarily for delivering propaganda coups, the first two *Sputnik*s had not been equipped for serious scientific work. Though the United States was far from immune to similar motivations, all of its satellites had also been outfitted to perform basic research (thus *Explorer*-1's discovery of the Van Allen belts). *Vanguard*-2, the second successful U.S. satellite, ascertained the pear-shaped form of the earth. And *Explorer*-3 collected important data on solar radiation and micro-meteoroids.[31] By the end of the decade, the U.S. had many more orbiting satellites than the USSR, most of which were also of greater scientific value. And the Soviets' cluster-rocket design was far from ideal. Yet frustratingly, for the Americans, the world's publics remained more easily impressed by headline-grabbing "firsts." And this was precisely what Korolev, pushed against his own better judgment by the giddy general secretary, continued to provide. In fact, the anonymous Chief Designer had hardly begun.

Beyond Earth Orbit

With three *Sputnik*s to his credit, Korolev began to think bigger still. In particular, the moon beckoned. But this was a very different target from the near-earth orbits so far attained. The *Sputnik*s had traveled about 150 miles above the earth. The moon, by contrast, was nearly a quarter of a million miles away. Korolev redesigned the R-7, adding an extra stage that would ignite once the rocket was already in space, thus providing the necessary thrust for breaking earth orbit and carrying an unmanned probe much further. He called the resulting craft *Mechta* (Dream) and thought of it as a steppingstone to his own greatest dream — that of sending a *man* to the moon. One after another, three *Mechta*s were launched — and failed — during 1958.

On 2 January 1959, however, Korolev's luck turned as the fourth *Mechta*, renamed *Luna*-1 (Moon-1) by his political bosses, did nearly everything it was supposed to, sweeping across sublunar space and eventually missing its target by only 3,700 miles — a cosmic hair's breadth. En route to the moon, in a spectacular piece of showmanship, *Luna*-1 waved back at astronomers the world over with a brilliant sodium flare released 62,000 miles above earth. Korolev had fought successfully to get scientific instrumentation on *Luna*-1 and was rewarded also with the significant discovery that the moon lacks a magnetic field. For an encore, the craft became the first man-made object to settle into solar orbit. It was on virtually all counts a great achievement, yet the Soviet authorities, embarrassed about having missed the moon (not that they had announced such a goal beforehand), felt it necessary to declare emphatically, just in case anyone was wondering, that a direct hit had never been intended. And when Korolev scored a perfect bull's-eye with *Luna*-2, fired on 12 September 1959, the Soviets coolly announced they had hit the moon on their first try. This launch, of course, had also been timed — at Khrushchev's orders — for maximum political effect. A few days later, with the moonshot still reverberating in the popular media, Khrushchev arrived confidently in the United States for a meeting with Eisenhower.

Working almost nonstop, Korolev and his team kept up the momentum. On October 4, the second anniversary of *Sputnik*-1, he launched *Luna*-3. This was an even greater success than the first two. Passing behind and around its target, *Luna*-3's cameras not only took the first ever photographs of the dark side of the moon, but even processed the film automatically and showed the images to an on-board television camera which relayed them to earth. This mission in particular helped Korolev — who continued to face competition for funds and support from other designers — into Khrushchev's good favors. Also impressive were the numerous innovations — in attitude control and stabilization, solar cells, and so on — that made it all possible. In all, during 1958–1959 the Soviets tried eight times to reach the moon and succeeded thrice. The United States, with its *Pioneer* program, tried and failed seven times (or six if one counts as successful *Pioneer*-4, which missed the moon by 37,000 miles).

With the Americans seemingly on the ropes, Korolev and his Soviet bosses pushed still harder for more and more spectacles. Activity at Korolev's design bureau, says one American writer, "was frenzied. On the agenda were spacecraft for the Moon, Mars, and Venus" (the latter two being tens of millions of miles away even at their closest passes to earth), as well as "communications, reconnaissance, and weather satellites."[32] And there were plans for the world's first manned space flight. It is one of the more remarkable things about Korolev and the Soviet space program in general that throughout the first half of the 1960s *all* of these various missions were actively pursued. Between 1960 and 1965 Korolev launched at least a dozen more rockets at the moon and sixteen at either Mars or Venus. The United States during the same period sent only two craft each to Venus and Mars (*Mariners* 1–4). In taking on these two planets, the Soviets again scored some good successes among the more numerous failures: *Mars*-1, launched 1 November 1962, traveled more than 63 million miles toward its target before becoming lost; *Zond*-2, launched 30 November 1964, came within about 1,000 miles of the Red Planet; *Venera*-2 (launched 12 November 1965) flew within 15,000 miles of Venus; and its follow-up, *Venera*-3, crashed into the same planet on 1 March 1966 after a journey of three-and-a-half months. (Of the four U.S. *Mariner* craft, the first failed completely to reach Venus while *Mariner*-2 came within 22,000 miles of it; *Mariner*-3 missed Mars "by a wide margin," and *Mariner*-4, by far the most successful, came within 6,000 miles and took the first ever close-up photographs of it.[33]

During these years Korolev was at the peak of his game. His "special gift" as Chief Designer was his ability to conceptualize systematically an entire rocket far in advance of its creation.[34] Virtually all of his waking hours were spent working, and there was hardly an aspect of the space program that he did not attend to personally, from top to bottom, technological, political, or personal. Officially, he interfaced with the political authorities via his immediate superior, D. F. Ustinov, who in turn reported to the Council of Ministers. Yet he also sometimes went around the bureaucracy, pitching directly to Khrushchev and others who visited his facilities. At the other end of affairs, Korolev is reputed to have been something of a pragmatic populist, contemptuous of narrow specializations and territorialism, always interested in the contributions even of the lowest-level workers. Both the hagiographies produced by the Soviets and the more sober Western and post–Soviet Russian accounts agree on this point — though the latter also note more frequently his ability also to deliver furious and stinging ad hominem scoldings of anyone he thought to be slacking. Though he lived frugally himself, Korolev had access to large amounts of cash, the specific provenance of which still eludes historians. Supposedly he used some of it to take care of needy or deserving subordinates.

The breadth and range of his skills have led to the question whether he is best considered a scientist-engineer or an administrator. Clearly he was both: a "new type of scientist-organizer," a "scientist-manager," in the words of one of his contemporaries.[35] But despite his considerable talents of salesmanship and management, many times Korolev was frustrated by what he felt were ridiculous knots of red tape, funding shortfalls, or plain stonewalling from the authorities. Keeping the Soviet space program functioning was an ongoing headache. Sometimes, he was unhappy with the quality of product he received, or the delays in manufacture at subordinate bureaus, factories, workshops, and so on. In these cases he often resorted to having work done in-house, by people he knew and trusted and could supervise more directly. Overall, he and his coworkers had to improvise endlessly, making up in sheer determined creativity what they lacked in funding, materials, and technology.

The First Man in Space

Although his efforts toward Venus and Mars captivated both the public and the scientific community, by far the greatest impression was made by Korolev's crowning achievement of 1961— and probably of his life — the successful launch of the world's first astronaut (or cosmonaut), Iurii Gagarin. Already by the end of 1959, Korolev was tiring of *Sputniks* and

Lunas. It was, he felt, time to put a man into space. Selling the idea to Khrushchev as another important "first" proved relatively easy. Actually doing it was another thing.

From the start Korolev felt deeply the difference between sending up a machine (or even a dog for that matter) and launching a human being. Whoever the man would be (there was no talk of putting a woman in space at this point), Korolev was determined to do everything possible to secure his safe return. Not just the inherent risks of space travel made this a stiff challenge. From the beginning, Soviet rocket and space programs had suffered greatly, compared to their American counterparts, from the general weakness of the Soviet economy and the backwardness of the Soviet industrial base. Despite Korolev's successes at securing funding, the manned space program would also suffer from these shortcomings. Only extra effort, care, and imagination could offset them.

Soviet ingenuity had long been a staple ingredient in the successes of Korolev's R-7. Lacking the necessary combination of know-how and resources to build a single rocket booster capable of putting payloads into orbit (as the Americans were doing), Korolev and a codesigner, M. K. Tikhonravov, had combined smaller rockets into clusters — providing both sufficient thrust and a distinctive look. (Coincidentally, this technique — especially when contrasted with the American single-rocket approach — also provided an interesting sort of metaphor for the Soviet socialist system, with power deriving from the common purpose and unity of many small units rather than from the strength of one individual.) Even so, getting a man into orbit — along with the extra weight of his capsule, life-support system, and other vital supplies — required pushing the cluster approach to new limits. The obvious solution, strapping together even more rockets and adding further stages, threatened to create a "vicious circle" whereby each extra increment of thrust was offset by the added weight of every new rocket. Korolev overcame the problem not by adding more engines but by paying careful attention to the positioning of the existing rockets, by providing for the jettisoning of some clusters soon after takeoff, and by a vicious weight-saving strategy based on throwing away or eschewing everything not absolutely essential.[36] Among the victims of the latter approach were the large capsule parachute and braking system: the pilot would instead be ejected — landing with his own much smaller parachute.

These and other systems were tested in a series of unmanned flights starting 15 May 1960. On this occasion a *Vostok* prototype carried a mannequin through sixty-four orbits before malfunctioning irreparably. In July there was more bad news: Two dogs, Chaika and Lisichka, were killed in a launch-pad disaster. A much better result came on August 19 when two more dogs, Belka and Strelka, completed eighteen orbits then returned safely to earth by parachute after being automatically ejected. Then on October 24 at Baikonur a ballistic missile test went horribly wrong, exploding and killing more than 160 people. Though it was not directly connected to the manned space mission, still it cast a pall. A little over a month later, on December 1, two more dogs, Mushka and Pchelka were killed when their *Vostok*— on course for a landing outside of Soviet borders — was automatically detonated during reentry. Shortly thereafter, Korolev himself suffered a heart attack. Neither able nor willing to take the prescribed rest, he was back at work within a few weeks, putting in his usual long days and nights.

Three more launches — using dogs and dummies — carried out over the following few months, proved successful. The last two in particular, during March 1961, convinced Korolev and his political bosses to prepare for the real thing. But who would they send up?

By now, the search for the ideal pilot had in fact already long been under way. Recruiters had begun by investigating and interviewing as many as 3,000 fighter pilots. Not a one was told what the mission might be. Of these, some 200 were selected for transfer to Moscow's Scientific Research Aviation Hospital, where they were placed in centrifuges, subjected to sleep and oxygen deprivation, and in many other ways prodded, poked, and stressed to their physical and psychological limits. In this manner the field was quickly reduced to twenty candidates, all of whom were then trained for the first manned spaceflight. Living and working closely together, they came eventually to be known as "Gagarin's squadron"—after their most illustrious member, the eventual first man in space. Some of them would fly on later missions; others went on to have important military careers; others fell into obscurity.

Given the care accorded to their selection, it is perhaps strange to learn that these men were in fact being groomed to be simple passengers, not pilots. Neither the Soviets nor the Americans, who were also working toward their own manned mission, had any real idea how a man might respond—both physically and psychologically—to being locked into a tiny capsule and sent hurtling through space. Would he become incapacitated in some way? Would he go mad? The Soviets were unwilling to risk their first mission finding out. Everything would be done on automatic pilot. (In fact, this system was preserved for several subsequent flights. The first real exception was the flight of *Voskhod*-2 in 1965.[37]) Since flying experience and ability were no longer vital attributes, other criteria could be weighed more heavily, including weight and size (the smaller the better) and political and propaganda considerations.

In both these areas, one man shone above all others. His name was Iurii Alekseevich Gagarin—born 9 March 1934 in Klushino, west of Moscow. One of four children, he had everything Korolev and Khrushchev were looking for. He was of proletarian stock, the son of collective farmers (his father was also a trained carpenter). Starting out in foundry work, Gagarin had first enrolled in technical school in Saratov before training in Orenburg to be a pilot. Bright but not intellectual, in every circumstance Gagarin earned high praise for his dedication, hard work, and optimism. In 1957 he qualified as a military pilot and was sent to an air base near Murmansk. Gherman Titov, who would eventually become the second man in orbit, later summarized Gagarin's biography: "He was the son of a peasant, and lived through the fearful days of fascist occupation. Then a craftsman. A worker. A student, a member of an aviation club. A flier."[38] He also possessed an infectious smile and boyish demeanor that in other times and places might have made him a movie star or pop sensation.

Though Gagarin was officially chosen for the flight only days beforehand, he seems to have been the clear favorite almost from the start, even among most of his fellow candidates.[39] "I don't know of anybody who was liked by so many different types of people," remarked B. V. Volynov (one of the twenty).[40] Korolev too was charmed. Supposedly he had been particularly impressed when Gagarin, upon seeing the spherical *Vostok* capsule for the first time, humbly removed his shoes before getting in to try it out.[41] And at just five feet two inches and similarly light, he was irresistible. But the final decision was Khrushchev's, not Korolev's, and here what mattered was Gagarin's outstanding political pedigree and the propaganda use that could subsequently be made of him.

A final factor identified by some historians is Gagarin's national origin. All the candidates, of course, were Soviet, but not all were Russian. Some were of Ukrainian, Chuvash, or other origin. This, of course, should not have mattered. Official Soviet ideology loathed nationalism and sought, at various times, either a "brotherhood" or a complete "merging" of national identities into one Soviet people. This was as much propaganda as a real goal, however—the USSR being in many ways clearly just the latest incarnation of the old Russian

Empire. There is, thus, probably much merit to the opinion of the Soviet defector Leonid Vladimirov that Khrushchev wanted a "pure" Russian cosmonaut to secure the notion of the Russians as the political and ideological elder brothers of the wider Soviet family.[42] Here too Gagarin was a perfect fit.

Gagarin, aged twenty-seven, arrived at the Baikonur launch pad around lunchtime on April 11. Korolev took him up to the capsule and went over procedures. Gagarin then returned to the quarters he shared with back-up cosmonaut Titov. Neither man slept all that well, and both were roused at 5:30 A.M. After breakfasting Gagarin returned to the launch tower, suited up, and was helped into the tiny capsule perched atop Korolev's rockets. Then he was sealed in. Though scheduled only to make one orbit, Gagarin was packing ten days' worth of air, food, and water. This was Korolev's precaution against the possible failure of his craft's braking rockets, developed by another important Russian rocket engineer, A. M. Isaev. In the event of failure, the craft's trajectory would, supposedly, bring it back to into the earth's atmosphere in ten days.[43]

Gagarin now had to sit in position through hours of checks. Finally, at 8:19 A.M., a little music was piped into the capsule for his amusement. Somewhat over twenty minutes after that the launch tower pulled back, and the rockets started up. Another twenty-five minutes passed. Then at 9:07 A.M. Gagarin — his heart pumping at 157 beats per minute — was on his way into orbit and history. It was, of course, far more Korolev's achievement than Gagarin's. The one man had conceived and developed it all. The other sat back, tolerated the considerable g-forces, touched no controls whatsoever, and periodically reported his impressions back to earth. These reports, however, were critically important. No human had ever been in orbit before. What would the physical effects be of prolonged weightlessness and cramped confinement? Would internal organs function normally? What about blood flow? Could a person swallow in zero gravity? Would he vomit uncontrollably? And then there were the unknown psychological effects.

From the moment of liftoff, Korolev and the many others on the ground who tracked Gagarin's eastward-moving course continuously asked their pilot how he was feeling. Gagarin — seemingly cheerful through it all — provided only good news: "fine," "excellent," "no discomfort," and the like. Minutes into the flight, as the first and then the second stages fell away Gagarin also began reporting enthusiastically on the view: "I can see the earth through the porthole. I can make out the folds of the terrain, snow and forests.... I can see small cumuli and their shadows. It's beautiful!"[44] About five minutes into the flight, equipment on the ground indicated a problem with telemetry. There was momentary panic at Baikonur. One of the ground crew noticed the Chief Designer's hands shaking. "His voice changed, and his face lost its color — so much we could not recognize him."[45] It turned out to be a false alarm, a harmless and momentary interruption in the line of communication. "Such breaks," another of Korolev's associates later pointed out, "considerably shorten a designer's life."[46] Gagarin, oblivious to the drama below, continued with his impressions, noting the disappearance beneath thickening high cloud of the features he had earlier described.

By 9:21 A.M., the crushing g-forces having abated, Gagarin reported, "Weightlessness is having a pleasant effect on me. Nothing at all the matter with it."[47] This was particularly welcome news. By 9:57 A.M. the *Vostok* was where Khrushchev had most wanted it — above the United States. Its signal was picked up first by a station in the Aleutians. One minute later, Soviet media broke silence and inundated the airwaves with the joyous news: a man, a *Soviet* man, was in orbit! The news quickly reached Gagarin's wife, who had had no idea. Gagarin flew on.

So far the flight had been textbook perfect, but reentry — which Gagarin had feared above other parts of the journey — was nearly a catastrophe. A problem occurred as the braking rocket first fired. Gagarin's report, given the following day, was terse and dry, giving little sense of any emotions he might have experienced: "The g-load began to rise a little, and then weightlessness came abruptly back.... The braking rocket operated for exactly forty seconds.... [Then] there was a sharp jolt, and the craft began to rotate around its axis at a very high velocity." Gagarin was spinning, but he does not seem to have panicked. "First I see Africa ... then the horizon, then the sky.... I waited for the separation [of his capsule from the reentry rocket stages]. There wasn't any."[48] Gagarin continued to rotate, falling fast into the atmosphere. Then the outside of his craft heated and turned red. He reported hearing burning and crackling sounds from outside. Suddenly, ten minutes behind schedule, separation occurred. The danger was past.

It would later turn out that during the original attempt at separation, although the braking rockets had worked perfectly, some cables had jammed in place, holding the two parts of the craft together. This would certainly have proven fatal, but fortunately the heat of reentry melted the cables. Thus saved, Gagarin was ejected without incident and soon found himself descending smoothly toward a plowed field in the village of Uzmor'e on the left bank of the Volga River not far from Saratov, where he had earlier trained. He landed comfortably enough and, still in his spacesuit, ascended a hill where he saw and apparently startled a woman and a young girl. Gagarin later described the moment: "I then began to wave my arms and yell, 'I'm one of yours, a Soviet, don't be afraid, don't be scared, come here!' It's hard to walk in a space suit, but I was doing it anyway.... I went up to her and said that I was a Soviet and that I had come from space."[49] The whole flight had taken 108 minutes.

The world's media erupted in applause and amazement. Even more than *Sputnik*, Gagarin's flight caught the world's imagination and convinced millions that America was losing an important race. This impression was probably strengthened over the following months as the Americans Alan Shepard and Gus Grissom set U.S. altitude records flying *sub*orbital paths.

Despite wanting to, Gagarin never returned to space. His fame and achievement now made him a priceless political asset — much too valuable to risk on further space flights. Reinvented as a poster boy and ambassador for the Soviet system, he was sent instead on a series of speaking tours. Though he shouldered his new responsibilities as best he could, he missed flying. At the same time, sudden fame led to marital, drinking, and other problems. A minor political career in the Supreme Soviet followed, and then a return to the Star City astronautical training facility near Moscow, but only for design work. It was not until 1967, after several other Russians had flown in space (making Gagarin less unique and the whole enterprise appear somewhat safer), that Gagarin was again approved for flight — though only as a backup — on *Soiuz*-1. This turned out to be to his good fortune. Vladimir Komarov, who ended up flying the *Soiuz*, was killed tragically on reentry on April 24. Gagarin's own luck ran out the following year, however. During a routine flight, while retraining as a fighter pilot, he was killed when his MiG-15 crashed near Kirzhach, midway between Vladimir and Moscow. Gagarin reportedly struck the ground at well over 400 miles per hour and the wreckage was strewn over many miles. Only a small bagful of body parts was ever recovered. These were placed in his casket and cremated. Amid a national outpouring of grief, Gagarin was placed in the Kremlin wall with full honors.

Soviet Space Achievements After Gagarin

On 6 August 1961, less than four months after Gagarin's epochal flight, Korolev sent a second cosmonaut, Gherman Titov, into orbit in *Vostok*-2. The timing, as usual, was politically motivated. A few days later, as the world again cheered Soviet space prowess, Khrushchev ordered construction of the Berlin Wall. But Titov's flight was also a significant step forward in the conquest of space. Gagarin had orbited only once and flown for just 108 minutes. Titov made seventeen orbits in twenty-five hours — and suffered accordingly from motion sickness. Like Gagarin, Titov flew under autopilot and was ejected after reentry, parachuting safely — though narrowly missing a passing train — to a point near the launch site at Baikonur. "Bump, and I was on my feet," he later reported. Like Gagarin's, his landing attracted onlookers. Titov much later related the following terse conversation he had with one of a trio of motorcyclists at the scene:

> "Are you Titov?"
> "I'm Titov."
> "Good stuff, Titov!"[50]

Then two cars arrived. A woman with a bloody forehead jumped out of one of them. Apparently the sight of Titov descending had caused her to veer into a ditch!

Titov's much longer flight, compared to Gagarin's, provided further insights into the challenges of living in zero gravity. "Weightlessness continued to play tricks with me," he later noted, "and for a long time I could not cope with my arms. As soon as I began to doze, they would rise up and hang in the air."[51] But perhaps most memorable, for him and for anyone reading about his journey, is the impression he got from looking at the earth from space: "I saw it, our earth, I saw it all. It is lovely, but it is really small, when you look at it from space. And, remembering the earth as I saw it *from out there*, knowing I could direct my ship to any point on the planet, I suddenly realized with all my being how careful we must be with it, how we have to work and think so as to have peace reign eternally on all six continents."[52] Virtually everyone who has ventured into orbit since Titov has felt or described similar sentiments.

On 20 February 1962, six-and-a-half months after Titov's flight, the American John Glenn orbited earth three times in *Mercury-Atlas* 6. Three months later his compatriot Scott Carpenter did the same in *Mercury-Atlas* 7. The Space Race was on in earnest.

Insofar as public and political attention remained fixed on firsts and other easily quantifiable achievements — rather than solid science and engineering — Korolev and his team were able to keep up the appearance of being ahead. Glenn and Carpenter's three orbits each were answered in mid–August by the near-simultaneous launching of two Soviet craft — *Vostok*-3 and *Vostok*-4 — whose cosmonauts knocked off sixty-four and forty-eight orbits, respectively. The two craft passed at one point within three miles of each other, hinting at the possibilities of space-docking in the near future. The American ripostes came in the form of six orbits from *Mercury-Atlas* 8 in early October and twenty-two with *Mercury-Atlas* 9 the following May.

Valentina Tereshkova: First Woman in Space

With the United States quickly gaining ground in terms of number and length of orbits achieved, the Soviets switched tack and focused on sending the first woman into space. Khrushchev's primary interest was propaganda as usual. In this case he sought to make a statement about the supposed equality of the sexes that had been achieved under the conditions of Soviet socialism. As with the male cosmonauts, the selection process focused on the candidates' revolutionary credentials as much as on their skill, physique, or fitness. From an initial pool of some 400 pilots, five finalists were quickly chosen and given the same basic training as the men. Their names were Tatiana Kuznetsova, Irina Soloveva, Zhanna Ierkina, Valentina Ponomareva, and the eventual winner, twenty-six-year-old Valentina Tereshkova. Tereshkova's major advantage seems to have been her background, which, as with Gagarin before her, read in many respects like the ideal Soviet biography. Born in 1937 to collective farm workers, her father had died fighting in World War II. Upon finishing school, Tereshkova had worked — and become politically active — in a tire factory. By 1961 she was chapter secretary of the plant's Communist Youth League and later joined the Communist Party itself. From age twenty-two she had also trained as a skydiver. Her selection was approved — perhaps even made personally — by Khrushchev.

Tereshkova's flight was eventually scheduled as one half of another two-craft mission, officially dubbed a "group flight." Preceding her into orbit, Valerii Bykovskii (a man) was launched from Baikonur on 14 June 1963 in *Vostok*-5. On the 16th Tereshkova blasted off in *Vostok*-6. Both flights were successful. Bykovskii completed a record eighty-one orbits and spent 199 hours in space. Tereshkova flew forty-eight orbits over three days. At their nearest pass the two craft were only a little more than three miles apart. As she flew, Tereshkova — code named *Chaika* (Seagull) — radioed politically correct greetings for all to hear: "Warm greetings from space to the glorious Leninist Young Communist League which reared me"; and "Everything that is good in me I owe to our Communist Party and Young Communist League."[53] The flight was not without its difficulties, however. From her capsule Tereshkova soon began reporting multiple symptoms: tiredness; knee pain caused by her cramped position; shoulder pain from her helmet; loss of appetite. Psychologically, too, she seemed to be under considerable stress. She wanted to come down, she said. She is reported to have cried. When eventually she landed safely in the southern Urals she was in poor shape, suffering nausea and perhaps spasms. She had eaten little or nothing for three days.

Given that her flight was marketed and consumed around the world as a great statement of Soviet gender equality, there is, perhaps, some irony in the response her complaints received on the ground. At one point Korolev himself reportedly cursed her out: "I've had it working with women! [*shtoby ia kogda-nibud' sviazalsia s zhenshchinami!*]" Later the same day Korolev told his wife that "space is not for women! [*babam v kosmose delat' nechego!*]."[54] Tereshkova — who went on to enjoy a successful political career — seemed to agree, later commenting: "I believe that a woman should always remain a woman and nothing feminine should be alien to her.... I strongly feel that no work done by a woman in the field of science or culture or whatever, however vigorous or demanding, can enter into conflict with her ancient 'wonderful mission' — to love, to be loved — and with her craving for the bliss of motherhood."[55] Although, like Gagarin, Tereshkova usually spoke from carefully prepared scripts, there has been little if any reason to suggest she thought differently herself. In any case, there were no more female Soviet cosmonauts until 1982.

The *Voskhod* Program

Tereshkova's flight was also the end of the line for the highly successful *Vostok* spacecraft. It was succeeded by a new vehicle called *Voskhod*. The first launch, planned for 12 October

1964, called for placing a three-man team into orbit. Nothing of the sort had ever been done, and a Soviet success would certainly impress the Americans. In fact, the mission has been fairly described as "another of Korolev's illusions."[56] Rather than an important technological leap forward, *Voskhod* was only a modest reworking of its predecessor. Getting three men into space would be achieved not by the deployment of new, more powerful engines, nor by using a much larger capsule, but mainly by a desperate — if inventive — regime of space-saving tactics. In other words, Korolev essentially set out to stuff three men into a capsule designed for one. To this end the ejection seat and apparatus, themselves part of the earlier *weight*-saving regime, were now removed: the cosmonaut-sardines would land *in* the capsule this time, using newer and lighter braking mechanisms. More risky still was the idea, mooted by a young engineer named Konstantin Petrovich Feoktistov[57] — one of the three cosmonauts who would go on to fly the mission!— to do away with the bulky space suits altogether. The cosmonauts would fly in simple overalls. This would save space *and* weight, making the whole scheme possible. But it meant leaving the cosmonauts completely unprotected in the event of any air leak or other problems. Further room was saved by placing the seats tightly together.

Time and resource constraints allowed only a single unmanned test. Yet remarkably, *Voskhod*-1 was a complete success. The three cosmonauts landed safely on October 13 after sixteen orbits, convincing the world once again of the superiority of Soviet over American space technology. The only participant who did not fare terribly well was Khrushchev himself, who was removed from office the same day by a group of political opponents centered around his own protégé, Leonid Brezhnev.

The next mission, *Voskhod*-2, attempted yet another spectacular first — a spacewalk. Two cosmonauts were chosen: Aleksei Arkhipovich Leonov (1934–present), who was to carry out the "walk," and copilot Pavel Beliaev. The major technological challenges this time were to create an airlock and a spacesuit that could function outside the craft. As usual, things were rushed and improvised in order to beat U.S. plans — this time for a manned *Gemini* mission on 23 March 1965. For an airlock, Korolev came up with a simple "inflatable section attached to a special door on the one side of the cabin."[58] The suit was more difficult. In space there is no atmospheric pressure. Any astronaut exiting a pressurized cabin would immediately be at risk of a fatal bout of decompression sickness. Preventing this required pressurizing the suit — but this brought its own problems. Once outside the capsule, any level of air pressure *within* the suit would tend to make it inflate like a balloon — potentially reducing internal pressure, presenting major mobility problems, and raising the possibility of leaks. The Soviets' solution was to construct a reinforced suit that would function with an internal pressure of six pounds per square inch, less than half that of normal cabin pressure.

Leonov and Beliaev were launched, flawlessly, on the 18th (five days ahead of *Gemini*). The real tests lay ahead, however. Once in orbit, Beliaev readied the airlock while Leonov added an oxygen backpack to his spacesuit. Leonov then entered the airlock and underwent decompression. Moments later he emerged through the exit hatch and drifted out to the full extension of his lifeline. For several minutes he dangled there — the first spacewalker. It was by any measure an amazing achievement and an overwhelming experience. Leonov later wrote of it: "I was attached by just an umbilical chord of cables to our space craft ... as it orbited ... at 30,000 kph. Yet it felt as if I were almost motionless.... Lifting my head I could see the curvature of the Earth's horizon.... For a few moments I felt totally alone in the pristine new environment, taking in the beauty of the panorama below me with an artist's eye. Then a voice filled the void: 'Attention. Attention.' It was my commander, Pavel Beliaev, addressing me and, it seemed, the rest of mankind. 'Your attention, please,' [he] said, ... 'A human being has made the first ever walk in open space.' It took me a moment to realize he was talking about me."[59] Moments later, while still floating, Leonov received a transmission from Soviet leader Leonid Brezhnev, which must have stretched the surreal nature of the moment to an extreme.

After a few minutes it was time to return to the craft. But now a problem appeared. Even at the low pressure of six pounds per square inch, Leonov's suit had still inflated and become rigid nearly to the point of immobility. No matter how he tried, he could not pull his legs forward far enough, or make himself small enough, to get into the hatch. He began to panic. His visor steamed and he started to perspire freely. With his air supply already low, his pulse and breathing rates spiked dangerously. If unable to repressurize he would soon get the bends — if he did not run out of air first. The situation suddenly seemed dire. But Leonov was equal to it. Completely improvising, he let some air out of his suit, dropping it to just four pounds per square inch. This put him in even more imminent danger from decompression. But it gave him the vital flexibility he needed to pass through the hatch. A moment later and he was safely inside and repressurizing. In all, he'd been outside for twelve minutes and nine seconds, including eight minutes struggling at the hatch.[60]

As it turned out there were more dangers ahead. After Leonov's reentry the *Voskhod*'s life-support systems — responding automatically to an imperfect seal on the hatch — suddenly began pumping too much oxygen into the cabin, raising the possibility of a catastrophic fire or explosion. This, however, was averted. Then, as the two men prepared for reentry, the autopilot malfunctioned, failing to slow the craft properly. The only hope now was for the crew to make reentry on manual controls — something never done before by the Soviets. At ground control, and with only a few minutes remaining before the *Voskhod* faced disaster, Korolev and others scrambled in near panic, trying to calculate, check, and recheck the needed trajectory. Finally, the numbers were sent up to the crew. Inputting them manually required a little on-board gymnastics — Beliaev had to lie across both seats, with Leonov out of his. This, of course, slightly altered the craft's center of gravity for a few moments, bringing its own risks. Reseated, the two men fired the retro-rockets and hoped for the best. Incredibly, it worked. A short time later Leonov and Beliaev were back in the earth's atmosphere headed for a safe landing — more or less.

The earlier problems with reentry had put them on course for a landing in the Urals — well within the USSR but nearly 2,000 miles from the intended site in Kazakhstan. And here they encountered one final set of challenges. The capsule landed without serious event and lodged between two trees above deep snow. In bitter cold the two cosmonauts struggled out of their craft and managed to light a fire only to be forced back inside by a pack of hungry wolves. Unable to properly reclose the door, they spent much of the night fighting the animals off. They were finally rescued around dawn.[61]

Voskod-2's spectacular if nail-biting success marks the beginning of the end of Korolev's anonymous reign as the world's greatest space pioneer. By now the Americans were increasingly finding their own footing and, able to marshal much greater resources, were quickly closing the Space Race gap. Soon they would move ahead. The United States had developed *Gemini* — a much more advanced craft sporting on-board computing and two-astronaut capacity. On March 23, flying in *Gemini-3*, Gus Grissom and John Young carried out first-ever maneuvers in orbit. In June, Edward White bested Leonov's spacewalk, spending twenty-two minutes on total extravehicular activity — and wearing a more cooperative space-

Soviet Academicians and Cosmonauts at a Meeting in Moscow. They are (from left to right) academicians Anatolii Blagonravov, Mikhail Millionshchikov, cosmonauts Vladimir Komarov, Boris Egorov, Konstantin Feoktistov, Valentina Tereshkova, academician Sergei Korolev, Academy of Sciences president Mstislav Keldysh, cosmonauts Pavel Popovich, Andriian Nikolaiev, Iurii Gagarin, Gherman Titov and Valerii Bykovskii. Photographed in 1964 (Ria Novosti/Photo Researchers, Inc. SPL Reference Number: C007/5026. Images and Text Copyright © 2011 Photo Researchers, Inc. All Rights Reserved).

suit! During a week-long flight in late August, the crew of *Gemini*-5 (the first craft to use fuel cells) flew a record 120 orbits. And in December *Gemini*-7 made it 220 orbits. Even more impressively, during the same flight *Gemini*s-6 and -7 maneuvered to within one foot of each other. And more was to come.

In May 1961 the race to the moon began — at least in the United States. Going specifically to the moon, rather than anywhere else, was at this time an American goal, not a Soviet one. The R-7, exceptionally well suited for earth orbital missions, could not lift the necessary amounts of fuel and other equipment. If the Soviets wanted to send a man to the moon and bring him back they would have to start more-or-less from scratch with a totally new craft. This, of course, was exactly what the Kennedy administration liked about the project. For his part, Korolev did not need U.S. competition to urge him to set his sights on a manned moon mission — he had been dreaming of this for decades. The U.S. announcement did, however, encourage him to push the project more aggressively with his political bosses. Since 1959 Korolev had even been working at OKB-1 on plans for an appropriately powerful rocket, the N-1. Packing enough thrust to lift fifty tons — and considerably more in subsequent redesigns — thus far the N-1 had been intended for military applications. It could, he argued, be adapted for a manned lunar expedition. Tepid political support, dispute over the appropriate type of fuel system, and other problems slowed progress, however, at a time when the American *Apollo* program was moving quickly ahead.

Korolev's Death

As it turned out, *Voskhod*-2 was Korolev's last manned mission. For many years his health had been steadily declining. Ever since his ordeal in the Gulag he had been affected by kidney and heart problems. After his 1960 heart attack, doctors' recommendations for rest and recuperation had been ignored. Instead, constant pressure to outdo the Americans, threats from the authorities to transfer funding and support to one or another of his engineering rivals, and Korolev's own fanatical devotion to his labors combined to create an extraordinarily frenetic and unhealthy work regime. By 1965 Korolev's list of complaints was ominous: a bout of internal bleeding, persistent heart arrhythmia, inflamed gall bladder, hearing loss, fatigue, and chest pains. His final demise came on 14 January 1966, caused by complications during a procedure to remove intestinal polyps. The operation, carried out by no lesser a person than the Soviet health minister, B. V. Petrovskii, is generally considered to have been botched. Korolev died on the operating table.

In death Korolev attained the public recognition he had been systematically denied in life. The transformation was instant and complete. Two days after his death his photograph and a lengthy obituary ran in *Pravda*. The following day he was given a hero's funeral at Red Square. In attendance were all the major political figures, including Brezhnev and other Politburo members; Chief Designers, scientists and engineers; academicians; the cosmonauts — including Gagarin, Titov, Leonov, and Tereshkova; and Korolev's family, relatives, and friends. There were numerous speeches. Gagarin spoke last. Korolev's ashes were placed in the Kremlin wall.

Although Korolev continues to be exalted for his numerous achievements and stupendous efforts, there have been in recent times minority opinions to the effect that he has been praised beyond his merit and to the detriment of other members of the Council of Chief Designers who deserve to share in the glory — including his archenemy Glushko.[62]

The Soviet Space Program after Korolev

Korolev was succeeded as Chief Designer by his former deputy, Vasilii Mishin, who struggled to pick up where the great man had left off. It is extremely unlikely that even Korolev could have continued any longer to keep the Americans from overtaking the Soviets, the gap in resources being just too great. But it was under Mishin's watch that the baton was clearly passed, as arguably the greatest prize of all went to the Americans who landed on the moon in 1969.[63] Nonetheless, Mishin did preside over some important scientific successes, including the soft landing of an unmanned research-probe (*Luna*-9) on the moon on 3 February 1966 (only two weeks after Korolev's death), the first probe to enter Venus's atmosphere (*Venera*-4, launched 12 June 1967), and the first transmission of data from the surface of Venus (by *Venera*-7 on 22 July 1970). Mishin also continued work on Korolev's dream rocket, the N-1, which remained the Soviets' best shot at a manned moon mission. The project continued to fare poorly, however. In the end only four N-1s were ever tested — between February 1969 and November 1972. They all blew up during liftoff or shortly after. In 1974 Mishin was dismissed in favor of Korolev's old rival Valentin Glushko, who immediately cancelled the N-1 altogether.

Long before his removal, however, Mishin enjoyed what became in retrospect not only his greatest personal success, but also the beginning of a whole new phase of Soviet and Russian space achievement. This was the launch on 19 April 1971 of *Saliut*-1— the world's first orbiting space station. Although the event was marred by the tragic death of its crew during the return flight, *Saliut*-1 provided these cosmonauts a home in space for a total of twenty-three days. It remained in orbit for six months. Other *Saliuts* soon followed. The

United States responded with its own orbiting space station, *Skylab*, launched in May 1973. After extensive repairs in space, *Skylab* quickly outperformed the first three *Saliuts*, allowing the United States to set consecutive space endurance records, ending with eighty-four days beginning that November. But under Glushko's authority from 1974 on, the *Saliuts* became a particularly bright spot in the ongoing Soviet space program. With the Soviets beaten to the moon, and the absurd pressures for novel space stunts abated somewhat, this fruitful area of endeavor was allowed to progress, with significant results. Beginning with *Saliut*-4, launched 26 December 1975, the Soviets in fact found themselves catching up, and then moving ahead of the Americans in space endurance: thirty days in 1975 (*Saliut*-4), and then a series of records on *Saliut*-6: ninety-six in 1977–1978, 140 in 1978, 175 in 1979, and 185 days in 1980. *Skylab*, by contrast, fell into disrepair and was deorbited in 1979. This left the field to the Soviets, who followed the last *Saliut* (number 7, launched April 1982) with a new generation space station called *Mir*, the first components of which were launched in 1986, the last a decade later. *Mir* continued to allow Soviet crews to push the frontiers of human endurance in space — culminating so far in a record of more than 437 days, set by Valeri Poliakov during 1994–1995. After the collapse of the USSR in 1991, U.S. crews and other nationals visited (including the Englishwoman Helen Sharman). Mir was deorbited in 2001.

Since the demise of the Soviet Union, and to the present day, Russia has remained on the forefront of space exploration and development, particularly in the areas of commercial satellite launch and space endurance. The Russians are also a key player in the development of the International Space Station, having signed onto the project in 1993. It was Russia that on 20 November 1998 launched the first component part of the station — the *Zaria*/FGB control module, sent up from Baikonur, a facility the Russians now lease from independent Kazakhstan. The Russians have also helped pioneer space tourism — having since 2001 taken a handful of high-paying individuals to and from the International Space Station using their reliable *Siouz* rockets — fittingly, a Korolev design. In this area, however, the Russian space program looks set to face stiff competition in coming years from private commercial interests in the West, including Richard Branson's much-anticipated Virgin Galactic service. Whatever the future of space travel, Russia's place in pioneering it is assured.

Further Readings in Russian and English

Biriukov, Y. V. "The History of the Designing of Liquid-Propellant Rocket Engines as a New Type of Rocket Engine." Viniti. USSR Academy of Sciences, Moscow, 1966. English translation in NASA 10 TT F-540, 3.

Cadbury. Debora. *Space Race: The Epic Battle Between America and the Soviet Union for Dominion of Space.* New York: HarperCollins, 2006.

Feoktistov, Konstantin Petrovich. *Zato my delali rakety. Vospominaniia i razmyshleniia kosmonavta-issle-dovatelia.* Moscow: Vremia, 2005.

Gagarin, Iurii. *Road to the Stars.* Told to Nikolay Denisov and Serhy Borzenko. Edited by N. Kamanin. Translated by G. Hanna and D. Myshnei. Moscow: Foreign Languages Publishing House, 1962.

Golovanov, Iaroslav. *Korolev: Fakti i mifi.* Moscow: Nauka, 1994.

Gurney, Clare, and Gene Gurney. *Cosmonauts in Orbit: The Story of the Soviet Manned Space Program.* New York: Franklin Watts, 1972.

Harford, James. *Korolev: How One Man Masterminded the Soviet Drive to Beat America to the Moon.* New York: Wiley, 1997.

Neufeld, Michael J. *Von Braun: Dreamer of Space, Engineer of War.* New York: Knopf/Smithsonian National Air and Space Museum, 2007.

Oberg, James. *Uncovering Soviet Disasters: Exploring the Limits of Glasnost.* New York: Random House, 1988.

Pervushin, Anton. *Bitva za zvezdy.* 2 vols. Moscow: Voenno-istoricheskaia biblioteka, 2003.

Raushenbakh, B. V., ed. *S. P. Korolev i ego delo: svet i teni v istorii kosmonaftiki: izbrannie trudi i dokumenty.* Moscow: Nauka, 1998.

Riabchikov, Evgeny. *Russians in Space.* Translated by Guy Daniels. New York: Doubleday, 1971.

Scott, David R., Alexei Leonov, and Christine Toomey. *Two Sides of the Moon: Our Story of the Cold War Space Race.* New York: Thomas Dunne Books, 2004.

Shelton, William. *Soviet Space Exploration: The First Decade.* With an introduction by Gherman Titov. London: Barker, 1969.

Sokolskii, Viktor. "Work on the Theoretical Foundations of Cosmonautics and Evolution of Rocket Technology in the USSR Prior to 1945." In *History of the USSR: New Research.* 5. Moscow: "Social Sciences Today," 1986, 64–92.

Suvorov, Vladimir, and Alexander Sabelnikov. *The First Manned Spaceflight: Russia's Quest for Space.* Commack, NY: Nova Science Publishers, 1997.

Vladimirov, Leonid. *The Russian Space Bluff: The Inside Story of the Soviet Drive to the Moon.* Translated by David Floyd. New York: Dial Press, 1973.

Conclusions

In the introductory chapter I argued that the history of Russian exploration, rather than simply a collection of separate narratives, presents a coherent overall *story* with certain distinctive features and themes — such as the preference for contiguous expansion and the tendency, compared with other imperial countries, to comingle concepts of state, nation, and empire. This story seems also to be set into distinct chapters or stages. In other words, looking back over the centuries of Russian travel one gets the impression of a general progress, over time, from one *sort* of exploration to another. For the most part, the sixteenth- and early-seventeenth-century operations of men such as Ermak, Stadukhin, or Atlasov seem relatively spontaneous and unsophisticated — a simple matter of piracy, plunder, and conquest. Furs were the great prize — whether gained as tribute or taken directly by hunting. Conquered lands and peoples were themselves valued primarily insofar as they could provide this one thing. These early conquests also display a certain amateurishness. Both *promyshlenniki* and official men went forth in small numbers, with little planning and few resources. They endured what they could, improvised endlessly, and won or lost more or less as the fates decided. They kept scant records or none at all. In their zeal for fur and conquest, they sometimes seem, at least to the modern mind, almost criminally oblivious to the many other riches of Siberia — including its diverse cultures, other natural resources, and its great beauty. No doubt these things are more easily appreciated from the relative comfort and prosperity of the modern age.

By the eighteenth century, however, much had changed. Expeditions were far more complex undertakings. Explorers enjoyed significant state backing, and they pursued far more ambitious goals. The two great Kamchatka Expeditions of the eighteenth century, for example, involved literally thousands of people and, in comparison with the modest affairs of the previous century, cost equally inflated sums of money. They also incorporated science in ways that had not been done before. In Ermak's day, science — if it was understood at all, was spurned and mistrusted in Russia as an alien and corrupting influence, contrary to tradition and true religion. By the eighteenth century, thanks largely to the westernizing efforts of Tsar Peter the Great, it had become central to the enterprise of exploration and expansion. Consequently, expeditions were now led and staffed not by freebooters and pirates but by educated and credentialed men such as Bering and Chirikov. There was sometimes even room for relatively tender and sentimental souls, such as Steller. The inventorying of plants, animals, and peoples, and studies of the motions of the planets as viewed from different locations had all become as critical to exploration as the gathering of tribute had been to Ermak and Ivan.

These new circumstances did not, however, mean that the basic urge to conquer or plunder had been deprioritized. Rather, they were symptomatic of an *expansion* (and perhaps also a refinement) of Russian imperial ambition—based on a growing awareness of the political and strategic importance of geographical knowledge, of the value and diversity of Russia's vast natural resources, and of the potential these things offered for national aggrandizement. Other aspects of eighteenth-century exploration also remained unchanged from earlier times. In particular, nothing could yet ameliorate the hardships involved in trans–Siberian crossings or northerly maritime navigations. Thus, men—and as the story of Mariia Pronchishcheva shows us, women also—suffered and died just like their predecessors from the despotisms of climate, distance, and terrain.

With the turn of the nineteenth century, exploration shifted again. Having largely completed their reconnaissance and conquest of Siberia, and with a growing foothold also in Alaska, Russians now gazed upon more distant, transoceanic horizons. Each in his own way, Kruzenshtern (in the tropical Pacific), Bellingshausen (in Antarctica), and Miklukho-Maklai (in Papua New Guinea) took up the great challenge presented by Bering and Chirikov's discovery of Alaska back in 1741—the task of transitioning from a tradition of mostly land-based, incremental, and contiguous exploration on and beyond the shifting Russian frontier to the different rigors of maritime navigations across vast spaces toward ever more remote and scattered destinations. This involved not only a physical and geographical change of focus, but also a shift of culture and perspective. It required, in a sense, that Russian explorers—and the state behind most of them—assume a similar kind of cocksure global-imperialist outlook as their counterparts from Great Britain and western continental Europe. This, however, the Russians ultimately could—or perhaps would—not do. Although they navigated, explored, studied, and contributed in ways that made them these other countries' peers, the Russians also showed their differences. In abandoning Alaska in 1867, in choosing not to pursue colonial or annexationist policies in Papua New Guinea (despite Miklukho-Maklai's pleadings), or in Hawaii, and in discovering but then forgetting Antarctica, the Russians slowly but surely, and perhaps without really being aware of it, reaffirmed their commitment to a uniquely Russian concept of state expansion: one that blended notions of empire and nation under the traditional desire, or historical instinct, for geographical contiguity. This reaffirmation is evident not only in the travels of Nikolai Przheval'skii and his associates into Central Asia, but also in Vilkitskii's achievements along the Russian Arctic coast.

It took a profound rupturing of tradition to shake the Russians out of this mindset, and to set them once again chasing distant horizons. The Bolshevik Revolution of 1917 brought to power individuals committed to furthering man's conquest of nature, and to surpassing all her supposed limitations. This, and the stridently internationalist perspectives central to Revolutionary Socialism inspired an enthusiastic return to internationalism in Russian exploration, too. Prior to the Second World War, efforts were focused on the North Polar region. But after 1945—in the context of the Cold War—the Soviets reached out to the South Pole and, most spectacularly, into Space. Post-Soviet Russia continues on the forefront of these endeavors.

I noted in the introduction that Russian contributions to the history of geographical exploration have not found a place in popular memory equivalent to their overall historical significance. I also offered a few suggestions as to why this might be, and deferred to this section a few more thoughts on the matter. It is to this question that we return now, starting first with a further look at the Russians' penchant for contiguous (and often land-based) expansion—as opposed to the Western European model of far-flung and scattered maritime imperialism.

Writing in different contexts, historians have noted an important consequence flowing from these different approaches, one we shall expand upon here. Specifically, whereas Western Europeans generally drew a clear distinction between themselves and their empires, for Russians, the two often blurred toward the point of synonymy. Victorian Britons, for example, understood India as part of their empire, but did not at all consider it part of the British state itself. The same is true even in the case of British settler-colonies such as Australia or Canada, whose demography and culture were often nearly identical to that of the home country, at least at first; these places too were understood also as empire (and later as commonwealth), but were never construed as part of Britain itself. A similar point could be made for the Dutch colonies in Indonesia, and — with exceptions such as Algeria — for much of the French Empire, too.[1] Most Russian conquests, by contrast, from the enormous expanses of Siberia to Arctic Islands, were not understood as empire in this sense — even if the word *empire* was often used. Rather, these lands were treated as permanent acquisitions — absorbed into the Russian state politically and in terms of national identity; and there they have remained ever since. For this reason, Russian explorations — at least of Siberia and the Arctic — may strike us as uniquely Russian phenomena, rather than as part of a common human story. Thus, perhaps, many of us have not identified with it as we have with other episodes of exploration and expansion.

Outside of Siberia and the Russian Arctic, however, exactly the opposite logic seems to operate. In the Pacific, for example — in Hawaii, Papua New Guinea, the Caroline Islands, and elsewhere — the footprints Russians left were so light, and have so nearly completely vanished, that we are almost unaware of them. In these places, the Russians created neither an expanded state nor a distant empire — not even a lasting impression. Thus, the much more permanent imprints left in the region by other nations' explorers — such as the Englishman Cook and the Frenchman Bougainville — have wiped the Russian ones from our memory.

The one major exception to these patterns, we have noted, is Alaska. Only a relatively short sail east from the Russian coast, this was nearly — but ultimately not quite — a case of further contiguous Russian expansion and incremental absorption. On the other hand, the Russian footprint in these lands was not so light that it could be easily washed away. Russian Alaska endures — both as a living culture and in the Western historical imagination. Alaska, in fact, serves in some ways as the critical boundary between Russia's contiguous and noncontiguous expansion — as the point at which the former sort of expansion began to break down, and beyond which all further exploration became merely a sort of imperial "window-shopping" or political promenading.

The historical memory of Russian journeys and discoveries has perhaps suffered also from a sort of "language problem" — by which I mean that compared to their Western European counterparts, Russians have not been so successful in naming places. Thus, while Russian names were attached, as we have seen, to a great many islands in the Arctic, Antarctica, and the tropical Pacific, these destinations typically do not have the historical weight or current significance of America (named for the Italian mariner Amerigo Vespucci), or of the various places named for Columbus (including Colombia and British Columbia). Often, also, Russian names did not stick. Many of the Russian discoveries in the Tuamotu and Caroline Island groups, for example, are now known by other names.

These are interesting points to consider. One might counter, however, that they are all somewhat incidental — and that the fundamental reason Russian explorers are not credited as highly as they might be is simply that they did not win the greatest prizes. Following this line, one might argue that Columbus discovered America while the Russians discovered only a *part* of it (Alaska); or that while Russians made many important global circumnavigations, Magellan — a Portuguese — made the first one. Similarly, where Russia *did* discover a whole new continent — as in the case of Bellingshausen in Antarctica — it was uninhabited and has remained marginal to history. To make matters worse, there is a strong rival claimant to the discovery itself (see chapter 7).

Fair points, perhaps, but not entirely convincing. If reality is perception, one must also consider the role of pure salesmanship — the marketing, if you will, of historical events, and here, I think, the Russians have not done as well as they might. Ask almost anyone what was the pivotal achievement of the Space Race and you are likely to be told that it was the landing on the moon. Russians, though, may more often tell you it was the successful launch of *Sputnik*, the world's first artificial satellite, or of Iurii Gagarin, the first person in space. There is, of course, no obviously correct answer to the question, but it is hard to deny that the achievements of the American Apollo crew and project have benefited globally more than have their Russian counterparts from effective publicity, even down to the carefully crafted and highly effective short speech given by Armstrong as he set foot on the moon: "That's one small step for man, one giant leap for mankind." This beautiful couplet explicitly claims the moon landing as a monumental achievement of all humanity, and it smells grandly of history. Gagarin's often-quoted words at his own liftoff — "Let's go!" — seem almost quaint by comparison.

One of my original hopes in researching and writing this book was that it might stimulate further interest and research into some of the topics it raises, many of which — especially those involving Russians in what I have termed "warmer climes" — remain greatly understudied. A substantial amount of the primary materials — written documents, charts, specimens, and more — gathered by Russian expeditions from various centuries remain to this day woefully underutilized, including materials collected by Steller, Przheval'skii, and Langsdorf. As of 2004, the "bulk of the documents" generated by the Krenitsyn-Levashov voyage of 1768–1769, "including detailed charts of the eastern Aleutian coasts, their description, and ethnographic data" remained unanalyzed.[2] I am unaware of this having changed since. These facts are both sobering and intoxicating — at once illustrating the degree to which past events and achievements can be ignored or forgotten, but also indicating exciting and rich fields for future research.

In the meantime, while Russian explorers of the past await their due acknowledgement, their modern counterparts continue to press along the paths they opened. Where will they go? One can certainly expect the current generation of Russians to contribute further to space exploration — a field they pioneered and of which they are intensely proud. They will no doubt continue also to make advances mapping and studying the Arctic Sea floor, motivated especially by the lure of profits from oil and gas reserves and by international competition for the rights to these resources. Ongoing global warming, and the resulting reduction in Arctic Sea ice, will help this endeavor, and will also encourage the Russians to devote more time and resources to navigation and research along the long and storied coastline once known as the Northeast Passage. Beyond this, one can only guess. What seems certain, however, is that the Russians, with four centuries of exploration behind them, are far from ready to abandon this rich heritage.

Notes

Introduction

1. Glynn Barratt, *Southern and Eastern Polynesia*, vol. 2 of *Russia and the South Pacific 1696–1840* (Vancouver: University of British Columbia Press, 1988), xii.

2. Geoffrey Hosking, *Empire and Nation in Russian History* (Waco, TX: Markham Press Fund, 1993). See also Geoffrey Hosking and Robert Service, eds., *Russian Nationalism, Past and Present*, Studies in Russia and Eastern Europe (New York: St. Martin's Press, 1998).

3. Richard Pipes, *Russian Conservatism and Its Critics: A Study in Political Culture* (New Haven: Yale University Press, 2005), 182.

4. Valerie Kivelson, *Cartographies of Tsardom: The Land and Its Meanings in Seventeenth-Century Russia* (Ithaca: Cornell University Press, 2006), 192–93.

5. Ibid., 1. Kivelson's excellent study delves deeply into questions of early Russian mapping and the Russian imagination.

6. Alix O'Grady, *From the Baltic to Russian America, 1829–1836: The Journey of Elizabeth von Wrangell*, ed. R. A. Pierce, Alaska History, no. 51 (Fairbanks: Limestone Press, 2001).

7. James Forsyth, *A History of the Peoples of Siberia* (Cambridge: Cambridge University Press, 1992); Yuri Slezkine, *Arctic Mirrors: Russia and the Small Peoples of the North* (Ithaca: Cornell University Press, 1994); Michael Khodarkvosky, "The Non-Christian Peoples on the Muscovite Frontiers," in *The Cambridge History of Russia*, vol. 1, ed. Maureen Perry (Cambridge: Cambridge University Press, 2006), 317–37; and the same author's *Russia's Steppe Frontier: The Making of a Colonial Empire, 1550–1800* (Bloomington: Indiana University Press, 2002).

8. A somewhat typical Soviet Russian account, for example, asserts that unlike the other European empires, which were built on the violent and immoral exploitation of native peoples, the construction of the Russian Empire, especially in Siberia, presents "a great history of progressive events" in which both Russian and non-Russian peoples participated and from which both benefited more or less equally. (G. P. Basharin, *Nekotorie voprosy istoriografii vkhozhdeniia Sibiri v sostav Rossii* [Iakutsk: Iakutskoe knizhnoe izdatel'stvo, 1971], 3.) This particular source explicitly rejects all notions of any Russian "conquests" in Siberia or Central Asia, arguing instead that these areas were instead "included" into a growing Russian world.

Chapter 1

1. There remains some controversy about when the expedition actually began. The issue is discussed at greater length elsewhere in the chapter.

2. Russian campaigns as far east as the Irtysh River date to 1483. It was not until a century later, however, that Russians were able to begin establishing themselves even nearly this far east.

3. Largely but not entirely. Small numbers of Novgorodian merchants had traded with native peoples from and beyond the Urals as early as the eleventh century and may have visited the area from the twelfth century.

4. Major sources include a series of seventeenth-century chronicles of various authorship, traditional Russian epic stories (*byliny*), folk songs, and so on. Each of the three main relevant chronicles — the Stroganov, the Yesipov, and the Remezov — paints Ermak's adventure in highly religious and patriotic terms. The Remezov Chronicle in particular views the whole campaign as the work of God's will, aimed at driving out "heathens" and Christianizing the land. The chronicles are widely available in print. In English translation, see Terence Armstrong, ed., *Yermak's Campaign in Siberia: A Selection of Documents*, trans. Tatiana Minorsky and David Wileman (London: Hakluyt Society, 1975). Russian *byliny* treating Ermak are analyzed in detail in A. A. Gorelov, "Trilogiia o Ermake iz sbornika Kirshi Danilova," in *Russkii fol'klor: materialy i issledovaniia* (Moscow-Leningrad: Akademiia nauk,

1961), 345–76. A good treatment of the nature and problems of relevant source materials is in R. G. Skrynnikov, *Sibirskaia ekspeditsiia Ermaka*, 2nd ed. (Novosibirsk: Izd-vo "Nauka," 1986), 12–81.

5. It is probable that an account of Ermak's campaigns was composed by one of the participants. Unfortunately, this is known only by reference in later chronicles. Ermak is thus known primarily from information in fairly lengthy chronicles detailing his exploits and most likely written in the first half of the seventeenth century. Shorter references to his campaign exist in other accounts. There are also a number of folk songs and tales mostly dating from the seventeenth century or later that have provided scholars with useful, if not always reliable or consistent information.

6. The most authoritative narrative, including copious analysis of sources and discrepancies, is Skrynnikov, *Sibirskaia ekspeditsiia Ermaka*.

7. A good sense of the level of development of pre-Mongol–conquest Siberia, and of the pernicious effects thereupon of Mongol victories in the region, is given in Igor V. Naumov, *The History of Siberia*, ed. and trans. David N. Collins, Routledge Studies in the History of Russia and Eastern Europe 6 (London and New York: Routledge, 2006). See especially 45–46.

8. Erwin Lessner, *Cradle of Conquerors: Siberia* (Garden City, NY: Doubleday, 1955), 246.

9. Ibid., 246–47.

10. Carol B. Stevens, *Russia's Wars of Emergence, 1460–1730* (Harlow, UK: Pearson-Longman, 2007), 16.

11. Prior to and during the Mongol-Tatar era, Russia was known as *Rus'*.

12. A good, recent survey of early Muscovite consolidation and expansion is Donald Ostrowski, "The Growth of Muscovy (1462–1533)," in *The Cambridge History of Russia*, vol. 1, ed. Maureen Perry (Cambridge: Cambridge University Press, 2006), 213–39.

13. Forsyth, *History of the Peoples of Siberia*, 28.

14. Ibid.

15. The Crimean, Kazakh, Astrakhan, Kazan, Nogai, Uzbek, and Sibir' khanates.

16. Forsyth, *History of the Peoples of Siberia*, 29.

17. Armstrong, *Yermak's Campaign in Siberia*, 64.

18. Isker is also known as *Qashliq* (variously spelled) and as *Sibir'*. The latter designation has been avoided here so as to avoid confusion with the larger khanate of the same name.

19. By 1662, the total Siberian population had grown to approximately 330,000. By 1815, it had reached one million, and in 1850, two million. The 1897 Russian Empire census shows 5.75 million. By 1914 it had reached ten million. Virtually the entire increase was due to Russian in-migration. The figures are from R. A. French, introduction to *The Development of Siberia: People and Resources*, ed. Alan Wood and R. A. French (Basingstoke, UK: Macmillan, 1989), 6.

20. To reflect the variations present in different sources I have here offered the modern names for three Siberian peoples. In general, the naming of Native Siberian peoples is a complex and shifting undertaking, foundering on a bewildering array of older or newer and popular or scientific titles, as well as on old hurts, political considerations, and the desire to address people respectfully in terms of their own making rather than in those imposed on them by outsiders. I do not pretend to be entirely conversant with these subtleties. Furthermore, older sources tend to lump together groups now separated by anthropologists and linguists. Names once in widespread use have in many cases changed or been dropped. For those wishing to delve further into this rich and difficult area of study a good resource is Dmitry Funk and Lennard Sillanpää, eds., *The Small Indigenous Nations of Northern Russia* (Vaasa, Finland: Åbo Akademi University, Social Science Unit, 1999). Also worthwhile, if a little politicized, is *The Red Book of the Peoples of the Russian Empire*, available on-line at http://www.eki.ee/books/redbook/introduction.shtml. A helpful guide to variant and overlapping namings, from the same book, is at http://www.eki.ee/books/redbook/reference.html. A good narrative and analysis of Russian colonization from the point of view of the affected native peoples is Marjorie Mandelstam Balzer, *The Tenacity of Ethnicity: A Siberian Saga in Global Perspective* (Princeton: Princeton University Press, 1999). Also valuable is James Forsyth, *A History of the Peoples of Siberia: Russia's North Asian Colony 1581–1990* (Cambridge, UK: Cambridge University Press, 1992). Finally, a very concise overview of the main groups' old and new names and geographical positions is in Naumov, *History of Siberia*, 48.

21. Kuchum's rule was effectively ended with Ermak's conquest of his capital, Isker, in 1582. His rule dates are usually extended to his death in 1598, however, since he never accepted his losses nor gave up trying to recoup them.

22. Armstrong, *Yermak's Campaign in Siberia*, 11. This account of Ermak's life comes from a source known as "The Cherepanov Chronicle," dating from 1760 and taken more or less seriously by different historians since that time.

23. Ibid., 12.

24. R. G. Skrynnikov, "Ermak's Siberian Expedition," *Russian History/Histoire Russe* 13 (1986): 1–39. The reference is to the Livonian War.

25. One source — the so-called Cherepanov Chronicle of 1760 — has Ermak born and bred in or around Stroganov lands and an employee of the same family, in which case his movements here perhaps constituted a return to a former employer or protector after a period of piracy. See, for example, Armstrong, *Yermak's Campaign in Siberia*, 10–11.

26. Lessner, *Cradle of Conquerors*, 259.

27. Skrynnikov, *Sibirskaia ekspeditsiia Ermaka*, 98.

28. Lessner, *Cradle of Conquerors*, 259.

29. "A Letter Patent From Tsar Ivan Vasilevich to Grigorii Stroganov Granting Financial, Judicial and Trade Privileges on Uninhabited Lands along the Kama River," 4 April 1558, in Basil Dmytryshyn, E. A. P. Crownhart-Vaughan, and Thomas Vaughan, eds., *Russia's Conquest of Siberia: A Documentary Record, 1558–1700*, vol. 1 (Portland: Western Imprints, Press of the Oregon Historical Society, 1985), 3–6.

30. "A Letter Patent From Tsar Ivan Vasilevich to Iakov and Grigorii Stroganov Granting Twenty Years' Exemption from Taxes and other Obligations for their Lands and their Settlers on those Lands in Takhcheia and along the Tobol' River," 30 May 1574, in Dmytryshyn, Crownhart-Vaughan, and Vaughan, *Russia's Conquest of Siberia*, 1:9–12.

31. Benson Bobrick, *East of the Sun: The Epic Conquest and Tragic History of Siberia* (New York: Poseidon Press, 1992), 40.

32. "A Letter Patent From Tsar Ivan Vasilevich to Iakov and Grigorii Stroganov Granting Twenty Years' Exemption from Taxes and other Obligations for their Lands," 30 May 1574, in Dmytryshyn, Crownhart-Vaughan, and Vaughan, *Russia's Conquest of Siberia*, 1:10.

33. Noted in Ivan's charter as Cheremis, Ostiaks, Votiaks, and Nogai: "A Gramota from Tsar Ivan Vasilevich to Iakov and Grigorii Stroganov Concerning Reinforcements to Subdue the Cheremis and Other Natives Plundering along the Kama River," 6 August 1572, in Dmytryshyn, Crownhart-Vaughan, and Vaughan, *Russia's Conquest of Siberia*, 1:7.

34. See, for example, Maureen Perrie, "Outlawry (*Vorovstvo*) and State Service: Ermak and the Volga Cossacks," in *Moskovskaia Rus' (1359–1584): Kul'tura i istoricheskoe samoznanie/Culture and Identity in Muscovy, 1359–1584*, ed. A. M. Kleimola and G. D. Lenhoff (Moscow: "Garant," 1997), 530–42. The notion has also been advanced by Russian historians including R. G. Skrynnikov.

35. Lessner, *Cradle of Conquerors*, 286–87.

36. This and all dating for Ermak's career have proved controversial and problematical in various ways and cannot be resolved here. Among the relevant issues: Did Ermak depart the Stroganovs, cross the Urals, and enter Sibir' all in the same season? Or did he depart earlier and then spend a winter camped near the Urals, before continuing on the following year? Both scenarios, of course, would put Ermak's actual conquest in 1582, which is now the widely (but not unanimously) accepted year. Dating problems, which continue to bedevil the literature in English and Russian, are considered in Armstrong, *Yermak's Campaign in Siberia*, 1–13; R. G. Skrynnikov, "Podgotovka i nachalo Sibirskoi ekspeditsii Ermaka," *Voprosy istorii*, 8 (1979): 44–56; and Skrynnikov, *Sibirskaia ekspeditsiia Ermaka*, 10–11, 150–51.

37. The latter position has been argued by Terence Armstrong, *Yermak's Campaign in Siberia*, 6, and at great length by R. G. Skrynnikov, *Sibirskaia ekpeditsiia Ermaka*, 191–206.

38. "The Conquest of Siberia by Ermak Timofeev and his Band of Cossacks as Reported in the *Stroganov Chronicle* (Excerpts)," in Dmytryshyn, Crownhart-Vaughan, and Vaughan, *Russia's Conquest of Siberia*, 1:14.

39. Armstrong, *Yermak's Campaign in Siberia*, 69. From the Yesipov Chronicle.

40. One of the chronicles, the Remezov, gives a figure of 5,000 men.

41. "The Conquest of Siberia by Ermak Timofeev," 14.

42. Lessner, *Cradle of Conquerors*, 289.

43. The account given here largely follows dates established by the Russian historian Bakhrushin, which are accepted by a large number of historians. See S. V. Bakhrushin, *Nauchnye trudy*, 4 vols. (Moscow: "Nauka," 1952–59). On the influence of Bakhrushin's dating, see Armstrong, *Yermak's Campaign in Siberia*, 7.

44. "The Conquest of Siberia by Ermak Timofeev," 14.

45. Route noted in Armstrong, *Yermak's Campaign in Siberia*, 19.

46. "The Conquest of Siberia by Ermak Timofeev," 15.

47. Ibid.

48. Armstrong, *Yermak's Campaign in Siberia*, 137.

49. "The Conquest of Siberia by Ermak Timofeev," 16.

50. Armstrong, *Yermak's Campaign in Siberia*, 150. In the Remezov Chronicle.

51. "The Conquest of Siberia by Ermak Timofeev." Excerpted with permission of the Press of the Oregon Historical Society, 1985, 16–17.

52. Ibid., 17.

53. Armstrong, *Yermak's Campaign in Siberia*, 72. In the Yesipov Chronicle.

54. "The Conquest of Siberia by Ermak Timofeev," 18.

55. Ibid.

56. Bobrick, *East of the Sun*, 44.

57. Alternatively, *November* 5 in some sources.

58. "The Conquest of Siberia by Ermak Timofeev," 19.

59. The Stroganov Chronicle has him going himself. Ibid., 20.

60. Lessner, *Cradle of Conquerors*, 308.

61. *Istoriia Sibirii*, vol. 2, *Sibir' v sostave feodal'noi Rossii* (Leningrad: Nauka, 1968), 35.

62. A very good account of the history of Ermak studies is in R. G. Skrynnikov, *Sibirskaia ekspeditsiia Ermaka*, 3–11.

63. Forsyth, *History of the Peoples of Siberia*, 31.

64. See, for example, scholarship by B. P. Polevoi and others in N. N. Bolkhovitinov, et al., *Istoriia russkoi Ameriki: 1732–1867*, 3 vols. (Moscow: Mezhdunarodnye otnosheniia, 1997–99).

65. S. V. Bakhrushin, *Nauchnye trudy*, vol. 3, pt. 1 (Moscow; "Nauka," 1959), 145. Also cited in Skrynnikov, *Sibirskaia ekspeditsiia Ermaka*, 9–10. See also the same author's *Ocherki po istorii kolonizatsii Sibiri v XVI i XVII vekakh* (Moscow: Izdatel'stvo M. i S. Sabashnikovykh, 1927).

66. See, for example, V. I. Shunkov, *Voprosy agrarnoi istorii Rossii* (Moscow, 1974) and the same author's *Ocherki po istorii kolonizatsii Sibiri v XVII — nachale XVIII vekakh* (Moscow and Leningrad, 1946). Other important Soviet writers on Ermak and the Russian conquest of Siberia include A. P. Okladnikov and A. I. Andreev.

67. Z. Ia. Boiarshinova, "K voprosu o prisoedinenii Zapadnoi Sibirii k russkomu gosudarstvu," *Tr. Tomskogo gosudarstvennogo universiteta* 136 (1957): 147–56.

Chapter 2

1. Depending on whether or not one accepts that Ermak was authorized by the tsar, at least indirectly (via the Stroganovs), to embark on his enterprise. See chapter 1.

2. A. R. Artem'ev, "*Zemleprokhodets Semen Dezhnev i ego vremia*," review article in *Otechestvennaia istoriia* 1 (2002): 196.

3. N. I. Nikitin, *Zemleprokhodets Semen Dezhnev* (Moscow: Rosspen, 1999), 12.

4. There are occasional generic references to women in the literature. Almost nothing specific is known, however.

5. G. A. Ushakov, *Po nekhozhenoi zemle* (Moscow: Izdatle'stvo "Mysl'," 1974), 20–21. On this find, see also Bobrick, *East of the Sun*, 66; and P. A. Gordienko, "The Arctic Ocean: An Account of Soviet Investigations...," *Scientific American* 204 (1961): 88.

6. *Istoriia Sibiri*, 2:41–42.

7. Ibid., 42.

8. Ibid., 47.

9. Ibid., 46.

10. Located between Ust-Kut and Bratsk, near Baikal where the Lena River passes close to the Ilim, a tributary of the Angara, itself a tributary of the Enisei.

11. Bobrick, *East of the Sun*, 57.

12. "Report to Tsar Mikhail Federovich from the Streltsy Sotnik Petr Beketov concerning His Expedition on the Lena River," in Dmytryshyn, Crownhart-Vaughan, and Vaughan, *Russia's Conquest of Siberia*, 1:137.

13. Forsyth, *History of the Peoples of Siberia*, 90.

14. Declining state revenues collected by the Chancery resulted in the Bureau being revived in 1730. It was finally and permanently abolished in 1763. A good summary history of the Russian administration of Siberia is in Naumov, *History of Siberia*, 69–72.

15. *Istoriia Sibiri*, 2:49.

16. Bobrick, *East of the Sun*, 60.

17. Forsyth, *History of the Peoples of Siberia*, 76–78.

18. Ibid., 79.

19. *Istoriia Sibiri*, 2:157.

20. "Documents concerning the Expedition Led by Vasilii Poiarkov from Iakutsk to the Sea of Okhotsk," in Dmytryshyn, Crownhart-Vaughan, and Vaughan, *Russia's Conquest of Siberia*, 1:209.

21. Ibid.

22. W. Bruce Lincoln, *The Conquest of a Continent: Siberia and the Russians* (New York: Random House, 1994), 64. Dmytryshyn, Crownhart-Vaughan, and Vaughan, *Russia's Conquest of Siberia*, puts it at forty-three men (1:210).

23. "Documents concerning the Expedition Led by Vasilii Poiarkov," 1:215.

24. Naumov, *History of Siberia*, 66.

25. Ibid., 65–66.

26. Cited in Kivelson, *Cartographies of Tsardom*, 124.

27. The main biography is Leonid A. Gol'denberg, *Semen Il'inovich Remezov, sibirskii kartograf i geograf, 1642-posle 1720* (Moscow: "Nauka," 1965). In English the best source is the relevant chapters in Kivelson, *Cartographies of Tsardom*.

28. *Khorograficheskaia kniga* (Chorographic Sketchbook), 1697–1711; *Cherteznaia kniga* (Sketchbook), 1699–1701; and *Sluzhebnaia chertezhnaia kniga* (Working Sketchbook), 1702–30.

29. J. L. Black, "J.-G. Gmelin and G.-F. Müller in Siberia, 1733–43: A Comparison of Their Reports," in *Development of Siberia*, ed. Alan Wood and R. A. French, 36.

30. Strahlenberg's accounts were published as *Das nord und östliche Theil von Europa und Asia* (Stockholm, 1730).

31. Black, "J.-G. Gmelin and G.-F. Müller in Siberia," 37.

32. The work of these two is treated in some detail in ibid., 35–49.

33. Lincoln, *Conquest of a Continent*, 119.

34. As Stepan Petrovich Krasheninnikov, *Opisanie zemli Kamchatki* (St. Petersburg, 1745).

35. Particularly interesting is his *Puteshestvie po raznym provintsiiam Rossiiskoi imperii* [Travels in Various Provinces of the Russian Empire], published in multiple volumes (1771–76 in German; 1773–88 in Russian). Pallas's correspondence has recently been published in Russian: *Nauchnoe nasledie P. S. Pallasa. Pis'ma, 1768– 1771*, comp. V. I. Osipov, V. I. Osipova, G. I. Federovoi (St. Petersburg: Tialid, 1993).

36. An example of the former might be G. A. Leont'eva, *Zemleprokhodets Erofei Pavlovich Khabarov* (Moscow: 1991). One of the latter is Daniil Romanenko, *Erofei Khabarov: Roman* (1946; Moscow: Moskovskii rabochii, 1969).

37. See the list of suggested readings at the end of this chapter.

38. Since the demise of the USSR three separate major rescripts of forest law have been passed in 1993, 1997, and 2007.

Chapter 3

1. The dates of both expeditions are sometimes rendered differently, and for a variety of reasons. For example, the exact date Peter gave his instructions to Bering is usually given as 23 December 1724, though sometimes as 6 January 1725. (I use the latter date hereafter.) Differences in the Western and Russian calendar do not appear fully to explain this difference. There is also the question whether to date the expedition from Peter's order or Bering's departure; conversely, the expedition's end is variously dated at 1742–3 depending on whether one focuses on the movements of men and ships or on official formalities. Other, comparable issues complicate the establishment of other expedition dates. Some of these issues are discussed briefly in Raymond A. Fisher, *Bering's Voyages: Whither and Why* (Seattle: University of Washington Press, 1977), 23.

2. Mairin Mitchell, *The Maritime History of Russia, 848–1948* (London: Sidgwick and Jackson, 1949), 74.

3. Ibid., 75–76.

4. Leonid Sverdlov, "Russian Naval Officers and Geographic Exploration in Northern Russia (18th through 20th Centuries)," *Arctic Voice* 11 (27 November 1996): 1.

5. Lydia T. Black, *Russians in Alaska, 1732–1867* (Fairbanks: University of Alaska Press, 2004), 3.

6. Leo Bagrow, *History of Cartography*, revised and enlarged by R. A. Skelton (Cambridge, MA: Harvard University Press, 1964), pl. LVIII.

7. Ibid., 109 and pl. LXI.

8. Bolognino Zaltieri's map of North America clearly shows the continents separated by a strait. Mercator's world chart of this year does likewise. See ibid., 136, and Pl. LXX, respectively.

9. Mitchell, *Maritime History*, 73–74.

10. Ibid., 82.

11. Vasilii A. Divin, *The Great Russian Navigator, A. I. Chirikov*, trans. Raymond H. Fisher (1953; Fairbanks: University of Alaska, 1993), 6.

12. Julia Schleck, "'Plain Broad Narratives of Substantial Facts': Credibility, Narrative, and Hakluyt's *Principall Navigations, Renaissance Quarterly* 59, no. 3 (2006): 768–94.

13. Also spelled "Borough."

14. "A Gramota from Tsar Mikhail Federovich to the Voevoda of Mangazeia...," in Dmytryshyn, Crownhart-Vaughan, and Vaughan, *Russia's Conquest of Siberia*, 1:75.

15. Ronald H. Fritze, *New Worlds: The Great Voyages of Discovery, 1400–1600* (Stroud, UK: Sutton, 2002), 178.

16. Skrynnikov, *Sibirskaia ekspeditsiia Ermaka*, 104. Hudson's voyages, for example, though made during the reign of Ivan IV's successor, Fedor, were just such a cooperative venture, organized by the Muscovy Company.

17. Ibid., 108.

18. Bans on foreign shipping were reiterated thereafter. In 1619, Tsar Mikhail ordered the Russian coast east of the White Sea closed to all foreign shipping. These restrictions lasted until the middle of the century.

19. Skrynnikov, *Sibirskaia ekspeditsiia Ermaka*, 108–10.

20. Ibid., 105.

21. Bobrick, *East of the Sun*, 61.

22. Skrynnikov, *Sibirskaia ekspeditsiia Ermaka*, 111.

23. *Istoriia Sibiri s drevneishikh vremen do nashikh dnei*, vol. 2, Akademiia nauk SSSR (Leningrad: Izdatel'stvo 'Nauka', 1968), 49.

24. "*Vazhneishie pokhody zemleprokhodtsev i nauchnye ekspeditsii v Sibiri kontsa XVI-XVIII vv*," map, supplemental to vol. 2 of *Istoriia sibiri*. Hereafter designated as *Istoriia sibiri*, map 2 supplement.

25. Black, *Russians in Alaska*, 17.

26. The ambivalence concerns the credit for discovery, not the historicity of Dezhnev's travels, which is widely accepted.

27. One of the more detailed treatments of Dezhnev's early life (amounting only to a single paragraph!) is in M. I. Belov, *Russians in the Bering Strait, 1648–1791*, trans. Katerina Solovjova, ed. and with an introduction by J. L. Smith (Anchorage, AK: White Stone Press, 2000), 25.

28. It has also been suggested he was born farther south, at Velikii Ustiug.

29. N. I. Nikitin, *Zemleprokhodets Semen Dezhnev i ego vremiia* (Moscow: Rosspen, 1999), 53–55.

30. It is traditional to put the voyage's start at Nizhne-Kolymsk. Recent archival evidence, however, may favor Sredne-Kolymsk. See B. P. Polevoi, "Novoe o Semena Dezhneve," *Dal'nii vostok* 1 (1989): 134–35. See also N. N. Bolkhovitinov et al., *Istoriia russkoi Ameriki*, 1:26.

31. Nikitin, *Zemleprokhodets Semen Dezhnev*, 76.

32. The evidence is assessed in Nikitin, *Zemleprokhodets Semen Dezhnev*, 87–89.

33. Recent Russian scholarship divides — as with many facts of Dezhnev's expedition — over the number of ships lost before or within the straits. The Russian historian M. I. Belov believes four, not two, koches made it through the Bering Straits (cited in L. M. Demin, *Semen Dezhnev*, Zhizn' zamchatel'nykh liudei, Malaia seriia [Moscow: Molodaia gvardia, 1990], 211). Bolkhovitinov et al., *Istoriia russkoi Ameriki* raises the number to six! (1:30).

34. This is the opinion of, for example, M. I. Belov. Belov also believes natives killed most or all survivors of the original wrecks. See Belov, *Russians*, 27.

35. Stepan Petrovich Krasheninnikov, *Opisanie zemli Kamchatskoi* (Saint Petersburg, 1745). Available in translation as *The History of Kamtschatka and the Islands Adjacent; Illustrated with Maps and Cuts*, trans. James Grieve (Glocester: R. Raikes, 1764; reprint, 1962).

36. On the fate of Ankudinov and Alekeseev, Belov states that they landed on the east coast of Kamchatka and "lived [there] for a long time" (Belov, *Russians*, 27).

37. The idea is reviewed in Demin, *Semen Dezhnev*, 197. The likely factuality of Russian visits and at least one settlement in Alaska as early as the 1660s is argued in L. M. Sverdlov, "Russkoe poselenie XVII veka na dalekoi reke Kheuveren (k voprosu o pervootkrytii Aliaski," in *Tri stranitsy iz istorii Russkoi Ameriki* (Moscow, 1999).

38. Nikitin, *Zemleprokhodets Semen Dezhnev*, 135; Demin, *Semen Dezhnev*, 198–200. Both sources discuss the possibility and some of its historiography.

39. Demin, *Semen Dezhnev*, 198.

40. Bolkhovitinov et al., *Istoriia Russkoi Ameriki*, 1:31–34, for example.

41. On the historiography of legends of Russians in Alaska before 1741, see C. G. Federova. *Russkoi naselenie Aliaski i Kalifornii. Konets XVIII veka-1867* (Moscow, 1971), 45–96, and C. G. Federova, "K voprosy o rannikh russkikh poseleniakh na Aliaske," *Letopis' Sever* (Moscow, 1964), 4:97–113.

42. Bobrick, *East of the Sun*, 63–64.

43. A. A. Burykin, "Pokhody Mikhaila Stadukhina i otkrytie Kamchatki," Elektronnyi zhurnal "Sibirskaia Zaimka," no. 6 (2000), accessed 10 January 2008, http://zaimka.ru/to_sun/burykin1.shtml.

44. Ibid., 63–65.

45. Stadukhin has found a recent defender in the Russian scholar A. A. Burykin, who finds his subject "an outstanding person," an "indefatigable and fearless explorer," and a man deserving of greater respect than is usually accorded. A. A. Burykin, "Pokhody Mikhaila Stadukhina i otkrytie Kamchatki."

46. Kurbat Ivanov's travels are outlined in *Istoriia Sibiri*, 2:29–30, 157.

47. Quoted in Bobrick, *East of the Sun*, 65.

48. This point is raised by Nikitin, *Zemleprokhodets Semen Dezhnev*, 171.

49. For example, R. A. Pierce, *Russian America: A Biographical Dictionary* (Kingston, ON: Limestone Press, 1990, 121).

50. See for example, F. A. Golder, *Russian Expansion on the Pacific, 1641–1850* (1914; reprint, Gloucester, MA: Peter Smith, 1960), 77–95. See also, L. Neatby, *Discovery in Russian and Siberian Waters*. (Athens: Ohio State University Press, 1973), 47–48. A good overview of the historiographical disputes about Dezhnev (up to the early 1980s) is given in N. N. Bolkhovitinov et al., eds., *Zarubezhnye issledovaniia po istorii russkoi ameriki (konets XVIII-seredina XIX v)*, Seriia: Problemy vseobshchei istorii. (Moscow: Akademiia nauk SSSR, 1987), see 17–23. Some Russians have also claimed recently that not Dezhnev but Alekseev led the expedition and thus deserves the credit. This is also a minority position. See Bolkhovitinov et al., *Istoriia russkoi Ameriki*, 1:25.

51. Nikitin, *Zemleprokhodets Semen Dezhnev*, 136, 174–76. Nikitin, one of Dezhnev's Russian boosters, has also advocated a "halfway" position, granting Bering priority for the straits and Dezhnev credit for discovering the northeastern extremity of the Eurasian continent (ibid., 180).

52. The voyage was discovered by B. P. Polevoi. See his "Zabytoe plavanie s Leny do r. Kamchatki v 1661–1662 gg. Itogi arkhivnykh izyskanii 1948–1991, *Izv. RGO*, no. 2 (1993): 37. See also Nikitin, *Zemleprokhodets Semen Dezhnev*, 174ff.; and Bolkhovitinov et al., *Istoriia russkoi Ameriki*, 1:34–39.

53. Nikitin, *Zemleprokhodets Semen Dezhnev*, 174.

54. Belov, cited in Black, *Russians in Alaska*, 19.

55. Nikitin, *Zemleprokhodets Semen Dezhnev*, 176.

56. Ibid., 179.

57. Bolkhovitinov et al., *Istoriia russkoi Ameriki*, 1:17.

58. Most accounts give this river; however, a recent multi-authored Russian study claims this is in error and gives instead the name "Nudima." Bolkhovitinov et al., *Istoriia russkoi Ameriki*, 1:18.

59. Ibid.

60. Black, *Russians in Alaska*, 23.

61. The question is treated quite thoroughly in Burykin, "Pokhody Mikhaila Stadukhina."

62. In Atlasov's time, the Ainu also inhabited parts of Kamchatka and southern Sakhalin.

63. Other important eighteenth-century reconnaissances of sections of the Okhotsk coast include those by Krasheninnikov, 1737–41; V. A. Khmetevskii, 1743–44 (along the coast route between Okhotsk and just north of Iamsk Bay); I. Balakirev, 1761–62 (by land along the Okhotsk coast from north of Iamsk Bay to the Penzhina River, then south along the west coast of Kamchatka as far as about 61°N latitude); Kirill Grigorevich (Erik) Laksman, 1792–93 ([sometimes misidentified as A. Laksman] along the coast by land from Gizhiginsk Bay southwest to Okhostk, then to Japan).

64. Black, "J.-G. Gmelin and G.-F. Müller in Siberia, 1733–43," 38.

65. Orcutt Frost, *Bering: The Russian Discovery of America* (New Haven: Yale University Press, 2003), 19.

66. Ibid., 20–22.

67. Since 1721, a fairly accurate map of the Kamchatka Peninsula was available to Russians. Between this date and Bering's departure, other maps of the regions to which Bering was heading also became available. But these left unanswered many basic questions about the geography of the north Eurasian Pacific region. On these maps, see ibid., 34–40.

68. Fisher, *Bering's Voyages*, 20. Fisher, 8–21, offers a good overview of the various possibilities and their historiography up to the 1970s.

69. Frost, *Bering*, 40. Russians such as Bolkhovitinov have emphasized the opposite idea — that Peter's priorities were to discover America from the west and to answer finally the question of any straits separating the two.

70. A leading Russian scholar of the expedition who has reaffirmed that Peter's priority in 1725 was indeed to find Alaska and the Bering Straits is N. N. Bolkhovitinov. See his *Rossiia otkryvaet Ameriku, 1732–1799* (Moscow, 1991).

71. F. A. Golder, *Russian Expansion on the Pacific, 1641–1850* (1914; Gloucester, MA: Peter Smith, 1960), 136.

72. Frost, *Bering*, 43–44.

73. Ibid., 44.

74. Golder, *Russian Expansion on the Pacific*, 139.

75. Ibid.

76. Frost, *Bering*, 46.

77. Ibid., 48–49.

78. There does not seem to be agreement or clarity about this landing. Many accounts make no mention of it. J. L. Smith confirms it, however, citing two other sources, in his introduction to V. A. Divin, *To the American Coast: The Voyages and Explorations of M. S. Gvozdev, the Discoverer of Northwestern America*, trans. Anatoli Perminov (Anchorage, AK: White Stone Press, 1997), 1.

79. Fisher, *Bering's Voyages*, 82.

80. Golder, *Russian Expansion on the Pacific*, 144.

81. See, for example, V. A. Divin, *Velikii russkii moreplavatel' A. I. Chirikov* (Moscow, 1953). This was the first book-length study of Chirikov. It has been translated as *The Great Russian Navigator, A. I. Chirikov*, Rasmuson Library Historical Translation Series, vol. 6 (Fairbanks: University of Alaska Press, 1993).

82. Frost, *Bering*, 58.

83. Ibid., 59.

84. *Istoriia sibiri*, 346.

85. Accounts of the Great Northern Expedition variously refer to four or seven detachments. The four noted here are those sent to map the Eurasian Arctic coast. Operations in or from Kamchatka, the Kuriles, and so on, including Bering's and Chirikov's, are considered separately.

86. *Great Soviet Encyclopedia*, s.v. "Stepan Gavrilovich Malygin."

87. *Istoriia sibiri*, 345.

88. The middle "M." is given in most sources. The English translation of the *Great Soviet Encyclopedia*, however, lists him as Vasilii Vasil'evich Pronchishchev.

89. *Istoriia sibiri*, map 2 supplement. Even Tolstoukhov was almost certainly not the first Russian to round

the peninsula. Other, unknown sailors had almost certainly made the trip, traveling from west to east, no later than 1617. See N. A. Gvozdetsky, *Soviet Geographical Explorations and Discoveries*, trans. Anatoly Bratov (Moscow: Progress Publishers, 1974), 13. For a more detailed account of the archeological evidence used to determine the existence of this earlier voyage, see Ushakov, *Po nekhozhenoi zemle*, 20–21.

90. Divin, *Great Russian Navigator*, 243. The Laptevs are in fact listed variously as brothers, half brothers, or cousins.

91. The beginning of a tradition of cartography in Russia, leaving out isolated exceptions, is usually dated to the late sixteenth century and connected with Ermak's opening of Siberia to the Russians. A recent and very good history of Russian cartography is A. V. Postnikov, *Karty Zemel' Rossiiskikh: ocherk istorii geograficheskogo izucheniia i kartografirovanniia nashego Otechestva* (Moscow, 1996). See also the same author's "Outline of the History of Russian Cartography," in *Regions: A Prism to View the Slavic-Eurasian World. Towards a Discipline of "Regionology,"* ed. Kimitaka Matsuzato (Sapporo, Japan: Slavic Research Center, Hokkaido University, 2000). The best source on the period through the end of the seventeenth century only is Valerie Kivelson's excellent monograph, *Cartographies of Tsardom: The Land and Its Meanings in Seventeenth-Century Russia* (Ithaca, NY: Cornell University Press, 2006).

92. Belov, *Russians*, 3, 28–29.

93. Kivelson, *Cartographies of Tsardom*, 21. Remezov is treated briefly in chapter 2.

94. Belov, *Russians*, 6; on early maps of the Bering Straits, see also *Istoriia sibiri*, 2:6–10.

95. *Istoriia sibiri*, 2:348.

96. Ibid., 2:349.

97. A. V. Postnikov, "Outline of the History of Russian Cartography," 36, accessed 18 December 2007, http://src-h.slav.hokudai.ac.jp/sympo/98summer/pdf/post36–42.pdf. The article also appears in *Regions: A Prism to View the Slavic-Eurasian World. Towards a Discipline of "Regionology,"* ed. Kimitaka Matsuzato (Sapporo, Japan: Slavic Research Center, Hokkaido University, 2000).

98. Starting in Baltic waters these routes led west through the North Sea and then either south and east around the Cape of Good Hope to the Indian and Pacific Oceans, or south and west across the Atlantic to Cape Horn and the Pacific. Even the shorter of these routes stretched well over 15,000 miles. The Passage, on the other hand, was half this length. Even the Suez Canal, which opened in 1869, does not offer a route nearly so short as the Northeast Passage.

99. Black, *Russians in Alaska*, 83.

100. Clive Holland, ed., *Farthest North: The Quest for the North Pole* (London: Robinson, 1994), 15.

101. Black, *Russians in Alaska*, 94.

102. Belov, *Russians*, 49.

103. Ibid., 54.

104. See B. P. Polevoi, "Novyi document o pervom russkom pokhode na Tikhii okean ("Rasprosnye rechi" I. Iu. Moskvitina i D. E. Kopylova, zapisannye v Tomske 28 sentiabria 1645 g.), in *Trudy Tomskogo oblastnogo kraevedcheskogo muzeia* 6, no. 2 (1963): 25–35. Cited in Bolkhovitinov et al., *Istoriia russkoi Ameriki*, 1:18, n. 26.

105. John J. Stephan, *Sakhalin: A History* (Oxford: Clarendon Press, 1971), 40.

106. Ibid., 11–12.

107. L. M. Starokadomskiy, *Charting the Russian Northern Sea Route: The Arctic Ocean Hydrographic Expedition, 1910–1915*, ed. and trans. William Barr (Montreal: McGill-Queen's University Press, 1976), 30.

108. Concerns about possible British intervention ruled out use even of the Suez Canal, forcing Russians all the way round the Cape. As Russia's position against the Japanese deteriorated, a second wave of ships *did* risk the Suez route, but to no ultimate avail.

109. This issue in particular is explored in John McCannon, *Red Arctic: Polar Exploration and the Myth of the North in the Soviet Union, 1932–1939* (New York: Oxford University Press, 1998).

110. Gvozdetsky, *Soviet Geographical Explorations*, 16.

111. Ibid., 19. On the history and nature of these organs, see M. I. Belov, *Istoriia otkrytiia i osvoeniia Severnogo Morskogo Puti*, 4 vols. (Leningrad: GUSMP, Morskoi transport and Gidrometeorologicheskoe izdatel'stvo, 1956–1969), esp. vols. 3–4.

112. McCannon, *Red Arctic*, 55.

113. Ibid., 29.

114. The difference between these two categories of ships — partly an issue of horsepower — is frequently glossed over, and the *Sibiriakov* appears in numerous sources, Russian and English, as an "icebreaker," which it was not. For more on the distinction, see Konstantin Krypton, *The Northern Sea Route and the Economy of the Soviet North* (New York: Frederick A. Praeger, 1956), 113–14.

115. Ibid., 113.

116. McCannon, *Red Arctic*, 62.

117. The best recent treatment of Siberian native culture and history is James Forsyth, *A History of the Peoples of Siberia: Russia's North Asian Colony, 1591–1990* (Cambridge: Cambridge University Press, 1992).

118. McCannon, *Red Arctic*, 65. McCannon also notes that the oft-cited figure of 12,000 convicts is now widely considered to be greatly exaggerated, but offers no alternative number (192, n. 7).

Chapter 4

1. Noted in Black, *Russians in Alaska*, 19. Sverdlov's article itself is only available in Russian: "Russkoe poselenie XVII veka na dalekoi reke Kheuveren (k voprosu o pervootkrytii Aliaski," in *Tri stranitsy iz istorii Russkoi Ameriki* (Moscow, 1999).

2. Black, *Russians in Alaska*, 22.

3. The overall expedition, incidentally, was loosely coordinated with Bering's Great Northern (or Second Kamchatka) Expedition.

4. Quoted in Divin, *To the American Coast*, 60.

5. W. Bruce Lincoln makes this claim. See Lincoln, *Conquest of a Continent*, 123.

6. Cited in Divin, *To the American Coast*, 65.

7. Black, *Russians in Alaska*, 26.

8. Steller's notes (as opposed to his more famous journal) from the Second Kamchatka Expedition remained unedited, unpublished, and largely unknown until 2003 with the publication of them as Georg Wilhelm Steller, *Steller's History of Kamchatka: Collected Information Concerning the History of Kamchatka, Its Peoples, Their Manners, Names, Lifestyle, and Various Customary Practices*, trans. Margritt Engel and Karen Willmore, ed. Marvin W. Falk, Rasmuson Library Historical Translation Series, vol. 12 (Fairbanks: University of Alaska Press, 2003).

9. Frost, *Bering*, 133.

10. Ibid., 128

11. Divin, *Great Russian Navigator*, 129.

12. Ibid., 156

13. Ibid., 159.

14. The Tlingits, and their interactions with the Russians, are treated in A. V. Grinov, *Indeitsy tlinkity v period Russkoi Ameriki (1741–1867 gg.)* (Novosibirsk, 1991).

15. Black, *Russians in Alaska*, 41.

16. Distinct groups, the Tlingit mainly occupied the northwest American continental coast and nearby major islands; the Aleuts, conversely, were originally dominant along the Aleutian Island chain.

17. Divin, *To the American Coast*, 69.

18. Frost, *Bering*, 134–35.

19. Georg Wilhelm Steller, *Journal of a Voyage with Bering, 1741–1742*. Ed. O. W. Frost; trans. Margitt A. Engel and O. W. Frost (Stanford, CA: Stanford University Press, 1988), 60–61.

20. Ibid., 64.

21. Ibid., 65, 67.

22. Ibid., 67.

23. Ibid., 67–69.

24. Ibid., 71.

25. This unit of measurement varies depending on context. It can mean the full length of an arm or just the distance from elbow to wrist. It is unclear what exactly is intended here.

26. Steller, *Journal of a Voyage with Bering*, 82.

27. Ibid., 123.

28. Frost, *Bering*, 260.

29. Herb and Miriam Hilscher, *Alaska, USA* (Boston: Little, Brown, 1959), 5.

30. Cited in Divin, *Great Russian Navigator*, 175.

31. *The Great Soviet Encyclopedia*, translation of the 3rd ed. of the *Bol'shaia sovetskaia entsiklipedia*, vol. 1 (1970), s.v. "Alaska."

32. Much of this research derives from — or is summarized in — Frost, *Bering*, chapter 1. Frost is perhaps the strongest recent advocate of Bering's achievements and merits.

33. Hilscher, *Alaska*, 6.

34. Frost, *Bering*, 281.

35. Black. *Russians in Alaska*, 65.

36. The company is usually considered a creation of both Grigorii Shelikhov and Nikolai Rezanov, even though by the time the company was officially chartered in 1799, Shelikhov had been dead four years. The attribution makes sense, given that the company was a progression of the Shelikhov-Golikov Fur Company in which Rezanov had become involved.

37. The full, cumbersome name of the ship in Russian is *Tri Sviatitelia vasilii Velikii, Grigorii Bogoslov i Ioann Zlatoust*.

38. These were named Giorgevskoe, Pavlovskoe, and Nikolaevskoe.

39. List adapted from Nikolai N. Bolkhovitinov, *The Beginnings of Russian-American Relations, 1775–1815*, trans. Elena Levin (Cambridge, MA: Harvard University Press, 1975), 176.

40. Particularly valuable, and up-to-date is Black, *Russians in Alaska*. For the Russian population in Alaska see Svetlana Grigor'evna Fedorova, *Russkoe naselenie Aliaski i Kalifornii* (Moscow: "Nauka," 1971).

41. Black, *Russians in Alaska*, 103.

42. "Vazhneishie pokhody zemleprokhodstev...," map supplement to *Istoriia sibiri*, vol. 2.

43. Ibid.

44. James Van Stone, ed., *Russian Exploration in Southwest Alaska: The Travel Journals of Petr Korsakovskiy (1818) and Ivan Ya. Vasiliev (1829)*, trans. David H. Kraus, Rasmusson Library Translation Series, vol. 4 (Fairbanks: University of Alaska Press, 198), 8.

45. This was one of the major companies in operation prior to the consolidation of all such activity under the monopolistic Russian-American Company in 1799.

46. "Vazhneishie pokhody zemleprokhodtsev...," map supplement to *Istoriia sibiri*, vol. 2.

47. Asserted in Black, *Russians in Alaska*, 194. See also Stone, *Russian Explorations*, 6.

48. Korsakovskii's and Vasil'ev's travel journals are available in English, with a useful introductory essay and bibliography, in Stone, *Russian Explorations*.

49. L. M. Starokamdomskiy, *Charting the Russian Northern Sea Route: The Arctic Ocean Hydrographic Expedition, 1910–1915*, ed. and trans. William Barr (Montreal: McGill-Queen's University Press, 1976), 172. Zagoskin's account is titled *Peshekhodnoi opisi chasti russkikh vladenii v Amerika*. A translation is available in H. N. Michael, ed., "Lieutenant Zagoskin's Travels in Russian America, 1842–44," in *Anthropology of the North*, no. 7 (Toronto: University of Toronto Press, 1967).

50. A. I. Alakseev, *The Odyssey of a Russian Scientist: I. G. Voznesenskii in Alaska, California, and Siberia, 1839–1849*, trans. Wilma C. Follette, ed. Richard A. Pierce (Kingston, ON: Limestone Press, 1987), 5.

51. Black, *Russians in Alaska*, 282.

52. More specific steps in this troubled history include the following: In 1821, the Russian tsar Alexander I banned foreign ships from sailing along Russian-Alaskan shores, only to be pressured into backing off in 1824 (in the case of the United States) and 1825 (in the case of Great Britain). In 1834 the Hudson Bay Company, with support from the British government, attacked the Russians at Stikine River. The ensuing conflict lasted until 1839, at which point the British switched their regional resources towards prosecuting the First Opium War against China. By this time, the British nonetheless had won from the Russians a lease on the latter's coastal possessions between 54° 40' and 58° 20'N.

53. Bolkhovitinov, *Beginnings of Russian-American Relations*, 175.

54. See V. N. Ponomarev, "Istoriia russkoi ameriki, 1732–1867," review article in *Otechestvennaia istoriia* 5 (2003): 163.

Chapter 5

1. Russell H. Bartley, "The Inception of Russo-Brazilian Relations (1808–1828)," *Hispanic American Historical Review* 56, no. 2 (1976): 217.

2. Glynn Barratt, *The Russians and Australia*, vol. 1 of *Russian and the South Pacific, 1696–1840* (Vancouver: University of British Columbia Press, 1988), 29–30.

3. Ilya Vinkovetsky, "Circumnavigation, Empire, Modernity, Race: The Impact of Round-the-World Voyages on Russia's Imperial Consciousness," *Meeting of Frontiers/Vstrecha na granitsakh*, accessed 31 May 2007, http://www.loc.gov/rr/european/mofc/vinkovetsky.html.

4. Barratt, *Russians and Australia*, 52.

5. A. I. Alakseev, *Osvoenie russkimi liudmi dal'nego vostoka i russkoi ameriki, do kontsa XIX veka* (Moscow: Izdatel'stvo "Nauka," 1982), 8. On these follow-up voyages, see N. A. Ivashintsov, *Russian Round-the-World Voyages, 1803–1849 With a Summary of Later Voyages to 1867*, Materials for the Study of Alaska history, no. 14 (Kingston, ON: Limestone Press, 1980).

6. Lydia T. Black argues against the tradition of solely crediting Rezanov, noting that Aleksandr A. Baranov had been "reconnoitering the situation [the possibility of establishing a Russian presence in California] since 1803–06" (Black, *Russians in Alaska*, 175).

7. Langsdorf's work in this area is surveyed in Richard G. Beidelman, *California's Frontier Naturalists* (Los Angeles: University of California Press, 2006), 42–47.

8. Black, *Russians in Alaska*, 169.

9. Bolkhovitinov, *Beginnings of Russian-American Relations*, 178–81.

10. This enterprise is rehearsed and analyzed in detail in Kenneth N. Owens and Alton S. Donnelly, *The Wreck of the Sv. Nikolai* (Portland: Western Imprints, Press of the Oregon Historical Society, 1985).

11. Oliver Jones Jensen, ed., *America and Russia: A Century and a Half of Dramatic Encounters* (New York: Simon and Shuster, 1962), 53.

12. The classic study, and the origin of this term, is Richard A. Pierce, *Russia's Hawaiian Adventure, 1815–1817* (Berkeley: University of California Press, 1965). A more recent monograph — focusing on the same set of circumstances but from the Hawaiian perspective — plays off Pierce's title: Peter R. Mills, *Hawaii's Russian Adventure: A New Look at Old History* (Honolulu: University of Hawaii Press, 2004). The most recent authoritative account in Russian is N. N. Bolkhovitinov, "Russkie na Gavaiakh (1804–1825)," in Bolkhovitinov et al., *Istoriia Russkoi Ameriki*, 2:275–302.

13. Arguments for and against are presented in Pierce, *Russia's Hawaiian Adventure*, 3–4.

14. "Letter, Baranov to King Kamehameha, about October 1, 1816, to be Delivered by Schäffer," in ibid., 45.

15. Olive Wyndette, *Islands of Destiny: A History of Hawaii* (Rutland, VT: Charles E. Tuttle, 1968), 69–70.

16. Harold Whitman Bradley, *The American Frontier in Hawaii: The Pioneers, 1789–1843* (Gloucester, MA: Peter Smith, 1968), 50.

17. Particularly in German- and English-language accounts, the name is spelled *Langsdorff*.

18. See Richard Pierce's introduction to Georg Heinrich von Langsdorff, *Remarks and Observations on a Voyage around the World from 1803 to 1807*, ed. Richard A. Pierce, trans. Victoria Joan Moessner (Kingston, ON: Limestone Press, 1993), esp. xxv–xxix.

19. K. V. Aleksandrova, *Akademik G. I. Langsdorf i russkaia ekpeditsiia v Braziliiu v 1821–36* (Bibliografich-eskii ukazatel') (Leningrad: Akademiia nauk, SSSR, 1979), 5.

20. Langsdorf's own account was published in English as G. H. von Langsdorff, *Voyages and Travels in Various Parts of the World during the Years 1803, 1804, 1805, 1806, and 1807*, 2 vols. (London, 1813–14). A shorter account is given in B. N. Komissarov, Grigorii Ivanovich Langsdorf (Leningrad: "Nauka," 1975). An excellent recent translation, with a useful introductory essay, is Langsdorff, *Remarks and Observations on a Voyage around the World*.

21. For example, *Cultura e Opulencia do Brasil por suas drogas, e minas*, a Portuguese-authored study that somehow made it to press in 1711 was quickly destroyed. Seven copies are known to remain, however. Prior to the nineteenth century, Portuguese secrecy was undermined only a few times, and without doing much more than whetting the appetites of foreign scholars. On all of this, see Roderick J. Barman, "The Forgotten Journey: Georg Heinrich Langsdorff and the Russian Imperial Scientific Expedition to Brazil, 1821–1829," *Terrae Incognitae* 3 (1971): 67–96.

22. Aleksandrova, *Akademik G. I. Langsdorf...*, 7.

23. Some sense of Langsdorf's ideas in this regard can be seen in Richard Pierce's introductory essay to Langsdorff, *Remarks and Observations on a Voyage around the World*.

24. Barman, "Forgotten Journey," 81–84.

25. Cited in B. N. Komissarov, *Grigorii Ivanovich Langsdorf, 1774–1852* (Leningrad: "Nauka," 1975), 99.

26. Barman, "Forgotten Journey," 91, mentions the possibility of intermittent periods of lucidity. A report published in the press in Germany in 1831 also suggests Langsdorf may have recovered somewhat once back in Europe: see Langsdorff, *Remarks and Observations on a Voyage around the World*, xxii. On the other hand, accounts published by some of the non-Russian expedition members suggest that Langsdorf was subject to periodic psychological problems long before his illness.

27. G. G. Manizer, *Ekspeditsiia akademika G. I. Langsdorfa v Braziliiu, 1821–1828*, ed. N. G. Shprintsin (Moscow: Geografgiz, 1948).

28. L. A. Shur, ed., *Materialy ekpeditsii akademika Grigoriia Ivanovicha Langsdorfa v Braziliiu v 1821–1929 gg. Nauchnoe opisanie* (Leningrad: nauka, 1973).

29. The historiography and bibliography of Langsdorf's expedition up to 1979, including materials focusing on some of his coexpeditionists, appears in Aleksandrova, *Akademik G. I. Langsdorf*. A brief overview of scholarship to 1993 is given in Richard Pierce's introduction to Langsdorff, *Remarks and Observations on a Voyage around the World*.

30. Langsdorff, *Remarks and Observations on a Voyage around the World*, xxii.

31. A notable exception among English-language writers is Glynn Barratt, who has written a series of excellent books on various aspects of this subject. A list of some of them appears in the list of suggested readings. Among a larger number of Russian sources on the topic, see V. A. Divin, *Russkie moreplavaniia na Tikhom okeane v XVIII veke* (Moscow, 1971).

32. E. V. Govor and A. Ia. Massov, comps., *Rossiiskie moriaki i puteshestvenniki v Avstralii* (Moscow: Nauka, 1993), 3.

33. Ibid., 4.

34. See Barratt, *Russians and Australia*, 100–07.

35. These are surveyed throughout Barratt, *Russians and Australia*, and in Govor and Massov's *Rossiiskie moriaki i puteshestvenniki v Avstralii*.

36. See in particular chapter 6 of Barratt, *Russians and Australia*.

37. A point made in Govor and Massov, *Rossiiskie moriaki i puteshestvenniki v Avstralii*, 5.

38. Barratt, *Southern and Eastern Polynesia*, 129.

39. Barratt, *Southern and Eastern Polynesia*, 201.

40. Glynn Barratt, *Melanesia and the Western Pacific Fringe*, vol. 3 of *Russia and the South Pacific 1696–1840* (Vancouver: University of British Columbia Press, 1990), 95.

41. Glynn Barrett, *Russia in Pacific Waters: A Survey of the Origins of Russia's Naval Presence in the North and South Pacific* (Vancouver: University of British Columbia, 1981), 204.

42. It is possible that the "eastern part" of the Riurik chain had in fact been seen earlier by Captain James Cook, and still earlier by the Dutchman Jakob Roggeveen.

43. Alternatively, Louis Choris.

44. Tikahau, Fangahina, and Aratika. Aspects of the work of Kotzebue, Chamisso, and Eschscholtz (aboard the *Riurik* and the *Predpriatie*) are surveyed in Richard G. Beidelman, *California's Frontier Naturalists* (Los Angeles: University of California Press, 2006), 48–55.

45. Among the current Federated States of Micronesia, the Senyavins comprise the island of Pohnpei and the atolls of Ant and Pakin. They are named for Russian admiral Dmitrii Seniavin (Senyavin).

46. He also had three brothers.

47. E. M. Webster, *The Moon Man: A Biography of Nikolai Miklouho-Maclay* (Berkeley: University of California Press, 1984), 28.

48. As elsewhere in this book, I am following the Old Style (Julian) calendar in use in Russia at the time. Maklai's own published journal, however, follows the New Style or Gregorian calendar. Readers comparing this account to Maklai's journal must therefore add twelve days.

49. Webster, *Moon Man*, 52.

50. N. N. Miklukho-Maklai, *Sobranie sochinenii v shesti tomakh*, vol. 1, *Puteshestviia 1870–1874 gg. Dnevniki putevye zametki, otchety* (Moscow: Nauka, 1990), 80.

51. Webster, *Moon Man*, 52.

52. Miklukho-Maklai, *Sobranie sochinenii*, 1:92.

53. Webster uses the appellation for the title of his biography.

54. Webster, *Moon Man*, 89.

55. The observation was made first by the Polish anthropologist (and continuer of Miklukho-Maklai's work in New Guinea), Bronislaw Malinowski (1884–1942).

Chapter 6

1. See his three-volume work, translated into English as *Travels of the Russian mission through Mongolia to China, and residence in Peking, in the years 1820–1821. By George Timkowski. With corrections and notes by Julius von Klaproth* (1824; London: Longman, Rees, Orme, Brown, and Green, 1827).

2. Cited in W. Bruce Lincoln, *Petr Petrovich Semenov-Tian-Shanskii: The Life of a Russian Geographer* (Newtonville, MA: Oriental Research Partners, 1980), 27.

3. Ibid., 30.

4. Ibid., 32.

5. I have used here, as throughout the book, Library of Congress transliteration spellings for Russian names. Przheval'skii's name is commonly rendered variously: Przhevalsky, Przewalski, Prjevalsky, among several others.

6. Foster Stockwell, *Westerners in China: A History of Exploration and Trade, Ancient Times through the Present* (Jefferson, NC: McFarland, 2003), 105.

7. Donald Rayfield, *The Dream of Lhasa: The Life of Nikolay Przhevalsky, Explorer of Central Asia* (Columbus: Ohio University Press, 1976), 3.

8. The left bank of the lower two-thirds of the river formed the new Chinese-Russian frontier and was, thus, under Chinese control.

9. Rayfield, *Dream of Lhasa*, 22.

10. I. V. Kozlov, *Velikii puteshestvennik: Zhizn i deiatelnost N. M. Przheval'skii, pervogo issledovatelia prirody Tsentral'noi Azii* (Moscow: Mysl', 1985), 34.

11. Rayfield, *Dream of Lhasa*, 28.

12. Kozlov, *Velikii puteshestvennik*, 26.

13. Ibid., 47.

14. At first Przheval'skii took two boys. The other one — a personal acquaintance by the name of Povalo-Shvyikovskii — was let go early in the expedition, however, apparently due to his inability to carry out simple but vital tasks. Przheval'skii's first choices of companions, incidentally, his previous partners Pyl'tsov and Iagunov, were both unavailable. Pyl'tsov had married and was unwilling to travel. Iagunov had recently died.

15. Lop Nur's position, as Przheval'skii found it, disagreed with existing Chinese maps in the possession of European experts. In fact, both Przheval'skii and the Chinese maps were correct. The lake literally moves — under the combined influence of shifting water-flow volumes and the courses of its feeder rivers. This fact was not properly cleared up until well after Przheval'skii's death.

16. Rayfield, *Dream of Lhasa*, 132.

17. Kozlov, *Velikii puteshestvennik*, 88–89.

18. Rayfield, *Dream of Lhasa*, 136.

19. Kozlov, *Velikii puteshestvennik*, 96–97.

20. Ibid., 107.

21. N. M. Przheval'skii, *Ot Kiakhty na istoki zheltoi reki: Issledovanie severnoi okrainy Tibeta i put' cherez Lob-Nor po basseinu Tarima* (Moscow: OGIZ, 1948), 84.

22. Ibid., 6.

23. Ibid.

24. Ibid., 19–20.

25. Rayfield, *Dream of Lhasa*, 187.

26. Stockwell, *Westerners in China*, 111.

27. Many of the original specimens collected in Central Asia and China by Prezheval'skii may be viewed on-line at the website of the Komarov Botanical Institute in St. Petersburg: http://www.mobot.org/MOBOT/Research/LEguide/index.html This excellent on-line source also allows access to the collections of well over 100 other Russian explorers across numerous regions.

28. Kozlov, *Velikii puteshestvennik*, 5.

29. The mineralogy and geology of parts of Central Asia were, of course, studied by others as well. Particularly important in the early period was Ivan Vasil'evich Mushketov (1850–1902). His studies in the Tian Shan, Syr-Dariia basin, and other parts of Turkestan during the 1870s resulted in much new knowledge and an important two-volume work, *Turkestan* (1886–1906).

30. On Pevtsov's life and career, see V. G. Selikhanovich, *M. V. Pevtsov: Puteshestvennik, geograf, astronom* (Moscow, 1956). Pevtsov's own published works include *Puteshestvie po Kitaiu i Mongolii* (Moscow 1951) and *Puteshestvie v Kashgariiu i Kun'-Lun'* (Moscow, 1949).

31. Rayfield, *Dream of Lhasa*, 202.

32. Kozlov's journey, and the circumstances surrounding it, are discussed in Alexandre Andreyev, *Soviet Russia and Tibet: The Debacle of Secret Diplomacy, 1918–1930s* (Leiden: Brill Academic Publishers, 2003).

33. *Great Soviet Encyclopedia*, 3rd ed., s.v. "Fedchenko, Aleksei Pavlovich."

34. Published in serial form in the journal *Izvestiia obshchestva liubitelei estestvozananie*.

35. V. V. Obruchev, "Introduction" to V. V. Sapozhnikov, *Po Russkomu i Mongol'skomu altaiu* (Moscow: Gosudarstvennoe Izdatel'stvo, 1949), 3.

Chapter 7

1. Rumored to have been sighted first in 1865 by Rønnbeck and Aidijärvi (Norwegian sealers) in the *Spidsbergen*, but discovered officially at noon on 30 August 1873 by Austro-Hungarian expedition of Karl Weyprecht and Julius Payer, the Franz Josef Land archipelago (early believed to be a single continental mass) was further charted and explored over the following decades by British, American, and Norwegian expeditions. The first Russian involvement (not counting Weyprecht and Payer's rescue on 24 August 1874 by Russians near Novaia Zemlia) came in 1930 when a Soviet research base was established there. See the introductory essay in E. B. Baldwin, *The Franz Josef Land Archipelago: E. B. Baldwin's Journal of the Wellman Polar Expedition, 1898–1899*, ed. P. J. Capelotti (Jefferson, NC: McFarland, 2004).

2. The American Robert Peary was first to the North Pole (1909).

3. Gvozdetsky, *Soviet Geographical Explorations*, 36.

4. Ibid., 15.

5. L. M. Starokamdomskiy [Starokamdomskii], *Charting the Russian Northern Sea Route: The Arctic Ocean Hydrographic Expedition, 1910–1915*, trans. William Barr, Arctic Institute of North America (Montreal: McGill-Queen's University Press, 1976), 299, n. 43.

6. Ushakov, *Po nekhozhenoi zemle*, 22–23.

7. Starokadomskiy, *Charting the Russian Northern Sea Route*.

8. Ibid., 22.

9. Ibid., 54.

10. Ibid., 114.

11. Ibid., 135.

12. Ushakov, *Po nekhozhenoi zemle*, 24.

13. Starakadomskiy, *Charting the Russian Northern Sea Route*, 136. Excerpted with permission of McGill-Queen's University Press.

14. Ushakov, *Po nekhozhenoi zemle*, 24.

15. Both had set off in 1912 on separate Arctic expeditions, Georgii Lvovich Brusilov on the *St. Anna* and Vladimir Aleksandrovich Rusanov on the *Hercules*. The only survivors ever found were two members of Brusilov's expedition.

16. Starokadomskiy, *Charting the Russian Northern Sea Route*, 209.

17. Similarly, Malyi Taimyr was originally called Tsarevich Aleksei Island, after the tsar's son and heir.

18. Cited and trans. in Gvozdetsky, *Soviet Geographical Explorations*, 25. Several expeditions were sent to Severnaia Zemlia in the early 1930s. Among their discoveries were the Krasnoflotskye Islands (eight in total) and Vize Island. The latter is located roughly equidistant between Severnaia Zemlia and Franz Josef Land. Its existence had been predicted by Russian naval officer V. Y. Vize, based on a study of the drift of the icebound *St. Anna*—

Brusilov's earlier-noted and ill-fated ship — during 1912–14. By "tracing all the zig-zags made by the *St. Anna* and checking them against the direction of the wind, Vize determined that between" 70°–80°N "there must have been some obstacle preventing the ship from proceeding eastward." Vize even drew the hypothetical island on a map in 1924. It was discovered in 1930. In fact, the obstacle was not Vize, much too small to have the effect, but rather "an enormous shoal ... running north-south at approximately 80°E," to which Vize Island was connected (Gvozdetsky, *Soviet Geographical Explorations*, 33–35).

19. See, for example, Derek Hayes, *Historical Atlas of the Arctic* (Seattle: University of Washington Press, 2003).

20. Vilhjalmur Stefansson, *The Adventure of Wrangel Island* (New York: Macmillan, 1925), 393.

21. Ibid., 16.

22. See, for example, ibid., 17.

23. That of Sir John Franklin (1786–1847). Franklin had set off in search of the Northwest Passage. He wrecked sometime after 26 July 1845 (NS) in the vicinity of Melville Bay, Canada. No trace of him or his expedition was ever found.

24. The theory held that the ice habitually encountered by ships starting anywhere between 75°–82°N, was simply a ring encircling an ice-free ocean further north. An early exponent of it was the English eccentric Daines Barrington (1727–1800). The theory persisted until the early 1880s, by which time it had caused the deaths of many explorers operating on its principles.

25. Black, *Russians in Alaska*, 84.

26. 80° 30' according to *Istoriia sibiri*, 350.

27. Holland, *Farthest North*, 29.

28. This expedition was led at first by Luigi Amedeo di Savoia, duke of the Abruzzi, and ultimately by his lieutenant, Umberto Cagni. Cagni reached about 86°34'N.

29. The first claim to have achieved the Pole was made by Frederick Albert Cook, an American physician turned explorer, who professed to have arrived there 21 April 1908. Cook's claim was quickly met with skepticism and he is now widely but not universally considered a fake. Peary reached the pole on 6 April 1909 and is generally granted priority. However, some controversy still persists whether or not Peary, too, actually reached the Pole or only came very close to it.

30. Wellman's comment, quoted in Holland, *Farthest North*, 187.

31. Starokadomskiy, *Charting the Russian Northern Sea Route* 305, n. 18.

32. The American Richard Evelyn Byrd is usually considered the first person to fly to the Pole (without landing). He did so 9 May 1926. His claim is less than perfect, however, since it is generally accepted that he only reached a little north of 88°, though by mistake not subterfuge.

33. McCannon, *Red Arctic*, 71.

34. Ibid., 68–69.

35. The first South Polar station, still in operation, is Orcadas Base. It was established on Laurie Island in 1903 by the Scottish National Antarctic Expedition and has been run continuously since by Argentina.

36. McCannon, *Red Arctic*, 75.

37. Ibid., 79, discusses this theory.

38. Holland, *Farthest North*, 298–99.

39. The point is made in Holland, *Farthest North*, 292.

40. Gvozdetsky, *Soviet Geographical Explorations*, 250.

41. This was the famous Decembrist Revolt, staged following the death of Tsar Alexander I by hopeful but poorly organized liberal revolutionaries in search of a constitution. Torson's name had been originally given to Vysokii Island, one of the islands discovered by Bellingshausen's expedition.

42. F. F. Bellingshausen, *The Voyage of Captain Bellingshausen to the Antarctic Sea, 1819–21*, 2 vols., ed. Frank Debenham, 2nd series, nos. 91–92 (1945; Kraus Reprint: Nendeln, Liechtenstein, 1967). See also, Alan Gurney, *Below the Convergence: Voyages toward Antarctica, 1699–1839* (New York: Penguin, 1997), 161.

43. Michael H. Rosove, *Let Heroes Speak: Antarctic Explorers, 1772–1922* (Annapolis, MD: Naval Institute Press, 2000), 8.

44. Bellingshausen, *Voyage*, xv.

45. Ibid., 71–72.

46. Listed as a Russian discovery, for example, under "Annenkov Island" in the *Great Soviet Encyclopedia*, 3rd ed.

47. I have used the accepted English spellings here.

48. Bellingshausen, *Voyage*, 96–97.

49. Gurney, *Below the Convergence*, 166.

50. A group of rocks and islets to the northwest of South Georgia discovered by Cook.

51. Bellingshausen, *Voyage*, 110.

52. Ibid., 117.

53. Ibid., 117, n. 2. Here, Bellingshausen's editor, Debenham, says "a few miles, not more than twenty." Bellingshausen's logbooks, which might shed much light, are unfortunately lost.

54. Gurney, *Below the Convergence*, 166.

55. Bellingshausen, *Voyage*, 117.

56. Cited in Rosove, *Let Heroes Speak*, 10.

57. Terence Armstrong, "Bellinghausen and the Discovery of Antarctica," *Polar Record* 15 (1971): 888.

58. The point was made by the Russian historian M. I. Belov. Cited here from Armstrong, "Bellinghausen and the Discovery of Antarctica," 887–89.

59. Ibid. Also see "Comment by Professor M. I. Belov," *Polar Record* 15 (1971): 887–91.

60. Bellingshausen, *Voyage*, 121.

61. I have given old and new style dates here since Bransfield's discovery is always noted according to the Western calendar. For explanation of further complications with dates and times relevant to Bellingshausen's voyages, see A. G. E. Jones, *Antarctica Observed: Who Discovered the Antarctic Continent?* (Whitby, UK: Caedmon, 1982), 87–88, and Armstrong, "Bellingshausen and the Discovery of Antarctica," 887.

62. Nonetheless, there have been and remain controversies regarding Bransfield's claims. See, for example, Debenham's comments in *Voyage of Captain Bellingshausen*, xxiv–xxviii. For more detailed treatment of the various priority controversies see: William Herbert Hobbs, *The Discoveries of Antarctica within the American Sector, as Revealed by Maps and Documents* (Philadelphia: University of Michigan, 1939); R. T. Gould, "The Charting of the South Shetlands, 1819–28," *Mariner's Mirror* 22, no. 3 (July 1941); and Jones, *Antarctica Observed*.

63. Bellingshausen, *Voyage*, 128–29.

64. The comment is Debenham's in ibid., 128. See also n. 1 from the same page.

65. Ibid., 410–11.

66. Ibid., 419–20.

67. Ibid., 421.

68. Jones, *Antarctica Observed*, 101

69. McCannon, *Red Arctic*.

70. Gvozdetsky, *Soviet Geographical Explorations*, 198.

71. These include: in 1928, the first flight in a plane over the continent by Australian Hubert Wilkins; in 1935, the first woman on the Antarctic continent (Mrs. Klarius Mikkelsen); also in 1935, the first trans-Antarctic flight, by the American Lincoln Ellsworth.

72. Gvozdetsky, *Soviet Geographical Explorations*, 251–52.

Chapter 8

1. Although Russians—rather than other Soviet nationalities—dominate the USSR space program (and this chapter)—others besides participated in important roles. It is also possible to argue about the "actual" national identity of some of the major personalities usually designated as Russian. Most important here is Sergei Korolev, the primary architect of the whole program. Korolev has been claimed by both Russians and Ukrainians (he was born and raised in Ukraine but was of Russian background and spoke Russian). The issue cannot be resolved here.

2. See, for example, James Harford, *Korolev: How One Man Masterminded the Soviet Drive to Beat America to the Moon* (New York: Wiley, 1997), 242. Here, Harford also cites and translates a Russian source: Leonard Nikishin, "Space Dramas: We Knew Nothing of Some, Others Did Not Really Occur," *Novoe Vremiia* (1991).

3. For a sense of the debate, see James Oberg, *Uncovering Soviet Disasters: Exploring the Limits of Glasnost* (New York: Random House, 1988).

4. Especially useful are Iaroslav Golovanov, *Korolev: Fakti i mifi* (Moscow: Nauka, 1994); B. V. Raushen-bakh, general ed., *S. P. Korolev i ego delo: svet i teni v istorii kosmonaftiki: izbrannie trudi i dokumenty* (Moscow: Nauka, 1998)—mainly a large collection of original documents; and Anton Pervushin, *Bitva za zvezdy*, 2 vols. (Moscow: Voenno-istoricheskaia biblioteka, 2003).

5. A good example, presenting a highly sanitized and idealized life of Korolev, is A. Iu. Ishlinskii, "O zhizni i deiatel'nosti akademika Sergeia Pavlovicha Koroleva," in *Iz istorii sovetskoi kosmonaftiki: Sbornik pamiati akademika S. P. Koroleva* (Moscow: Nauka, 1983), 6–25.

6. Konstantin Ivanov, review of Konstantin Petrovich Feoktistov, *Zato my delali rakety. Vospominaniia i razmyshlenniia kosmonavta-issledovatelia* (Moscow: Vremia, 2005), in *Neprikosnovennyi zapas*, no. 1 (2006), accessed 17 August 2007, http://magazines.russ.ru/nz/2006/1/re30.html.

7. Originally published 1928–32. Available in an English translation as Nikolai Rynin, *Interplanetary Flight and Communication* (Jerusalem: Israel Program for Scientific Translations, 1970). It combines entries on space flight, science fiction, astronomy, and other related matter.

8. Harford, *Korolev*, 8, 123. On the history of nineteenth-century Russian plans and dreams involving rocketry and space travel, see Viktor Sokolskii, "Work on the theoretical Foundations of Cosmonautics and Evolution of Rocket Technology in the USSR Prior to 1945," in *History of the USSR: New Research* 5, Social Sciences Today (Moscow, 1986), 64–92.

9. The couple had a daughter in 1935. They divorced in 1948, apparently over Korolev's marital infidelities. He married his second wife, Nina, in 1949. He continued to have affairs, however, say his biographers.

10. Leonid Vladimirov, *The Russian Space Bluff: The Inside Story of the Soviet Drive to the Moon*, trans. David Floyd (New York: Dial Press, 1973), 26.

11. A. Iu. Ishlinskii, "O zhizni i deiatel'nosti akademika Sergeia Pavlovicha Koroleva," in *Iz istorii sovetskoi kosmonavtiki: Sbornik pomiati akademika S. P. Koroleva* (Moscow: Izdatel'stvo "Nauka," 1983), 12–13.

12. Golovanov, *Korolev: fakty i mifi*, 136.

13. Korolev's arrest date, along with a number of other dates in his biography, vary slightly from source to source. In such cases I have followed the chronology printed in Raushenbakh, *S. P. Korolev i ego delo*.

14. Golovanov, *Korolev: fakty i mifi*, 257.

15. Harford, *Korolev*, 50–51.

16. Ishlinskii, "O zhizni i deiatel'nosti akademika Sergeia Pavlovicha Koroleva," 13.

17. He was officially rehabilitated only in 1957, however.

18. Raushenbakh, *S. P. Korolev i ego delo*, 14.

19. Harford, *Korolev*, 65–66.

20. An excellent new biography of von Braun has recently been published: Michael J. Neufeld, *Von Braun: Dreamer of Space, Engineer of War* (New York: Knopf/Smithsonian National Air and Space Museum, 2007).

21. Debora Cadbury, *Space Race: The Epic Battle Between America and the Soviet Union for Dominion of Space* (New York: Harper-Collins, 2006), 101. Estimates of the numbers involved vary; 5,000 is also a commonly cited figure.

22. IGY was actually an eighteen-month period from 1 July 1957 to 31 December 1958. Timed to coincide with a particularly active period in the solar sunspot cycle, it attracted participation from about seventy countries. It has also sometimes been noted that US interest in IGY may in part have been inspired by the scientific-humanitarian cover it offered for the launch of a spy satellite.

23. The official but fake address of the main Soviet launch site. The actual site was near Tiuratam, some 150 miles away from the town of Baikonur.

24. After 1958 the United States moved ahead of the USSR in the mass production of ICBMs.

25. Golovanov, *Korolev: fakty i mifi*, 465.

26. The word means "fellow traveler" in Russian.

27. Cited in Ia. Golovanov, "Perekrestki zvezdnykh dorog," in A. Leonov and A. Sokolov, *Chelovek i vselennaia* (Moscow: Izdatel'stvo iskusstvo, 1976), section 1 (no page numbers).

28. One might quibble that Laika was the first in *orbit*, but not in space. Back in 1951 the Soviets had fired two dogs (Dezik and Tsygan) to an altitude of about sixty-two miles, usually considered the beginning of space. (Harford, *Korolev*, 161).

29. Golovanov, "Perekrestki zvezdnykh dorog," section 2 (no page numbers).

30. Vladimirov, *Russian Space Bluff*, 73.

31. Harford, *Korolev*, 137.

32. Ibid., 148–49.

33. Ibid., 153–54.

34. Raushenbakh, *S. P. Korolev i ego delo*, 29.

35. The Russian academician P. L. Kapitsa, cited in Raushenbakh, *S. P. Korolev i ego delo*, 8.

36. Vladimirov, *Russian Space Bluff*, 78–83.

37. Korolev had to fit all his craft with a logic lock. Only by opening this lock could the pilot access the manual controls. For security purposes parts of the code were known only to ground control, to be radioed up in the event of necessity. Neither Korolev nor his cosmonauts liked this system at all. And it seems that Korolev in fact regularly violated it, secretly providing his pilots with the numbers before launch.

38. *Gherman Titov, First Man to Spend a Day in Space: The Soviet Cosmonaut's Autobiography as Told to Pavel Barashev and Yuri Dokuchaev, Novosti Press Agency Correspondents* (New York: Crosscurrents Press, 1962), 90–92.

39. A Russian specialist who has interviewed most of the other nineteen finds that only three thought someone other than Gagarin would be chosen. Golovanov, *Korolev: fakty i mifi*, 628–29.

40. Ibid., 629.

41. Cadbury, *Space Race*, 209.

42. Vladimirov, *Russian Space Bluff*, 91–93.

43. Ishlinskii, "O zhizni i deiatel'nosti akademika Sergeia Pavlovicha Koroleva," 22.

44. Yaroslav Golovanov, *Our Gagarin* (Moscow: Progress, 1978), 136–37.

45. Cadbury, *Space Race*, 238.

46. Golovanov, *Our Gagarin*, 137.

47. Ibid., 139.

48. Harford, *Korolev*, 172–75.

49. Ibid., 175.

50. *Gherman Titov, First Man to Spend a Day in Space*, 100–02.

51. Ibid., 99–100.

52. Ibid., 110.

53. Oberg, *Uncovering Soviet Disasters*, 68.

54. Golovanov, *Korolev: fakty i mifi*, 701.

55. Oberg, *Uncovering Soviet Disasters*, 70–71. Tereshkova went on to hold positions in government (in the Supreme Soviet 1966–74 and the Presidium thereof from 1974 to 1989) and in the Party (she was a member of the Central Committee from 1969 to 1991). Over the years she collected a huge array of Soviet and foreign awards and honors — including Hero of the Soviet Union, the Order of Lenin, and the United Nations Gold Medal of Peace. In November 1963 she married cosmonaut Andrian Nikolaev (1929–2004), though less out of love than under pressure from Khrushchev, who saw political mileage in the arrangement. They divorced in 1982.

56. Cadbury, *Space Race*, 281.

57. Feoktistov has recently published his memoirs: *Zato my delali rakety. Vospominaniia i razmyshleniia kosmonavta-issledovatelia* (Moscow: Vremia, 2005).

58. Oberg, *Uncovering Soviet Disasters*, 80.

59. David Scott and Alexsei Leonov with Christine Toomey, *Two Sides of the Moon* (New York: Thomas Dunne Books/St. Martin's Press, 2004), 1.

60. There are discrepancies across accounts regarding the total time Leonov spent "walking." Sometimes twenty-two minutes is cited. The difference appears to depend on whether one counts time in space only, or time outside the capsule, including in the airlock.

61. Oberg, *Uncovering Soviet Disasters*, 80–83.

62. Harford, *Korolev*, 14–15, notes some of these claims, though he then dismisses them. Other of Korolev's designers and engineers who may have been underrated include Mikhail Iangel (a fuels specialist) and Vladimir Chelomei (a rocket-engine designer).

63. Although it has become customary in the West to consider the moon the main goal of the Space Race, and the United States thus as the race's winner, this is in some respects an arbitrary judgment. There is no reason why the Soviets' main achievements — first satellite and first person in space — should not be considered the most important milestones. Indeed, Soviet and Russian writers have made this very point more than once.

Conclusions

1. In the nineteenth century, Algeria came to be designated a full French Department (essentially the equivalent of statehood in the United States). This both reflected and helped to create a French sense of possession and incorporation that goes beyond "mere" empire.

2. Black, *Russians in Alaska*, 91.

Index

Page numbers in *bold italics* indicate illustrations.

DATE DUE
